SPHERES OF INTERVENTION

SPHERES OF INTERVENTION

US FOREIGN POLICY AND THE COLLAPSE OF LEBANON, 1967–1976

JAMES R. STOCKER

CORNELL UNIVERSITY PRESS
Ithaca and London

First published 2016 by Cornell University Press
Printed in the United States of America

Library of Congress Cataloging-in-Publication Data

Stocker, James R., 1980– author
    Spheres of intervention : US foreign policy and the collapse of Lebanon, 1967–1976 / James R. Stocker.
        pages cm
    Includes bibliographical references and index.
    ISBN 978-1-5017-0077-4 (cloth : alk. paper)
    1. United States—Foreign relations—Lebanon.
    2. Lebanon—Foreign relations—United States.
    3. Lebanon—History—Civil War, 1975–1990
    4. Lebanon—History—1946–1975   I. Title.
    DS87.5.S76 2016
    956.9204'3—dc23

                                                2015036172

Cornell University Press strives to use environmentally responsible suppliers and materials to the fullest extent possible in the publishing of its books. Such materials include vegetable-based, low-VOC inks and acid-free papers that are recycled, totally chlorine-free, or partly composed of nonwood fibers. For further information, visit our website at www.cornellpress.cornell.edu.

Cloth printing   10   9   8   7   6   5   4   3   2   1

CONTENTS

ACKNOWLEDGMENTS

Funding for this book came from a variety of sources, including the Graduate Institute of International and Development Studies (formerly l'Institut de Hautes Études Internationales), the Swiss National Science Foundation, the Gerald R. Ford Presidential Foundation, and Trinity Washington University.

I am deeply grateful to Jüssi Hanhimäki for his guidance and support. Mohammed-Reza Djalili of the Graduate Institute and Douglas Little of Clark University provided useful feedback that improved the manuscript. David Painter of Georgetown University and Samir Seikaly of the American University of Beirut kindly welcomed me to their respective institutions and opened doors to a variety of resources. In Beirut, Ambassador Abdallah Bouhabib of the Issam Fares Center for Lebanon, Habib Malik of Lebanese American University, and Niqula Nassif of *al-Akhbar* newspaper shared their time, advice, and assistance in a variety of ways. My gratitude is also due to the many Americans, Lebanese, and Syrians who agreed to be interviewed for this project. I alone am responsible for any errors of fact or judgment.

The staff members at the Nixon and Ford presidential libraries, the National Archives II facility in College Park, the Danish Institute in Damascus, and the Jaffet Library at the American University of Beirut were generous with their time and knowledge. My sincere thanks are due to Michael McGandy of Cornell University Press for shepherding this work through the peer review process and into publication.

Among personal debts, friends and family too numerous to list provided food, shelter, conversation, and inspiration in Geneva, Beirut, Damascus, Washington, Arkansas, and elsewhere. My wife, Yelena Osipova, read the manuscript several times and provided essential intellectual and moral support. This work is dedicated to her.

SPHERES OF INTERVENTION

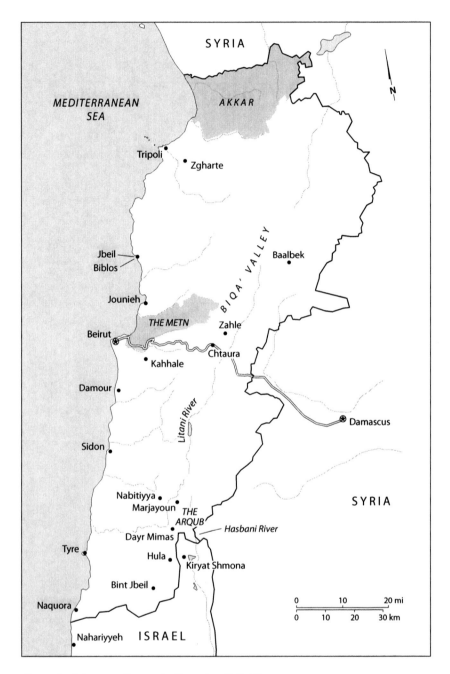

FIGURE 1. Lebanon and its surroundings, circa 1967–76.

Introduction
"This Is the American Policy"

On Martyr's Day, November 11, 2010, speaking live over an Internet video connection, Hizbullah secretary general Hassan Nasrallah gave a history lesson. At the time, the Special Tribunal for Lebanon investigating the murder of Lebanese prime minister Rafiq Hariri was expected to soon issue criminal indictments for numerous suspects, including Hizbullah members. In his speech, Nasrallah repeatedly asserted that the tribunal was a US and Israeli plot to undermine the stability of Lebanon. Then, announcing that he was addressing his opponents in the March 14 coalition, particularly the Christian youth, the party leader proceeded to trace the origins of contemporary US policy back to the days of Henry Kissinger. In June 1976, Kissinger sent a response to an open letter written by Maronite Christian politician Raymond Edde. Edde's letter had accused Kissinger of attempting to destroy and partition Lebanon. In his response, according to Nasrallah, Kissinger explained that Lebanon's formula of coexistence threatened US interests in the region, which depended on "sectarian states" such as Israel. For this reason, Kissinger allegedly wrote, the United States had manufactured the Lebanese Civil War. This admission, Nasrallah proclaimed, should be "taught in the educational curricula in Lebanon and the Arab world" and "printed and circulated so that every Lebanese man, child and old man reads it." After all, he continued, "this is America and this is the American policy."[1]

FIGURE 2. "Dr. No: Engineer of the War in Lebanon!" Henry Kissinger was sometimes compared with Dr. No, the first Bond villain. Cover, *al-Hawadith* magazine, June 18, 1976. American University of Beirut/Library Archives.

Soon after his speech, reporters and political opponents of Hizbullah in Lebanon pointed out that the Kissinger letter was not real, but rather a 1976 satirical piece published in the pages of *al-Hawadith*, a now-defunct Beirut-based leftist newspaper.² A few days later, the author of the fake letter, journalist Salim Nasar, told the story of its creation. At the height of the Two Years' War, just a few days after the Syrian military intervention in June 1976, Nasar was at his home in the mountains. A journalist from *al-Hawadith* came to Nasar's house, needing material for the latest edition of the paper and carrying editions of several local papers to discuss. In one of these was Edde's open letter. Nasar then decided to write a response based on what he thought Kissinger would answer. However, thirty-five years later, Nasar still insisted that the information that he put in the fake letter came from Lebanese officials and a former White House translator, and that Nasrallah's characterizations of US policy in his speech were "100% true."³

The interesting part of this story is not whether the Hizbullah leader had all the details correct in his speech. Rather, it is that it illustrates how widespread the viewpoint is that the United States played an important role in Lebanon's nearly sixteen-year-long civil war. Not only did a major Lebanese political figure tout this letter as a real historical document, but he also weaved it together with current political developments into a larger narrative of the history of US–Lebanese relations. The fact that the letter's author confirmed Nasrallah's analysis, even as he acknowledged that the document was made up, suggests not just the influence of Hizbullah in contemporary Lebanon but also the power of the narrative itself. Many who have spent time in Lebanon have heard some version of this interpretation of US policy. But with a few exceptions, most Western accounts of the Lebanese Civil War ignore this narrative and its implications.⁴

Rather, accounts of Lebanese history in the years between 1967 and 1976 usually portray a period of destabilization culminating in civil war. Internal tensions, already running high in the aftermath of the 1967 Arab-Israeli War, erupted in January 1969 following an Israeli attack on the Beirut airport. Within a few months, the Lebanese army clashed with Palestinian militias present on Lebanese territory, sparking a crisis that would last until November, when an agreement was signed in Cairo between the Lebanese government and the fedayeen, as the militants were known. The country was again thrown into crisis by clashes between Christian militias and fedayeen in the spring of 1970. The political conflict dragged on throughout the summer, abating only after the Palestinians were defeated in September 1970, not by the Lebanese security forces, but by the Jordanian army, hundreds of miles away. Fighting broke out again in May 1973 as the Lebanese army confronted the fedayeen once more. Finally, the country entered a continuous state of conflict from April 1975 until the achievement of an Arab-brokered peace accord in October 1976. These eighteen months of bloodshed, often called the Two Years' War, set the stage for nearly fifteen more years of civil war in Lebanon.[5] Estimates of the number of lives lost during 1975 and 1976 alone range between twenty-five thousand and forty thousand.[6]

These years were also a transitional period in US relations with the Middle East. After Israel's victory in the 1967 war, the Johnson administration refused to press Israel to withdraw from territory it had occupied without some concessions from Arab states. In January 1969, President Richard Nixon took office, marking the start of an era in which the United States would become more deeply involved in the Arab-Israeli conflict than under any previous US administration. During 1969 and 1970, under Secretary of State William Rogers, the State Department launched two diplomatic efforts to broker a settlement to the Arab-Israeli conflict, as well as another failed attempt in 1971. Beginning in 1971, US Middle East policy was increasingly dominated by National Security Advisor Henry Kissinger, who sought to prevent any new diplomatic initiatives. This changed after a regional war broke out in October 1973. Kissinger, now secretary of state, undertook his own diplomatic initiative, which achieved two initial disengagement agreements between Israel and the Arab states in the first half of 1974. Following Nixon's resignation later that year, Kissinger continued to pursue Middle East initiatives during the administration of Gerald Ford, achieving a second disengagement agreement between Egypt and Israel in September 1975. This agreement brought Egypt decisively into the US orbit, while excluding the Palestinians and the Syrians. Ford's electoral defeat in November 1976 put an end to the Kissingerian period of Middle East diplomacy, leaving behind a region transformed but still far from at peace.

This book examines the intersection of these two processes: the collapse of the Lebanese state and the evolving US role in the Middle East. At its core are two related arguments. First, US policy toward Lebanon was subordinated to strategies toward the Cold War and the broader Middle East. During this period, both strategies would undergo changes that would have a great impact on US-Lebanese relations. At least during the early part of the period, Lebanon was still seen as a strategic asset for the United States within the broader context of the Cold War and regional politics. Over time, as Kissinger took over the reins of Middle East policy from the State Department, Lebanon became more marginalized, particularly as the United States became involved more deeply in mediating between Israel and the Arab countries following the October War. Lebanon would only resume its importance after conflict broke out in 1975, though this time in a negative manner: no longer viewed as an asset, Lebanon had now become a potential threat to US interests in the Middle East that needed to be isolated from broader regional affairs.

Second, the United States played a role in the process of Lebanese state collapse. Throughout this period, US policymakers attempted to walk a fine line between contributing to Lebanon's stability and taking sides in a complex conflict that involved many different sects, ideologies and nationalities. This was not easy. Numerous parties within Lebanon solicited US support, including money, weapons, diplomatic assistance, and promises of military intervention. Most of the time, US officials refused their entreaties, but not always. The United States intervened in internal Lebanese politics in a variety of ways, from providing assistance to the Lebanese state to helping Lebanese militias arm themselves. Through these actions, US officials hoped to have an impact on the balance of power in the country. Beyond this direct role, US policies toward the Middle East, particularly toward the Palestinians, also indirectly contributed to the crisis.

This study sheds light on a number of disputed aspects of the history of US foreign policy and of Lebanon's national history, including the role of Lebanon in US Middle East policy, the impact of US policy on the Lebanese state, and the origins of the Lebanese Civil War. Three main questions drive the book's narrative: First, what factors motivated US policy toward Lebanon during this period? Second, how did US policy relate to the origins and outbreak of the Lebanese Civil War? Third, once the conflict broke out, how did the US react to it? The answers to these questions are complicated, but in short, while there is no evidence to support conspiracy theories like Nasrallah's, US behavior did, in more subtle and indirect ways, profoundly shape Lebanon's internal politics in the late 1960s and 1970s.

US Interests in Lebanon

To the casual observer of history, the ebb and flow of US policy toward Lebanon may appear to lack rhyme and reason.[7] Twice during the Cold War, the United States deployed troops to Lebanon. The first time was in 1958. During this time, the United States feared growing Soviet influence in the Middle East, which it saw manifested in an increasingly assertive Egypt, led by Arab nationalist president Gamal Abd al-Nasser. By the mid-1950s, domestic discontent was growing in Lebanon, particularly among its Muslim and leftist populations, who resented President Camille Chamoun's vocally pro-Western foreign policy and apparent intent to revise the constitution to permit himself another term in office. Violence broke out in mid-1958, as loosely organized Muslim, Christian, and leftist groups clashed. After a coup in Iraq toppled the pro-Western monarch in that country, the Eisenhower administration responded to Chamoun's pleas with fourteen thousand US Marines to help restore order. By that time, the violence was already dying down, but a US mediator who accompanied the troops did broker a truce to the conflict. Most historians agree that the Eisenhower administration viewed this action in the context of the Cold War, rewarding Chamoun for his embrace of the Eisenhower Doctrine.[8]

The second time was nearly twenty-five years later. In 1982, Lebanon had been a war zone for the better part of a decade. Hoping to rid its northern neighbor of the Palestinian militias, thereby protecting itself from having to make compromises with its Arab neighbors, Israel invaded southern Lebanon. Despite a promise to the United States that it would stop south of the Litani River, the Israeli army continued northward to Beirut. President Ronald Reagan sent in marines once again, this time under the cover of a so-called Multinational Force that included French, Italian, and British units. The US goal was to facilitate a cease-fire and the evacuation of Palestine Liberation Front (PLO) forces, and then a transition to a new government under the leadership of Bashir al-Gemayel, a polarizing Christian politician and militia leader handpicked by Israel as the next president. Unlike the previous intervention, this one went horribly wrong. Gemayel was assassinated by a massive bomb in the Phalange Party headquarters. Under the cover of the Israeli army, Christian militiamen retaliated by slaughtering thousands of Palestinians at the Sabra and Shatila refugee camps in the south of Beirut. Just over a year later, the Fultinational Force was the target of a suicide bombing that killed more US troops than had been killed at any point since the withdrawal of US ground forces from Vietnam ten years before.

What explains the timing of these interventions, as well as the lack of interventions in other cases? The first encounters between the United States and Lebanon had little to do with geopolitics, but rather with cultural matters. Over the course of the nineteenth century, US missionaries began to move to the Levant region, with the goal of Christianizing, or rather Protestantizing, segments of the local population.[9] But by the post–World War II period, a combination of three factors pushed the United States to engage more deeply with the country: (1) Cold War strategic interests, (2) economic interests, and (3) the Arab-Israeli conflict.

First, during the Cold War, concern about expanding Soviet influence was reflected in military and economic assistance, political intervention, and covert action. In the aftermath of World War II, the Truman administration sought to cooperate with Britain, which was reasserting its influence in the region, as a bulwark against the spread of communism.[10] The Eisenhower administration involved itself more actively in the region, initially hoping that a military alliance would emerge to resist communist advances. However, US officials were also sensitive to Arab public opinion, which opposed the so-called Baghdad Pact because Great Britain adhered to it. Therefore, the US government encouraged its allies not to join the pact.[11] By the early 1960s, efforts to encourage an acceptable Western-leaning regional alliance had failed, and the Kennedy and Johnson administrations concentrated on improving their bilateral relations with Middle Eastern states that they viewed as friendly to US interests, including Lebanon. This trend would continue under the Nixon and Ford administrations.

Second, although US officials did fear the expansion of Soviet influence, explanations that concentrate on the Cold War obscure the fact that the United States had economic interests that may have had little to do with the Soviet Union. Oil was the most important of these. The United States was involved in the search for petroleum in the Middle East well before the advent of the Cold War.[12] As the Middle East's share of world petroleum production and measureable reserves increased, so did US economic interests in the region. From the 1930s, Lebanon was the terminus point for an oil pipeline from Baghdad, and then, from the early 1950s, for the Trans-Arabian pipeline (TAPLINE) from Saudi Arabia. These lines provided a significant source of oil imports for Europe. In addition, the United States and Western powers had a number of other economic interests in the country, including trade, industrial investment, banking, and the aircraft industry. Some revisionist accounts have therefore argued that economic interests did play a role in US policy toward Lebanon during this period. However, even these accounts acknowledge that US economic interests cannot fully explain US attention to Lebanon.[13] By the late 1960s, structural changes within the oil industry, as well as political problems and pricing disputes, had reduced TAPLINE's strategic importance as a supplier of oil to Europe.[14]

Third, following World War II, successive US administrations grew increasingly interested in what would become the Arab-Israeli conflict. After supporting the creation of Israel as a Jewish state in 1948–49, the Truman administration hoped to preserve the status quo by limiting arms shipments to the region.[15] By the mid-1950s, as Egyptian president Nasser grew in power and influence in the Arab world, the United States began to link his ideas with the expansion of Soviet influence and increasingly came to see Israel as a strategic asset. Still, under President Eisenhower, the United States preserved a modicum of neutrality in the conflict, for instance, by opposing the British, French, and Israeli attack on Egypt during the 1956 Suez Crisis. During the early 1960s, the Kennedy and then Johnson administrations began to more actively support Israel, including selling the country major weapons systems for the first time.[16] After the 1967 war, the Johnson administration backed Israel more openly, hoping to "use the new asymmetrical situation to extract peace treaties and recognition of Israel's existence from the Arabs."[17] These hopes did not materialize, at least in the short run.

Lebanon has not received much attention in Western histories of US policy toward the Arab-Israeli conflict. According to William Quandt, US policymakers saw one of the primary US interests in the Middle East as protecting the so-called moderate Arab states, including Jordan and Lebanon, from Soviet influence.[18] Strikingly, however, Lebanon is virtually absent from his and every other narrative of US diplomacy during the Nixon and Ford administrations.[19] Readers are left with little idea of how these countries figured into the policy debates of the period, or whether they mattered at all. Instead, histories of US Middle East diplomacy have often focused on efforts to achieve peace agreements between Israel and Egypt on one hand, and Israel and Syria on the other.[20] This author has attempted to redress this balance in his own work, and this book will serve as another step in that direction.[21]

By contrast, as mentioned above, Lebanese, Palestinian, and other Arab accounts of these years often portray Lebanon as a centerpiece of US policy toward the Arab-Israeli conflict, a phenomenon usually connected with the person of Henry Kissinger. There are several versions of what is often called the Kissinger Plan (*khatat kisinjar*) or the Kissinger Plot (*muamarat kisinjar*), in which the US national security advisor and later secretary of state allegedly attempted to solve the Middle East conflict, particularly the question of the Palestinians, at Lebanon's expense.[22] One version asserts that Kissinger sought to settle the Palestinian refugee population in Lebanon on a permanent basis.[23] Others have asserted that the US caused the conflict in Lebanon in an attempt to destroy the Palestine Liberation Organization (PLO).[24] Some believe that the United States encouraged the Lebanese government to be tough on the Palestinians during the years prior to the outbreak of the civil war, a hypothetical policy often referred to as "Ammanization," in reference to nearby Jordan, whose regime cracked down on and then expelled the Palestinian militants.[25] Others focus on the regional geopolitical situation, arguing that in the aftermath of the 1973 war, the United States sought to divide Lebanon between Israel and Syria to keep both countries within the US orbit.[26] Although these works offer little documentary evidence that such a plan actually existed, they help explain why Lebanese political figures, such as Hassan Nasrallah today, readily embrace the idea that the successive US governments sought to sacrifice Lebanon for its regional interests.

One final consideration must be taken into account in evaluations of US-Lebanese relations. It is possible that US policy toward Lebanon may not have been a product of interests (whether strategic, economic, or other), but simply of neglect.[27] Thus, in one interpretation, these years may have simply been one of the "ebb" periods in US attention toward Lebanon, when US policymakers were focused on events in Vietnam and other parts of the world. Neglect may also be read in a different way: as a side effect of the subordination of Lebanon to the larger interests of US policy on the Arab-Israeli conflict. Whether or not US officials consciously thought about it as such, Lebanon could still be seen as a containment pen for the Palestinian militant groups while the United States dealt with other issues. Indeed, the US focus on the interests of states such as Egypt may have implicitly required that Lebanon and the Palestinians be de-prioritized. Such an argument supports Jüssi Hanhimäki's interpretation of Kissinger's foreign policy as a "flawed architecture" that paid insufficient attention to local and regional conditions around the world.[28]

Causes of the Lebanese Civil War

To understand how US policy may have contributed to the outbreak of the Lebanese Civil War, it is necessary to discuss the broader historical debate over its causes. At least seven categories of explanations have been offered for this conflict: (1) weaknesses in the Lebanese political and social system, (2) changes in demography, (3) socioeconomic developments, (4) the rise of militias, (5) foreign political involvement, (6) attacks on Lebanese territory from outside of Lebanon, and (7) the Arab-Israeli conflict. Many of these are closely interrelated, making it difficult to analyze them separately. Today, nearly all historians acknowledge that the war's causes were multiple, and no single one by itself could have produced the conflict. Still, the debate over the relative importance of these factors remains heated, in part because the narrative of the civil war ties into the country's current political divisions, and many of those who tell it are personally invested with one side or another.

Some have argued that aspects of the Lebanese political and social system were inherently flawed. In 1943, Lebanese political leaders established the National Pact, an unwritten political agreement that established a government system based on a fixed structure of power-sharing among different religious communities. There are seventeen recognized sects in Lebanon, each with its own internal politics. Traditional community leaders, known as *zuama* (singular: *zaim*), play a role in both local politics and on the national stage. Important political positions in government are filled by members of specific sects: the president is a Maronite Christian; the prime minister is a Sunni Muslim; and the speaker of the parliament, a Shi'a Muslim. Other important political and security posts are also reserved for individuals from specific sects. The commander of the army, for instance, is generally a Maronite Christian. Parliamentary seats and civil service positions are allocated on a proportional basis for each sectarian group, including (at this time) a six-to-five ratio of Christian to Muslim deputies in Parliament.[29]

Lebanese state institutions were (and remain) relatively weak. After the country gained independence in 1943, it developed a relatively laissez-faire economy, which earned it the moniker "Merchant Republic." Under the presidency of Fouad Chehab (1958–64), and at least during the first years of the mandate of Charles Helou (1964–70), the state became somewhat stronger. The army and its intelligence branch exercised extensive control over the media and other forms of public expression, and often intervened directly in domestic politics. However, as will be discussed later, a popular backlash and change of regime in 1970 resulted in a change of leadership in the army, weakening the state security forces significantly.

Changes in the country's demography placed strains on the confessional political system. The six-to-five ratio of Christian to Muslim deputies was based on a census from the 1930s that, by the 1960s, no longer corresponded to the actual population, which likely had a higher percentage of Muslims. In addition, Maronite control of two powerful positions, the presidency and the commander of the army, meant in effect that they had more power than other groups. Accounts that portray the Maronites as monopolizing power are somewhat exaggerated.[30] Nonetheless, the confessional system remained a key issue of dispute. Soon after the civil war broke out in 1975, "deconfessionalization" became one of the demands of the Lebanese National Movement, a coalition of leftist and Muslim parties allied with the Palestinian guerrilla factions.

Socioeconomic factors also pushed the country toward conflict, though in complicated ways. In the early years of the war, Lebanese leftist leaders employed the Marxist rhetoric of class conflict to explain the outbreak of the conflict.[31] Today, many scholars continue to argue that socioeconomic factors played an important role, but in a qualified way. Fawwaz Traboulsi, for instance, argues that socioeconomic issues ruptured the fabric of Lebanese society, while also acknowledging that the presence of Palestinian militant groups in Lebanon had much the same effect.[32] The unequal economic development of the country, concentrated on Beirut and other urban areas to the exclusion of many impoverished and rural ones, particularly South Lebanon, fueled instability. Strikes and other civil disturbances were often driven by economic concerns. Those who categorically dispute the role of economic factors in the outbreak of the civil war generally do not address the indirect effects of these social dislocations, which undermined faith in the state and traditional societal institutions.[33]

The rise of the Lebanese militias was both a response to feelings of insecurity and a cause of that insecurity. Armed nonstate groups representing both confessional and ideological causes had been present long before the fedayeen groups began to gather in Lebanon. In modern times, they played a prominent role in the 1958 internal crisis. Many have pointed to the crises of 1969 as the time in which the Christian militias began to train and rearm again.[34] This rearmament is often absent in accounts of the period leading up to the conflict, which present the appearance of these groups as a natural reaction to the presence of the Palestinian militias. By the time of the outbreak of the Lebanese conflict in 1975, the arming of the militias had contributed to a cycle that might be seen as an "intrastate security dilemma," in which various armed groups within the same state could not assess the others' intentions and therefore hoped to arm themselves before their opponents did.[35] Undoubtedly, the presence of these militias reflected the weakness of state institutions, but it was also a manifestation of ingrained social networks that persisted no matter how strong and intrusive the state.

In addition to these internal causes, external ones played a role in the political, social, and ideological polarization of this period. Most scholars recognize the presence of Palestinian armed militias on Lebanese territory as the most important catalyst of the conflict. Arab residents of Mandatory Palestine first sought refuge on Lebanese territory during the 1948–49 Arab-Israeli war. In its aftermath, the Lebanese army and security services strictly controlled these refugees to prevent them from organizing politically or militarily. However, the June 1967 war discredited Arab regimes like Lebanon and undermined their ability to control the emerging Palestinian militias. Much of the time, the argument was phrased in terms of state sovereignty. Those advocating for Lebanese state sovereignty felt that an armed militia on the country's territory was a threat to its identity and security; those advocating for Palestinian national rights felt that the armed struggle was essential for the Palestinians to achieve these rights. But this dispute often had a sectarian element to it. Lebanese Muslims tended to support hosting the Palestinian militant groups, while many though not all Christians opposed this.[36] Even many Palestinian leaders believed that a confrontation between the Lebanese state and the Palestinian "revolution" was probably unavoidable.[37]

The impact of these militias cannot be understood without taking into account the actions of other countries, whose activities undermined the power and legitimacy of the Lebanese state. Such diverse actors as Arab states, Western countries, and the Soviet Union all exerted influence in Lebanon during these years. These interventions included funding media organizations, political parties, and civil society groups; exerting pressure on or bribing politicians; and providing arms to their allies. Arab countries in particular gave significant amounts of money to groups in Lebanon to advance what they saw as their own interests.[38]

The two countries with the most influence on Lebanon were Syria and Israel. In particular, Syrian governments had long seen their security and ideological interests intertwined with those of its neighbor. During a lengthy period of instability in Syria from 1949 until the early 1960s, Lebanon served as a haven for Syrian opposition leaders plotting against the regime in Damascus.[39] By 1970, however, Hafiz al-Asad managed to consolidate control over Syria, which left him less vulnerable to domestic threats. Still, Lebanon retained an important role in Syria's strategy toward the Arab-Israeli conflict. From the late 1960s, Syria provided support to Palestinian militias based in Lebanon. The militias' launching of periodic attacks across the border was a thorn in Israel's side that constituted a potential negotiating chip for Syria in any future peace agreement. At the same time, Syria worried that an Israeli invasion of its own territory could be launched through Lebanon's Biqa Valley.[40] In addition to these security motives, some see pan-Syrian or pan-Arab ideological motivations as responsible for Syria's behavior in Lebanon, which was separated from Syria by the colonial powers in the early twentieth century.[41] However, as the late Lebanese journalist Samir Kassir pointed out, Syria's desire to increase its profile regionally required regional stability, which implies a need for prudence that would tend to preclude the notion that Syria intended to establish direct control of Lebanon's territory.[42]

Israel's policy toward the country on its northern border also focused on ensuring its security, which during the period in question primarily revolved around the issue of the Palestinian guerrillas located on Lebanese territory. Soon after its establishment in 1949, Israel began to conduct reprisal raids against Arab targets to discourage what it saw as a "quest to destroy the Jewish state" by groups based on Egyptian, Syrian, Jordanian, and Lebanese territory.[43] Through these reprisals, Israel sought not just to punish the fedayeen but also to put pressure on the Arab governments to control the militants and, in some cases, to consider peace negotiations.[44] On some occasions, this strategy worked, provoking government crackdowns. However, the attacks often had other effects, including making at least some Arab states more resolutely opposed to compromise with Israel.[45] Moreover, in Lebanon and Jordan, the reprisals undermined public trust in the ability of the state and the army to defend the country. One writer compared this effect to a "vicious vice": if the Lebanese government did not crack down on the commandos, the Israelis would "tighten the screw with massive retaliatory raids which undermine the legitimacy of the regime due to its inability to protect its citizenry." On the other hand, if the government did use force against the fedayeen, "potential domestic discord exert[ed] an equal and opposite pressure."[46] The reprisals also had long-term economic and social effects, contributing to a mass exodus of individuals from the south of Lebanon to the northern cities, particularly Beirut, creating a new class of urban and often politicized Shi'a.[47] These new disenfranchised groups added to those that opposed the Lebanese state, making civil conflict more likely.

Reprisal attacks were not the only feature of Israeli policy toward Lebanon. As Frederic Hof has pointed out, throughout its history, Israel has exhibited a "mild" form of irredentism toward South Lebanon.[48] Israeli leaders occasionally spoke of acquiring territory and waters of Lebanon's south, but there is little evidence during this time period that they seriously planned to annex territory from Lebanon. In addition to irredentism, Kirsten Schulze has noted that in contradiction to the "conventional view" that Israel did not get involved in the domestic affairs of its neighbors, intervention to affect domestic politics and the regional balance of power was a constant feature of its policy toward Lebanon.[49] Israeli leaders had specific ideas about how they wanted the Lebanese government to behave and took more than just defensive actions to achieve this.

Other regional states, including Egypt and Jordan, also played major roles in Lebanese politics, even if their physical distance from the country sometimes limited their ability to influence events there. Under Nasser, Egypt attempted to impose a form of hegemony on Lebanon, much as it did throughout the rest of the Arab world, in part through popular appeals to the country's people in the name of Arab nationalism. This particularly resonated among Lebanon's Muslim population.[50] From 1952 onward, Egypt played an important role in Lebanese politics, including mediating between disputing factions during times of crisis. This role diminished somewhat after Nasser's death in 1970, but Anwar Sadat, his successor, continued to take an interest in Lebanon. Jordan, too, followed closely events in Lebanon, which (like itself) was seen as a weak, "moderate" Arab state whose government wanted to minimize its role in confronting Israel and which also had to deal with the increasing concentration of Palestinian guerillas on its territory. Yet Hussein's influence on Lebanon was also limited by this history. During much of the period in question, Jordan was a relative pariah state among Arab countries for its role in repressing the fedayeen, at least until it began to grow closer to Syria in the aftermath of the 1967 Arab-Israeli War. In addition to these two countries, Libya, Saudi Arabia, Kuwait, Iran, and many others all played minor roles in Lebanese politics during these years, each for their own reasons.[51]

A final factor influencing Lebanon's stability was the course of the negotiations in the Arab-Israeli conflict. If there was to be an end to the presence of the fedayeen on Lebanese territory, it would most likely come through one of two paths: a confrontation between the Lebanese state and the Palestinians that would result in the disarming of these groups, or the conclusion of a Middle East peace agreement that would allow the Palestinians to leave Lebanon. Popular Lebanese support for the fedayeen and Arab pressure on their behalf eventually ruled out the use of force to control the fedayeen. If regional diplomacy closed off options to address the issue of the Palestinians, this could discredit "moderate" groups in Lebanon that supported the diplomatic process and provide spoiler groups with an incentive to launch attacks across the border into Israel. As we will see, the closure of the diplomatic option for dealing with the Palestinians contributed to the dilemma described above.

These factors listed above offer a framework for evaluating the role of the United States in Lebanon's slow descent into civil war. Naturally, not all of these factors bear relevance to the United States. Most "internal" factors, including demography and socioeconomic conditions, were far removed from US influence. For instance, the United States had little say over the creation of the confessional system within Lebanon, and could hardly have borne responsibility for rising birth rates among the Muslim population. Indeed, it would be somewhat foolish to assume that any external power could be entirely responsible for a complex civil war in another country. Still, there are at least three ways that the United States can be seen as deeply complicit in Lebanon's long slide into conflict.

First, perhaps most importantly, US diplomacy in the Arab-Israeli conflict intentionally neglected the issues that were most crucial to Lebanon, particularly the status of the Palestinians. In the late 1960s, when the Palestinian militia groups rejected negotiations with Israel outright, there may have been little that US diplomats could have done to persuade Israel, or indeed these groups themselves, to bring them into peace negotiations. In fact, as this author has argued elsewhere, the State Department's diplomatic initiatives in the early years of the Nixon administration were designed at least in part to lessen Arab pressure on so-called moderate states like Lebanon and Jordan that refused to take militant and pro-Palestinian stances in the Arab-Israeli conflict.[52] Although these efforts did not lead to a peace agreement, they may well have helped countries such as Lebanon and Jordan. But after 1971, the US government ceased initiatives until the outbreak of the 1973 October War, allowing pressure within Lebanon to wax. Moreover, in the period after 1973, when Arab states and some Palestinian leaders indicated their desire to participate in a US-sponsored negotiations process, the United States still refused to address Palestinian concerns head-on. As Rashid Khalidi has argued, the US-brokered disengagement agreements following the 1973 October War, which did not address the concerns of the Palestinians, "had the effect of intensifying the conflict on other Arab-Israeli fronts, and contributing measurably to the consequent devastation of Lebanon."[53]

Second, from the late 1960s, as the cycle of attacks and reprisals between Lebanon and Israel deepened, US diplomats put themselves at the center of a dialogue between the two countries. These officials hoped to broker understandings between two allies to minimize and control the violence along the border. In some cases, as we will see, this may have helped the Lebanese government to work out a modus vivendi with both Israel and the fedayeen that temporarily ended the reprisals and allowed the border to remain calm. As it began to concern dozens of instances of reprisals over many years, however, the benefits of this dialogue became harder to identify. Repeated outbreaks of violence steadily reduced faith in the Lebanese state. Overall, the effect was simply to perpetuate the vicious cycle of reprisals and pressure on the Lebanese government, as described above. Moreover, overall US policy toward the reprisals was primarily guided by an interest in maintaining good relations with Israel, as well as the genuine belief of many US policymakers that Israel had a right to respond to fedayeen attacks. Lebanon's stability, by contrast, was less often the main object of their concern.

Finally, the longstanding relationship of the United States with the Christian community in Lebanon contributed to the willingness of the Lebanese Christian militias to resort to violence. During the years before the outbreak of conflict, Lebanese Christian and other leaders regularly requested assistance from the United States. Most of time, US leaders refused this. However, in several cases prior to the outbreak of the conflict, there is strong reason to believe that the US government helped facilitate the transfer of weapons to the Christian militias from third parties. The type and amount of assistance appears to have been limited, probably reflecting US fears about the discovery of such efforts. However, there is more to this issue than the question of whether and how many guns and dollars were provided. Even a small amount of aid might have persuaded Christian and other militia leaders that more assistance would come, whether in the form of aid or intervention. A number of diplomats, historians, and political figures have suggested that certain Lebanese believed that the United States or other powers would intervene, a belief that reinforced their unwillingness to compromise with their opponents.[54] In fact, the Ford administration did help arm the Lebanese military, knowing that certain elements of this institution were likely to help the Christian militias in the event of a civil war. In short, a failure to adequately set the expectation that no assistance would come in itself contributed to the conflict.

The Course of the Conflict, 1975–76

Whatever US intentions toward Lebanon may have been prior to the civil war, once the fighting broke out, US policymakers were forced to devise a strategy to deal with it. For the most part, the United States attempted to keep its distance from the details of the fighting, but US officials took a keen interest in the progressive regionalization of the conflict, as other countries, including Syria, Egypt, Israel, Libya, and Iraq became increasingly involved. As before, despite the deteriorating humanitarian situation, the United States government did not treat Lebanon simply in isolation, but rather as a function of its impact on the Arab-Israeli conflict.

In 1978, Arab scholar Marwan Buheiry contrasted two interpretations of US policy toward the war: on one hand, that US policymakers had no "master plan" for the Lebanese crisis, which left them "confused and perplexed"; or on the other, that US policy toward Lebanon was a "ruthless exploitation of internal weakness that crowned Kissinger's Middle East policy in 1975–76."[55] Many accounts of US policy during this period echo the first: the US simply reacted to events as they occurred, with the goal of stopping the conflict in Lebanon from preventing US diplomatic initiatives in the Arab-Israeli conflict from going forward.[56] Others, however, suggest that Kissinger actively sought to fan the flames of conflict in order to advance the US regional agenda, for instance, by sowing tensions between Arab parties (Syrians/Palestinians and Syrians/Egyptians).[57] Some accounts straddle the fence, noting that the United States derived a number of benefits from the conflict, while recognizing that this does not necessarily mean that it intended to exacerbate it.[58]

Buheiry's latter interpretation comes closest to capturing the intentions of top US policymakers, particularly Henry Kissinger. The United States may not have had a master plan for Lebanon, but its officials had a strong sense of interests in the region that guided their policy. Kissinger came to see the intra-Lebanese feuding and accompanying inter-Arab strife as a dangerous threat to US interests. In the short term, it may have distracted Syria, the PLO, and other parties from the Arab-Israeli conflict, but it also threatened to radicalize these groups in a way that could spark regional violence that could undermine the steps already taken in the Arab-Israeli negotiations. To prevent this, the US government acted in two ways to affect the course of the fighting.

First, the United States drew on its diplomatic relations with other countries in an attempt to control outside intervention. The United States government had close relations with other involved states including Israel, Syria, Egypt, Jordan, and Saudi Arabia, not to mention various Lebanese groups. Kissinger later even claimed that the United States was the "only country in contact with all the factions" in Lebanon.[59] Here, as elsewhere, the secretary of state exaggerates, since France and Britain, too, had contacts with all of the countries and Lebanese factions, as well as much stronger contacts than the United States to the PLO. However, neither of these had the financial and military means of the United States, or its close relations with Israel. The State Department began to consult closely with other states about the Lebanese conflict only in October 1975, some six months into the fighting, and did not send a mediator until April 1976, when former diplomat Dean Brown visited Lebanon for a six-week mission.

These overt efforts at mediation were less important than those that took place behind the scenes. The US government moved from facilitating communications between the Lebanese army and Israel to passing signals from Israel to Syria and back. These steps were designed to control the manner in which the regionalization of the conflict occurred. As will be argued, these steps were probably *less* consequential than some have imagined, but they may well have helped smooth the way to a settlement of the conflict that did not involve a regional war. Most importantly, the allegation that the United States helped facilitate the Syrian intervention in Lebanon by communicating a set of "red lines" is misleading. In many cases, the Syrian and Israeli governments seem to be sending the exact same messages through their press statements. It was the fact that they were sending messages through these back channels, rather than the content of the messages, that was novel. This process of communication helped underline to Syria that its intervention should take place in a careful, controlled manner.

Second, US government officials arranged for some support to be provided to the Maronite militias via other countries, which likely contributed to lengthening the conflict rather than shortening it. Some accounts have speculated that the United States may have provided some direct assistance to these groups after the fighting broke out in 1975.[60] Declassified documents suggest that this option was considered and then dismissed. Kissinger, apparently on his own authority, encouraged the Israelis to provide weapons to the Christians, but there is no evidence that the United States government supplied these groups directly in 1975–76.[61] It has been suggested that, in addition to Israel, Jordan and Iran may have also been likely channels of aid to the militias.[62] Thus far, no documentary evidence has come to light that demonstrates US collusion in arms shipments from countries other than Israel during this period of the Two Years' War, though toward the end of 1976, Jordan did inform US officials that it was planning on shipping weapons to the Christian militias. Whatever the extent of the coordination, top US officials knew of and supported the strategic logic of these Israeli and Jordanian arms transfers.

The expectations of the local parties in regard to support from the United States may have also had an impact on the conflict. As we saw above, many have assumed that the Maronite Christian militias expected US intervention in the conflict, which might have encouraged them to adopt more aggressive military strategies and negotiating positions than they might have otherwise. In fact, the Maronites were extremely disappointed in what they saw as a lack of support from the West, even though they made few requests for support directly to the US government. The Palestinians, the Lebanese National Movement, and other opposition forces may also have been either emboldened or deterred by their perceptions about the likelihood of a US intervention. For instance, the Christian leaders' opponents, particularly Kamal Jumblatt, concluded in spring 1976 that US opposition to Syrian intervention was actually benefiting them. But even if the parties' assumptions were divorced from reality, the fact that they made them still suggests that the international sphere had a deep impact on the conflict itself. In this way, beliefs about what the United States might do were nearly as important as what it actually did.

The Ford administration also contemplated the possibility of taking a different approach to the Lebanese conflict that would have required a reevaluation of its policy toward the Arab-Israeli conflict. In 1975 and 1976, at several junctures, US policymakers considered bringing the PLO into the Arab-Israeli peace process, or even conducting talks with the PLO in the context of mediating in the Lebanese Civil War, either of which could have facilitated a resolution to the conflict in Lebanon. Such a move would have meant that the Christian groups would have had less reason to fear that the Palestinians would take over the Lebanese state; the Palestinians, on the other hand, would have had an incentive not to provoke conflict in Lebanon. However, this would have contradicted key parts of Kissinger's dual goal of shielding Israel from the claims of the Palestinians and the Ford administration from the potential domestic repercussions of adopting a strategy that would have been considered by many Americans to be hostile toward Israel. Though the secretary of state was tempted by this possibility at times, he did not allow this to occur, cutting off at least one possible route to resolving the Lebanese imbroglio.

All this adds up to the conclusion that the US role in Lebanon was limited but essential. By passing messages, sending signals, and often holding out the tantalizing impression of support, the United States contributed to the deepening of the conflict there. But this does not mean that the war should be interpreted as a US conflict alone. Lebanon was a battleground in which many different parties—including Syria, Israel, Egypt, Libya, the PLO, the United States, and the Soviet Union, not to mention the Lebanese factions themselves—saw their national interests or even survival at stake. The priority of most of these parties was to prevent a defeat rather than to score an absolute victory. The result, intentions notwithstanding, was an absolute tragedy.

This book has three parts. The first three chapters address the period between 1967 and 1970, including the impact of the 1967 war on the political situation within Lebanon (chapter 1); the US-Lebanese relations during the run-up to the signature of the 1969 Cairo Agreement between the Lebanese government and the Palestinian militias (chapter 2); and the period until the events of Black September in Jordan restored a measure of calm in the country (chapter 3). The next two chapters discuss the years between 1970 and 1975, including the reemergence of the conflict between the Lebanese government and the Palestinians in 1972–73 (chapter 4) and the somewhat hopeful period between the 1973 October War and the April 1975 outbreak of the civil war (chapter 5). The last three chapters look at the first two years of the Lebanese Civil War in 1975–76, including the US reaction to the outbreak of conflict (chapter 6), the establishment of the so-called Red Line Agreement (chapter 7), and the events following the Syrian intervention in Lebanon up until establishment of a temporary peace and the end of the Ford administration (chapter 8). The book ends with a brief epilogue, drawing parallels to the present day, at which time various Lebanese groups continue to try to draw the United States in their ongoing battles.

CHAPTER 1

Sparks in the Tinderbox

The United States, the June War, and the Remaking of the Lebanese Crisis

Near the end of the 1960s, Lebanon was shaken by two events: the June 1967 Arab-Israeli War and the December 1968 Israeli attack on the Beirut airport. Each prompted a major popular backlash against the Lebanese government and Western interests in Lebanon, straining the country's confessional political system and calling into question its traditional neutrality in regional and international affairs. Many consider these events to be the regional triggers that set the country on the path to civil war.

If these were earthquakes, however, tensions had long been building up along the country's fault lines. Lebanon's sectarian political system had already been tested nearly a decade earlier during the 1958 civil war. In the aftermath of that conflict, a new ruling coalition struck a balance on the internal and foreign policy issues that divided the country. By the late 1960s, the coalition had begun to dissolve in the face of internal and regional pressures, including increasing political interference by the Lebanese military, heightened violence and rhetoric in the inter-Arab and Israeli-Arab conflicts, and a new global wave of revolutionary spirit that was sweeping across the Middle East, and indeed, much of the Third World.

Throughout the 1960s, the United States played a passive yet important role in internal Lebanese politics. In the first years of the decade, the Kennedy and Johnson administrations paid relatively little attention to Lebanon. But as regional politics heated up over the course of the decade, so too did the US interest in Lebanon. US officials attempted to stay close to Lebanon through arms sales and small amounts of economic aid, though neither could defuse the opposition within Lebanon to US policy toward the Arab-Israeli conflict.

Meanwhile, Lebanese interest in the United States was growing. Both the government and various other groups solicited US support in their internal struggles. At the same time, groups opposed to Western influence in Lebanon launched a coordinated attack on US interests in the country. The 1967 war and the Israeli attack on the Beirut airport strengthened these forces considerably, increasing their prominence and influence over the country's government, which would ultimately allow the gathering of Palestinian militant groups on its territory.

Lebanese Domestic Tensions on the Eve of the June War

Lebanon's internal political situation on the eve of the June 1967 war was a direct legacy of the 1958 civil war. During this conflict, Sunni Muslim, Nasserist, and leftist groups rose up against mostly Christian forces loyal to President Camille Chamoun. This coalition resented many aspects of Chamoun's rule, but the most galling were his announcement of support for the Eisenhower Doctrine in 1957, his US-funded intervention in the 1957 parliamentary elections, and his 1958 attempt to modify the Lebanese constitution to allow his reelection. Not all Christians supported the president. The Maronite patriarch clashed with Chamoun, while Pierre Gemayel's Phalange Party (also known by its Arabic name, al-Kataib) stayed largely neutral during the fighting. Nor did all Muslims support the opposition, as Prime Minister Sami al-Sulh remained loyal to the president.[1] Nevertheless, the conflict took on strong sectarian overtones, cracking the foundation of sectarian cooperation that was supposed to be the basis for the Lebanese state. The Lebanese army wisely refused to get directly involved in the conflict, instead playing a peacekeeping role between the two sides. Now, in his time of crisis, Chamoun called for the United States to send troops in to restore order. Following a coup against the Western-aligned Hashemite ruler of Iraq, the United States obliged, deploying marines to Lebanon to facilitate an end to the conflict.

A key to the resolution of this crisis was the election of army commander Fouad Chehab to a six-year term as president.[2] Chehab's election ended the rebellion and facilitated the formation of a new government that attempted to deal with the issues of internal development and foreign policy that had led to the conflict in the first place.[3] To address the country's unequal distribution of wealth, his regime undertook a program of modernizing and building up the Lebanese state, expanding state services such as running water and electricity to many rural parts of the country that had previously had neither. Through vocal support for the Arab cause, as well as by aligning himself closely with Gamal Abd al-Nasser, Chehab earned the support of much of Lebanon's Muslim population.

To his critics, however, Chehab was an aloof ruler with autocratic tendencies whose foreign policy unnecessarily exposed Lebanon to danger. Over time, Chehab gradually extended the control of the army's intelligence branch, the Deuxième Bureau (DB), over the country's internal politics, particularly after a 1961 coup d'état attempt by the Syrian Socialist National Party. Following this incident, the DB began to intervene more heavily in the country's political life, tapping phone lines, censoring the media, and interfering in elections. At least initially, Chehab drew support from across the Lebanese political spectrum. Some Christian groups, such as Pierre Gemayel's Phalange Party, supported Chehab's programs; however, they paid a price for this in support among the Christian population, many of whom saw the Chehabists as catering too much to "Arab" opinion, meaning paying lip service to the idea of Arab nationalism while voicing vocal opposition to Israel. Others, such as Chamoun's National Liberal Party and Raymond Edde's National Bloc, vocally opposed the Chehabists, resenting the military's frequent intervention in domestic affairs.[4]

The continuity of Chehab's political legacy was established with the 1964 election of his handpicked successor, Charles Helou, as president. Born in 1913, Helou made his name as a journalist with the French-language newspaper *Le Jour*. During the 1958 uprising, Helou and several others had established themselves as part of a so-called Third Force that sought a middle ground between the belligerents.[5] Helou was elected largely on the basis of his reputation and his association with the Chehabist political movement.[6] Over time, however, Helou would develop significant disagreements with the Chehabists and the DB, a political bloc known as the Nahj, whose loyalty to the former president often undermined Helou's authority. Pensive and prone to periodic bouts of depression, Helou would try to toe the line between two opposing groups, the Chehabists and their mostly Christian opposition. However, this would open him up to charges of weakness and vacillation from both sides.

The increasing radicalization of the Arab world, and the implications that this had for Lebanon's role in regional politics, greatly complicated Helou's balancing act. Nasser's Egypt, or the United Arab Republic (UAR), as the union of Egypt and Syria between 1958 and 1961 was known, had long exerted a strong influence in Lebanese affairs. During the 1950s and 1960s, the so-called Arab Cold War grew more intense. After the 1961 breakup of the UAR, a deep mistrust reigned between Egypt and Syria. Tensions between Egypt and Saudi Arabia fueled civil wars in Yemen and an insurgency in Oman.[7] Competition between Egypt and Syria on one hand, and Egypt and Saudi Arabia on the other, manifested in a number of disputes in Lebanon, in the press and elsewhere.[8] Meanwhile, regimes with even more militant foreign policy positions than that of Nasser took root in Iraq in 1958 and consolidated power in Syria in 1963. In addition, newly formed Palestinian fedayeen groups, as well as the creation of the PLO as an umbrella group in 1964, added strong voices to those pushing for radical action against Israel. Fatah, a new organization under Yasser Arafat, launched its first attack into Israel from Jordanian territory in 1965.[9] As a result, the Arab "center" shifted decidedly toward militarism, subjecting Lebanon to a wide variety of pressures from Arab states.

Given that intra-Arab feuds tended to fuel conflicts within Lebanon, one might have expected an Arab reconciliation to have had a net benefit on the country's internal politics. However, this was not the case. Relations between Syria and Egypt improved by the mid-1960s, in part because of an agreement to focus on the two countries' common enemy, Israel. This only brought new pressures to bear on Lebanon's long-standing neutrality in the Arab-Israeli conflict. At the 1964 Cairo Summit of the Arab League, some Arab regimes began to push Lebanon to participate in a number of elements of an Arab "common defense strategy" against Israel, such as diverting the waters of the Jordan River, which flowed through southern Lebanon into Israel, and stationing troops from other Arab countries on Lebanese territory. Aware of the sensitivities of the Lebanese internal situation, Egyptian president Nasser personally intervened to prevent Helou from having to host Syrian forces on his country's territory, telling Helou that in case of trouble, he could call for Egyptian forces instead. However, Nasser still insisted that Lebanon begin work on diverting the Jordan River.[10]

One important change in the Lebanese domestic political landscape during this period was the growing role of leftist and Arab nationalist political parties. Such groups had been present since before the founding of the Lebanese state in 1943, but they initially played a relatively small role in Lebanese politics. The Lebanese Communist Party (LCP) had had a presence in Lebanon since 1925. Although it was officially banned in 1948, it continued to organize its activities openly, though it had little success in affecting the country's domestic affairs.[11] The Movement of Arab Nationalists (MAN), originally founded by students at the American University of Beirut (AUB), had branches and operations in a variety of Arab countries, particularly Yemen and Oman. With the exception of a small role in the 1958 crisis, MAN's activities in Lebanon remained limited. Smaller Baath and Nasserist parties had influence in some localities, but they had no broad base of support. The exception to this general rule about the weakness of the Left was the Progressive Socialist Party (PSP) of Druze leader Kamal Jumblatt. Jumblatt's position as a traditional zaim meant that he enjoyed the support of a large part of the Druze community, even as he advocated progressive political positions.[12] However, apart from the 1958 civil war, there was little effective cooperation between these groups.

During the 1960s, due in part to regional and international developments, these parties began to focus increasingly on common issues. Some in the Lebanese Left were exposed to the international influences of the 1960s, traveling to youth and student conferences and meeting other Third World leaders in Africa and Latin America.[13] The increasingly militant positions of Nasserism and the escalating war in Vietnam contributed to an atmosphere in which these groups began to overcome some of their ideological differences. In the mid-1960s, they began to work together, in large part because of a growing focus on the Arab-Israeli conflict. In March 1965, the LCP's Central Committee began to advocate involvement in Arab issues and joining forces with groups such as the MAN and the PSP.[14] Among the Arab Nationalists, by the 1960s, splits had begun to develop in the leadership over several issues, including how close they should remain to Nasserism and whether the group should pursue armed action to liberate Palestine. In consonance with Nasser's wishes, the MAN did not push for military action against Israel, though it began military training.[15] Jumblatt played a leading role in exploring alliances with these leftist groups. In 1965, he formed the "Front of Progressive Parties and Powers and Nationalist [wataniyya] Personalities," which provided a forum for cooperation among these marginal (and marginalized) parties, including the LCP, Baath, and Arab nationalist movements, to affect national politics in a way that their small size might not have otherwise allowed.[16]

As the leftists were uniting in opposition to the government, two groups who might well have cooperated in support of the status quo in foreign policy—the army and the traditional Maronite Christian leaders—were hardly on friendly terms. Chehab initially enjoyed the support of some Christian leaders. However, the concessions that Chehab and Helou made to Nasserism, including embracing a role within the new common defense strategy against Israel, alienated much of the Maronite population, which began to unite in opposition to the Chehabists. In early 1967, three of the country's most important Maronite Christian zuama, Pierre Gemayel, Camille Chamoun, and Raymond Edde, formed a political grouping called al-Hilf al-Thulathi (usually shortened to Hilf), or Tripartite Alliance, to oppose the Chehabists. This also began to affect President Helou, who understood that the Lebanese president was considered the representative of the Christian population, much as the Sunni prime minister would be expected to represent the interests of Lebanon's Sunni population.

At this time, the dispute over the country's role in regional affairs did not yet focus on the Palestinian militias that had begun to proliferate across the Arab world. Prior to the 1967 Arab-Israeli war, Lebanon had a restrictive policy toward the Palestinian refugees within its borders. The DB kept a close watch over the Palestinian refugee camps to prevent groups from arming. Still, the guerillas did have a clandestine presence in the camps. One fedayeen member, Jalal Kaawash, died at the hands of Lebanese army interrogators in December 1965.[17] The army often arrested fedayeen who crossed from Syria into southern Lebanese territory to infiltrate Israel. Rarely did this result in cross-border incidents, though in one case in 1965, Israel did launch a retaliatory raid into Lebanon.[18] In 1966, the army arrested and interrogated Yasser Arafat himself in South Lebanon, only later recognizing who had been captured.[19] Some important Lebanese groups did support the fedayeen at this time, including Sunni Muslim leaders, the Lebanese Left, and Kamal Jumblatt, who, even prior to the 1967 war, had argued that the fedayeen should be allowed to pursue their armed struggle from bases in Lebanon.[20] Even though the idea of letting Palestinians organize from Lebanon had some supporters at the time, this was not nearly as widespread as it would become later.

The United States and Lebanon in the 1960s

After the US forces departed in 1958, the United States and Lebanon resumed a relationship that, although not completely trouble free, would seem near-idyllic by comparison less than a decade later. At that time, the US embassy in Beirut enjoyed relatively cordial relations with individuals from most Lebanese sects and political groups. Both President Fouad Chehab and his successor, Charles Helou, as well as the army leadership, met frequently with the US ambassador. Beirut was also a hub for US economic and political activity. Many US corporations had branch offices there. At any given time, around twenty officials from the State Department, the CIA, the US

Information Agency (USIA), and other government departments pursued Arabic language studies in Beirut, leaving many with fond memories of the country and a familiarity with its complex politics.[21]

US policy toward Lebanon during the early 1960s reflected a broader global and regional policy, particularly toward the Arab world. From the late 1950s, the Eisenhower administration had worked to improve relations with the Arabs, especially with Nasser and Egypt.[22] By the early 1960s, however, US relations with Egypt began once again to encounter problems, as the Kennedy and then Johnson administrations increased their support for Israel, to whom they provided new types of weapons and consistent diplomatic support.[23] Still, the Kennedy administration initially attempted to court Nasser's regime to keep it out of the Soviet sphere of influence.[24] By the time of Kennedy's assassination, tensions between the United States and Egypt had been heightened by US opposition to Egypt's policy in Yemen, but the two powers tried hard to keep their differences under control.[25]

In the early 1960s, the Arab-Israeli conflict still played a relatively small role in US-Lebanese relations, reflecting the fact that the United States still sought to stay out of the feud. US administrations had as yet made few efforts to broker a Middle East peace. During the 1950s, the Eisenhower administration had made several secret efforts, known as the Alpha and Gamma projects, to promote behind-the-scenes talks between the Arabs and Israelis.[26] After these failed, US officials stopped these initiatives, viewing the issue as essentially a lost cause. In 1962, Kennedy authorized Dr. Joseph Johnson, the head of the Carnegie Endowment for Peace, to propose a solution to the Palestinian refugee problem, resulting in what would be known as the Johnson Plan.[27] However, this plan was rejected by Israel.[28] Despite Israel's refusal, in 1962 the Kennedy administration decided to sell Hawk missiles to Israel, angering many in Lebanon and throughout the Arab world.[29] In the eyes of many Arabs, this sale of weapons diminished the ability of the United States to serve as a neutral arbiter in the region.

Although US officials in Beirut did not intervene in Lebanese politics during this period, the legacy of Eisenhower's Lebanon policy left many in that country with the impression that the United States might well do so. Not only had the Marines landed in Beirut, but, as the memoirs of several CIA operatives later revealed, the US had also helped fund the campaigns of Chamoun's allies during the 1957 parliamentary.[30] During the 1964 presidential election, many Lebanese and other parties sought US support again. Some wanted the US embassy to help persuade Chehab to serve another term as president, while others desired support for their own candidates. In a summary cable to Washington, a US political officer provided a partial list of individuals "upon whose ears counsels of moderation had fallen with some effect," which included nineteen Lebanese politicians and religious figures, as well as the UAR ambassador, who had passionately argued in favor of extending Chehab's term. In the election, however, the US ambassador remained staunchly neutral.[31]

By 1964, the worsening Arab-Israeli conflict once again put this issue at the center of US relations with the region, including US-Lebanese military cooperation. As Lebanon came under pressure to participate in common Arab defense plans, its government and army turned to the United States for military equipment. From the beginning of the decade, the United States had already been discussing the sale of high-performance aircraft to Lebanon, first F-4s and then F-8As.[32] At the January 1964 Cairo Summit, the Arab League decided to award funds to Lebanon to purchase military equipment, including aircraft, to help with the common Arab defense. Soon thereafter, the US State Department began to worry that assistance to Lebanon would fuel a regional arms race.[33] US officials started to urge their Lebanese counterparts to think twice about purchasing any planes, warning that they would likely be ineffective against Israel's French-built Mirage aircraft, not to mention expensive to maintain. For their part, many political figures within Lebanon, including Helou, were not particularly eager to acquire the planes, seeing the purchase as a political necessity rather than a military one.[34] By January 1966, the US informed Helou that it needed all the F-8A planes for Vietnam, in effect refusing the Lebanese request.[35] Soon after, Lebanon purchased ten advanced Mirage III aircraft from France instead. US and Lebanese officials also discussed the sale of Hawk surface-to-air missiles and the deployment of a US civil defense adviser in Lebanon, but after numerous delays, these plans were effectively cancelled by the outbreak of the 1967 Arab-Israeli War.[36]

The US State Department also took up contacts with the Israelis on behalf of the Lebanese. In 1965, Israel repeatedly threatened to use military force to halt Lebanese efforts to divert the Jordan River. US officials encouraged their Israeli counterparts not to resort to the use of force, particularly in view of what they called Lebanon's "delicate political situation."[37] Though it is unclear whether such representations were decisive, Israel did not attack the Lebanese projects. The US government also encouraged Israeli restraint in response to fedayeen attacks from Syria into Israel that occasionally crossed Lebanese territory.[38]

By late 1965, both the Lebanese government and the US embassy in Beirut were growing increasingly concerned about the rising influence of the Soviet Union and the Lebanese Left. The new ambassador at that time was Dwight Porter, an austere Midwesterner whose father had been a classics professor. Porter came into office with a good knowledge of Lebanese politics, having previously served as a senior assistant for Robert Murphy, the US envoy during the 1958 crisis.[39] In late September 1965, Helou asked for US assistance in the economic field, stressing the importance of this for his own political position, which was being challenged by the Lebanese left for not doing enough to address the country's economic and social problems. Porter suggested that Helou needed to exert more personal control to combat the Left. The two then decided that the US embassy, or rather an "Embassy annex"—obviously a reference to the intelligence services—should work more closely with the director of Sureté Générale, Lebanon's internal security force.[40] Two weeks later, the two again discussed in detail the rise of the Left and Soviet influence in Lebanon. Porter suggested to Helou that his Foreign Ministry and other sources were probably not secure. Helou agreed, saying that he also had doubts about members of his directorate. Porter gave Helou an intelligence report on Soviet activities in Lebanon, which claimed that five newspapers in Beirut received regular Soviet subsidies in exchange for printing anti-US propaganda.[41]

Over the next two years, growing anti-US sentiment was expressed in regard to visits of the US Sixth Fleet. At this time, the Sixth Fleet conducted regular visits to the port of Beirut about twice a year, allowing sailors an opportunity for leave.[42] Leftist and Nasserist newspapers often launched invectives against the visits, but these generally had little impact.[43] By 1966, however, this began to change. In May of that year, the US ambassador reported that local leftist groups had begun an "intense and vehement anti-American campaign" as a result of a meeting of US ambassadors in Beirut and the recent visit of the US Sixth Fleet to that city's port.[44] By early June, many Lebanese, including those who were often pro-American, were furious that the United States had agreed to sell A-4 Skyhawk planes to Israel.[45] Soon thereafter, the Lebanese government asked for a postponement of a planned fleet visit. The US military had little choice but to accede to the Lebanese request, which both sides agreed to keep quiet.[46] Still, other scheduled visits took place over the fall. During one port call by the USS *Independence* at the end of October, the sailors performed volunteer work, while nearly eight thousand members of the public toured the ship. A missile demonstration was even arranged for the members of science clubs at AUB and Haigazian College. Although a few Lebanese newspapers lambasted the ship's visit, Lebanese government officials welcomed its arrival.[47] At least for the moment, the US reputation appeared to have been restored.

Some Lebanese groups courted US support against what they portrayed as Nasserist and Soviet influences, including (according to them) the Chehabists. Not all these groups were Christian. In January 1967, Shi'a leader Kazim Khalil approached a US embassy official to request financial support for the new Tripartite Alliance, saying that "other governments" were supporting the other groupings and that it would be cheaper to support them now than later, when it would be more expensive, "as was the case in 1958." The US embassy in Beirut recommended against this, and there is no evidence that any support was provided.[48] Khalil's request reflected increasing political tensions in the public sphere that stemmed in part from the broader Arab-Israeli conflict. In early March 1967, Pierre Gemayel sent an open letter to President Helou complaining about Egyptian political interference in Lebanon. Around the same time, the pro-UAR and leftist Lebanese press began an intense campaign against what they portrayed as interference by the US ambassador.[49]

At this point, developments in the Arab-Israeli confrontation squelched plans for another Sixth Fleet visit, this time in a much more public way. In early April, while the Lebanese government was considering a US request for a Sixth Fleet visit beginning May 26, Israeli prime minister Levi Eshkol told a journalist that the United States had offered him "solemn promises" that Israel did not need to purchase US arms, implying that the Sixth Fleet would be used to guarantee Israel's security.[50] In an angry speech, Syrian prime minister Nuraddin Atassi demanded that Lebanon prevent the fleet from visiting.[51] Even Soviet general secretary Leonid Brezhnev jumped on the bandwagon, claiming in an April 24 speech that there was no reason for the Sixth Fleet to be in the Mediterranean twenty years after the end of World War II.[52] On May 15, President Helou reluctantly asked Porter to postpone the visit indefinitely, worrying that it might bring down the government of Prime Minister Rashid Karame.[53] On May 18, the government made the official announcement that although the visit had been approved "in principle," it would not take place at this time—a face-saving compromise that barely masked the fact that the ship's visit had been jettisoned. The cancellation was a blow to US prestige, but it would seem relatively mild in comparison to what was to come after the outbreak of war just a few weeks later.

Lebanon's Six Day War

The dispute over Sixth Fleet visits to Lebanon played out against the background of heightened tensions between Israel and its Arab neighbors. These strains eventually culminated in the outbreak of war on June 5, 1967. Historians have placed responsibility for this war on nearly all of its participants and both superpowers.[54] In the months prior to the outbreak of war, attacks by Palestinian militants across the Syrian and Jordanian borders had become an increasing menace to Israeli villages, particularly those in the country's north, near the Golan Heights.[55] Israel's own behavior had been provocative, particularly along the Golan Heights, where the Israeli military often deliberately provoked the Syrian army so that it could launch reprisals. Nasser's motives remain unclear, but his actions helped precipitate the crisis. As the war of words escalated between Israel and Egypt, on May 16, Nasser requested that the UN withdraw the forces that it had stationed along that border following the 1956 Suez Crisis. On May 23, Egypt closed the Straits of Tiran to Israeli shipping, giving that country what it considered to be a casus belli, or legitimate grounds for using military force. Some historians have contended that Nasser's actions were at least partially motivated by false intelligence reports, provided by the Soviet Union, of an impending Israeli attack on Syria, though there has been a significant amount of dispute over whether the Soviets really intended to bring about a war.[56]

The Johnson administration's attitude toward the growing tensions prior to the Six Day War is also a matter of dispute. Avi Shlaim argues that the Johnson administration, via Secretary of Defense Robert McNamara, gave Israel a straightforward "green light" to intervene.[57] William Quandt, by contrast, has suggested that the administration eventually gave Israel a "yellow light" prior to the war, which the Israelis took to mean "green."[58] Douglas Little suggests that US officials were doing their utmost to prevent hostilities prior to the conflict.[59] Whatever the case, the administration certainly feared the implications of a conflict for US interests in the region, particularly its relations with its moderate allies. As the cancellation of the US Sixth Fleet visit had illustrated, US relations with friendly Arab states depended in part on the status of the Arab-Israeli conflict. This concerned not only Lebanon. Indeed, US relations with countries such as Jordan, a frontline state in the conflict, and Saudi Arabia, a key oil producer, may well have been considered more important. In any case, by the end of May, the administration saw little that it could do to stop the conflict. If it used its influence to force Israel to back down, Nasser would be strengthened, while Israel and the moderate Arab states would be weakened. If Israel attacked, the conflict could also cause a backlash against US interests in the region. This conundrum was exacerbated by the signature of a mutual defense pact between Nasser and King Hussein of Jordan on May 30. In such an atmosphere, the administration began to grasp for any possible solution. Perhaps wishfully, National Security Council (NSC) official Harold Saunders wondered whether it might be best to "allow fighting to ensue," so that Israel would take the blame for any confrontation, rather than the United States.[60]

Once the war broke out on June 5, the fighting itself was quickly settled. The Arab armies were unprepared and overwhelmed by the Israeli attacks, which destroyed most of the Egyptian air force during the first day of combat. The Johnson administration was incensed by Nasser and Hussein's accusations that the US and UK warplanes had participated in attacks on Arab forces, as well as their decision (along with five other Arab states) to break off relations with the United States and Great Britain.[61] In part for this reason, during the conflict, the Johnson administration was unwilling to push Israel to stop its advance on the West Bank and Jerusalem, though it did transfer an offer of a cease-fire by Hussein to Tel Aviv on June 7.[62] Israel refused. By June 10, Israel was in control of the entire West Bank of the Jordan River, the Syrian Golan Heights, and Egypt's Sinai Peninsula up to the Suez Canal.

Although not a single bomb had fallen on its territory, Lebanon was deeply shaken by the war. After the Israeli attack began, other Arab countries and a vocal minority within Lebanon pressured the government to join the fighting. Had the war dragged on longer, this might well have occurred. On June 6, a worried President Helou told Porter that Lebanon might be forced to undertake a "limited" military initiative against Israel or allow Syrian troops to pass through its territory. Syria, he said, was pressuring Lebanon through demonstrations by Syrian workers and Palestinian refugees, as well as via Lebanese politicians such as Kamal Jumblatt. Porter warned Helou that Israel could be expected to respond to any attack from Lebanese soil.[63] In reality, the protests were probably genuine expressions of popular sentiment, rather than foreign manipulation. Certainly they were felt at the highest levels of power. According to news reports, on June 7, Lebanese prime minister Rashid Karame ordered army commander Emile Bustany to attack Israel, though the latter apparently refused to do so. Some Lebanese officials later denied that this had occurred, but the announcement itself was enough to raise tensions throughout the country.[64]

US officials had hoped that they would not be blamed for the war, but this turned out to be a pipe dream. As the scale of the Arab defeat became clear, the calls for an attack on Israel died down but anti-Western demonstrations continued. Public anger against the West was magnified by accusations of US and UK participation in the Israeli attack on Egypt. In the Hamra neighborhood of West Beirut, protesters armed with Molotov cocktails attacked the US embassy. One succeeded in breaking into the second floor and setting a small fire, though it was extinguished quickly.[65] Other sites in

Lebanon linked to Western interests were attacked, including the Mobil Oil headquarters, Shell Oil storage tanks, the Saudi embassy, and the St. George Yacht Club. Fearing attacks against US citizens, the US embassy in Beirut ordered the evacuation of about three thousand US nationals living in Lebanon.[66] Under pressure from Muslim and leftist groups, the Lebanese government recalled its ambassador from Washington and requested that the United States recall Porter. The ambassador returned to Washington for several months, but relations between the two countries were not severed.[67]

Pro-Western rightist groups in Lebanon feared that these demonstrations were designed to force the country to abandon its ties to the West. Maronite political parties, particularly the Phalange, made every effort to prevent the Lebanese government from breaking off diplomatic relations with the United States and the United Kingdom. According to US embassy reports, during the war, the Phalange sent militiamen to stop pro-Nasser demonstrators, reportedly killing up to fifteen people. The group also offered to guard the US embassy if Lebanese security forces could not.[68] On June 18, the Tripartite Alliance leaders met to settle on a strategy. Two days later, Gemayel issued a statement calling for the "internationalization and guaranteed neutrality of Lebanon" in the Middle East, drawing criticism in the left-wing and pro-UAR press. On June 26, the Christian leaders pressed Helou to bring back the US and UK ambassadors and to refuse to participate in the Arab economic boycott against these countries. Helou resisted returning the ambassadors right away but gave assurances that Lebanon would not fully participate in the boycott. Gemayel allegedly called Helou "weak" during the meeting.[69]

These same groups also appealed directly to the US embassy officials for support. Representatives of the Phalange and the National Liberal Party (NLP) peppered the US embassy with requests for arms and financial assistance throughout June and July. In a report, the US chargé noted that while he did not yet recommend this, the "relevant committees" should be notified so that in the event his recommendation changed, the proper "financial assistance" could be considered.[70] On June 30, Chamoun asked for arms and financial assistance on behalf of his, Gemayel's, and Edde's parties, claiming that they needed to be prepared to counteract the influence of Jumblatt and other Muslim extremists. Nasser, the Christian representatives insisted, continued to provide arms to his allies, so the United States should help theirs. The US chargé listened but did not offer any support.[71] In July, Druze leader Rashid Hamade told US officials that Jumblatt was organizing a militia of three thousand to four thousand men, supported by the Soviets, "to influence the internal political situation in Lebanon at the appropriate moment," and in the "cause of progressive Arab Socialism." If this organizing continued, he claimed, the "moderate Druze community" would be forced to take up arms as well. Hamade claimed to be in touch with Chamoun, Gemayel, and Edde, and asked for US assistance. Again, the US reporting officer made no commitments.[72]

Publicly, the Lebanese government and army tried to steer a middle path between the two sides. In private, however, they too were exploring the possibility of assistance from the United States as a last resort. Army commander Bustany requested a meeting with the US chargé d'affaires, Adrian Middleton, which took place on July 12. Bustany said he had asked for the meeting at the request of the president. Bustany seemed to be probing for how the US could help the army control dissent from "Muslim elements within Lebanon" or curtail efforts by "Communist elements outside Lebanon" to take action against US interests or against Israel. The commander told him that without a "clear US guarantee" the government might have to cave in to a boycott or other actions against the United States and United Kingdom, which could eventually lead to a crisis or even civil war. Although Bustany did not explicitly ask for a commitment to a military intervention, Middleton thought that he was not excluding a request along these lines. The chargé did not provide any such guarantee.[73] In any case, this demonstrates how concerned the army and government leadership were about the possibility of popular uprisings.

Over the summer, militant forces successfully pushed for additional measures against US interests. Resistance to visits from US military ships expanded into opposition against the visit of any US-flagged vessel. One protest even targeted merchant ships carrying supplies for the United Nations Relief and Works Agency (UNRWA), the body charged with the welfare of Palestinian refugees, in Jordan.[74] Lebanon's Council of Ministers passed a resolution calling for a boycott of US companies such as Ford, RCA, and Coca-Cola.[75] President Helou, however, took pains to assure the US chargé that these would be implemented slowly, if at all.[76] Leftists took a strident anti-American line. In a press conference on August 2, Jumblatt issued a call for Arab states to take a variety of measures against Western interests, including stopping oil pumping; withdrawing deposits in US, UK, and West German banks; closing foreign military bases in the Arab world; establishing compulsory military service; and even backing "Negro revolts" in the United States and Quebecois separatists in Canada.[77] While this rhetoric may have been exaggerated, it set the tone for the public mood.

Now that the war had ended, the administration had to deal with the fallout for US interests across the region, particularly on its moderate allies. Jordan seems to have drawn the US attention more than Lebanon. Having lost the West Bank, including the city of Jerusalem, King Hussein was deeply shaken.[78] There were two basic ways the Johnson administration could try to offset these trends in the moderate states. First, at least in theory, the administration could pressure Israel to offer significant concessions to the defeated Arab countries, such as withdrawing from occupied territory, as they had after the 1956 Suez Crisis. This would strengthen the position of the US allies and the administration's own image in the Arab world. Although some in the Johnson administration, including National Security Advisor Walt Rostow, thought that Israel should eventually return to its 1967 borders, the administration refused to press Israel to withdraw from the territories it had occupied without any Arab concessions.[79]

Second, the United States could offer economic and military assistance to allied Arab governments to strengthen their domestic positions. During the conflict, the United States suspended the shipment of military equipment to all Arab states, including Lebanon and Jordan.[80] US officials now increasingly saw a need to demonstrate their support for moderate allies. Former national security advisor McGeorge Bundy, who still communicated with the Johnson administration even after leaving office, suggested specifically that the US government should help out "the strong Lebanese general who seems to have kept the Lebanon out of the war," referring to Bustany.[81] By June 20, Johnson had authorized the resumption of full economic relations with Lebanon and other states that had not broken off diplomatic relations. By the beginning of July, transfers of military supplies had resumed.[82] Even if the Johnson administration was willing to provide aid, however, it was not easy for the Lebanese to accept it out of fear of being too closely linked to the US government. Immediately after the conflict, Helou decided to postpone acceptance of US offers of CCC and PL-480 food aid.[83]

Although the Lebanese army had not fired a shot, the situation along its southern border grew more hostile after the war. Calling Prime Minister Rashid Karame's orders to send troops to fight Israel a declaration of war, Israeli officials proclaimed the 1949 Lebanese-Israeli armistice agreement null and void, although they claimed that Israel would take no measures to upset the cease-fire between the two countries. Still, Lebanese officials took this seriously. At Lebanon's request, US officials privately protested these statements, as well as Israeli prime minister Levi Eshkol's comment on September 8 that "some of the Litani River's waters (in south Lebanon) flow unused into the sea."[84]

In the months that followed, tensions in the region and in Lebanon abated temporarily, reflecting a complex set of circumstances. On one hand, the

Arab defeat in the 1967 war had weakened the influence of Syria and UAR in Lebanon.[85] That fall, Syria experienced yet another change in government, as a new faction of the Baath party consolidated power. Moreover, the Arab-Israeli military front remained calm. Being hardly in a position to challenge Israel militarily, the Arab states focused on diplomatic efforts. At the Khartoum conference in September, the Arab League settled on a policy that became known as the "three no's": no peace with Israel, no recognition of it, and no negotiations with it. Still, there was no decision for the Arab countries as a bloc to cut off diplomatic relations with the Western powers, and the agreement allowed for steps short of peace treaties, as well as indirect negotiations. In conversations with US officials, Hussein spun the results of the conference as a "complete victory for the moderates."[86] Moreover, the Khartoum agreement signaled a détente between Egypt and Saudi Arabia that would tone down the ideological war in the Lebanese print media.[87] That same month, the US and British ambassadors returned to their embassies in Beirut. By early 1968, tourists and foreign capital seemed to be returning to Lebanon.[88]

Partially as a result of this relative relaxation, the United States paid somewhat less attention to the situation in the Middle East. In November, members of the UN Security Council (UNSC) reached agreement over the language of Resolution 242, which called for Israeli withdrawal from "occupied territory" and the termination of hostilities, as well as the "right to live in peace within secure and recognized boundaries." This was to provide an ostensible basis for a diplomatic resolution to the conflict. Swedish diplomat Gunnar Jarring was chosen as a mediator in the conflict.[89] Johnson also made a gesture that suggested a tilt back toward neutrality, rejecting a request from Israeli prime minister Levi Eshkol for advanced F-4 Phantom planes from the United States.[90] In December 1967, the CIA argued strongly in favor of providing military aid to Jordan to shore up its government, lest other moderate governments in the area be weakened.[91] Jordan received some US arms shipments over the next few months.

The 1967 war had left an impact that could not be erased from the region in general, or from Lebanon in particular. The rioting during the war had marked the country's worst internal violence since the 1958 conflict, bringing sectarian tensions back to the surface of the country's politics. Lebanon's neutral position in the global and regional order had been thrown off balance. Faith in the existing Arab governments had been shaken, opening the possibility of more radical governments. The temporary calm would prove misleading, as the tensions began to manifest themselves again the following year.

Pepsi-Cola Hits the Spot

By the spring of 1968, the seeds of disaccord planted the previous year had sprouted anew in Lebanon. Since the fall, the parliamentary elections in March and April 1968 had been the most important item on the country's domestic political agenda. Prior to the elections, the Chehabists made it clear to the United States that they intended to intervene in the elections to ensure their control over the country. In February, Chehab himself told the US ambassador that the army must, and would, play a role in the country's political life, though he made it clear there would be no outright coup.[92] Both the Chehabists and the Christian opposition inquired about whether the United States would be willing to support them.[93] Even Helou sent several messages through intermediaries urging some US help for pro-Western candidates.[94] US officials were resolved to make clear that, regardless of what other countries were doing, they intended to stay out of the Lebanese elections.[95] Despite the Chehabists' best efforts, the Tripartite Alliance ended up doing relatively well in the elections, infuriating their opponents. The Chehabists and the leftists accused the Maronites of stoking confessional tensions for their own political advantage. In a sign of the times, on May 31, Camille Chamoun was shot in the shoulder by a would-be assassin linked to pro-Nasser groups, though his wounds were relatively minor. In the spring of 1968, student protests at the American University of Beirut and other Lebanese universities broke out, halting classes.[96] Meanwhile, Lebanese leftist political parties, including the Communist Party and the MAN, focused increasingly on the Arab-Israeli conflict.[97]

Perhaps the most visible consequence of the failure of Nasserism was the increase in support for the Palestinian fedayeen. In late March 1968, a combination of Jordanian army units and Palestinian guerrilla fighters succeeded in turning back an Israeli armored assault on the village of Karame in Jordan. Although the army's artillery units probably knocked out the Israeli tanks, the victory was credited to the Palestinian movement.[98] After the 1967 war, the Lebanese government began allowing press releases from organizations such as al-Asifa, the military wing of Fatah, which had previously been censored, to appear in the Lebanese press.[99] Massive demonstrations took place in Beirut during the April 1968 funeral of Khalil al-Jamal, a Lebanese who died fighting with the fedayeen. Prime Minister Abdullah al-Yafi posthumously awarded al-Jamal a medal.[100] Fatah sponsored the development of the Lebanese Movement in Support of Fatah (al-Haraka al-Lubnaniyya al-Musanida li-Fath), an organization that began to raise funds for the group.

The fedayeen also began to establish a military presence in Lebanon itself, though at this time, its forces remained covert. Hundreds of Palestinian and Lebanese volunteers began military training in the Lebanese mountain village of Kayfun and in Syria.[101]

In May 1968, new tensions began to appear along Lebanon's southern border. On May 12, allegedly in response to a fedayeen infiltration attempt, Israel shelled the Lebanese border village of Hula.[102] Several Lebanese newspapers announced that this was designed to isolate Lebanon from other Arab states and push it into the US fold.[103] In a May 14 meeting, Helou complained to Porter that the attack threatened the very existence of the Lebanese state. In his report, Porter noted that the US embassy "basically supports Helou's analysis of situation." He suggested that the State Department urge Tel Aviv to again hold meetings of the Israel-Lebanon Mixed Armistice Commission (ILMAC), the coordinating body that since 1949 had been responsible for implementing the truce along the border of the two countries but had been suspended after the 1967 war.[104] The State Department concluded that even minor Israeli reprisal attacks had the potential to undermine Lebanese internal stability, the government's ability to control the fedayeen, and the country's orientation to the West.[105] However, it is unclear whether the United States actually took up this subject with Israeli officials at this time. After Israel shelled Hula again on June 15, US ambassador to Israel Walworth Barbour was finally instructed to tell his hosts that the State Department believed that these "trigger happy" actions would make the Lebanese job of controlling terrorism more difficult.[106]

Over the summer, the arming of militias continued. On August 6, in an article in the leftist newspaper *al-Muharrir*, Jumblatt warned that "large quantities of light weapons have been smuggled from Israel to Lebanon and distributed to members of the proscribed Syrian Nationalist Party and to Camille Shamun['s] followers" to provoke strife.[107] Jumblatt offered no proof, but pro-Western militias were renewing their requests to the United States for military and financial support. In October 1968, a Phalange organizer told a US embassy officer that the organization might approach the United States for assistance in arming their militia. He claimed that the Phalange had a paramilitary capacity of five thousand men, as well as a "commando force" of between fifty and seventy. They had sufficient stocks of light weapons but needed to standardize them and acquire heavier weaponry. According to the report, the US representative made clear that the United States would not support the group's efforts to arm.[108] Druze leader Fadhullah Talhuq also renewed his request for US arms, claiming that Jumblatt continued to receive weapons from Syria.[109] Around this time, a Fatah guerrilla unit was deployed in the Arqub region in southeast Lebanon with the assistance of Lebanese leftist groups, including the Baath and the LCP.[110]

In this renewed atmosphere of tensions, parallel protests increasingly threatened the safety of US officials in the region. In July 1968, when US ambassador to the United Nations George Ball visited Beirut with future Assistant Secretary of State for Near Eastern Affairs Joseph Sisco, the two felt these tensions firsthand. A small crowd of several hundred leftist and pro-Palestinian demonstrators had gathered. As the US officials rode out of the airport in Ambassador Porter's car, the protesters threw two Coca-Cola bottles that flew through the vehicle's open window, shattering and spraying glass, which cut Ball on the hand. Ball joked that it was a good thing that they were Coke bottles, since Pepsi-Cola "hits the spot," as the beverage's slogan went at the time.[111] While not exactly an assassination attempt, the incident demonstrates the public hostility toward US officials.

By then, an increasing number of US officials were coming to believe that the political stalemate in the region, combined with the fighting, was threatening the United States' Arab allies. This led some officials to believe that the United States needed to get more actively involved in brokering a peace between Israel and the Arab states.[112] In March, the NSC argued that the United States had to decide between letting "terrorism versus retaliation play itself out, with all its dangers" and telling Israel "to soften their political positions" and support Jarring's efforts.[113] By May, Hussein had suggested to both Israeli and US officials that he risked being overthrown if the stalemate continued, asking the latter for a statement on the US attitude toward Jordan's independence and territorial integrity.[114] Secretary of State Dean Rusk, National Security Advisor Walt Rostow, and his brother, Undersecretary of State Eugene Rostow, felt that the United States should do something.[115] However, the Johnson administration still did not put major pressure on Israel to withdraw from Arab territory or make other concessions.

In October and November, Lebanon's political situation deteriorated once again. Amid chaos over the formation of a new government, President Helou offered his resignation, which he withdrew after a four-man ruling cabinet was finally selected.[116] The following month, after clashes in Jordan between the government and the fedayeen, protests and fighting broke out in Beirut.[117] On November 14, street protests in support of the fedayeen took place in many parts of Lebanon, including Tripoli, resulting in more clashes between members of these organizations and the Phalange.[118] The State Department was concerned enough to request an evaluation of the Lebanese government's ability to protect US citizens.[119]

Nearing the end of its term in office, the Johnson administration finally took a stronger position on the shape of an eventual Arab-Israeli peace treaty. In November, Dean Rusk privately told Egyptian foreign minister Mahmud Riad at the United Nations in New York that the US government interpreted UN Resolution 242 as requiring an "Israeli withdrawal from UAR territory," by which it meant the entire Sinai Peninsula, which had been occupied during the 1967 war. Meanwhile, another official passed this message to Israeli ambassador Yitzhak Rabin, who argued that this was a change in the US position.[120] At least in part, the Johnson administration hoped that these efforts to push the parties to reach an agreement on the conflict would resolve the tensions in the Middle East. However, since the US position remained secret, it had little impact on the public mood in the region in general or in Lebanon in particular, which was about to take a turn for the worse.

The Beirut Airport Raid

On the night of December 30, 1968, a team of Israeli commandos landed at Beirut International Airport, blowing up thirteen civilian airliners in retaliation for a Popular Front for the Liberation of Palestine (PFLP) attack on an Israeli El Al plane at the Athens airport a few days earlier. This attack would cause the collapse of the Lebanese government and polarize the country even more than the 1967 war. It also posed a final challenge in the Middle East for the Johnson administration, which was set to leave office. The administration responded with perhaps the harshest public criticism it had ever directed toward Israel, though the response was still rather limited.

Many in the Lebanese public were dismayed that such a brazen attack had met no resistance from the military and demanded answers from the government. Some historians have questioned whether the army leadership even knew of the attack before it was over.[121] Other accounts have maintained that they did anticipate it. Several suggest that after the incident in Athens, the army and civilian leadership had warned that Israeli military reprisals against Lebanon were likely. At an emergency meeting the morning of the attack, the army leadership instructed its regional and special command to take measures to protect the areas under their responsibility, mentioning the port of Beirut and the Beirut airport as likely targets. The military commander of the Beirut region, Iskandar Ghanim, was specifically instructed to watch those targets.[122]

Whatever the case, the Lebanese Left was resolved to take action to protest the government's failure to resist the attack. Initially, the leftists were split on the strategy they should pursue. At a meeting at Kamal Jumblatt's home in Mukhtara, major factions of the MAN and traditional Baath, along with "Socialist Lebanon," argued for taking an extreme line against the government, while Jumblatt and the PSP, supported by the LCP, stressed the need to work within the political system. All the groups were united behind the goal of supporting the fedayeen.[123] In the end, the leftist groups settled on a common set of demands that included instituting compulsory military service, protecting and organizing the fedayeen, and training southern villagers in the use of weapons for self-defense against Israeli attacks.[124] Some of the student movements were even more radical. Striking students at the Lebanese University issued a statement claiming that their movement sought to "eliminate the substance on which the existing Lebanese regime is based—sectarian and class divisions and foreign concessions."[125] The student strikes were so effective that they prompted the resignation of Prime Minister al-Yafi. They continued throughout the month of January, until Rashid Karame, a protégé of Fouad Chehab, agreed to take over as prime minister.

The Johnson administration understood that the attack had threatened the internal stability of Lebanon. The State Department wrote up an assessment that the Lebanese popular reaction to the attacks could bring down the government, force Helou's resignation, cause "communal strife," damage US interests, and even result in increased freedom for the fedayeen or a more radical position by Lebanon in Arab affairs.[126] A little over a week later, an NSC paper warned that the Israeli raid had "placed [the] continued existence of a moderate, pro-US regime in Lebanon in doubt," probably resulting in a radical regime more amenable to fedayeen raids that would invite more Israeli reprisals.[127]

Publicly, the Johnson administration offered some criticism of the Beirut raid. Walt Rostow called it "a grave matter for regular forces to attack a civil international airport in a country which has been striving towards moderation in the [Middle East]."[128] This was enough to anger some of Johnson's Jewish supporters.[129] The United States also decided to support Lebanon over Israel at the United Nations Security Council, where Lebanon had filed a complaint, the first of many over the next few years. On December 31, the Security Council adopted a consensus statement condemning Israel for the attack.[130] Behind closed doors, the Johnson administration also made their concern clear to the Israelis. In Tel Aviv, US ambassador Barbour urged the Israeli government to exercise restraint toward Lebanon and Jordan, saying that the United States "believed Lebanon that there are no training camps or military headquarters for fedayeen there."[131] The Israeli government protested the US demarche.[132] It also hoped to influence the administration that would take office in January. In a secret message sent to incoming national security advisor Henry Kissinger about "Arab terrorism," the Israeli government complained that several hundred guerrillas were gathering in the Lebanese south between Marjayoun and Mount Hermon.[133]

There was some disagreement between the US and Lebanese governments about whether the United States should do more. On January 5, Helou's adviser, Michel Khoury, asked the US ambassador for a concrete expression of US support for Lebanon, such as a visit of the US Sixth Fleet to Beirut, possibly accompanied by a US statement of support for Lebanese independence and territorial integrity. Khoury, the son of the first Lebanese president, Beshara al-Khoury, was an influential adviser to Helou and played an important role in the relationship between Helou and the United States, acting as a messenger when Helou was unable to meet with Ambassador Porter. Porter told Khoury that because of the sensitive internal situation in Lebanon, "a visit by any country's fleet might be a mistake at this moment."[134] The US embassy in Tel Aviv thought that any statement of support should include recognition of Israel's problem with terrorism.[135] Neither of these measures was taken at the time, but both public statements and the military movements would be employed several times over the next few years to influence the situation in Lebanon.

Instead, the State Department sought to help the Lebanese in more discreet ways. A few days after the attacks, US diplomats became directly involved in passing messages between the Israelis and Lebanese, a role the State Department would continue to play intermittently over the next few years. In a January 3 ILMAC meeting, Israeli military representatives gave their Lebanese counterparts a letter from Israeli prime minister Eshkol to Helou. The Lebanese officers initially took the letter but later returned it to a UN liaison officer, maintaining that the military authorities were not authorized to pass on such a message.[136] The Israeli government then asked the US diplomats to pass the letter to the Lebanese. The letter stated that the attack on the Beirut airport was intended to "influence your government in eradicating the practice of attacking civil aviation." Eshkol observed that the Israeli-Lebanese relationship had in practice been cooperative for twenty years and added, "My government sees no reason to change its policy in the future, provided the Government of Lebanon takes all the necessary measures to prevent its territory from being used as a base for hostile actions against my country."[137] This attempt at a private communication essentially contained the same message that the Israelis were also delivering in public: control the fedayeen, or your interests will suffer.

The State Department hesitated to pass on this letter directly. To do so would risk associating itself with the message, whose content, if made public, would embarrass the Lebanese government and damage US credibility in the Arab world. This risk was underlined by Israeli leaks to the press that that the Israeli government would pass on a "warning" via a "third-party." With Israel's approval, US officials briefed Lebanese ambassador Najati Kabbani on the substance of the letter, without passing on the actual text.[138] On January 8, Kabbani told the State Department that he had passed the content of the message to Helou as "information." State Department officials, however, urged the Lebanese to keep the letter the next time, since the Israeli action served as a tacit recognition of ILMAC, and thus of the armistice.[139]

This exchange exemplified a dilemma in US policy toward Lebanon over the next few years: whether to push Lebanon to control its border and allow Israel to respond militarily when the army failed to do so, or whether to recognize that Lebanon would not be able to control its border in every case and urge restraint on Israel. Nowhere was this debate more visible than in the cables sent from the US embassies in Beirut and Tel Aviv. Porter in Beirut maintained that the United States should restrain Israel in order to create a political breathing space in which the Lebanese government could assert its control over the fedayeen.[140] Barbour in Tel Aviv repeatedly argued that the United States should recognize the difficulties that the terrorist attacks posed for Israel and should not pressure the Israelis to refrain from retaliating.[141] To a certain extent, this can be seen as a typical example of Foreign Service officials empathizing with their host governments, but it also reflected a difficult decision: Washington was being forced to choose between the interests of two friendly countries.

Despite the initial US condemnation of the attack, the pro-Israel instincts of the administration won the day, much to the chagrin of some officials within the State Department. One such official was Talcott Seelye, a talented Arabist born in Beirut to an AUB professor and his wife. At the time, working on the Lebanon desk, he expressed disappointment that although the State Department had planned to issue a presidential statement of support for Lebanon, "certain factors" had kept the US from doing so—obviously a hint at US relations with Israel.[142] At the UN in New York, Dean Rusk allegedly told Egyptian foreign minister Mahmud Riad that the "Johnson's administration ends at the end of next month, so do not expect it to put pressure on Israel."[143] The question for the states of the Middle East, including Lebanon, was whether the incoming Nixon administration in Washington would be any different, and if so, how.

By the end of 1968, regional events had contributed to a redefinition of the US role in Lebanon. Ten years earlier, when the Eisenhower administration thought that US influence in the region was threatened, it had been able to send the Sixth Fleet to the shores of Lebanon to mediate an internal conflict in that country. If not greeted with open arms, the US presence was nonetheless accepted. By the end of 1968, however, such a deployment would have been virtually unthinkable. The 1967 war had resulted in the ejection of the US ambassador and attacks on US institutions, while the Israeli attack on the Beirut airport had toppled the entire Lebanese government. In short, US ability to act in Lebanon had been curtailed.

CHAPTER 2

Compromise in Cairo

The Nixon Administration and the Cairo Agreement

At the beginning of 1969, the outlook for Lebanese president Charles Helou looked grim. The attack on the Beirut airport had shaken Lebanese internal politics, bringing down the government. The Palestinian militias enjoyed the support of most of the country's Muslims and a significant portion of the Christian population, and had powerful allies among Sunni Muslim, Druze, and leftist political leaders. Over the course of 1969, the situation in Lebanon would worsen, as domestic crises in April and October led to the November 1969 Cairo Agreement, which granted the Palestinian fedayeen a legal right to station guerillas on Lebanese territory.

The existing historical accounts of these events present little analysis of the role of the United States.[1] In his memoirs, Lebanese president Charles Helou implicitly denied that he sought external support for his government, claiming that during the October crisis, "I was convinced that, even if it was desirable, even if we asked for it, we could not have the effective support of any foreign friend."[2] Helou had a good reason to downplay efforts to get support from the United States and other Western powers. Had this effort become known, it would have drawn criticism from a significant portion of the Lebanese population, undermining the government's legitimacy and possibly leading to his downfall.

But the Lebanese president's denial was misleading. Throughout 1969, the Lebanese government sought and the US government provided support to help it resist pressure to allow the fedayeen to organize in Lebanon. US policymakers attempted to convince other states to take actions that would ease the pressure on Lebanon's government. They urged Israel to refrain from reprisal attacks, while asking conservative states in the region to provide aid to the Lebanese government and pressure the fedayeen to curb attacks from Lebanon. Perhaps most importantly, the State Department advanced ambitious plans to broker a peace to the Arab-Israeli conflict, which US officials saw as key to preventing the spread of what they perceived to be radicalism in the region. However, at least at the time, the United States itself provided little direct economic and military aid to Lebanon.

As Helou feared, this support was ultimately ineffective. But that did not stop him from repeatedly seeking US and other assistance, even to the point of contemplating US military intervention in Lebanon along the lines of 1958. In the end, the United States declined to intervene, fearing that military action would be ineffective at best and, at worst, bring about the very consequence it sought to prevent—the downfall of the government, or even the political regime. However, other parties within Lebanon may have thought that the possibility of overt or covert US intervention was real and at times acted in a more reserved manner as a result. Fears of US intervention thus had a deterrent effect that extended beyond any actions the US government took.

"Trying to Be Helpful"

When the Nixon administration came to office, just a few weeks after the Israeli attack on the Beirut airport, Lebanon was low on its list of priorities. Top US officials on the Middle East spent much of their first few months concerned with the broader situation in the region, particularly the conflict between Egypt and Israel playing along the military front in the Sinai Desert, known as the War of Attrition, a state of low-intensity warfare featuring frequent shelling, raids, and bombing attacks. Over time this would change, and the administration would pay more attention to the situation of Lebanon and Jordan, whose governments appeared increasingly threatened by growing radicalism, embodied most strongly by the Palestinian fedayeen.

Although the National Security Council and the US State Department initially worked well together, there were deep differences in their assessments of the importance of the Arab-Israeli conflict. Under the leadership of Secretary of State William Rogers, the State Department saw the Middle East as a time bomb, which officials hoped to defuse by brokering an Arab-Israeli peace agreement. These efforts were spearheaded by Joseph Sisco, described by a former colleague as "the closest thing within the State Department to a road builder's steamroller," as the head of the Near East and South Asian Affairs division.[3] Bright, energetic, and argumentative, Sisco quickly became an enthusiastic proponent of US mediation in the Arab-Israeli conflict. For National Security Advisor Henry Kissinger, an Arab-Israeli peace was a long shot that could only be achieved with massive US pressure on Israel, which he thought should not be applied without significant concessions from the Soviet Union on issues such as Vietnam. Nixon seemed to agree with the State Department that the situation was dangerous and with Kissinger that the chances of achieving a peace agreement were slim. The president was therefore prepared to leave the initiative on this issue to the State Department, which began a series of talks with the Soviet Union about the possibilities for an Arab-Israeli agreement, while at the United Nations, US, Soviet, French, and British diplomats undertook the so-called Four Power talks on the region's problems, with little success.[4]

Over time, the split between the different factions of the Nixon administration grew increasingly worse. Kissinger began to actively oppose the State Department's efforts to broker an agreement between the Arab countries and Israel. From his office in the West Wing basement, the national security advisor drafted message after message to the president arguing against the State Department's strategy. In an April 1969 memo, Kissinger contended that although in the current situation, "moderate regimes like Lebanon's suffer," a stalemate in the region was still in the United States' interest. For him, the arguments in favor of making a proposal for a settlement of the Arab-Israeli conflict were "that a settlement would: 1. Help our moderate friends— Lebanon, Jordan, Saudi Arabia; 2. Undercut the fedayeen; 3. Improve our position with all the Arabs by gaining us the credit for a settlement." However, he noted, "forces are at work in the Arab world that feed on more than the Arab-Israeli problem," meaning that US intervention, even if successful, might not help the situation in these countries. In light of this, US interests required that "on a quite Machiavellian level, we should see that the USSR is the one that presses its clients into making unpalatable concessions." Thus, Kissinger believed that allowing the stalemate to continue would force Moscow to compromise first, even though he understood that the situation might well destabilize US allies such as Lebanon. The State Department, on the other hand, believed that its efforts would help the Lebanese, Jordanian, and other moderate governments.[5]

In addition to exploring the long-term solution of a regional peace, US officials also consulted with Lebanon's government about other actions to help to ease pressure on its government in the short term. One possibility was an international security presence in the country. Helou and his advisers wanted a UN force along Lebanon's border with Israel.[6] In principle, such a force could help to physically stop the Palestinian shelling and infiltrations, as well as the resulting Israeli reprisals. Even if the attacks continued, the force would reaffirm the legitimacy of the 1949 armistice between Israel and Lebanon, and provide political cover for the Lebanese government, which could blame the UN force for failing to stop any attacks. Not surprisingly, Israel cited this latter consideration to justify their opposition to a UN force, refusing categorically to host such forces on their own soil, claiming that it would "lessen [the] GOL's [Government of Lebanon's] feeling of responsibility for controlling [the] fedayeen." In Beirut, Ambassador Porter found the Israeli refusal "depressing."[7] State Department officials tried to advocate the possibility of hosting a UN force only on the Lebanese side of the border, but these came to naught.[8] The Lebanese tried to get the British and the French to support the idea of such a force, but to little avail.[9] No UN force would be stationed in South Lebanon until 1978, when the UN Interim Force in Lebanon was created in the aftermath of an Israeli invasion.

Helou also asked the United States to convince other Arab countries with whom it had ties to support Lebanon. Wealthy Gulf states such as Saudi Arabia and Kuwait had ambivalent attitudes toward the guerillas. On one hand, these countries also provided subsidies to the guerillas, and allowed them to fund-raise directly in their countries. On the other hand, these conservative leaders feared the more radical of the fedayeen, which enjoyed incredible popularity—perhaps even more than their own monarchies. Thus, Helou had some reason to think that they might be willing to help him. In early February, Helou planned to send private representatives to Jidda, Kuwait City, and Tripoli, bypassing the foreign ministry, to urge these governments to use their influence to calm the fedayeen groups in Lebanon. He and his advisers wanted the State Department to make similar demarches. In his report back to Washington, Porter warned of the risk of "engaging in what appears to be anti-fedayeen activity."[10] Within ten days, Helou's plan had been leaked to opposition leaders, forcing him to drop the plans, which (fortunately for him) were not made public.[11] By March, US officials had decided to delay their approaches to Arab governments.[12]

Although the US could have tried to convince the conservative monarchies to intervene with the fedayeen, the Arab countries that could best help Lebanon were on less than friendly terms with the United States. By virtue of his popularity across the Arab world, Egyptian leader Gamal Abd al-Nasser had some influence over the fedayeen. However, US diplomats had little influence with the Egyptians, who had broken off diplomatic relations with the United States in 1967. Instead, the Lebanese made their own approaches via the army's DB, which had close connections to the Egyptian regime. In February, Nasser's subordinates told an emissary from the Lebanese army that Egypt supported the intensification of the fedayeen activities in order to maintain the pressure on the Israeli army and people.[13] In a subsequent meeting, Nasser himself told DB official Sami al-Khatib that he understood Lebanon's predicament. Al-Khatib met with Fatah leader Yasser Arafat on February 7, reaching an agreement to cooperate along the border. However, in his report at the end of that trip, sent to the Lebanese army leadership, the president, the prime minister and others, al-Khatib opined that Arafat would not be able to keep his commitments, that Nasser would not help them much, and that the Lebanese should rely on themselves.[14]

By this time, some Lebanese Christian leaders had begun to ask the United States for assistance in arming their militias. In early 1969, Chamoun and Gemayel began to reactivate their supporters.[15] On January 28, Chamoun sent an emissary to the US embassy to request arms for his militia and that of the Phalange, as well as to discuss the possibility of taking action to bring the Karame government down through strikes and demonstrations. The embassy officer categorically refused, stating that the US would not provide weapons, and "disagreed completely" with their plans to bring down the government.[16] The Kataib also made a request during this month for aid in the event of an internal conflict.[17] At this time, President Helou opposed any US aid for either demonstrations or the militias, specifically asking Porter for US "support to convince militant Christians they were running [the] risk of precipitating a battle, which they could not win and which would in [the] long run destroy them and [the] concept of a confessionally balanced Lebanon." Porter agreed to try to do so.[18]

In 1969, the bulk of the Palestinian militias were in Jordan, though they had begun to increase their numbers in Lebanon. By the beginning of April, the number of fedayeen in the south of Lebanon had reached around eight hundred, due in large part to an increased presence of Saiqa, a Syrian-controlled Palestinian militia set up to challenge Fatah.[19] As the crisis worsened in early April, Helou tried to coordinate his actions with Karame. In most accounts of this period, Karame has been portrayed as opposing the use of force against the fedayeen.[20] However, in conversations with US officials in Beirut, Helou and his advisers painted a more nuanced picture of the prime minister's attitude. While Karame wanted to avoid shooting incidents, he was also concerned with preventing the access of the fedayeen to the border.[21] On April 6, Helou, Karame, and army commander Emile

Bustany decided to continue a policy of establishing army cordons around the pockets of fedayeen, authorizing the use of force if necessary.[22]

Fighting broke out between the fedayeen and the army on April 15 in the small village of Dayr Mimas, some two miles from the Israeli border. This sparked a series of demonstrations and further clashes throughout the country, including an April 23 strike in Beirut and Sidon. The strike was organized by a coalition of Lebanese leftist parties, including the Lebanese Communist Party, the Ishtirakiyya Lubnan (Socialist Lebanon), the pro-Iraqi Baath party, and smaller groups, who saw the strike as "a revolutionary event of unprecedented importance."[23] At first, Kamal Jumblatt did not endorse the strike.[24] But he soon changed his position. A later account portrayed Lebanese communist leader George Hawi as entering Kamal Jumblatt's office with bloodstained clothes to force Jumblatt to back the strike, which he did, along with the Sunni Mufti and other leaders.[25]

At least initially, Karame appears to have supported Helou, who assured Porter that the decision to confront the fedayeen had the Sunni prime minister's approval. The fedayeen had been informed of the Lebanese government's willingness to confront them, which Helou hoped would act as the "ultimate deterrent."[26] In "secret discussions" with Helou, Karame had also agreed in principle that the Lebanese government would make approaches to the conservative Arab states that were supporting the fedayeen financially. However, the problem remained of how to keep this from becoming public, thereby undermining Karame's support among the pro-fedayeen Muslim population. As a sign of the difficulties in implementing this strategy, a Lebanese ambassador of the Sunni confession had recently been sent to Kuwait to pass on this message but, once there, apparently decided not to take up the subject with the Kuwaitis, for fear of having his position exposed.[27] By April 23, the political pressures had caught up with Karame, who resigned his post.

The State Department applauded Helou's use of force and did what it could to offer him moral support. Following the outbreak of violence on April 15, Porter congratulated Helou on what he called a "wise and courageous decision" to crack down on the fedayeen.[28] Already on April 7, perhaps in anticipation of the coming conflict, Khoury had requested that the United States use its influence to restrain Israel from launching raids during this period.[29] As tensions rose, the State Department now assured Tel Aviv that it believed the Lebanese were doing their best to control the border, so as to discourage them from putting extra pressure on Lebanon.[30] Following the April 23 strike, the State Department began a period of expanded, if relatively fruitless, diplomacy in support of the Lebanese. The State Department instructed its ambassadors to Saudi Arabia, Kuwait, and Libya to express their concern about these governments' support for the fedayeen, which it complained posed a threat to the "internal stability of moderate regimes," both in Jordan and increasingly in Lebanon.[31] They also asked France and the Soviet Union to discuss the situation with Syrian officials.[32]

At the same time, Helou and his advisers considered the possibility of requesting a US or other foreign military intervention, beginning a dialogue with the US ambassador on this subject that would be repeated intermittently over the next few years. On April 7, Khoury mentioned to Porter that the Lebanese government had considered requesting an increased UN military presence on the Lebanese-Israeli border, or unilateral military support from France or the United States. However, he confessed, all these measures seemed impractical. Porter warned him not to expect US military involvement in Lebanon. Khoury responded that France had given him the same answer.[33] On April 23, as the strike worsened, Helou again contacted Porter via Khoury with an urgent message: "In the event of civil disturbances which might overtax [the] limited capacity [of the] Lebanese security forces . . . what was [the] possibility of outside assistance to assist him to restore stability." Porter again ruled out any possibility of a military intervention.[34]

Although Porter played it down, the possibility of a US military intervention in Lebanon was at least conceivable, if unlikely. Soon after taking office, Nixon had asked at an NSC meeting whether the military was capable of executing a "Lebanon-style" mission, referring to the 1958 intervention. Secretary of Defense Melvin Laird answered that it was.[35] Nixon's question was probably not made with Lebanon specifically in mind, but rather referred to any intervention in a small country. Yet, even if the physical capacity for a US military intervention still existed, US officials understood that there were political limits on their military options. US troop commitments in Vietnam discouraged any thoughts of intervention elsewhere. Perhaps more importantly, a US military intervention would be extremely unpopular in the Arab world and could bring about a backlash against US interests in the region. Indeed, an unpopular US intervention could actually make the conflict worse by discouraging compromise between the groups. At the end of 1968, for instance, the US embassy in Beirut had concluded that in the event of "confessional strife," the State Department should "not encourage Christian leaders to assume that they enjoy a special protective relationship with the United States," except in a case such as "a serious threat of genocide against the Christian and/or foreign community."[36] During April, there seemed to be little serious consideration in Washington of the possibility of an intervention. Contingency planning documents suggest that the United States had excluded the possibility of introducing US forces to Lebanon, except to evacuate US nationals.[37]

As the crisis deepened in early May, however, Helou continued to seek US support. On May 2, Helou asked Ambassador Porter in general terms what help could be expected from the United States if the situation deteriorated. The Lebanese president suggested that "it would enable him [to] act more decisively in handling [the] internal situation if he felt his hand was strengthened by assurances [of] US support 'as a last resort,'" which "would embolden him to resist tremendous pressures upon him to 'strike a bargain' with [the] fedayeen—a step which he does not wish to take, knowing it would be [the] beginning of [the] loss of Lebanon's sovereign control over its own policies and destiny." Porter's immediate response was that he could not discuss "realistic possibilities of US assistance in hypothetical circumstances."[38] However, he sent Helou's query to Washington.

Despite skepticism among State Department officials about military intervention, they now considered some sort of limited military action, such as a movement of the Sixth Fleet in the Mediterranean as a show of force. They even submitted a draft cable to the NSC for clearance to be sent to Middle East posts, requesting assessments of their host governments' likely reaction to such a move.[39] In the end, the plan was dismissed because of Department of Defense objections and State Department doubts.[40] On May 6, the State Department replied to Helou's approach, commending him for his stand against the fedayeen, while telling Porter that department officials "wish[ed] to be as responsive as possible without committing ourselves to any sort of intervention." Porter was authorized to convey US willingness to make a public statement of support, but the State Department thought it unlikely that they could get Syria to stop its intervention. The United States was now making "renewed efforts in Riyadh, Kuwait and Tripoli" to convince these governments to curtail their support for the fedayeen, as well as "encouraging [the] Saudis to continue to be responsive to urgent Lebanese arms needs." Finally, Porter was to encourage Helou to talk to UN secretary-general U Thant about the possibility of a UN intervention.[41] Once again, the State Department wanted to avoid giving the Lebanese any hope of a unilateral US military intervention.

When Porter passed on these messages the next day, Helou made it clear that he hoped the United States would continue consultations with Saudi Arabia, Kuwait, and Libya. Helou told Porter that he had persuaded former prime minister Hussein al-Oueini to talk to Saudi King Feisal about the fedayeen threat.[42] In addition, Helou wanted the United States to urge Israel to refrain from attacks, though he knew that he was "exposing himself dangerously" if this should be revealed. The possibility of a direct US military intervention was still on the Lebanese president's mind as well. Helou stated that "he fully understands USG reluctance [to] serve as [the] world's policeman in intervening in local or regional conflicts, particularly as [a] result [of] US experience in Vietnam," but "as chief of state, he had to study what options he had available to him to deal with the threats to his country's territorial integrity and sovereignty." Porter felt that he was thinking as a "Christian President," trying to protect the Christian population.[43]

Even if the United States government was unable to intervene militarily, Helou explored the possibility of installing a stronger UN force in Lebanon. On April 29, Helou discussed with Porter a range of possibilities for increased UN involvement, including introducing new forces, or even granting UNRWA personnel, who were primarily civilian administrators, a security role in the camps. The State Department was not opposed to an expanded UN presence, but it wanted Porter to let Helou take the initiative in asking for it, probably because a US request would have upset both Israel and the Arab countries.[44] On May 7, Helou told Porter that he was ready to appeal to the UN for "emergency forces," if necessary, and wanted to know whether the Nixon administration would consider dispatching troops "as a first contingent" of a UN emergency force if there were political difficulties in approving it—in other words, whether the US would send troops to Lebanon before an international mandate for the force was approved. Porter invoked the likely opposition of Congress and US public opinion, trying to "inject realism into his [Helou's] thinking re limitations on US capabilities to assist, and above all to intervene militarily."[45] The ambassador did approach UNRWA director Laurence Michelmore about giving UNRWA a security role of some sort in the Palestinian camps. However, this idea was dropped after objections from UN headquarters in New York.[46]

In addition to Helou, Lebanese Christian leaders contacted the US embassy again about the possibility of aid. On April 28, Phalange chief Pierre Gemayel repeated his request from the previous January for arms in case confessional fighting broke out. Porter refused their requests, encouraging them instead to support President Helou. In his report, the ambassador noted he was seeing Camille Chamoun the next day and expected a similar request.[47] The State Department responded that it "strongly endorse[d]" Beirut's counsel to Christian leaders to support Helou and thought that Porter should "meet Phalangist and other requests for arms by reaffirming US confidence in [the] Lebanese structure and maturity of its leadership."[48] Perhaps expecting a negative response, Chamoun did not request arms directly, instead stressing the importance of building up Lebanon's security forces.[49]

Even former president Chehab was willing to take drastic measures to try to stop the fedayeen. During their meeting, Chamoun had suggested to Porter that a public Israeli warning about commando activity might have the effect of "bringing to their senses those Muslim extremists who advocate complete freedom for fedayeen activity in Lebanon," as well as gaining support for the army. On April 30, Porter asked former president Chehab whether he thought that such a statement would be useful. After reflection, Chehab called him back the next day to say that he agreed that it would be helpful. However, Porter still recommended against it, since the Israelis would probably make such a statement again soon anyway and might find it peculiar, considering recent US requests for restraint.[50] The State Department concurred, adding that such a statement would "provide grist for Soviet and extremist propaganda mills" and rally support for fedayeen, in addition to risking embarrassing leaks.[51] Chehab also asked the United States to request that Israel increase their patrols along the border with Lebanon to prevent fedayeen infiltration.[52] When the United States passed this message on, Israeli embassy officials in Washington told their US counterparts that although they had "respect" for Chehab, Israel did not have the forces to seal the border or apprehend infiltrators—though they expected the Lebanese to do so.[53] Although unsuccessful, Chehab's involvement in such a risky endeavor reflects how far the situation had deteriorated.

In the end, the State Department sought to make clear that it was unlikely to be a significant source of help to Helou. On May 12, Porter was instructed to deliver the message that would ultimately sum up US policy toward Lebanon at the time: "Helou should clearly understand that Lebanon's future rests essentially in his hands and in [the] hands of [the] Lebanese collectively. Outside help can be marginal at best and he should avoid looking to external factors as [a] crutch."[54] On May 26, Porter delivered this message in a "rather unhappy exchange," while telling Helou that "his diplomatic position would be strengthened in proportion to the stand he adopts in defending Lebanon's sovereignty and independence."[55] Porter thus placed the burden of Lebanon's future squarely on Helou's shoulders, with little hope of outside relief.

With most of his international options closed, Helou had little choice but to consider compromise with the fedayeen. The Lebanese president was ready to strike a deal that would allow the guerillas to remain in Lebanon, but he was determined not to compromise on the principle of Lebanese sovereignty. On May 3, Helou began to negotiate with the fedayeen under Egyptian auspices.[56] Following a meeting between Helou, Karame, Arafat, and an Egyptian delegation on May 7, Helou and Karame asked the army to enter a direct dialogue with the Palestinian leadership under army chief of staff Yusif Shamayyit.[57] On May 14, Khoury told Porter that Helou planned to meet Karame the next day to seek an agreement that would allow the fedayeen presence in a small area of southern Lebanon, on the condition that they not engage in operations against Israel, expand outside an agreed area, increase their numbers, or engage in subversion in Lebanon. If they did, Lebanon would be authorized to use military force to stop them. Privately, Helou added that he expected the fedayeen to break the agreement at times and wanted to be "sure that in such event Karame will at least acquiesce to a quick response by the Lebanese military."[58]

Within a week, a tacit agreement seems to have been reached. According to Helou's memoirs, on May 20 he told Karame that he was ready to let the future government regulate Lebanese-Palestinian relations, provided two conditions: that no facility would be given to the Palestinian resistance without the approval of the army commander in chief, and that no changes would be made to the status of the Palestinians in the camps. Karame apparently accepted these conditions, resuming his position as prime minister that he had resigned after the attack on the Beirut airport.[59] Still, over the summer, the country's internal divisions would continue without resolution, as Karame was unable to form a government. Meetings with the fedayeen continued, including a high-level meeting of government and military leaders on June 10,[60] as well as a secret meeting between al-Khatib, Arafat, and others in Amman.[61]

US officials admired Helou's stance and actions. In Washington, Seelye praised Helou's "stiff back."[62] After a meeting with the Lebanese president on June 28, Porter reported that Helou did not intend to back down from his "refusal to negotiate away Lebanon's sovereignty by bits and pieces." In the meeting, Helou had first claimed that he would rather resign than capitulate, then later maintained that he would not "'abdicate' whatever the consequences, even if this meant 'never leaving Baabda (the Presidency) alive.'" At the same time, in a pragmatic moment, he admitted that his policy was not a solution and "was only buying time." Helou also criticized the Christian leadership, including Chehab, who was "a captive of his 'sense of realism" in wanting to compromise. Gemayel was advocating the creation of an "'inner cabinet' which would deal with the fedayeen problem in secret," which Helou said was "of pure form and no substance." Chamoun and other Christian leaders, whom Helou called "pitiful bastards," now understood the situation and agreed with his policy.[63] Yet, Helou continued to seek US support for the Lebanese government, including the possibility of a military intervention, but Porter still urged the Lebanese president to accept that the United States would not make any military commitments.[64]

Maronite Christian and other traditional leaders continued to seek weapons and funding from the United States. At the end of June, Chamoun urged the US embassy to help the Christians arm, arguing that "a strong and militant Christian community would be a substantial deterrent to confessional strife." Porter told him that he would report his views to Washington but promised no change in policy. Chamoun argued that he saw no US policy in the region, maintaining that the domino theory applied to Saudi Arabia, Jordan, and Lebanon.[65] In mid-July, a Phalange representative presented US deputy chief of mission Bob Houghton with a formal request from the party's Central Committee for small arms to protect the Christian community in the event of a civil conflict. Houghton declined. Disappointed with this response, the representative then asked whether the US diplomats might ask the Saudis to give them the weapons.[66] Soon thereafter, during a courtesy call by a US officer, Pierre Gemayel condemned the US government for abandoning its friends in Lebanon, noting that the Phalange could not hold out much longer without money and arms from the West. Druze leader Fadlallah Talhuq also requested and was refused such aid. Talhuq responded that "if that is your policy . . . then Lebanon will not survive much longer."[67]

By this point, Porter's attitude toward providing weapons to the Christian militias had begun to change. In an internal report in August 1969, Seelye wrote that he thought Porter wanted the US government to provide weapons to the Christians. Seelye rejected this outright: "I am dead set against our supporting any factions in Lebanon and I am convinced that our efforts should be directed at encouraging the Christians to accommodate to their environment. They must realize that times have changed and that it is no longer practicable for them to rely on an outside protector to save them from their neighbors. (The same thing, of course, might be said about the Israelis!)" Still, Seelye was not optimistic about the Christian groups' willingness to "accommodate adequately," and thus thought that "confessional strife may again erupt." He did feel that in the unlikely event that a "sort of genocide" erupted, the State Department should look at all options, including providing assistance to the Christians.[68]

Thus, up until the end of the summer of 1969, the United States did not seriously consider providing weapons to the Christian militias in Lebanon, much less intervening military. These debates seem to have been contained within the State Department, with little reaction from the National Security Council, which would have to take part in any real decision about intervention or crisis management in Lebanon. The NSC staff was, however, aware of the futility of US efforts in Lebanon. As Harold Saunders summarized in a memo to Kissinger in late May, the State Department's diplomacy was "largely an exercise to show that we are trying to be helpful but cannot commit ourselves to intervene."[69]

The August Attacks and the Rogers Plan

By the end of the summer of 1969, the situation in much of the Near East had begun to grow more tense. Increased Israeli bombing raids against Egypt, renewed clashes along the Lebanese-Israeli border, and clashes between the Palestinian militants and the Lebanese and Jordanian governments made the situation the most potentially explosive it had been since 1967. Meanwhile, in Jordan, Israel for a second time struck sections of the Ghor Canal, the country's most important irrigation project, undermining the rule of King Hussein.[70] As a result, members of the National Security Council staff began to worry that the moderate governments could fall or be pressured into agreements with the Palestinians.[71] As if proving the theory, the pro-Western government of Libya fell on September 1, which the United States judged to be largely an "internal manifestation," but one signaling a general move toward support for the Palestinians. Although the State Department thought that a renewal of general hostilities in the region was unlikely, the positions of the parties were hardening.[72]

In August and early September, Israel undertook a series of brutal reprisal raids against Lebanon for fedayeen attacks, bringing new life back to the Lebanese crisis, which had been languishing quietly throughout the summer. Against US advice, the Lebanese requested a UN Security Council meeting. In this meeting, the Lebanese representative announced that the country could not take responsibility for the actions of Palestinians on its territory. Following the first raid, an Israeli government spokesman had announced that "the GOL was secretly pleased" by their raid, which further undermined the Lebanese government.[73] The United States sought a compromise resolution with language more partial to Israel, but Israeli officials protested the fact that the resolution mentioned the Armistice Agreement of 1949.[74] On August 22, the State Department informed the US embassy in Beirut that "the White House has taken an interest" in the Lebanese Security Council complaint, which was complicating the situation.[75] In the meantime, the Lebanese requested that the United States urge Israel to stop the attacks.[76] The State Department did so in late August, and also after attacks on September 5 and September 15.[77]

Following the September 5 attack, Helou again asked the United States for assistance, focusing on three areas: persuading Saudi Arabia and Iran to improve their relations with Lebanon, obtaining a two- to three-week moratorium on Israeli attacks in order to form a government, and issuing a statement about the situation in Lebanon, such as referring to "traditional US interest and concern for independence and integrity of Lebanon."[78] On Porter's recommendation, the State Department attempted to do these things, although this helped Helou only to a limited degree and, in some ways, may have even undermined his position.

First, the State Department reached out to Jidda and Tehran, but neither seemed willing to do much for Lebanon, since each had a beef with the Lebanese government. The Saudis wanted to build an oil refinery in the country, while the Iranians were seeking the extradition of the former head of the Iranian intelligence service, who was wanted on corruption charges and living in Lebanon.[79] The Saudis told the US chargé in Jidda that it would be useful if the Lebanese were to dispatch a high-level mission to the king.[80] In Iran, the shah told the US chargé that he recognized the danger in Lebanon and was prepared to take steps to strengthen Lebanon internally, including providing support to Shi'a and possibly even Christian groups, though he hinted that this might depend on the return of the Iranian official.[81] Despite these efforts, there is no concrete evidence that either Saudi Arabia or Iran provided any material support to Lebanon or the Lebanese militias at this time.

Second, the State Department sought unsuccessfully to help the Lebanese reach a tacit agreement with Israel on control of the border. However, Lebanon asked that the State Department make no mention of the fact that it was trying to form a government, information it feared would be leaked by the Israelis.[82] The US chargé in Beirut supported this, noting that Israeli newspapers had recently portrayed Helou as a friend of Israel, which had undermined him at home.[83] Khoury later stressed to Houghton that because of Helou's past experience, as well as that of other leaders such as King Hussein, Helou "would prefer that a morat[oriu]m not be requested rather than use his name." Houghton and Khoury worked out a general approach in which the US officials would ask Israel for "a period of calm" to restore stability and contain the fedayeen.[84] The Israeli ambassador in Washington responded that "Israel and its people cannot be expected to endure shellings and casualties simply to give President Helou time to form [a] moderate government in Lebanon."[85]

Helou also had alternate lines of communication to the Israelis. Israeli foreign minister Abba Eban later told US officials that on September 10, the same day Helou requested a moratorium on Israeli attacks, Israel received a message from Helou "through other channels," probably the Vatican, stating that his government understood the problem that the fedayeen posed to Israel but that they could not completely stop infiltration from Syria. The message asked the Israelis to agree "not to conduct war against Lebanon or occupy Lebanese territory even temporarily," saying that "such assurances would help Helou handle [the] fedayeen problem." Eban asked the State Department to convey to the Lebanese that Israel was "interested in maintaining Lebanon's integrity, special character, and democratic system," although Israel would still "take the minimu[m] actions necessary to defend its citizens."[86] When Porter delivered this message, Helou said that it "showed favorable n[ua]nce in [the] Israeli position which [was] not previously evident." Although Helou "could not take cognizance of Eban's message as [a] direct communication to [the] GOL," he would refer to it as a "friendly message" from the United States.[87] By late September, the Israeli strikes across the border had largely ceased, as another series of low-level clashes between Lebanese army and the fedayeen ensued.[88]

Other prominent Lebanese may have also been in touch with the Israelis at the time. In private, Israeli officials somewhat cryptically told their US counterparts that "certain Lebanese have confidentially told them that they welcome occasional Israeli attacks against fedayeen bases in Lebanon." Seelye felt that this did "not represent the Lebanese Government or Lebanese opinion," and hoped that Porter's counsels would keep the Christian groups from "going to the street."[89] The identity of these individuals, as well as the impact of their coordination, remains unknown. However, since such statements had come from such diverse figures as former presidents Chehab and Chamoun, the comments could have been from many different individuals.

Third, the US government complied with the Lebanese request for a public statement about Lebanon's integrity, though the statement did not help much. During September, for a variety of reasons, plans to issue the statement were repeatedly delayed.[90] Finally, at an October 10 dinner at the Middle East Institute, Assistant Secretary of State Joseph Sisco issued the "long-planned" statement on Lebanon.[91] The assistant secretary declared that the US opposed any "aggression" against Lebanese territory, and his message was soon followed by a statement issued by the US embassy in Beirut.[92] However, like other US pronouncements at the time, including a speech by President Nixon at the UN General Assembly the previous month, this statement was heavily criticized in the Arab media.[93] In Lebanon, a meeting of Muslim leaders (including Karame) under Mufti Khalid Hassan issued a joint communiqué rejecting the statement, which it said "only protects Israeli interests."[94] While thanking Porter for the US message, Michel Khoury called the response "predictable," noting that the Lebanese regime and the United States government were "in [the] same boat in [the] M[iddle] E[ast]." Porter responded that he hoped Helou understood that the United States would not guarantee a military intervention but had "taken a calculated risk that the fedayeen and radical Arab states would misread our intentions."[95]

Adding to the problems of the Lebanese government, an unrelated incident at the end of September damaged Lebanon's relations with the Soviet Union and the United Arab Republic. Over the previous few years, Egypt had tried several times to convince the Lebanese to provide them with one of the French Mirage fighter planes that Lebanon had purchased several years before, which would then be turned over to the Soviet Union. However, the Lebanese refused, since this would violate their end-user agreement with France. During the summer of 1969, the army had either discovered or was informed of a plot by the Soviet Union to steal one of these planes. The DB leadership was apparently incensed by this plot and decided to publicize the incident and arrest the two Soviet embassy officers involved.[96] During the arrest raid, both diplomats were shot, one fatally, sparking angry protests and denials from the Kremlin. According to a former KGB officer, the GRU, Soviet military intelligence, was responsible for the plot, and the KGB *rezidentura* in Beirut was not even aware of their plans before the raid.[97] Afterward, the surviving officer was whisked from the country, but the incident nonetheless damaged Lebanese-Egyptian and Lebanese-Soviet relations at a time when the government would soon need their assistance.

Although State Department officials were concerned about the tensions in Lebanon and Jordan, the main way they hoped to help these states was to kick-start negotiations between the Arab states and Israel. By that time, US mediation had been effectively stalled since June. In September, the State Department was preparing to propose a new regional peace plan to Israel and Egypt that would emphasize an Israeli withdrawal from all Egyptian land in exchange for a peace settlement. Moreover, even if this initiative was not accepted, US officials considered whether to reveal this position publicly to reduce US isolation in the Arab world, as well as to decrease the tensions in Jordan, whose government—even more so than the government in Lebanon—was coming under increasing pressure from Palestinian militant groups.[98] This effort would eventually develop into the so-called Rogers Plan. Yet just as US diplomats began consultations with Egypt in mid-October, a full-blown conflict broke out in Lebanon.

October Crisis and the Cairo Agreement

On October 18, 1969, the Lebanese army began a campaign to reassert its authority in the south by cutting supply lines to the fedayeen. Following a few isolated clashes, Lebanon erupted into crisis on October 23.[99] This time, the conflict was larger in scale than the previous spring and involved Lebanon's neighbors to a greater extent. Fighting broke out in the Nahr al-Barid and Baddawi refugee camps in Tripoli and the Burj al-Barajna camp in Beirut's southern suburbs, as well as along the Syrian border. To put pressure on the Lebanese government, Syria closed its borders to Lebanon, Libya cut off diplomatic relations, and Iraq asked its citizens to leave the country.[100] Over the next few weeks, although the United States would pay more attention to Lebanon's situation than at time that year, the declining US image in the Arab world caused the Lebanese government to remain effectively cut off from the United States, unable to request any assistance or even consult about the situation.

For the first time that year, the National Security Council and the White House took a serious interest in the situation in Lebanon, in part because of the Syrian and Iraqi actions. Kissinger reported that his "contingency planning group" was working on plans to intervene for the evacuation of US citizens, "preserving the moderate government or protecting the Christian community," and "reacting to foreign invasion." The crucial difference between this event and 1958, he presciently argued, was that US status in the Arab world had been much better in 1958. In handwritten notes at the bottom of the document, Kissinger added that "in short, the situation must be seen in the context of the general Middle East, about which I am doing a separate memorandum."[101] The memo shows that Kissinger now recognized the serious risk to the moderate government of Lebanon, which he had downplayed during the previous spring and summer. The US government searched for steps that it could take to help Helou, but the decline of US status in the region made any direct involvement dangerous. The State Department suggested issuing another public statement in support of the Lebanese government.[102] The US embassy in Beirut, however, thought that a unilateral statement would aggravate the situation unless it was issued jointly with the Soviet Union. If this were not possible, Porter felt the French should issue a statement alone. He also urged that the Israeli government stay silent and that US representatives avoid implying that they were coordinating with Helou.[103] The State Department agreed, specifying that they did not mean to suggest a statement without the Soviet Union.[104] That these US officials were unwilling to even issue a statement about the conflict on their own is a sign of their desperation. The State Department contacted British and French officials, who also had few ideas.[105]

The State Department was able to provide some support for the Lebanese government by providing a channel of communication to Israel. On October 23, via US diplomats and the special Lebanese channel, Israel again sent Helou guarantees that it was not trying to annex Lebanese territory.[106] Whether or not Israel was coordinated with the Lebanese, the Israelis did use their own deterrent power. On October 24, Israeli deputy prime minister Yigal Allon publicly warned Arab nations and Palestinian guerrillas that Israel "will not stand idle if [the] Lebanese government is overthrown from without." This statement was not coordinated with the US State Department, which instructed the embassy in Tel Aviv to tell Israeli officials that it was not helpful.[107] More importantly, by October 27, the State Department had secured a promise from the Israeli government that it would not launch reprisal attacks in Lebanon during this period, allowing the Lebanese to redeploy three battalions from the border to other areas, thus providing a small margin of military maneuver for the Lebanese security forces.[108] Finally, at Khoury's request, the State Department sent word to Ambassador Rabin that they had information that an Israeli official in Paris was telling colleagues that there was an agreement between Helou and the Israelis. Rabin promised to investigate.[109]

Lacking any option for Western assistance, Helou again looked to Nasser to mediate the crisis. Nasser's intentions regarding Lebanon remain something of a mystery. Farid el-Khazen and others have argued with reason that Nasser sought to defuse the crisis in order to focus his energies on formulating a response to the Rogers Plan.[110] Initially, Nasser exchanged a series of letters with Helou that addressed the fedayeen situation, while Egyptian diplomats also tried mediating between parties in Lebanon. Khoury initially told Porter that Helou was encouraged by Nasser's mediation and the UAR ambassador's actions up until that point.[111] Two days later, however, he complained about Egypt, noting that Nasser's followers were placing barricades in the streets even as the Egyptian ambassador tried to get them taken down.[112] Nasser's inter-Arab diplomacy sent mixed signals about his intentions as well. On October 27, Nasser had sent an emissary to Damascus and Amman to consult about the situation, but soon thereafter, the United Arab Republic, Syria, and Libya issued a statement supporting freedom of action for the fedayeen. At the same time, the Egyptian leader had sent word to Helou that the United Arab Republic was sympathetic to Lebanon's position.[113] Nasser seemed to be playing to all sides.

In general, US officials thought that Egypt was playing a constructive role in Lebanon. Instead, US suspicions focused on the Soviet Union and Syria. Although US officials doubted that the Soviet Union wanted chaos in Lebanon, they believed that the USSR sought to use the situation to expand its influence and embarrass the United States. Sisco told Kissinger on October 25 that he was sure that the Soviets were involved in Lebanon, possibly by putting Syrian soldiers in fedayeen uniforms.[114] That same day, a report by Tass, the official Soviet news agency, warned against "outside interference by a big power" in Lebanon.[115] This comment, clearly aimed at the United States, aroused Nixon's interest in the issue. That day, the president ordered Kissinger to put together an NSC meeting on Lebanon, as well as on the situation in Libya.[116] Nixon asked for a tough response to the Tass statement; however, the State Department and NSC staff proposed a relatively mild statement to avoid inflaming the situation.[117] In a face-to-face meeting, Sisco reprimanded Soviet ambassador Anatoly Dobrynin. Sisco reported that he "felt that he had struck the note K[issinger] wanted him to," suggesting that Kissinger had asked for the hard line to be taken in private rather than in public.[118] Rogers took a similar tone in an October 31 meeting with Dobrynin, in which the secretary called the Soviet statement "disappointing."[119]

These US measures were not coordinated with the government in Beirut. Hostility toward the US government limited the ability of US officials even to meet with most Lebanese government officials, Christian or Muslim, though Porter had been able to meet with former president Chehab.[120] Soviet representatives, on the other hand, met with both Christian and Muslim officials. On October 27, the Soviet ambassador met with Helou for the first time since the Mirage incident and spent four hours in a meeting with Karame.[121] On October 29, the State Department asked for Porter's views on the desirability of "raising our profile in Lebanon slightly as [to] offset what seemed to [be] public credit being given to Soviets for alleged successful peacemaking efforts."[122] Porter responded that he was not avoiding top officials, but rather that they did not want contacts with the US ambassador to be publicized and could not meet, even in private.[123] Even if US officials had wanted to be more active on the ground, there was little more that they could have done.

In the meantime, the United Arab Republic and the Soviet Union apparently warned the Lebanese government against US intervention. Khoury told US embassy officials that the Soviet ambassador's meeting with Helou on October 27 had held no surprises. The ambassador had assured the Lebanese president that the "Soviet Union did not want the destruction of

Lebanon." He said that the Soviets had been in contact with the Syrian government but did not reveal the details of these demarches, saying that the Soviet government "considered the Lebanese problem as part of the Arab problem and could not disassociate Lebanon from the Arab world." The ambassador claimed that the Soviets opposed "external intervention" in Lebanon's affairs. Helou responded that as long as he was president and in control, there would be no requests for external intervention.[124] Tass subsequently announced that Helou had told the Soviet ambassador that he would not ask the US Sixth Fleet to intervene.[125] In Cairo, Bustany gave a similar message to the Egyptian foreign minister, Mahmud Riad.[126]

In fact, for the first time, the Nixon administration was seriously considering the possibility of a military intervention of some kind, whether direct or indirect. On October 29, the Washington Special Actions Group (WSAG), an inter-agency coordinating committee that met in times of crisis, met to discuss options for Lebanon. Kissinger noted that he had just met with Nixon, who wanted a "tough option" to deal with the situation in Lebanon. In terms of indirect aid, there were two main options for funnelling assistance to Lebanon: providing weapons to the Lebanese army or to the Christian militias.[127] Although a few attendees commented that providing weapons to the army would become known and perhaps provoke a backlash, Kissinger insisted that the United States needed to do so. Deputy assistant secretary of state Rodger Davies was charged with drafting a cable that contained an offer of arms to Lebanon. As for the Christian militias, the requests from these groups for arms and support had continued throughout the early fall.[128] All participants in the WSAG meeting agreed that a plan needed to be in place to provide weapons to the militias, but it remained to be decided under what exact circumstances and how they would be provided. Davies said that State believed that weapons should be provided to these groups only in the event of the collapse of the government. The CIA representative at the meeting, deputy director for plans Thomas Karamessines, stated that the plan was to allow a private US firm such as INTERARMCO to supply the weapons, which the US government would pay for. If necessary, the arms could also be delivered via air drop. When another participant asked why not just provide arms directly to the Phalange now, Kissinger argued that providing weapons to the Lebanese army was similar "because they are controlled by officers sympathetic to the Falange [sic]." This was, "in effect . . . support of the Falange by proxy, while retaining the option of covert support should the GOL show signs of imminent collapse."[129]

It is not entirely clear whether the United States actually supplied any weapons to the Christian militias at this time. At the height of the crisis, in an October 31 telephone conversation, Kissinger told Nixon that in addition to meeting Lebanese military requests, "we will also supply covert actions."[130] However, there is no concrete evidence that this occurred. Despite the enthusiasm in the WSAG meeting for this step, some in the US government continued to argue against it. The Department of Defense, for instance, warned that supplying arms to the Phalange "might encourage covertly that violent form of communal sectarianism discouraged officially in Lebanon."[131]

In addition to indirect aid, the US government considered the possibility of a direct military intervention in Lebanon, although the options for this looked poor. At the outbreak of the fighting, both Porter and the State Department agreed that the United States should not move its forces in the Mediterranean region unless they were needed for evacuating US citizens.[132] By October 26, the United States decided to move the Sixth Fleet within about 450 miles of Lebanon, which US officials hoped would signal concern to the Soviet Union while not aggravating the political situation.[133] On October 28, Saunders, at Kissinger's request, drafted a memo to the president on options for Lebanon, including military ones, which the president had requested in a note on his daily brief over the weekend.[134] By October 29, a carrier task force had been moved to four hundred miles off Lebanon, a Marine battalion landing team task force was just north of Crete, and a second task force was just west of Crete, approximately six hundred miles from Lebanon.[135] US officials expected the Soviet Union to pick up on these moves.[136]

At its October 29 meeting, the WSAG group also considered a US military intervention in Lebanon in the event of an internal conflict or external intervention. Several participants pointed out that the line between an internal and international conflict was likely to be blurred. Even in the current hostilities, at least 150 of those captured were Syrian regulars in fedayeen uniforms. Group members agreed that a purely internal conflict within Lebanon would not likely spark a US intervention, though it needed to be planned for. However, an external one might. An alternative to US intervention was an Israeli intervention in Lebanon. Kissinger suggested that this might be a preferable alternative, allowing the US to focus on keeping the USSR out of the battle through the principle of superpower non-intervention. But the plans for this needed to be refined.[137]

Though US and Lebanese officials knew that a direct US military intervention was a poor option, they tried to remain ambiguous about it publically, presumably to have a deterrent effect. On October 31, Helou told Porter that he was astonished by a report in *Le Monde* that the United States had no intention of intervening in Lebanon. Porter responded that the report was probably just "interpreting US public opinion (as had Helou himself) as being opposed [to] military intervention almost anywhere."[138] That same day, the media reported that US Navy secretary John Chaffee said that the US military "is not anxious to become involved in a land operation and would do so only if 'circumstances make it necessary.' "[139] The implication was that the US government *would* intervene militarily in Lebanon under certain unnamed circumstances. There are no documents suggesting that Nixon administration officials asked Chaffee to make this statement, though they did not back away from it, leaving it unclear whether this was another "calculated risk" on Washington's part. The next day, Porter warned again about the importance of leaving "legitimate doubts as to US intentions" to serve as a warning to the Syrians and fedayeen.[140]

For US policymakers, the deteriorating situation in Lebanon meant that US interests in the region were likely to suffer. A State Department analysis affirmed that the Lebanese would probably have to accept the fedayeen presence in Lebanon and that Karame would likely demand more freedom of action for the fedayeen as a price for agreeing to serve as prime minister.[141] The deterioration of the situation in Lebanon also risked having an impact in Jordan. Both Jordanian officials and the US ambassador worried about the United States associating itself with an agreement between the Lebanese and the fedayeen, because this situation would imply that a similar agreement would be acceptable for Jordan.[142] The State Department promised the embassy in Amman that it would not associate itself with any such agreement.

Indeed, the State Department's predictions soon came to pass. Beginning on October 29, Lebanese and fedayeen representatives met in Cairo under Nasser's auspices to negotiate an agreement. Khoury told the US that Helou had initially wanted to send Chief of Staff Shamayyit as the main Lebanese representative instead of Bustany, who Helou feared would give away too much, but the "Egyptians and Palestinians insisted on Bustany." The United Arab Republic wanted Bustany to have plenipotentiary powers, but Helou refused, saying "details had to be negotiated in Lebanon with the Lebanese government." Bustany, he said, had been authorized to compromise on military but not political issues.[143] Just as in May, Helou sought to preserve the principle of Lebanese sovereignty, even though he was forced to make concessions in a written form.

Once Bustany's party had left for Cairo, not even Helou, much less US officials, had any direct influence over the negotiations. The Lebanese president told US officials that he was again considering making an appeal to the Lebanese public, as he had done in May, to try to influence public opinion. However, Porter advised him, both in person and through Khoury, not to issue another public statement on the issue but that the Lebanese government should "maintain its cool, hol[d] firm to its position, and be prepared [to] take advantage of opportunities which conflicting forces may provide."[144] The vagueness of this advice, like the signing of the agreement itself, reflected the limits on US ability to impact events inside Lebanon at this time. The final Cairo Agreement was signed by Bustany and Arafat on November 3, 1969. Though it officially remained to be confirmed in Lebanon, it would have been extremely difficult to modify an agreement brokered by Nasser's government; thus, for practical purposes, the deal had been done.

The Cairo Agreement was both a political and a military document. On one level, it granted Palestinian refugees in Lebanon the right to work and move throughout the country, while also allowing for local committees to be formed in the refugee camps to represent Palestinian interests, albeit "in cooperation with the local Lebanese authorities within the framework of Lebanese sovereignty." At its core, though, it was a military arrangement, providing a basic framework for cooperation between the Lebanese army and the Palestinian "revolution." It permitted the militants to form military outposts in the camps, as well as to conduct "resistance" activities in the south, again "in cooperation with the Lebanese authorities."[145] Although its wording emphasized cooperation, the agreement merely glossed over the gap between the two sides. By any standard, it was a capitulation by the Lebanese government. The requirement of cooperation provided a thin rhetorical veil that could allow the Lebanese government to say that it was protecting the country's sovereignty. But most saw right through this.

The US was initially left in the dark about what had actually been agreed in Cairo. Khoury told US deputy chief of mission Bob Houghton on November 4 that the "Lebanese [had] achieved more or less what they expected in Cairo" and "compromised but did not capitulate." However, he "agreed that it obviously gave the fedayeen more freedom of action than previously," though the details were "to be worked out in Lebanon." A few days later, Khoury revealed that Boustany had "exceed[ed] his instruction[s] in the agreement he concluded in Cairo," and that even "Karame himself felt that Boustany had gone too far." However, Khoury had still not revealed its exact content, possibly for fear of leaks to the Israelis.[146]

Even though an agreement had been signed, tensions between the militants and the government were still running high. Although both Helou and the US government knew that a US military intervention had always been unlikely, other Arab states still considered it a possibility. On November 6, following the signature of the Cairo Agreement, Khoury explained that the Lebanese government had been pressured to renounce the possibility of US intervention. He thought that, at the Arab defense ministers' meeting in Cairo on November 8, there would be an attempt to pass a resolution preventing external security guarantees from non-Arab states. Khoury asked whether the United States could approach its friends to prevent this. Porter had reservations about whether this would work with Morocco or Saudi Arabia, but thought that a "direct approach to [the] Egyptians" might work, though it could also backfire.[147] The State Department agreed with Porter's skepticism and felt that it should take no action.[148] The upside of the situation, according to Porter, was that the Syrians and Palestinian militia leaders had not understood US intentions during the crisis, which had been helpful to Helou. The ambassador characterized it as "one rare situation where Arab proclivity to believe the worst about us may actually have had [a] stabilizing effect on [the] Lebanese situation."[149] The dark cloud of Arab suspicion thus had a silver lining for Helou, the army leadership, and the Christian parties.

Within the Nixon administration, there were different interpretations of the implications of the Cairo Agreement. Kissinger saw the events as a sign of increasing Soviet assertiveness in the Middle East, noting that their statement that foreign powers should not interfere with the Arab states was "reminiscent of the Brezhnev doctrine of limited sovereignty for Eastern Europe."[150] Sisco and the State Department, however, seem to have interpreted the fighting in the context of Israeli-Lebanese relations. In a draft cable to Tel Aviv, he noted that "events have borne out our somber predictions of the past that Israeli policy of substantial military retaliation against two remaining moderate regimes, Jordan and Lebanon, while militarily successful, has been a political disaster." Moreover, the crisis reinforced Sisco's belief in the need to continue to pursue an Arab-Israeli peace agreement and that Israel should rethink its "QUOTE seven-fold UNQUOTE retaliation on Jordanian and Lebanese soil."[151] For Sisco, however, like Kissinger, perhaps the most important lesson was that the Lebanese crisis had once again revealed US weakness. In a memo a few weeks thereafter, he noted that "we are giving very serious thought to other steps we might take in order to reaffirm that our power in the Middle East is still credible."[152]

The destabilization of the Lebanese internal political system during 1969 cannot be understood without reference to the role played by the United States. Throughout the crises of that year, US officials in Lebanon maintained an ongoing dialogue with the Lebanese government concerning Lebanon's internal security situation. The State Department also served as a mediator between Lebanon and Israel and pressed friendly Arab states to encourage the fedayeen to practice restraint. At times, they even considered the possibility of military action in Lebanon, though this never went beyond the planning stage. Yet, there were serious limitations on US ability to impact events. For instance, US support for Israel meant that it would never back Lebanon fully against Israeli reprisals. In addition, many US policymakers saw the merit in Israeli arguments that they should be allowed to strike within Lebanon in self-defense and that attacks were the main incentive for the Lebanese government to control the fedayeen. And even in the fall of 1969, when the Nixon administration appears to have been relatively successful in restraining Israel, this provided only short-term relief. But as long as all sides believed that the United States might intervene, the Nixon administration could maintain at least some influence.

CHAPTER 3

From Cairo to Amman

The United States and Lebanese Internal Security

The Cairo Agreement in November 1969 provided a temporary reprieve to the crisis in Lebanon, but it was not a permanent solution. The fedayeen remained in the refugee camps and in the south of the country, their presence now sanctioned by a still "secret" agreement, details of which were printed on the front pages of the major Lebanese newspapers. This agreement would only buy time until the next crisis, which came in late March 1970, when Christian militiamen ambushed a Palestinian convoy, sparking confrontations throughout the country. Tensions continued throughout the summer, not only in Lebanon but throughout the Middle East. In late summer and fall, a confluence of local and international factors would produce another temporary peace in Lebanon. The most important of these was the September 1970 civil war in Jordan, concentrated in its capital, Amman.

These two cities, Cairo and Amman, embodied two possible models for relations between the Arab government and the fedayeen. The first represented cooperation with the fedayeen, while the second stood for military control. Cairo appealed to Lebanese leftists, much of the Muslim population, and the fedayeen, who saw it as a viable model for allowing the Palestinian resistance to continue in cooperation with the Lebanese authorities. The notion of an Amman-style military solution might have tempted some

Christian leaders, but the events of the previous October had demonstrated that such a solution was impossible, at least at the moment.

Cairo and Amman also provided two possible models for US policy toward Lebanon: in the first, the United States remained distant from the conflict, allowing local and regional forces to play out; in the second, the United States would attempt to use its diplomatic and military power to shape events. During the negotiations leading up to the Cairo Agreement, the Nixon administration had been unable to provide significant support to the Helou government. In the year that followed, US officials would attempt to play a more active role in the conflict. This, in itself, did not produce a noticeable improvement in the situation in Lebanon. What did make a difference is that in the fall, the United States helped the Hashemite regime in Jordan to suppress the Palestinian guerillas located on its territory, which gave confidence to the Lebanese government, while reminding the fedayeen of the significance of outside support.

Post-Cairo US Assistance to Lebanon

The Cairo Agreement convinced the Nixon administration that it needed to provide aid to the Lebanese, but as we saw in chapter 2, the US government had to decide what type of support to give and, perhaps more importantly, whom to give it to. In Lebanon, two different groups were soliciting US help: the Lebanese security forces and pro-Western militias. The United States would have to make a decision about which of these, if either, to support. Neither seemed capable of successfully confronting the fedayeen. If the army tried to use force to confront the fedayeen, it risked falling apart as an institution. On the other hand, arming the militias could ultimately launch the country into civil war. In effect, the choice was between supporting the logic of the state and the logic of the militias. At least initially, the Nixon administration would choose the former, but they made arrangements in preparation for the latter as well.

The Lebanese army and government were anxious for military assistance. A few days after the signature of the Cairo Agreement, Ghaby Lahoud, the head of the army's intelligence branch, the Deuxième Bureau (DB), asked whether the United States could supply around ten thousand M-16s for the army, including three hundred right away for the combat officer corps.[1] US officials were unwilling to provide M-16s, the most advanced US rifle in production at the time, but they initially offered Lebanon ten thousand of the next best option, the M-14.[2] Justifying a request for these and a $1 million subsidy, Kissinger argued that "even the Israelis would like to see the US help Helou." Nixon agreed on December 6.[3] The final US offer appeared to be somewhat less than the original proposal, including six thousand M-14 rifles and a number of helicopters, with $5 million in military credits instead of a grant.[4] By standards of US aid to the region, this was a relatively small amount. Jordan, for instance, received $14.2 million in military grant aid in 1969, then nearly $59 million over the next two years.[5]

Although this offer came relatively quickly, several factors prevented the quick provision of weapons other than rifles. Anti-US sentiment made it difficult for the Lebanese government to discuss security planning with the United States openly. In January, Helou and Lahoud told Porter that any military purchases would have to be "in [the] context of an overall military sales agreement with [the] USG, the ostensible purpose of which was to improve effectiveness of [the] Lebanese army to resist Israeli aggression."[6] In addition, Lebanese political leaders were bent on replacing army commander Emile Bustany, which kept the government from submitting a list of equipment requirements for several months.[7] It was not until February 19 that the new army commander, Jean Noujaim, finally provided the Beirut embassy with a list of Lebanese arms requests, including fifty M-41 tanks, one hundred to two hundred .50 caliber anti-aircraft guns, five thousand mines, and ten bulldozers.[8]

In the meantime, with US help, the Lebanese army and internal security forces made efforts to improve their capacity to conduct internal security operations. The US government designed several programs in support of the Lebanese security forces, including USAID training programs for police and the provision of materials for the control of refugee camps and demonstrations. The agent of sale for the latter was Sarkis Soghanalian, a US citizen of Lebanese Armenian origin who would later became an important military supplier for the Christian militias in Lebanon.[9] Soghanalian originally sought to purchase tear gas for the Lebanese army but later found something called a "sickening agent" that he wanted to import instead. To hide the fact that it was purchased in the United States, he planned to "arrange at some transit point such as Vienna to modify shipping documents to obscure [the] origin of [the] gases." US munitions control officers informed him that "his application would be expedited."[10]

US willingness to provide aid to Lebanon was increased by concerns about the expansion of Soviet influence in the region. From the mid-1960s onward, the Soviet Union had repeatedly offered weapons to Lebanon, often on much more favorable terms than Western nations. Now, in early March 1970, Soviet ambassador Sarvar Azimov offered Lebanon any kind of military equipment its government wanted, including antiaircraft weapons and tanks, repeating an offer previously made to Karame.[11] Many within Lebanon, such as Kamal Jumblatt, had begun to campaign publicly for Lebanon to obtain weapons from any source possible, including from the Soviet Union. In March, he even asked the United States to provide Lebanon with arms, in particular antiaircraft and antitank weapons, and Porter believed that Jumblatt's request was serious.[12] In early March, Porter complained bitterly several times to the State Department that it was not being responsive enough to Lebanese needs.[13] His messages helped speed the wheels of bureaucracy.[14] In early April, the Lebanese received a positive response to their request.[15]

Although the US embassy in Beirut had thus far resisted the idea of arming the militias, as the October 29 WSAG meeting had shown, top US officials were increasingly considered the possibility. The US embassy knew that close relations existed between the Christian militias and certain officers of the army and internal security forces, which meant that aid to the Lebanese armed forces was more than just an alternative to arming the Christian militias. Porter reported that his advocacy of arms deals with Lebanon was designed in part to satisfy pro-Western Lebanese groups. The militias had asked that the army leadership support them and, in turn, offered the service of their paramilitary forces in fighting the fedayeen. However, according to Porter, "the army's (quite proper) response to them is that 'we will arm you when the time comes, but that time is not here.'" He expected that this knowledge would ease demands from "our friends here" for US support.[16] Porter thus understood that in an emergency, the army was likely to arm the Christian militia groups, foreshadowing events some four years later.

Following the signature of the Cairo Agreement, the WSAG continued to look into the question of whether to supply arms to the Phalange. In late November, the group decided if the President would agree to supplying M-14s to the Lebanese army, the plans to provide weapons to the Phalange would be discontinued.[17] Although Nixon agreed to provide the M-14s, the president and Kissinger apparently still remained committed to the possibility of arming the Christian militias. The two authorized the preparation of "contingency arrangements for the rapid covert delivery of approximately 3,000 weapons to the pro-Western, Christian [Ph]alange organization," which would be done "only in the event of a breakdown of internal security to assist the [Ph]alange in protecting Christian areas and the American community from attack." In addition, the embassy was to inform the Lebanese army of its willingness to sell or deliver seven thousand M-14 rifles, both to strengthen the military and to "create a reserve of replaced weapons which the Army high command could issue to selected auxiliary groups loyal to the regime if need arises."[18]

Again, there is no concrete evidence that these weapons were actually provided at this time or that the Phalange or other militias were notified of the US decision. Porter continued to refuse the militia's appeals for arms and money. On November 24, two Phalange representatives visited Porter to request arms and assistance, saying that they had raised "a substantial amount of money" and had contacted foreign arms dealers but "had been unable to get the Army's permission to import the arms," though some in the security forces wanted to help them. Porter turned down their request for guarantee of US intervention in case of an emergency, but assured them "that we had not, and would not, be idle." The two described their group's military planning, saying that the party had detailed plans to protect landing sites for weapons at the coastal towns of Batrun, Jbeil, and Damour in the event of conflict.[19] In addition to the Phalange, which sought five hundred weapons altogether, supporters of Suleiman Frangie, Camille Chamoun, and Raymond Edde were all looking to purchase weapons. Many had been "purchased from the fedayeen themselves, or from smugglers whose source seems primarily to be Syria."[20] Other groups also made requests for weapons to US officials in Beirut, including the Tashnag Party (the largest political party among the Lebanese Armenians) and Druze leader Fadlallah Talhuq, but Porter again rebuffed these requests.[21] The Maronite militias were also making requests to other countries for aid, particularly France, which had reportedly refused as well.[22]

President Helou, who had expressed his opposition to US support for the Christian militias the previous fall, now seemed more equivocal about the possibility. During a meeting on December 12, Porter told Helou that he had responded negatively to Christian requests for arms. The Lebanese president thanked him, but notably did not seem concerned about whether the US embassy armed them, saying "he could fully appreciate the combined frustration and anger of the Christians and thought it natural that they should seek arms, especially in the face of the arming of the refugee camps."[23] Although Helou was not requesting assistance for the militias, unlike the previous summer, he no longer warned against it.

The Lebanese government began to appeal to the United States on behalf of groups outside its control, though not for the organized militias. One area of focus was South Lebanon. By this time, the government and the army were trying to create friction between the fedayeen in the south and Lebanese villagers. In late January 1970, Khoury asked US embassy officials to help in their efforts, perhaps by making clandestine donations to religious or political foundations, or by helping them get assistance from the shah of Iran.

Porter promised nothing but made inquiries back in Washington.[24] It is unclear whether any assistance was provided. In early February, Khoury asked the United States to provide the Lebanese army with older weapons to give to sympathetic Christian and Shi'a villagers in the South, which would "be used ostensibly for border defense, but in fact to provide points of resistance against fedayeen." Khoury told Porter that the government knew which leaders could be trusted, arguing that the Syrians were distributing weapons through Saiqa to villages with large Baath party memberships.[25] By midmonth, an army official specified that they would like five thousand rifles or even old World War II carbines. Porter now endorsed the idea, noting that "even the radicals could not publically [sic] object" to the provision of arms to individuals in the South for self-defense.[26] At this time, Nasser and Arafat had also offered help to arm villagers in the south to protect them against Israeli incursions.[27] Again, it is unclear whether the US government ever provided these older weapons for distribution.

On the whole, US military aid does not appear to have contributed greatly to the ability of the Lebanese government to control the fedayeen. Few weapons were delivered to the army, and there is no indication that any aid was delivered by the United States to the Christian militias at this time. The significance of these discussions lies in what they reveal about US and Lebanese intentions: if a crisis did occur, the militias and the army seemed ready to work together, and the United States was ready to at least consider assisting them. These trends would only be strengthened in the period ahead.

Implementing the Cairo Agreement

Most of the Lebanese political class was unhappy with the Cairo Agreement, whether or not they admitted it publicly. There was open talk about the possibility of Helou resigning, although an opinion poll in November suggested that relatively few Lebanese wanted this.[28] However, most Lebanese leaders remained publicly silent, hoping to keep their future options open. Among Christian leaders, only Raymond Edde opposed the agreement publicly, while Chamoun and Gemayel appeared to accept it in a qualified way, probably hoping to increase their chances in the 1970 presidential elections.[29] The army's DB was also unhappy with the agreement, despite the fact that one of their officers, Sami al-Khatib, had accompanied Bustany to Cairo for the negotiations with the fedayeen.[30]

Nevertheless, the Cairo Agreement did offer at least a temporary reprieve from the internal political crisis. Karame, 215 days after his previous resignation, finally formed a government on November 25.[31] Kamal Jumblatt became interior minister, which put him in charge of implementing the Cairo Agreement, taking at least some pressure off Helou. In December and January, Jumblatt worked out a series of agreements on guerrilla activities in Lebanon, including regulations on fedayeen funerals and bans on firing weapons, bearing arms, and wearing uniforms in public areas.[32] At the same time, however, fedayeen units increased the flow of supplies into Lebanon and expanded their bases.[33]

In the meantime, Helou looked for ways to keep Lebanon from being drawn deeper into the fighting. At an upcoming Arab League summit in December at Rabat, Helou expected to receive pressure to station other Arab troops on Lebanese soil. He worried that he would face "fourteen and a half" opponents at the table, including Prime Minister Karame, who would be half with him and half with the other Arab leaders. Helou expected other moderate Arab states, such as Saudi Arabia and Jordan, to sacrifice Lebanon for their own interests, noting cynically that "he would be only too happy to do the same in the interests of his country."[34] Helou, Karame, and several DB officials decided to seek Nasser's support for the protection of the Lebanese vis-à-vis the fedayeen. Sami Al-Khatib and a DB colleague traveled to Cairo, where they met with Minister of Defense Mohammed Fawzy and Nasser's adviser Sami Sharaf, who assured them of the Egyptian president's support.[35] Indeed, just before the opening of the Rabat conference, Helou's predictions appeared to be coming true, as Libya asked Morocco on December 17 to station troops on the Lebanese border with Israel.[36]

US efforts helped Lebanon at the Rabat conference. The Rogers Plan was finally announced to the public at the Galaxy Conference on Education on December 9. On December 18, the State Department added a Jordanian component to the plan, including minor adjustments to the borders between Israel and Jordan and a choice for refugees between compensation and repatriation. Though Jordan seemed interested, the Israeli cabinet rejected the plan on December 22.[37] Although this plan did not lead directly to an agreement, at least in the short term, the State Department felt that it gave states like Egypt, Lebanon, and Jordan an excuse to avoid taking a more militant position at the conference.[38] US officials also believed that their provision of weapons to the armies of the moderate states helped these states resist arguments that they should station other Arab troops on Lebanese territory.[39]

During the first three months of 1970, the cycle of fedayeen raids and Israeli reprisals across Lebanon's southern border began again.[40] Israeli reprisal attacks increasingly affected citizens within Lebanon. After fedayeen seized an Israeli farmer in a cross-border raid, Israeli attacks on southern villages killed at least ten people, including a foreign correspondent.[41] Israeli troops seized numerous Lebanese civilians from southern villages, taking them back into Israel as hostages.[42] According to Foreign Minister Nasim Majdalani, during the previous few days, at least twenty thousand civilians had fled from the south, most of whom fled to the southern suburbs of Beirut.[43] The State Department resumed its role in mediating the violence across the Lebanese-Israeli border, telling Israeli officials in Washington that these attacks were harming the Lebanese government, which was "doing all it can within limitations of [the] Cairo Agreement to control [the] fedayeen."[44] Israeli foreign minister Abba Eban took exception to what he called the US effort to give "juridical weight" to the Cairo Agreement, but US diplomats in Tel Aviv told him that this was not their intention.[45]

By then, the Lebanese government was again communicating directly with the Israelis concerning the border situation. At the time, this communication seems to have involved little more than trading threats. On January 10, Helou told Porter that he had received a warning from Israeli minister of defense Moshe Dayan, delivered by a "bishop from Jerusalem of Lebanese origin," that if fedayeen attacks continued, "Israel would take measures such as at Irbid and other areas in Jordan, reducing Lebanon's border areas to unpopulated desert."[46] Helou said that he sent back three points to the Israelis, though he was "inhibited from making them too strongly for fear the Israelis would ma[k]e them public to embarrass him":

> Firstly, Lebanon is and has been Israel's policeman even though it can't admit it, and despite the imperfect way it sometimes performs that function. To destroy Lebanon for its shortcomings in this regard would be like eliminating the Haifa police department for its inability [to] stop sabotage acts there. . . . Secondly, continuation of unprovoked raids into Lebanon will set in train a series of events which will include stationing of foreign troops, perhaps Syrian, perhaps Iraqi, on Lebanese territory. While admittedly these troops would cause great trouble for [the] Lebanese regime, they will also be [a] problem for Israel. Helou's third point is that it [is] not in Israel's interest [to] destroy the only other democratic, non–Muslim, religiously mixed state in the area. However flawed their comprehension, the Lebanese at least have some understanding of Israel's problems. This could be a valuable asset for Israel should it eve[r] decide to be part of as well as in the Middle East [sic].[47]

Had this response been revealed publicly, it would have been extremely damaging to Helou. However, the response reflected an understanding, shared within the Lebanese government and political class, that preserving calm across the border would require some sort of understanding with Israel. Even Kamal Jumblatt understood this. A few days later, Foreign Minister Majdalani told Porter that "Jumblatt, as contrasted to his pessimistic attitude of a few days ago, now felt that it [was] possible to enforce [the] terms of the Cairo Agreement, but only if Israel would understand and cooperate."[48] Jumblatt brokered an agreement with the fedayeen on January 20 that banned the fedayeen from carrying weapons in the cities and moved heavy weapons away from villages near the border.[49]

Nonetheless, the fedayeen raids resumed in February, and in early March, the Israeli government began a series of well-publicized approaches to the United States, other Western countries, and the Vatican, asking for help in stopping the attacks.[50] Porter was instructed to pass on a message from Israel that Lebanon should "step up control measures to prevent further fedayeen actions originating from Lebanese territory."[51] Meanwhile, in a conversation at the border with the senior Lebanese delegate to ILMAC, the Israeli Northern Zone commander threatened to establish a "no man's land" along the border.[52] Israel leaked this threat to the press, as well as the fact that the US ambassador had been asked to intervene.[53] Sisco complained to an Israeli official in Washington that these leaks were "not helpful."[54] Porter had visited Helou on March 5, drawing headlines the next day that the US ambassador had given the Lebanese president assurances that the United States would use its influence with Israel to reduce the attacks.[55] In fact, the State Department saw little that could be done.

The situation in the south inflamed Lebanese public opinion, making it more difficult for the Lebanese government to work with the United States. On March 7, for the first time since 1949, a Lebanese soldier died in combat with the Israelis. Two days later, Helou told Porter that he might be the last US representative that the Lebanese could treat openly as a friend.[56] On March 10, the Beirut press began to repeat the story about Porter's delivery of an Israeli message to Majdalani on March 4. According to Porter, most of the Lebanese press "adopted the premise that the USG, having agreed to carry Israel's messages, has thereby assumed responsibility for Israel's subsequent actions." As a result, protests began outside the US embassy in Beirut.[57] Porter thought that in the future, Israel should use UN channels to communicate to Arab governments, because such incidents undermined US credibility.[58] In the meantime, the Lebanese and Israeli governments argued over whether a secret agreement had been reached in December regarding control of their border.[59] On March 20, Kamal Jumblatt announced that he had reached an agreement with the fedayeen to conduct joint patrols with the internal security forces, a move that was seen as a rebuke to the army.[60]

A tenuous peace held, but it would last only a few days, as a new internal conflict broke out that threatened to bring about a repeat of the previous October.

The Kahhale Ambush and the Exodus from the South

Against this background, an incident far from the border threatened to turn the Lebanese internal tensions into a civil conflict. On March 25, in the small mountain town of Kahhale, Christian villagers opened fire on a caravan of fedayeen returning from the funeral of one of their comrades killed in fighting in the south. At least eight fedayeen were killed.[61] Who was behind the attack remains a mystery. Some sources have suggested that this attack had the "discreet backing" of the DB and internal security forces.[62] News reports at the time blamed the Phalange.[63] Robert Oakley, a political officer at the US embassy from 1971 until 1974, has maintained that Camille Chamoun and some of his sympathizers later told him of their participation in these incidents.[64] The attack was probably intended as a show of force, though no explanations from its organizers were given.

Following this attack, clashes broke out between the fedayeen and Christian groups and the internal security forces in various locations, including near the Shatila camp on the outskirts of Beirut.[65] Pierre Gemayel's son Bashir, thought to have participated in the ambush, was taken prisoner at a checkpoint.[66] Bashir was later released as part of a deal, but the fighting left at least forty-one dead and seventy wounded. Helou refrained from using the army to control the situation, though the gendarmerie was deployed to various areas. Jumblatt negotiated a solution, which was seen as enhancing his prestige.[67] Egyptian foreign minister Mahmud Riad also assisted in the negotiations.[68]

The clashes had a negative impact on the standing of the United States in Lebanon. The leftist press blamed the incident on US collusion with Lebanese militias. One newspaper claimed that the individuals that fired at Kahhale were "the slaves of the American ambassador in Beirut." The paper also claimed that the United States had been furnishing the Christian groups with arms through a smuggler killed by the fedayeen on March 24, though there is no evidence of this in the US archives.[69] The incident was followed by direct attacks on US interests in Lebanon. On March 29, the PFLP attacked the US embassy and the offices of the American Life Insurance company, causing minor damage.[70]

Despite these events, many individual Lebanese Christian leaders contin-ued to petition the US government for support. On April 16, Nixon and former Lebanese foreign minister Charles Malik met for half an hour in the president's office, during which time Nixon telephoned CIA director Rich-ard Helms.[71] Malik and Nixon had known each other since the latter's days as vice president, when they worked together in the 1958 Lebanon crisis, during which Malik served as foreign minister. There is no record available of Malik's meeting with Nixon, but his recommendations to the president included consulting with conservative Arab states on cutting funds for the fedayeen, as well as providing arms to "certain private groups in Lebanon."[72] Malik also gave Nixon a letter from Maronite patriarch Meouchi, the content of which is unknown. Nixon did not reply until August, when, just prior to the outbreak of the crisis in Jordan, the State Department authorized the Beirut embassy to tell the patriarch of Nixon's concern for Lebanon.[73]

FIGURE 3.   By the early 1970s, fedayeen groups had established themselves on Lebanese territory. An American embassy officer took the two PFLP posters shown above off buildings in Beirut in 1970 and sent them back to Washington. On the left, the skull wears a top hat in the colors of the American flag, with Stars of David instead of regular stars. The hat and bow tie are meant to suggest capitalism and imperialism. King Hussein of Jordan pokes his head out of an eye socket, wearing an eye patch designed to evoke a comparison with Israeli minister of defense Moshe Dayan. The skull is eating bodies. On the right, in bright red and green, the poster announces "The Liberation of Palestine Is the Battle of the Arab Masses . . . and the Cause of Forces of Progress in the World." RRIJLS, Box 11.

In April and May, the Nixon administration offered Lebanon little beyond words. Porter delivered a message from Nixon to Helou expressing support for Lebanon's "stability and independence" against "outside interference."[74] During an April 15 visit to Beirut as part of a broader Middle East tour, Sisco could not discuss internal Lebanese security with Helou because the two met in the presence of other leaders, including Prime Minister Karame.[75] While the State Department remained focused on the Middle East, the National Security Council staff and the White House had other priorities. Other foreign policy issues, particularly the recent US military offensive in Cambodia, distracted them from the situation in the Middle East. In May, the national security advisor planned on holding a meeting of the so-called 40 Committee, which oversaw covert operations, to consider aid to Lebanon. However, the meeting was scheduled and cancelled four times because of Kissinger's prior commitments.[76] In the meantime, the situation in the Middle East, particularly on Lebanon's southern border, was approaching a new low. In response to fedayeen attacks across the border, including a May 8 attack on an Israeli school bus, Israel launched its fiercest reprisals into Lebanon yet. On May 12, clashes broke out between the Lebanese army and the Israelis in the south. Syria sent its air force and ground troops to the Arqub region, losing several planes.[77] The *New York Times* called the situation in Lebanon "even more perilous than the escalating Indochina conflict."[78]

At the time, the Nixon administration faced two major decisions regarding the Middle East: whether to provide Israel with orders of Phantom aircraft it had requested the previous year, and whether to launch a new peace initiative in the region. After his April trip, Sisco returned to the State Department determined to find a way to reinvigorate US diplomacy in the region, in large part because of his concerns about Lebanon and Jordan. To accomplish his aim, he proposed a new step: bringing the fedayeen directly into the negotiations. Though this idea was eventually rejected, Sisco's proposal marked a huge step forward in the range of possibilities being discussed within the US administration. Instead, in early June, Nixon finally authorized Rogers to propose a plan to stop hostilities, under the slogan "Stop Fighting and Start Talking." This new effort, dubbed the Rogers Initiative (in contrast to the Rogers Plan of the previous December), would be accompanied by a few measures to meet Israeli demands, such as delivering a few planes.[79]

While the initiative was being developed, events in Lebanon underscored the dangers. Concerned about Lebanese internal stability and preparing for the possibility of a new diplomatic initiative, the United States put pressure on Israel to withdraw its troops from Lebanese territory. On May 12 and

May 19, for the first time, the United States voted for UNSC resolutions demanding that Israel withdraw troops from Lebanon.[80] This did not stop the Israeli attacks. Jumblatt then proposed that the fedayeen withdraw from the area west of the Hasbani River back to the Arqub.[81] The State Department sought a military reprieve from Israel to allow the Lebanese to implement this agreement, while reminding the Lebanese government about the need to stop the attacks.[82] The Israelis, however, were not willing to grant this request.[83]

Whether due to the attacks or simply to Jumblatt's urging, some fedayeen groups in Lebanon now made concessions. On May 26, Khoury informed the US that Fatah had agreed to move east of the Hasbani. However, the group's leaders still had to get the assent of other groups. In the meantime, Helou had secretly sent letters to all Arab leaders requesting arms and money, while warning that the fedayeen raids were causing more damage to Lebanon and the Arab cause than to Israel.[84] A few days later, the Lebanese government adopted a series of potentially risky steps to control the fedayeen, including setting a time limit for the implementation of the Cairo Agreement by June 15.

As the Israeli patrols continued and refugees flowed into Beirut, the Lebanese again considered going to the Security Council.[85] At the time, the State Department, which was getting ready to launch yet another Arab-Israeli peace initiative, urged Helou to hold off.[86] In an ILMAC meeting, the Lebanese told the Israelis of their intention to complain to the Security Council. The Israelis replied that if Lebanon did not go to the UNSC, they would "'reduce' artillery bombardments and other activities." The Lebanese allegedly rejected this.[87] In any case, Israel finally ceased fire on June 2, while issuing an ultimatum to Lebanon in an ILMAC meeting: if the Lebanese complained to the UNSC, Israel would increase its military activity. Since the incursions had stopped, Helou just sent a letter of report to the Security Council, rather than a request for a meeting.[88]

At least, that was the story that the Lebanese told US officials. In fact, a tentative agreement between the Lebanese and the Israelis regarding border security may have been responsible for the cease-fire. According to Israeli officials, the Lebanese were secretly advancing "ingenious" ideas for coordination.[89] The Lebanese had set a number of conditions for Israeli reprisals. The Israelis should not shell civilians or damage property. Their ambushes should be at night and not penetrate too deep into Lebanese territory, involve constructing new roads on Lebanese territory, or use armored vehicles. Finally, the Lebanese did not object to the shelling of bases in the Mount Hermon (Arqub) area with "few" aircraft and "quietly."[90] The Lebanese themselves told US officials nothing about this agreement. From Beirut, Porter warned that the Lebanese government was "playing [a] very dangerous game," since a leak could "have serious political consequences."[91] The Lebanese did tell the United States that the Israelis were trying to send messages via a "Greek Catholic bishop"—possibly the same one that had previously transmitted a message from Dayan—that Israel had no territorial designs on Lebanon. However, Helou was hesitant to see the bishop for fear that the Israeli government would publicize the fact that they had sent a message.[92]

US officials were concerned that turmoil in other parts of the region would spread to Lebanon, possibly even leading to the fall of the government. After the revolution in Libya the previous year, that country's government had taken increasingly radical positions on regional affairs, something that was applauded by publics throughout the Arab world. Libyan leader Muammar Qaddafi visited Beirut on June 7, where a crowd of eighty thousand gathered along the road to the airport to greet him. Some supporters even took automatic weapons into the airport terminal and fired in celebration from the balcony overlooking the tarmac.[93] In Jordan, on June 9, a group of fedayeen opened fire on King Hussein's motorcade, killing one of his bodyguards.[94] A few days later, demonstrators burned down the Jordanian embassy in Beirut.[95] These events had no direct connection, but to observers at the time, they seemed to be related.

The State Department encouraged Israel to continue its secret talks with the Lebanese and to refrain from attacking.[96] After the Qaddafi visit and the Jordanian embassy fire, Israeli officials told their US counterparts that they now shared their concerns and had orders to ease the strain on Lebanon.[97] The Israeli army also proposed to the Lebanese to find a way to coordinate military actions more closely. One Israeli official told his US counterpart that about ten days before, the Lebanese had told the Israelis that they would take strong action against the fedayeen on June 15, though not in the Arqub.[98] In Beirut, Porter remained skeptical about whether the Lebanese could coordinate with the Israelis, arguing that the only solution was for Israeli patrols to stay out of Lebanon.[99]

As the June 15 deadline for the enforcement of the Cairo Agreement approached, the situation appeared somewhat less urgent. Porter felt that a stalemate existed in part because the fedayeen knew that if fighting broke out, the Christian militias might join in. In fact, Porter even suggested that these militias might be the "greatest deterrent" against the outbreak of fighting.[100] On June 15, with Arafat's approval, Jumblatt put into effect restrictions on firing across the border and carrying arms without permits.[101] The fighting had once again ended, at least temporarily. A few days earlier, the

Israeli army had made a proposal for military coordination with the Lebanese army, and the Lebanese now promised a response within a few days.[102]

However, there was still a danger to US citizens in Lebanon. On June 13, the Lebanese government told the United States that the radical fedayeen sought to remove the US presence from Lebanon.[103] A few days later, although the dangerous situation of the previous weekend had abated, Porter reported that things could change at any moment, particularly if the United States decided to sell Phantom fighter jets to Israel, since this could make some Lebanese military units hesitate to use force to defend the embassy.[104] Khoury told Porter that Helou and Noujaim had discussed the possibility of an attack on the US embassy and planned to use the army to keep mobs away. In the meantime, the US embassy prepared contingency plans for emergency situations.[105]

In Washington, US officials again considered the possibility of an internal collapse in Lebanon or Jordan, including whether or not the United States should intervene militarily.[106] At least two high-level meetings also addressed Lebanon. At a June 17 NSC meeting on the Mediterranean situation, President Nixon asked, "Let us suppose late in summer we get a request from Lebanon or Jordan for assistance, or something happens in Lebanon. What can we do?"[107] In his memoirs, Kissinger suggests that US contingency planning was "halfheartedly undertaken."[108] However, at least some officials were already pressing for a more positive attitude toward a US intervention. During one meeting, in response to a question from Nixon, Kissinger stated that the United States could put in ten thousand marines, though there would be a question of the Soviet reaction. Sisco stated that he supported US military action in the event of a Syrian intervention in Lebanon.[109] A meeting of the WSAG was held on June 22, at least in part to consider a US response—including military intervention—if "President Helou asks for U.S. assistance in the event of aggression by other Arab states." The memo notes that Jordan intervention plans were also to be discussed.[110] At the time, however, US preparations concentrated on Lebanon.

The military options for Lebanon were neither militarily nor politically appealing. The main logistical problem was finding a base from which to launch a US invasion.[111] US planners considered bases in Turkey, Cyprus (UK bases), Greece, or Italy, though each was problematic. In political terms, the United States would be seen as intervening to support Israel, undermining support from "Arab moderates and allies." Perhaps most damningly, even if the United States intervened, it was doubtful that the intervention would save the "moderate government" in Lebanon "in the long run."[112] In the end, the WSAG avoided a decision on the circumstances under which the

United States would intervene in Lebanon, instead ordering a general study on interventions in "friendly" Arab countries, such as Lebanon, Jordan, Kuwait, or Saudi Arabia.[113]

Though overt military intervention was unattractive, covert action remained an option. As Helou approached the end of his mandate, both the Lebanese government and the US embassy in Beirut were changing their attitudes toward the possibility of the US providing weapons to the Christian militias. In early June, Porter wrote a letter to Sisco asking the assistant secretary to reconsider the issue of aid to the Christian militias. Though this letter is not available in the archives, Sisco's response on June 12 thanked Porter for his suggestion that the United States "rethink the question of providing arms to various Lebanese constituents particularly the Christians." The assistant secretary agreed that "the situation is different today than in the past and we should take a fresh look at it" and assured Porter of his "direct and personal involvement in this since I too feel that we need to be more decisive along these lines in the days ahead."[114]

Helou's attitude toward the militias appeared to be changing as well. On May 18, Khoury had told Porter that he and Helou knew that certain Christian leaders, including the Maronite patriarch, were encouraging Israel to "have a bash at the fedayeen," though he thought this was dangerous.[115] On June 17, Khoury urged the United States to provide aid to the Christian militias, arguing their strength was a significant deterrent to the fedayeen.[116] On June 23, Helou sent word via Khoury urging the United States to provide weapons to the Christian militias. Porter responded that if the United States did provide weapons, they would not inform the Lebanese government and would deny it if asked. When Khoury said that Helou wanted the United States to "get credit with the Christian groups," Porter countered that the "US hand should not show."[117] On June 29, Helou personally requested that the United States provide arms to the Christian militias at the request of Camille Chamoun. His reasoning was "humanitarian grounds." The Lebanese president maintained that "he could not with [a] clear conscience [let the] Christians to go to bed each night in fear of being annihilated by better-armed Palestinians and their supporters." The main impact, he thought, would be psychological, though there was a risk that the militias might "miscalculate" and use the weapons in a crisis. Finally, Helou appealed to US interests, arguing that the militias might save the United States "from having to intervene militarily to rescue its citizens—an intervention which would have far-reaching consequences." Porter again assured him that they would listen to his recommendations, while noting that the United States would act "in complete secrecy." To Washington, he reiterated that "all of the old arguments (which I have supported for five years) against USG assistance in arming private Lebanese groups are, in my opinion, being rapidly overtaken by events."[118]

Did the United States actually provide weapons to these groups? Several years later, in 1973, Sisco noted in a document that, unlike in 1970, the United States would not consider providing weapons to the Christian militias in the event of an emergency, thus implying that in 1970, they had considered this.[119] However, there is no concrete documentary proof about whether any military assistance was provided at the time.

Causes of the Calm

After several turbulent months, a temporary relief came to the Lebanese government in the late summer and fall of 1970. A combination of factors, including Suleiman Frangie's election as president of Lebanon, the September crisis in Jordan, the death of Nasser in Egypt, and the change in the Syrian regime, all had led to a "tactical retreat" by the fedayeen.[120] In addition, Egypt and Israel's acceptance of the Rogers Initiative calmed the fighting between the countries.[121] The most important of these changes were the events in Jordan, in which US diplomacy played a significant role.

The question of support for the fedayeen was surprisingly muffled in the debates over who would be the next president of Lebanon. Instead, the major question was whether the Nahj would retain their control over the country. From several months prior to the election, former president Fouad Chehab himself appeared to be the candidate with the broadest support. However, general dissatisfaction with the Nahj had been growing over the previous decade for numerous reasons, including the DB's heavy-handed intervention in internal politics, the radicalization of broader regional politics, and the Chehabists' dispute with the Soviet Union. Chehab personally remained quite popular, and until the beginning of August, many believed that he would run for president. Had Chehab decided to run, there is a broad consensus that he would have been elected by the Lebanese parliament.[122] The biggest challenge to the Chehabists remained the Hilf of the three Christian zuama, Chamoun, Gemayel, and Edde, but the rivalry among these leaders prevented them from settling on a common candidate.[123] In late July, Chehab decided not to run, thus opening up a race with many candidates and no clear front runner.

Much of the Lebanese public believed that external powers, including the United States, would play a role in deciding the election. As a sign of this, a

FIGURE 4. The note on the door of the US Embassy reads "The attendance of a number of candidates for the Presidency at the American Independence Day Celebration." US ambassador to Lebanon William Porter greets the suits and uniforms, representing candidates in the upcoming election. Pierre Sadiq, *al-Nahar* newspaper, July 5, 1970.

cartoon in Beirut's *al-Nahar* newspaper portrayed Ambassador Porter viewing a stream of visiting tuxedoes and uniforms, representing Lebanese presidential candidates, at the US embassy's Fourth of July celebration.[124] Former president Camille Chamoun's supporters, including Charles Malik, fervently sought US support. Malik himself sent a fifty-one-page memorandum to President Nixon outlining what he saw as the dangers of Chehab's reelection.[125] Maronite patriarch Meouchi also warned the United States about the possible reelection of Chehab.[126] Chehab never personally solicited the United States for aid, but his supporters, including former prime minister Hussein Oueini, sent surrogates to meet with US officials to ask them to support Chehab.[127] The US embassy did not oppose Chehab, who told a colleague a few days before the election that the US ambassador had come by to say that the US government "approved of and hoped for" his election.[128] While there is no archival record of such a visit, Porter did hold the former president in high regard.

Other countries had more important roles. Ironically, the lack of Egyptian participation in the elections may have been the most important. For the Nahj, maintaining good relations with Egypt was key to ensuring the support of the Lebanese Muslims and thus to maintaining their control on power. Since at least October 1969, the DB had maintained contacts with Cairo to try to enlist Nasser's support for the Nahj.[129] Although the Egyptians had been angry over the September 1969 Mirage affair, one of Nasser's advisers had reaffirmed to al-Khatib Egypt's support for the Nahj and the Deuxième Bureau.[130] However, by summer, Nasser was refusing to endorse any candidate, thereby undermining the Nahj. The Soviet Union, on the other hand, still angry over the DB's role in the Mirage affair, tried to prevent a Chehabist from being elected. Some prominent Chehabists appear to have argued on Chehab's behalf to the Soviet Union, though unsuccessfully.[131] The Soviets consulted with Jumblatt and the leftists about who the next president would be. In a June 29 meeting, Helou told Porter that, several weeks before, Jumblatt had suggested that the best solution to the electoral question would be to renew Helou's mandate. Later, Ambassador Azimov confirmed to Helou that Jumblatt's offer was serious.[132] The Soviets also encouraged Michel Khoury to seek the presidency, promising Soviet support, as well as that of the Iraqi Baath, the Palestinians, and the Lebanese progressive parties.[133] In early July, Porter observed that many Lebanese politicians were courting the influence of the Soviet Union as if it were a new Sublime Porte.[134]

With Chehab out of the race and Nasser refusing to endorse a candidate, the field was essentially wide open, though Nahj candidate Elias Sarkis and the Central Bloc's Suleiman Frangie appeared to be the front runners. Sarkis had long been a functionary within the Chehabist government. Frangie, a Maronite zaim from the Zgharta region in the north, had taken over the family's political dynasty after his older brother Hamid Frangie suffered a debilitating stroke in 1957. In the third round of voting, Jumblatt switched part of the votes that he controlled from Sarkis to Frangie, ensuring the latter's victory. Why the switch? Phalange member Karim Pakradouni has stated that the Soviet Union asked Jumblatt not to vote for Sarkis because of the Mirage affair, which it blamed on the Chehabists. By contrast, former LCP leader George Hawi noted that as a condition of Jumblatt's support, Frangie had to promise to respect the Cairo Agreement and authorize the legalization of leftist parties (including the Lebanese Communist Party and the Syrian Social Nationalist Party).[135] Whatever Jumblatt's motives, Frangie's election would have enormous implications down the road. Soon after taking office, Frangie began sending many high ranking DB officers abroad in ambassadorial positions, in some cases threatening to arrest them should they return to Lebanon, thereby dismantling their intelligence network.[136]

Although the United States had not opposed Sarkis, US officials were happy with Frangie's victory, believing that he would be a strong leader capable of controlling internal security. Soon after Frangie's election, Porter was invited to dine with the new president and his family at their summer home in Ehden. During the course of a long conversation, Frangie told Porter that the fedayeen and Israeli retaliations in the south were his greatest concerns. At the end of the visit, Porter suggested that Frangie find someone to be an intermediary between the president and the embassy during crises, as Khoury had done.[137] On August 31, Porter received a visit from

Charles Malik, who said that Frangie had entrusted him to come up with "specific proposals" on the fedayeen.[138] Porter had reservations about using Malik as a channel, but if Frangie requested it, he was willing to do so. Malik also asked Porter to remind President Nixon of their conversation four months prior, which included arming certain militias.[139] Within a few weeks, however, Frangie had designated Lucien Dahdah, the brother-in-law of his daughter and a close adviser, as a contact.[140] The scene thus appeared to be set for a replication of the close relationship that had existed between Porter and Helou.

Meanwhile, in Jordan, a civil war was about to break out between the regime of King Hussein and the Palestinian guerrillas located in his country. On September 7, guerrillas from the PFLP hijacked three planes and landed them all in northern Jordan, eventually blowing them up after evacuating the hostages. One week later, the Jordanian army launched an attack on the Palestinian militias within the country, with the aim of permanently subjecting them to the authority of the state. The fate of the showdown in Jordan would have important implications for Lebanon, as well as for the role of the United States in the region.

Even prior to the hijackings, Jordanian and Lebanese officials were in touch about their mutual security situations. On August 13, DB members Sami al-Khatib and Ahmad Hajj traveled to Jordan to deepen political and military ties, meeting with key military leaders. During their visit, the two Lebanese also met with Arafat and other fedayeen leaders present in Jordan.[141] PLO leaders must have noticed the symbolic significance of the trip. The Lebanese situation also offered a potential model for the resolution of Hussein's conflict with the fedayeen. Egyptian foreign minister Mahmud Riad visited Jordan on August 20 and tried unsuccessfully to explore a settlement along the lines of the Cairo Agreement.[142] Some US officials worried that violence would spread from Jordan to Lebanon. At a September 9 meeting of the Joint Chiefs of Staff, Admiral Thomas Moorer warned of the possibility of a Syrian or Iraqi attack on Jordan and Lebanon and a decision was taken to prepare aid for Lebanon in the event of a confrontation with the fedayeen.[143]

After launching his attack on the fedayeen on September 16, King Hussein enlisted the help of the United States and Israel. On September 19, after reports that Syria had sent troops and tanks into Jordan, the United States arranged for Israel to conduct overflights of the area to collect intelligence. The United States and Israel also discussed the possibility of an Israeli military intervention to save Hussein's regime, though all sides had reservations about this. On September 22, as the Israeli military was poised to send a ground force into Jordan, the king's own air force attacked the Syrian tanks, which withdrew, leaving the Jordanian army free to continue their rout of fedayeen forces.[144] Still, the possibility of a US or Israeli military intervention appears to have deterred other Arab states from joining in the melee. Although a cease-fire was eventually reached, over the next nine months the Jordanian government would gradually push on with its offensive, resulting in the eventual expulsion of the Palestinian militant groups from the country in July 1971.

The events in Jordan would provide a model for a US reaction to a civil conflict in Lebanon. Lebanese officials saw the relevance of the situation in Jordan to their own country. As the Jordan crisis reached its peak, President-elect Frangie probed the possibilities of US assistance to Lebanon in the event of a similar crisis. On September 22, the day before officially taking over as president, Frangie, through what is referred to as his "confidant" (presumably Dahdah), inquired about the US "reaction and action" in the event of civil war in Lebanon due to Palestinian actions, or to Syrian actions "directly or in the guise of Palestinians," in particular if the Lebanese government— or Frangie himself—asked the United States to intervene. Plans were made to discuss Frangie's question at a September 24 WSAG meeting.[145] Houghton told Frangie that similar questions had been posed in the past and that he doubted that US answers had changed or that any new undertakings would be given, though he said he would report to Washington. In his report, Houghton stated that he thought it was significant that Frangie asked about the US response if the "GOL or President Frangie" requested interventions, which suggested that he understood that these were different situations.[146]

In Washington, US officials seriously considered responding to a crisis in Lebanon along the same lines as they had in Jordan. During the September 24 WSAG meeting, Kissinger asked whether there was a draft cable ready to be sent to Lebanon in case of emergency. His aides assured him there was one. However, some at the meeting expressed doubts about US ability to intervene in Lebanon effectively. CIA director Helms is recorded as saying, "The imagination boggles. It was bad enough in 1958, but now, with the fedayeen as a complicating factor!" Kissinger asked, "If we don't do it, would we have the Israelis do it—or anyone do it?" Saunders reminded the group that "we had an Israeli option."[147] The draft documents thus probably contained plans for a US military intervention (as had the plans in the summer of 1970), as well for an Israeli military intervention or deterring action in the case of outside interference. Many of the factors that made the US hesitate to endorse an Israeli ground action in Jordan, including the possibility that Israeli forces would not leave the territory, would apply in the Lebanese case. Still, in the aftermath of the Jordan crisis, had there been a similar confrontation in Lebanon, the United States would likely have been willing to try similar measures to help the Lebanese government.

As the crisis in Jordan wrapped up, the United States told the Lebanese government as much. On September 25, the State Department commended Houghton's response to Frangie's confidant, authorizing the Chargé to point out that "our vigorous diplomatic efforts together with contingency military steps which we took immediately undoubtedly helped contribute to obtaining Syrian withdrawal" from Jordan. The United States, the message continued, prized Lebanese national independence and stood ready to view its needs sympathetically.[148] The implication was that the United States would consider taking similar actions in Lebanon, including deterring a Syrian military intervention there in case of a confrontation between the Lebanese army and the fedayeen. On September 26, Houghton passed this on to Frangie's confidant, who was appreciative.[149]

US officials worried about the possibility of fedayeen relocating from Jordan to Lebanon.[150] Houghton reported that the Lebanese government shared this concern but felt it could handle the situation, in part because of "assurances that UAR, Soviet Union and Syria [do] not want [a] repetition of [the] Jordan crisis in Lebanon."[151] Frangie's confidant called Houghton to convey the Lebanese president's thanks for the US message, which Frangie felt was "stronger than those sent [to] Pres[ident] Helou." He also told Houghton that in Cairo, Frangie had twice met alone with Nasser, who conveyed to him his support, even in a confrontation with the fedayeen. The Lebanese president hoped that Nasser would visit Lebanon in the next two or three months.[152] This suggests that even the great Arab leader was growing weary of the fedayeen.

The Lebanese government was also a secondary beneficiary from the Jordanian crisis in terms of US military assistance. Prior to taking office, Frangie had twice raised the subject of arms with Porter, but the ambassador made clear the United States could not provide extensive economic or military assistance.[153] On October 3, the new US ambassador, William Buffum, who had since replaced Porter, strongly recommended military aid to help the Lebanese government "handle [a] Jordan-type situation in Lebanon," including armored cars, M-41 tanks, and .50 caliber antiaircraft guns, the antiaircraft guns "because of [the] high potential in its ground role as a deterrent against mob action."[154] By the end of the year, the United States had offered Lebanon $5 million in grant military assistance.[155]

Soon, Nasser's death and the coup by Hafiz al-Asad's "Corrective Movement" in Syria changed the regional landscape. Neither of these events marked an immediate change in the policy of these countries toward Lebanon. However, they contributed to an overall feeling of uncertainty, not just for the fedayeen, but also for the Lebanese government. On September 28, the same day that Frangie's confidant told Houghton of the meeting of the two presidents in Cairo, Nasser died of a heart attack, shocking the Arab world. His passing deprived the Lebanese government of a potential ally, albeit an unreliable one, in its attempts to control the fedayeen. In October, the change of regime in Syria led to the replacement of the leadership of the Saiqa group, temporarily weakening that group. Taken together, these two events also marked the beginning of a long-term trend that would have important consequences for Lebanon: namely, the increasing importance of Syria at the expense of Egypt as the Arab arbiter of Lebanese affairs. In the short term, however, neither was as important for Lebanon as the impact of the events in Jordan.

Ironically, although Amman had deeply influenced the situation, Cairo would remain the model for Lebanese-fedayeen relations. There was no full crackdown in Lebanon mirroring that which took place in Jordan. Having suffered a major defeat, the guerillas would behave more cautiously in Lebanon, at least in the short term. Fewer provocations along the border meant fewer Israeli reprisal attacks, which in the short term made the fedayeen presence more tolerable for the Lebanese government, which was unwilling to face the kind of Arab approbation heaped upon King Hussein for his actions in Jordan.

Following the Cairo Agreement, the United States had tried harder than before to try to help support the Lebanese government. Through military aid, mediating relations with Israel, and launching the Rogers Initiative, they had helped the Lebanese government navigate the crisis in relations with the fedayeen. But it was through the events in Jordan that the United States had its greatest direct impact on Lebanon. Both US leaders and local actors believed that US actions contributed to King Hussein's success in defeating the Palestinian militias, demonstrating the impact that the United States *could* have on the local situation in the region, at least in theory. This perception is as important as reality in helping understand the calm that developed in Lebanon during the next few years. With what was viewed as a tougher regime in place, and with the fedayeen still reeling from their defeat in Jordan, US officials could once again place the Lebanese cauldron on the back burner.

CHAPTER 4

Plus ça change

International Terrorism, Détente,
and the May 1973 Crisis

Although the fedayeen's defeat in Jordan eased
tensions in Lebanon, the country's problems never went away. Cross-border
attacks and Israeli reprisals in Lebanon soon resumed, though somewhat less
frequently than in 1970. Over the next two years, as the Jordanian army
wiped out the remaining pockets of fedayeen on their territory, Lebanon
would become the main host state for the Palestinian armed groups. At the
same time, the fedayeen strategy began to change. The militants began to
employ more frequent and more spectacular international terrorist attacks,
including against US targets, which prompted increasingly severe Israeli
reprisals on Lebanon. In April 1973, an Israeli raid in Beirut killed several
Palestinian leaders, sparking a conflict between the Lebanese government
and the Palestinians that would have more serious effects on the internal
political situation in Lebanon than any of the previous crises.

In many respects, the US role in the 1973 crisis in Lebanon was similar to
the one it had played in 1969 and 1970. Just as before, the Lebanese government inquired about the possibility of diplomatic and military assistance from
the United States. Yet, by then, changes had occurred in the regional and
global situation that gave outside parties a greater incentive to contain the
conflict. Syria and Egypt, now preparing to launch a major war against Israel, were determined to prevent a major crisis from occurring in Lebanon
to preserve Arab unity, even though they differed somewhat over their pol-

icy goals in that country. Increasing détente between the superpowers led the United States and the Soviet Union to seek to avoid a clash in the Middle East. The outcome of such a balance of factors was, again, a military and political stalemate between the fedayeen and the Lebanese government, just as in 1969 and 1970, but this time, the militias would draw different conclusions from the fighting.

The New International Terrorism

From the fall of 1970, Lebanon's border with Israel was calmer than it had been in years. The new Lebanese government under Suleiman Frangie took stricter measures to control the fedayeen, including putting at least three thousand soldiers on patrol along the frontier with Israel.[1] A new US ambassador in Beirut, William Buffum, reported that the Palestinians were in "disarray" after the Jordan clashes and that the "general security situation here [was] better than at any recent period."[2] Granted, fedayeen attacks did not stop altogether. Some thirty cross-border attacks were mounted from Lebanese territory in 1971 alone.[3] On the whole, though, Frangie's government was satisfied with its relationship with the fedayeen, in part due to what it saw as the moderating influence of Yasser Arafat.[4]

The appearance of increased stability reduced the perceived need for US involvement in both Lebanon and the Arab-Israeli conflict more broadly. The US government continued to provide weapons to the Lebanese army and mediated cross-border violence between Lebanon and Israel in isolated cases.[5] Still, the overall situation on Israel's borders with Lebanon and Jordan was calmer. Along the Suez Canal zone in occupied Egyptian territory, a tenuous stalemate also seemed to be holding. For these reasons, US policymakers felt less of an incentive to launch initiatives to broker an end to the Arab-Israeli conflict, though the State Department tried one last time, in the late spring of 1971, approaching Israeli and Egyptian officials about the possibility of an interim settlement between the two countries. Although this found some reception in Cairo, it was rejected in Tel Aviv.[6] Following this, the State Department's involvement in Arab-Israeli negotiations effectively came to a halt, reflecting Kissinger's new dominance on Middle East issues, US preoccupation with other issues such as Vietnam, and concerns about the domestic implications of putting pressure on Israel during the run-up to the 1972 US presidential elections.

During mid-1971, some Palestinian groups began to undertake a new strategy of attacks against international targets, including assassinations and

airplane hijackings. Though such operations had been conducted by the fedayeen previously, they now occurred more often and against a broader variety of targets, including Arab and Western ones. Many were conducted by
a new entity called the Black September Organization (BSO), organized in
secret by some Fatah leaders with members of the PFLP and other groups.[7]
The most convincing explanations for the new strategy emphasize frustration with the lack of success of the cross-border attacks and a desire for revenge after the events in Jordan, as well as competition for recruits among
the Palestinian groups.[8] Jordanian prime minister Wasfi al-Tal was assassinated
by BSO in November 1971, and an attempt on the life of his replacement
was made the next month.[9] By 1972, the group was targeting Western European interests as well. In mid-February, for instance, the PFLP hijacked a
Lufthansa plane in Aden, which they released only after the West German
government paid a $5 million ransom to the group in Beirut.[10]

Early in 1972, both the international attacks and cross-border infiltrations
began to intensify. On the night of February 23–24, fedayeen killed an Israeli couple in a bazooka attack on the pickup truck they were driving.[11]
Israel responded with ground attacks and air raids on Lebanon that left twelve
fedayeen dead. On February 28, in response to a Lebanese complaint, the
UN Security Council unanimously demanded that Israeli troops leave Lebanon. *Al-Nahar* newspaper reported that the Lebanese ambassador in Washington had spoken to Sisco, who contacted Israeli officials and insisted that
the Israeli troops withdraw immediately.[12] In the meantime, the Lebanese
government obtained an agreement with the fedayeen that would permit
their presence in the Arqub as long as they evacuated all villages and withdrew to at least ten kilometers from the border.[13]

Behind the scenes, the US embassy got more involved with the fighting
in Lebanon than it had since 1970. The two sides discussed the possibility of
outside support in the event of a crisis. Frangie told Buffum that he felt the
army could handle the fedayeen militarily, as long as Syria did not intervene.
If that happened, however, the president "might feel required to ask for some
sort of outside help."[14] Responding to a US request, Frangie authorized holding exploratory talks with the Israelis along the border regarding a way of
dealing with the fedayeen. However, after Israeli representatives refused to
remove an observation post they had set up in South Lebanon, Frangie withdrew this authorization.[15] Yet, he gave the United States permission to share
with the Israelis information about the agreement with the fedayeen, provided that it was kept confidential.[16] Lebanon asked the member-states of
the UN Security Council to augment the observer force along the Lebanese-
Israeli border, though they refused.[17]

In early summer, an attack within Israel itself prompted a new series of reprisals on Lebanon. On May 30, 1972, three Japanese nationals trained by the PFLP opened fire on travelers at the Lod Airport in Tel Aviv, killing, among others, sixteen US citizens on a pilgrimage to the Holy Land. At this time, the PFLP operated openly in Beirut, even issuing press releases to journalists there. Though the organization claimed sole responsibility for the attacks, Israeli prime minister Golda Meir accused the Lebanese government of assisting the group.[18] Israeli officials told US diplomats that the Lod attacks were planned and the terrorists were trained in Lebanon, urging the United States to make clear to the Lebanese government that they needed to "put an end to these activities."[19] The State Department passed on the message through the US ambassador in Lebanon and to Frangie's son, Tony, who was visiting Washington.[20]

In response, the Lebanese government began to take action against the fedayeen groups. On May 30, Prime Minister Saib Salam held a two-and-a-half-hour meeting with Arafat that led to an agreement for the fedayeen to "freeze" all operations from Lebanon.[21] The bulk of the Lebanese government's actions, however, focused on those groups they labeled as "extremists," particularly the PFLP. On June 2, Frangie publicly condemned the Lod massacre and announced that the Lebanese had "taken new measures" to stop the PFLP's "information activities" in Lebanon, including shutting the organization's office in Beirut.[22] At that moment, the US ambassador reported that the internal tensions within Lebanon were worse than at any time since the 1967 war.[23] Although the PFLP information office was transferred to Kuwait, at least officially, the organization did not shut down its activities in Lebanon altogether. For instance, "former" PFLP spokesman and *al-Hadaf* editor Ghassan Khanafani continued to give interviews from Beirut.[24]

As violence on the border increased, the United States faced what one official called a "familiar dilemma." US officials doubted the effectiveness of the reprisals but felt that they had limited influence over Israeli actions. The State Department thought that the best course of action would be a "low-key but unmistakable signal" to Israel that the United States disapproved of reprisals.[25] Barbour, however, argued that the Israelis would think that Washington did not take their concerns seriously. Thus, he suggested that the United States should forbear offering advice.[26] The State Department agreed, authorizing him to tell the Israelis that the United States has "foreborne [*sic*] to intervene or offer advice to GOI [the Government of Israel] but GOI would be mistaken if it misunderstood US silence as acquiescence in any act of violent retaliation."[27] US officials were under no illusions that this would prevent Israeli reprisals.[28] This debate resembled that of early 1969, but because Lebanon's internal situation was relatively stable and US citizens had been killed, the United States saw less reason to protect this government. At the time, the United States made some military equipment available to the Lebanese army, including the early delivery of fifty armored personnel carriers in what Harold Saunders of the NSC called "*preventive medicine* to try to avoid reaching the kind of situation Jordan reached in the summer of 1970."[29]

The Lebanese measures to restrict the PFLP were not enough for Israel, which continued to increase its pressure. On June 21, an Israeli force crossed the border, capturing a number of Syrian officers present in South Lebanon. Two days later, another Israeli attack into Lebanon killed twenty-one fedayeen and nineteen civilians.[30] Following the reprisals, negotiations under Arab auspices led to an agreement between the Lebanese government and the fedayeen. Frangie told Buffum that copies had been given to Kuwait and Saudi Arabia, which had made their financial support for the fedayeen dependent on their "full cooperation" with the agreement.[31] Most of the Palestinian organizations promised to discontinue cross-border operations, withdraw a majority of militants from the Arqub region, evacuate villages in the south, and refrain from carrying arms in public.[32] Following the conclusion of this agreement, the border remained relatively quiet for a few months, though the war continued unabated. On July 8, *al-Hadaf* editor Ghassan Khanafani, whose picture had appeared in a newspaper posing with one of the Japanese terrorists from the Lod attack, was assassinated in Beirut by a car bomb, presumably by Israeli intelligence.

That fall, a new terrorist attack prompted a rethinking of US policy toward the issue of terrorism. On September 5, members of the BSO kidnapped a group of Israeli athletes at the Olympic Games in Munich. The kidnappers killed several of the athletes during the initial hostage-taking. The rest were killed, along with all but three of the hostage-takers, during a botched rescue attempt by the West German security services. The events unfolded on live television, shocking the world. Now, the United States was even less inclined to press Israel for restraint in its reprisals.

Nixon initially pressed for a strong US reaction to the events in Munich. When notified by Deputy National Security Advisor Alexander Haig that the Israelis would likely strike in Lebanon, Nixon just commented rhetorically that "they have got to hit somebody, don't they?"[33] In another phone call a few minutes later, the president told Haig that United States should consider breaking off diplomatic relations with countries such as Jordan and Lebanon that harbored terrorists, asking, "Hell, what do we care about Lebanon [?]" Soon after that, Haig called Rogers. The two agreed that they should call for calm the next day. Haig lamented that Nixon "always wants to do something. We have to be careful not to do something he will regret."[34] After discussion, the US leadership eventually settled on a more measured response. They decided on taking a "delicate line" that "demonstrated justified sympathy for Israel but which did not serve to encourage Israeli retaliation which could only further escalate tensions and dangers in the Middle East."[35]

When the Israeli reprisals came, the United States continued to waver between protecting Lebanon and supporting Israel. On September 7 and 8, Israel launched an attack on Lebanon that was its most extensive against any Arab country since the 1967 war.[36] The United States passed Israel a message that expressed "strong concern" about the attacks, but it vetoed a UNSC resolution calling for an immediate halt, because it did not mention the Munich incident.[37] However, after a second set of Israeli strikes in Lebanon on September 15 and 16 in response to the killing of two Israeli soldiers by infiltrators, US officials lodged stronger protests with Israel, in part because of the attack's potential impact on superpower relations. Kissinger told Israeli foreign minister Abba Eban that his criticism was directed not at the attacks but at their timing: first, a day before he took trip to Moscow to prepare for a second superpower summit in 1973, and then the day after his return.[38] Kissinger's primary concern was for détente, rather than for Lebanon's stability.

The Lebanese government, meanwhile, had to do something about the Israeli reprisals and the Palestinian attacks. On September 16, anticipating another Israeli attack, one of Frangie's advisers asked US officials in Beirut for information about Israeli intentions, saying that they were going to hold a "very important" policy meeting that day.[39] The United States requested this information from Israel. Israeli officials briefed the United States on their plans to send troops into Lebanon, but they refused to allow US officials to share it with the Lebanese.[40] Israel launched a two-battalion strike into Lebanon that lasted until the next day. During these attacks, the Lebanese government decided to take new measures against the fedayeen. On September 18, the army moved into the south, setting up roadblocks and taking other measures to reduce the fedayeen's freedom of movement. Colonel Musa Kanaan, the senior Lebanese military officer responsible for controlling the fedayeen, maintained that the army was under instructions directly from the presidency, bypassing Prime Minister Saib Salam.[41]

The State Department was concerned about this violence for several reasons. First, some worried that the Lebanese army could crack under the strain between Muslims and Christians.[42] Second, there was concern that the attacks would increase Soviet influence in the region. In mid-September, the Soviet ambassador offered Frangie a defense agreement and to dispatch the Soviet fleet to Beirut to counter the recent Israeli "aggression."[43] Ambassador Buffum thought that the Soviet Union was "making a major play for Lebanon" to recoup some lost prestige after their military advisers had been expelled from Egypt that summer.[44] Israeli media reports stated that the government was considering further military action, including "regular patrols," in effect "'policing' Lebanon up to [the] Litani River."[45] To try to head this off, the State Department passed Israel information from Beirut about the new inspections and checkpoints in the south.[46]

Finally, the crisis was again temporarily resolved through another agreement between the Lebanese government and the Palestinians in early October. Like the Cairo Agreement, this one was brokered by Egyptian officials, though the mediation took place in Lebanon, not in Egypt. In some ways, this agreement may have been even more restrictive than the Cairo Agreement, as some fedayeen "headquarters" facilities were allegedly transferred to Damascus, and Arafat had to promise not to carry out raids across the southern border. To a certain extent, these new restrictions reflected a backlash against the fedayeen after the Munich incident, suggesting that the strategy of international attacks was failing. On the other hand, however, the new international strategy had drawn world attention to the Palestinian issue and had been wildly popular among the guerrillas' base of support. The international strategy would continue to have advocates for some time.

A New Request for Support

At that point, for the first time since 1970, the Lebanese government attempted to resume a dialogue with the United States about US support in the event of a crisis. On October 3, 1972, Lebanese foreign minister Khalil Abouhamad met Sisco at the Lebanese Consulate General in New York for a "discreet" meeting, which the assistant secretary later called "perhaps one of the most significant conversations we have held with the Lebanese in recent years." In this meeting, the foreign minister sought commitments for military and diplomatic assistance in the event of a crisis, including if Syria or the Soviet Union became involved in a confrontation between the government and the fedayeen.[47] The next day, Abouhamad repeated his requests in a meeting with Secretary Rogers. Back in Lebanon, on October 20, Abouhamad again brought up the subject of assurances in a conversation with David Korn, a visiting State Department official. Abouhamad warned that a "showdown" could occur in the next few months, and Frangie needed to know to what extent he could rely on the United States. Lebanese army commander Iskandar Ghanim endorsed Abouhamad's message the following day.[48] These men requested training and assistance for the army, as well as delivery of military equipment, including communications and jamming equipment. The government's plans, they stressed, had been held closely within Lebanon's Christian leadership. Both indicated that the Lebanese did not expect a direct US military intervention similar to that of 1958.[49]

However, US officials did not respond to the Lebanese demarche at this time. Initially, this was because the Nixon administration was preoccupied with the 1972 presidential elections. Still, US officials in Beirut were strongly concerned about a possible civil war in Lebanon.[50] In the meantime, the cycle of violence and US mediation repeated itself again after Israel announced a policy of "preventive attacks" on Lebanon on October 15.[51] Following the election, Secretary Rogers sent the NSC a memo arguing for a "prompt and forthcoming answer" to Lebanese queries. He included a draft cable assuring the Lebanese of continued military aid and offering to issue a statement of support for Lebanon. The cable also noted the possibility of coordination with Israel and Jordan for a "role in deterring [the] Syrians," a move clearly inspired by the September 1970 crisis in Jordan.[52] However, Haig requested that the draft telegram be sent back to the State Department to be made "even more noncommittal."[53] In any case, the Lebanese demarche went unanswered.

During this period, the Lebanese government also attempted to start a dialogue with the United States through normal diplomatic channels concerning consultations in the event of another Israeli attack on Lebanon. On October 20, Sisco told Lebanese ambassador Najati Kabbani that he could not give "concrete answers at this moment," though they would continue their discussions with the Israelis.[54] On November 1, the two met again to discuss Lebanese proposals for advance consultation in the event of an unprovoked Israeli attack, but Sisco said again that the State Department could not give them a reply based on hypothetical circumstances.[55] Considering that the Lebanese foreign minister had also requested military support directly from the United States, one wonders whether Kabbani's instructions were intended as a serious effort, or even served as a cover within the Foreign Ministry to mask the dialogue concerning the fedayeen.

The Lebanese government also sought more direct contacts with Israel, in the hope that it might provide a solution to the issue of reprisals. Many Israeli officials saw the latest agreement as a sign that their attacks were working. In early October, one Israeli official seemed convinced that the

Lebanese government could successfully carry out the "final suppression" of the fedayeen, though unlike in Jordan, this would have to take place over time, rather than in one fell swoop. Israel, she thought, could play a role in helping to bring this about, in part by acting as a deterrent to any Syrian intervention.[56] On October 20, following US encouragement, Abouhamad told Buffum and Korn that the Lebanese army would upgrade their ILMAC liaison officer to a more senior individual, who would be Christian instead of Muslim.[57]

Between September and early February 1973, Lebanon's southern border was largely quiet, as a result of the September agreement with Arafat and pressure from other Arab states. The calm may have also reflected increased cooperation between the Lebanese and Israeli governments. In December, Israel offered to remove an early warning station from within Lebanese territory in exchange for a written promise from Lebanon to prevent fedayeen attacks.[58] In January, UN Truce Supervision Organization (UNTSO) officials told US diplomats of further meetings between Lebanese and Israeli officials at Ros Hanikra, near the Lebanese-Israeli border.[59] Soon thereafter, Foreign Minister Abouhamad told Buffum that the Lebanese had been secretly holding negotiations with Israelis and that drafts of papers had even been exchanged, though no agreement was reached.[60] The US embassies in Beirut and Tel Aviv differed in their interpretations of how serious these exchanges were, but the fact that they occurred suggests that the Lebanese government felt confident enough to take this risk.[61]

As before, US willingness to support the Lebanese government depended at least in part on how stable the regime was. Now that Frangie's government appeared to have better control over the security situation, US officials were less likely to back Lebanese requests for support. For instance, early in the morning on February 21, 1973, Israel launched air raids on two targets near the refugee camps of Nahr al-Barid and Baddawi in northern Lebanon, claiming these were preventive strikes on institutions that had trained members of international terrorist organizations that had attacked Israel.[62] Israel claimed that only militants were killed in the raid, while Palestinian sources maintained that thirteen civilians died.[63] The Lebanese government requested US support for a complaint at the UN Security Council, arguing that they had succeeded in reaching an agreement with the fedayeen to keep them away from the border. However, the State Department refused to agree to this, seeing "no compelling domestic reasons" for the complaint.[64] The embassy made its recommendation despite the fact that later that same morning, an Israeli jet fighter shot down a Libyan civilian airliner headed to Cairo that had strayed into the Sinai desert, killing more than a hundred ci-

FIGURE 5. In this cartoon, published soon after the murders of two American officials in Sudan, a Palestinian militant tells the world, "So you know that when I speak, I act." *Al-Muharrir*, March 3, 1973.

vilians and shocking the Arab world.[65] In the end, Lebanon did decide to request a meeting of the Security Council.[66] In Washington, Ambassador Kabbani argued that "we cannot turn Lebanon into a concentration camp."[67]

In early March 1973, US officials were targeted for the first time by Palestinian groups, again prompting reconsideration of US policy toward international terrorism and toward Lebanon itself. On March 1, a group of armed Palestinians from the BSO burst into a party for a US official at the Saudi embassy in Khartoum, taking numerous captives, including two US diplomats, Cleo Noel and Curtis Moore, and a Belgian colleague, Guy Eid. Among other demands, the attackers sought the release of Abu Daoud, one of the plotters of the Munich incident, who was being held by the Jordanian authorities. When this was not immediately forthcoming, the kidnappers killed all three Westerners.[68] There were also attempts to attack targets in the United States. On March 6, FBI agents in New York found bombs at three locations near Israeli facilities.[69] Making matters worse, evidence soon emerged that Yasser Arafat may have been involved in the Khartoum assassinations, though this remains disputed.[70]

Whether or not Arafat was personally involved, this new threat against US officials and targets in the United States posed a dilemma. Up until this point, the US government had never actively targeted the fedayeen, although it had encouraged other states to control the groups present on their territory. Now, the attack sparked demands for reprisals such as those Israel regularly meted out. US ambassador to India Daniel Patrick Moynihan likely voiced the opinion of many US officials in a cable that he sent soon after hearing that Fatah leader Salah Khalaf (Abu Iyad) had allegedly planned the attack: "If we know his whereabouts, I hope by now the son of a bitch is missing a few front teeth."[71] In effect, the United States had to evaluate whether it was now at war with the fedayeen.

Though a military response was unlikely, US officials would have to determine whether or not they were going to push the moderate states to crack down further on the fedayeen. Several factors militated against a strong effort to do so. Attacks on US interests were still the exception rather than the rule. A countercampaign could escalate the violence, or damage other US interests in the region, including US relations with the Arab states. In addition, many US and Lebanese officials still believed that Arafat and Fatah were more moderate than other leaders and groups.[72] As NSC officials warned, too much pressure on Arab governments to crack down on the fedayeen would "play into Black September's hands because they would like to prevent a negotiated solution" to the Middle East conflict.[73]

The Nixon administration thus took a middle road, urging the Lebanese government to take measures against the better-known BSO leaders, while at least initially ignoring Fatah and Arafat. The State Department asked Buffum to press the Lebanese to deport the BSO leaders, repeating a December 28, 1972, request that Salah Khalaf (Abu Iyad) be arrested or expelled.[74] Beyond this, the State Department was divided on what measures to take. From Amman, US ambassador Dean Brown (who would later serve as US envoy to Lebanon) felt that Lebanon needed to be persuaded or forced to follow Jordan's example.[75] Buffum and others argued against this, protesting that the Jordanian example was not appropriate in Lebanon, which, unlike Jordan, lacked a strong government and military and was starkly divided along confessional lines.[76] In the end, the State Department did not specifically encourage the Lebanese government to expel the fedayeen. In Washington, Sisco sought to revive the question of US assurances to Lebanon, which had lain dormant since the previous fall, suggesting to Rogers that if the request was made in the context of the attacks in Khartoum, it might now get a response from the NSC, or rather, Kissinger.[77] But the Lebanese request remained unanswered. Nonetheless, the United States sped up deliveries of grenade launchers, ammunition, and communications and other equipment to Lebanon.[78] An army G-2 source told a US officer that Frangie had ordered the head of military intelligence to cooperate closely with the United States.[79]

Around this time, the Lebanese border with Israel began to heat up again. On March 10, the State Department instructed Buffum to express at a "high level" the US concern about these reports of fedayeen presence near the border.[80] Israel seemed determined to send a warning, both to Lebanon and to the United States. In a March 13 interview, Israeli foreign minister Abba Eban called US policy toward Lebanon "absolutely incomprehensible," since "on the one hand Lebanon enjoys support of America and Belgium while on the other the killing of American and Belgian diplomats was planned in Beirut."[81] On March 19, Lebanon's acting prime minister and defense minister met with fedayeen leaders, including Arafat, to insist they pull back from the southern border, refrain from public demonstrations, and stop building defensive trenches around the outside of the refugee camps, among other demands. Arafat promised a pull-back in the south, but was otherwise "evasive."[82] However, the government did not take any immediate military action.

Within the United States government, many officials began to push for a new US initiative to broker an Arab-Israeli peace, seeing this as a response to the increasing tensions in the area. Both the State Department and the National Security Council became involved, though they did not fully coordinate their strategies. In early January, the State Department instructed the US Interests Section in Cairo to propose talks toward an interim agreement between Israel and the United Arab Republic.[83] In Egypt, Sadat's adviser Hafiz Ismail, who was planning to visit Washington to meet with Kissinger at the end of February, rejected the State Department's approach.[84] Ismail's meeting with Kissinger failed. The State Department then suggested again that it undertake a diplomatic initiative. At this point, Nixon wrote, on one of Kissinger's memos, "I am determined to move off dead center. . . . This thing is getting ready to blow." The United States, Nixon ordered, should put pressure on Israel, who would otherwise maintain their "intransigent position," thinking the United States would "stand with them regardless of how unreasonable they are."[85] Nixon shared the State Department's sense of urgency, though it is unclear whether his concerns were about a war between states such as Egypt and Syria, or the implosion of a friendly government, such as Lebanon.[86] In any case, while the State Department was preparing a new proposal for the president, the situation in Lebanon exploded into yet another full-blown crisis.

The Israeli Raid on Beirut and the May Crisis

On the night of April 9, 1973, Israel launched an attack in Beirut that would have a deep impact on Lebanon. A small team of commandos, led by future prime minister Ehud Barak, slipped onshore via ship, then were driven to a residence in the Verdun neighborhood of West Beirut, where they entered two buildings, killing several important Palestinian figures: Muhammad Yusuf al-Najjar, an alleged Black September leader; Kamal Adwan, the PLO chief of operations in the West Bank and Gaza; and Kamal Nasser, a member of the PLO Executive Committee. Adwan's wife, numerous by-standers, and many Palestinian fighters were also killed in the process. Dubbed "Operation Spring of Youth," the mission was designed to send a message to the fedayeen that they were not safe anywhere.[87]

The killings again sparked a political crisis in Lebanon that led to a military confrontation between the government and the fedayeen. Accusing the army of incompetence, Prime Minister Salam demanded the dismissal of its commander, Iskandar Ghanim, threatening to resign if this did not happen. Frangie refused, and Salam carried out his threat. The break between these two had important implications for Lebanese internal politics.[88] Frangie had also isolated himself from Rashid Karame, another major Sunni political figure, over the previous years.[89] Frangie's damaged relations with these two important Sunni leaders would be a major liability during the crisis of that spring and summer, as well as in the period beyond.

The next morning, Kissinger informed Nixon of the news of the attack. Their conversation suggests that the fate of Lebanon was not initially their foremost concern. Nixon responded that he was "delighted." Kissinger noted that "all hell is breaking loose, now, of course, in Lebanon. . . . But basically there is nothing of any major consequence."[90] Just as with Nixon's reaction following the Munich incident, it is possible to read too much into this conversation. Nonetheless, these remarks suggest that Nixon and Kissinger had little sympathy for either the Palestinian groups or Lebanon. Perhaps even more tellingly—as Lebanese ambassador Kabbani later complained on behalf of his colleagues during a meeting of Arab ambassadors with Secretary Rogers—unlike in previous cases, the Nixon administration did not publicly condemn the Israeli attack.[91]

Following the raid, numerous media reports accused the US government of involvement, stirring up anti-US sentiment throughout the Middle East. On April 12, the CIA warned that Palestinians were mounting "a major campaign to incite anti–American sentiment and are staging incidents against US diplomatic installations in Beirut." Demonstrators inflicted minor damage to the US Information Agency building in Beirut, while the Algiers Voice of Palestine allegedly called on the Arab masses to "kill everyone who is American."[92] Palestinian WAFA radio reported that US Hercules planes evacuated the Israeli soldiers from Beirut, while Algiers and Damascus radio carried allegations attributed to Arafat that former US ambassador to Lebanon Armin Meyer, now serving as an adviser on terrorism to President Nixon, supervised the Israeli Defense Forces (IDF) raid.[93] On April 14, an oil refinery in Sidon owned by a US company was attacked.[94]

At that time and since, US officials have denied that they gave any support to the Israeli raid.[95] US diplomats protested strongly against the propaganda campaign, which US intelligence agencies believed was supported by the Soviet Union.[96] On April 12, Rogers called in thirteen Arab chiefs of diplomatic missions in Washington to tell them that continuing to allow media reports accusing the United States of complicity would impact their relations with the United States. Similar representations were made in the Arab countries themselves.[97] The United States also publicly announced that they had evidence that Fatah and the BSO were the same organization.[98] Less helpfully, from the US point of view, Israeli radio claimed that the CIA was conducting covert activities against BSO, prompting a US complaint to Israel.[99]

In the meantime, the political crisis in Lebanon was deepening.[100] Following Salam's resignation, Frangie appointed Amin al-Hafiz as prime minister, in part on Jumblatt's advice.[101] However, the Sunni establishment opposed Hafiz because of his relative lack of stature within the community.[102] A number of security incidents throughout the month contributed to the tensions.[103] At Frangie's request, Sadat's advisers urged the fedayeen to "transfer their operations from Beirut to Cairo."[104] Clearly, the fedayeen were not willing to adopt this suggestion.

In part to show that it was doing something, the Lebanese government filed a complaint about the incident at the United Nations. Initially, US officials tried to convince the Lebanese not to do so. Once the complaint had been made, the United States appealed to its allies for a "balanced" referendum and asked London and Paris to table a draft resolution in order to prevent an Arab one.[105] Israel opposed any resolution that condemned their attack and pressured the United States to veto rather than abstain.[106] In Lebanon, Buffum argued that in contrast to the situation in September, a veto "would seriously damage US interests here and throughout the Middle East," including Frangie's efforts to form a government.[107] Kissinger informed Nixon that "reliable clandestine reports indicate that the fedayeen intend to use a US veto as the occasion for widespread attacks on Americans in Beirut." However, he noted, the United States was still prepared to veto an unbalanced resolution.[108] Finally, a draft was produced that allowed the United States to abstain. It called on Israel to refrain from further attacks, but did not mention fedayeen raids on Israel.[109]

Although the United States had hoped that the Lebanese government would take action against BSO leaders, the intention was not to provoke a military conflict with the fedayeen. Following the Beirut attack, the Nixon administration finally began to take up Abouhamad's demarche from the previous fall. The State Department sent another draft telegram back to Nixon with a note from Rogers that suggested that US support could make the Lebanese government "more readily inclined to arrest or expel the terrorists."[110] The draft outlined the US belief that Lebanon could do something about the "BSO/Fatah problem . . . without provoking [a] showdown with Palestinian organizations and their supporters in Lebanon." To support this, it offered many of the same steps as had the one the previous fall, including the possibility of arranging outside military intervention or threats thereof by Israel or possibly Jordan to deter Syria.[111] Had this telegram been delivered immediately, it would have likely constituted the broadest security guarantees ever given by a US administration to an Arab regime—greater even than King Hussein had received prior to the September 1970 conflict. However, the White House had yet to give its clearance.

In early May, a confrontation broke out between the army and the fedayeen following the kidnapping of three army soldiers by the Democratic Front for the Liberation of Palestine (DFLP) on May 1.[112] The next day, the Lebanese army surrounded Palestinian camps in the Beirut area, while the air force attacked the outskirts of the Sabra and Shatila camps in the south of the city.[113] The CIA called the May 2 clashes "the most serious since those of 1969."[114] Fearing the worst, the US embassy in Beirut destroyed or shipped out many of its classified files.[115] At least initially, the fedayeen groups remained "largely on the defensive for fear of triggering Israeli intervention."[116] Instead, they concentrated on obtaining external support from other Arab states.

FIGURE 6.   A meeting between Lebanese president Suleiman Frangie (left) and PLO chairman Yasser Arafat (right). Arafat's bubble reads, "Fateh," the acronym for his guerilla organization. Frangie's bubble states, "Fatah al-hudud," meaning "Open the borders," a reference to the fact that during the previous month's fighting, Syria had closed its borders with Lebanon to pressure the Lebanese government to halt its offensive against the fedayeen. *Al-Muharrir*, June 2, 1973.

Indeed, Arab states would play the decisive role in the crisis. Although some initially expressed sympathy toward the Lebanese government's predicament, most opposed its crackdown.[117] Syria and Egypt, now preparing for war against Israel, sought to end the fighting between the Lebanese army and the fedayeen, though they took somewhat different attitudes toward the Lebanese government. Damascus was more aggressive, sending troops and armored vehicles just across the border to pressure the Lebanese to stop their offensive against the fedayeen.[118] Cairo initially sought to maintain a neutral position between the Lebanese government and the Palestinian militias, aiming to broker a peace between them and to moderate the Syrian position, which was more openly pro-Palestinian. Arab League secretary general Mahmud Riad traveled to Beirut on May 4 to mediate between the parties.[119] After no solution was reached, on May 7, the biggest military clashes up until that point broke out between the fedayeen and the Lebanese army. The next day, the Lebanese army used airstrikes again against the fedayeen.[120] At that point, Syria closed its border with Lebanon, while allowing hundreds of guerillas from the Palestine Liberation Army (PLA)'s Yarmuk brigade to enter the Lebanese south. At the same time, President Asad sent Foreign Minister Abd al-Halim Khaddam and General Muhammad al-Khuli to Beirut on a mediating mission.[121]

Of the conservative and moderate states, only Jordan seemed prepared to help Lebanon. On May 8, Jordanian prime minister Zaid Rifai warned US officials that Lebanese leftists "were using [the] fedayeen in [an] attempt to take over [the] Lebanese government." Comparing the crisis in Lebanon to the Jordanian civil war, Rifai said that the situation was moving "from June 1970 to September 1970," and asked the United States to consider moving the Sixth Fleet closer to Lebanon and think about "measures to intervene whether on [the] pretext [of] evacuation of Americans or for any other reason."[122] The Beirut embassy did not think the threat from the Lebanese Left was as serious as Rifai suggested, but rather stemmed from the more radical fedayeen groups. Still, Buffum suggested that the Jordanians pass word to the Syrians of Lebanon's importance.[123] King Hussein's government went even further than that. Soon thereafter, both of Jordan's two armored divisions, as well as an infantry division, were moved to the north of the country near the border with Syria.[124] Jordanian officials also offered the United States use of "Jordanian C-130 [planes] to deliver arms and ammunition to Lebanon if necessary," though this offer was politely refused.[125]

The Israeli government's attitude remained much the same as before. Israeli officials hinted publicly that, under certain circumstances, the IDF might intervene militarily in the crisis in Lebanon. Israeli defense minister Moshe

Dayan told a group of students that he did not think that Syria would intervene in Lebanon directly, but if it did, "Israel would consider itself . . . free to act."[126] This warning, similar to those issued during the 1970 crisis in Jordan, was intended to deter Syria. The Lebanese government may have welcomed this. Jordanian officials told their US counterparts that in a secret meeting in Tel Aviv on May 9, Golda Meir told King Hussein that Israel was in contact with certain Lebanese leaders, who believed that the threat of Israeli intervention would keep Syria from intervening in that country.[127] It is not clear what contacts Israel still maintained with the Lebanese government. It could have been the dialogue via ILMAC, or through other channels, such as the traveling bishop who had played an important role in 1970. Unlike during Helou's presidency, the Lebanese government did not inform the US embassy of these contacts.

When the fighting did not immediately stop, the Lebanese government began to look for assistance from the United States. On May 3, Director-General of the Presidency Boutros Dib requested that the Nixon administration consider what it could do if it was confirmed that Syrian forces had crossed into Lebanon. Tony Frangie, the president's son and minister of communications, was more straightforward, telling Chargé Houghton that the Lebanese government "wished USG assistance, the sooner the better."[128] That evening, the foreign minister stressed to Houghton that Syria was their main concern and mentioned his conversation with Sisco the previous summer.[129] Clearly, the Lebanese still hoped for US support along the lines they had discussed the previous fall.

As it had during the 1970 crises in Lebanon and Jordan, the Nixon administration reviewed its options for military intervention, which remained "generally unattractive, apart from some symbolic gestures." The NSC staff now agreed that the State Department's draft cable to the Lebanese should be more specific as to the limited possibilities for a military intervention.[130] Still, the draft cable to the Lebanese government had not been sent. On May 3, a new options paper provided a range of possibilities for military intervention, from a show of force to the use of air support in favor of the Lebanese, or even the use of ground troops.[131] However, the Nixon administration did not take any measures right away to support Lebanon. Kissinger left the United States soon thereafter to visit the Soviet resort of Zavidovo from May 4 to May 8 in preparation for Brezhnev's upcoming visit to the United States.[132] There are no records that suggest that he brought up Lebanon with the Soviets while there.

Nor did the Nixon administration make any great efforts to directly assist the Lebanese government. The United States had no influence over Syria and little over Egypt and other Arab states. US officials did consult with the Soviets, but with the new atmosphere of détente, they did not press them not to interfere.[133] Just as in 1969–70, the Soviet Union had a great diplomatic advantage over the United States, as its ambassador could meet openly with both Frangie and Arafat.[134] Still, the increased Soviet role in Lebanon concerned US officials there. Worrying that Ambassador Azimov may be trying to give Frangie assurances, as he had after the Israeli raid in 1972, the US chargé in Beirut suggested that Rogers send an oral message to Frangie.[135] The secretary did so that same day, stating that the United States valued Lebanon's independence and expressing confidence that the government would be able to "ride out the present storm."[136] The chargé passed it on the next day.[137] However, the United States provided little more than words, refusing even to sell the Lebanese army ammunition at a discounted price.[138] Later that month, the US government shipped some smaller military items, including mine detectors, alarm devices, and signal equipment, but these did not arrive in time to affect the fighting.[139]

By May 15, the Lebanese government was getting ready to sit down with the Palestinians for negotiations, although it remained interested in US support. Frangie sent a message via Foreign Minister Abouhamad requesting "strong USG support" in case of an "impending showdown with [the] fedayeen," as well as "assistance in beefing up Lebanese army as rapidly as possible should [the] fedayeen refuse." He hoped that the State Department would request that the Soviets put pressure on the fedayeen, as well as consider whether Jordan and Iran might also be able to deter Syrian and Iraqi intervention in case of a confrontation. Houghton told him that the United States had already made some demarches along those lines and promised to pass on the message to Washington. Abouhamad also asked about Israeli intentions, specifically whether they were willing to use force to deter fedayeen intervention, or whether they simply had designs on Lebanese territory.[140]

That same day, the Washington Special Actions Group (WSAG) finally met to discuss US options on Lebanon, particularly if Syria sent in troops.[141] Sisco prepared a briefing memo, which recalled that the 1970 contingency plans had included an option for providing weapons to the Phalange militia, "an action which we would find highly questionable today under any circumstances."[142] Among the possible options were a range of US military moves from a show of force to full military intervention, whether to evacuate US civilians or to impose a solution to the conflict.[143] The Jordanian example remained a model for a US response to the crisis, as yet another option was to urge that Israel make military moves as a deterrent against Syria. But like in 1970, the Nixon administration worried that an Israeli offensive into

Lebanon itself could result "with Israel in forward positions in Syria or even in control of Southern Lebanon." Other options included an airlift of military equipment to Lebanon, as well as diplomatic demarches to other countries.[144] During this meeting, both Kissinger and Sisco felt that they had to "reluctantly" acknowledge that Israeli pressure was indeed forcing the Lebanese government to confront the fedayeen. They also agreed to put aside the draft cable for a week or so, though even Kissinger thought that it should eventually be sent, and perhaps even strengthened from previous drafts.[145]

In the meantime, the State Department instructed its embassy in Beirut to tell the Lebanese that Washington would take some steps to help them. Following up on Frangie's request, US diplomats would talk to the Soviets, Saudis, Kuwaitis, Emiratis, Iranians, and Jordanians about measures to ease pressure on Lebanon. While they would await a list of specific military requests from Lebanon, once they received it, they would do what they could, including flying arms and ammunition directly into Lebanon, either themselves or via an intermediary. Finally, the State Department noted that it believed Israel would not intervene if Syria did not. Nothing was mentioned about arranging a US, Israeli, or other military intervention, though the message stated that the US government was undertaking contingency planning and asked for their suggestions.[146]

The US message came too late to have any impact on the crisis. On May 17, Lebanese and Palestinian representatives signed a new agreement that became known as the Melkart Protocols, after the Beirut hotel in which the talks were held. At least initially, both US and Lebanese leaders seemed happy with the agreement. Unlike the Cairo Agreement, this document was "comprehensive and detailed," explicitly calling for a suspension of guerrilla operations from Lebanese territories against Israel, among other requirements.[147] The State Department saw this as a complete adoption of the government's demands.[148] Indeed, the agreement seemed to include all the obligations agreed to the previous September.

After receiving the US message on May 18, a Lebanese official asked specifically what the United States would do if Syria intervened and Israel attacked Lebanon. Houghton told him that he could not answer such a question about "hypothetical" circumstances. The official approved the idea of US demarches toward other countries, though he emphasized that the Soviets were the most important.[149] The Lebanese emphasis on the Soviets may have been to put pressure on the United States for more concrete assurances or gestures of support, but as we have seen, the Soviet Union did seem to have more influence on the ground than did the United States. The official later confided that "the GOL knew that the Soviets 'signaled' the Syrians to stop supporting the infiltration of armed units across the Lebanese-Syrian border and knew that the Soviets undertook these representations after they were approached by the U.S."[150] This suggests that the US demarche to the Soviets on May 10 may have had some effect after all.

Perhaps somewhat hypocritically, considering its own lack of action during the crisis, the Nixon administration seemed disappointed with the behavior of most of its allies in the region, except for Jordan, the only country to offer material assistance (in the form of air-to-ground rockets) to the Lebanese.[151] In response to a question from Brown about what Jordan would do in case of a Syrian intervention, the king was pessimistic but responded that "if we should want him to attack Syria, we should let him know but be prepared to help him out when the rest of the Arabs fall on him like a ton of bricks."[152] To their other allies, including Saudi Arabia, Kuwait, and the United Arab Emirates, the United States expressed disappointment.[153] To avoid upsetting détente, US representatives in Moscow were instructed to discuss the issue of Lebanon "in terms of consultation with USSR on [a] problem of mutual concern," asking them to "play an important and constructive role by using its influence with Syria and with [the] fedayeen to assure that GOL-fedayeen arrangement is respected and applied effectively."[154] US officials were hesitant to risk their country's improved relations with the Soviets, or indeed much else, for the sake of Lebanon.

The Aftermath

Although the Melkart Protocols seemed on the surface to be just another peace agreement, the attitude of the main protagonists had changed. Each side saw itself as more threatened than ever before. The Lebanese army had managed to inflict a relatively serious blow on the fedayeen, but in the meantime, the country had drawn the ire of many of its neighbors. Syrian pressure on Lebanon continued. Even after the signing of the agreement, the Syrian government kept the border closed, and rumors circulated that it was considering taking measures to close Lebanese air space. The Sunni Muslim community and the Lebanese Left pressed for the resignation of the prime minister, echoing Arab nationalist themes similar to the Syrian position. Frangie's government took a defiant attitude, even as these local and regional forces strengthened.[155]

While this stalemate continued, a crisis of confidence broke out among the traditional Maronite leaders in the ability of the army and the state to guarantee their security. During the conflict, Palestinian positions had blocked a route between the Christian areas of the Metn and East Beirut that the Phalange considered vital for connecting the Christian areas of the country.[156] There were reports that right-wing militias in Lebanon participated in the May clashes in order to provoke a split between the Lebanese and the Palestinians.[157] Whether or not this was true, following the crisis, the Christian militias began to arm themselves more actively, while the Palestinians also increased their preparations for war.[158]

For the Palestinians, the May conflict had important implications as well. A contact in the Lebanese Foreign Ministry gave the US embassy a copy of a report written by the PLO Planning Center, a Palestinian think tank in Beirut initially formed by the PLO executive committee in 1968.[159] This memo portrayed the Lebanese military attack as part of an "imperialist-zionist-reactionist plan" against the Palestinians. Like the United States, the Palestinians were disappointed with their allies, in particular the slow reactions of Egypt and Kuwait. Still, the Palestinians were happy that except for the "puppet regime in Jordan," no Arab state had offered support to the Lebanese government, not even the Saudis. The report expected the United States to try to reinforce Saudi Arabia's position in the Arab world, to encourage Jordan to help Lebanon, to bring pressure on Egypt to be neutral through peace proposal, and to use Israel and Iran to deter Syria and Iraq respectively—an accurate assessment. Furthermore, the Palestinians believed that "the menace of an American interference [i.e., military intervention] in the region was growing, which made some of the Revolution's circles consider such an interference as a likely possibility." The report suggested that these events required the Palestinian groups to pay more attention to the internal Lebanese political scene, claiming that the guerillas had "no alternative but to endeavour to deep-root the national movement in Lebanon, reinforce it, strengthen it, and participate in unifying it and organizing it, in order to create the Lebanese national front which will then be pushed to raise the question of the regime strongly."[160] Thus, the May 1973 conflict underlined the necessity of intervening in Lebanese internal politics for the sake of the fedayeen's own survival.

At the same time, however, the US government also received signals from Palestinian leaders that it did not want a conflict with Lebanon. In the summer of 1973, key leaders of Fatah appear to have been reconsidering their attitude, not just toward the Lebanese but toward the United States and even Israel. As early as 1969, key Palestinian figures such as Ali Hassan Salame, Arafat's intelligence chief, had met with CIA operatives, including CIA officer Robert Ames, though this relationship allegedly ended abruptly after the US officials tried to pay Salame a bribe. After the assassinations in Khartoum, however, Ames wrote back to Salame to try to reestablish a connection.[161] In July 1973, Ames was recontacted by Salame, who said that the Palestinians were concerned that either right-wing Lebanese or the Jordanians would try to provoke another round of conflict. Arafat, he said, had decided that unless there was an all-out war on the refugee camps, the fedayeen would not respond to any provocations. However, should an attack on the camps occur, they would use squads stationed throughout the city to burn it down.[162] Despite this last bit of bluster, the message seemed to suggest that the PLO did not want a conflict in Lebanon.

The PLO Planning Center report also contained a reference to the Arab-Israeli conflict that was largely ignored by the US government. It noted that the Egyptian "regime's crisis is getting worse," which meant that a decision might be taken to implement "Haykal's theory of the '*limited war*.'"[163] The previous March, Muhammad Hassanayn Haykal—journalist, former minister of information and adviser to Sadat—had called for a "limited war" in which Egypt would seize some territory in the Sinai, thereby changing the attitudes of the United States, the Soviet Union, and Israel toward Egypt and the Arab world.[164] The report warned against this, arguing that the Palestinian movement should insist that a "people's war" was the only true path to liberation and that the fedayeen should resist any Egyptian attempt to include them in diplomatic negotiations.[165] Haykal and Sadat had made public pronouncements about the possible resumption of war, but few in the US and Israeli governments took them seriously.[166]

Even if Kissinger did not give much credence to Arab threats of war, State Department officials believed that the US government needed to take some sort of initiative on the Arab-Israeli conflict in order to reduce tensions. In early May, the State Department's March memo on the Middle East proposal was finally delivered to the National Security Council. The document now put the argument for US mediation in the conflict in terms of the fedayeen, noting that in the long term "movement toward peace . . . will provide the possibility for eroding the base of support for Palestinian terrorism, without which base the movement must ultimately begin to whither."[167] But the National Security Council did not take any action toward authorizing this initiative. In the meantime, Nixon was growing increasingly occupied by the Watergate investigation. As domestic criticism increased, the president felt the need to appoint a strong figure as secretary of state. He therefore asked for Rogers's resignation in August. Fearing that Kissinger would resign if anyone but he was appointed, Nixon gave the job to the national security advisor, while also allowing him to keep his former position.[168] Thus, Kissinger was left to dominate US foreign policy, including on the Middle East.

Over the summer, the Nixon administration sought to restrain Israel from reprisal attacks that could destabilize Lebanon or provoke a broader war, either of which could derail the US-Soviet conference scheduled for June.[169] Israeli officials asked the United States to request that Lebanon exert maximum control over the fedayeen, particularly with regard to their southern movements.[170] Although the State Department did so, embassy officials warned that the Lebanese government's capacity to exert control along the border was limited, since most of the army was deployed in a "defensive position" against Syria and in the area of Beirut.[171] The US embassy in Beirut expected "continued instability in Lebanon and threat of periodic crises," and even now recommended a gradual reduction of embassy staff members.[172]

Even as Frangie was encouraging the Christian militia leaders to build up their own forces, he continued to look for support from the United States, including via a special emissary. In June, former Lebanese foreign minister Charles Malik sent a message to the US embassy that he was traveling to the United States, to a conference in Colorado, and that Frangie had asked him to meet with Nixon to "discuss fundamental matters which cannot be put on paper." Malik's message said his mission was "top secret" and requested that the "Special Agent of the Denver Office of the FBI" get in touch with him. Malik then left before the US embassy could get in touch with him, though the director of the Foreign Ministry confirmed to Houghton that Malik carried a message from Frangie.[173] The State Department knew that Malik wanted meetings at the White House, but they did not make any such arrangements.[174] It is unclear whether these other officials did not meet with Malik simply because of their schedule or whether this was designed intentionally to avoid more entreaties on behalf of the Christian militias, as he had made during his previous visit.

Instead, Malik was granted an appointment with Secretary Rogers on June 26. After conveying a message of thanks from President Frangie for the US support for Lebanon during the crisis, Malik said that the Lebanese president now wanted to know "how far the US was willing to go to support Lebanon's integrity," particularly in the event of a Syrian invasion of Lebanon or Palestinian action against the government. Rogers reiterated that the US government would be "as responsive as possible to Lebanon's needs . . . though what we can do for Lebanon is not open-ended."[175] There is no indication that Malik asked Rogers for aid to the Christian militias, as he had done with Nixon in April 1970.

Once back in Lebanon, Malik wrote to William Baroody Jr., one of Nixon's advisers and the son of Malik's friend, American Enterprise Institute resident William J. Baroody. In his letter, Malik stated that Frangie had told him, "I should certainly fly to Washington again as soon as I receive a firm appointment with President Nixon." He emphasized that he would be representing the president of Lebanon and speaking in his name if he saw the president, Secretary of Defense Melvin Laird, or Kissinger.[176] Malik's determination to see these officials suggests that he hoped to renew back-channel connections for planning on security contingencies, including aid to the militias.

Even if Nixon and Kissinger avoided seeing Malik, they continued planning for Lebanon. On June 13, the WSAG held a meeting on the situation in Lebanon and the broader Middle East. No documents from this meeting have been released. However, a briefing paper sent by a State Department staffer to former ambassador to Lebanon Dwight Porter suggests that the questions asked at this meeting went to the very core of US relations with Lebanon. The questions included "How great, really, is our interest in Lebanon? Is this interest so great that we would seriously consider committing American ground forces for other than E&E [emergency and evacuation] purposes?" Finally, the meeting would address a question on the minds of many in the Middle East: "Is our thinking being guided by 1958?"[177] In other words, should the United States intervene? The fact that these questions were mentioned in this document suggests that they were being taken seriously at a high level within the US administration.

By the end of June, the State Department proposed sending the draft telegram from April, which it thought should discourage hopes of a US military intervention along the lines of 1958.[178] Even NSC staffers felt that it was becoming "increasingly embarrassing" that they had not yet responded to the questions from the previous autumn.[179] On July 6, the State Department finally issued the long-awaited instructions to Buffum to begin a dialogue with the Lebanese government about US assistance. As finalized, these instructions indicated that, in the event of "major Syrian action against Lebanon,"

Among possible steps [the] USG might take are:

A. Public statement reiterating USG support for independence and territorial integrity of Lebanon.
B. Some corollary steps in Eastern Mediterranean area which would demonstrate concrete support for this position. We would welcome hearing Lebanese views on what those steps might be.
C. High-level approach to USSR with [a] view to making clear our opposition to intervention in Lebanon by outside or regional powers and eliciting Soviet cooperation in preventing such intervention. As GOL knows, we spoke to Soviets about restraining Syrians in [the] recent crisis.

D. In our judgment consultations between Israel and Lebanon might be
   required regarding possible Israeli role in deterring Syrians. We
   would be ready to play a role, if appropriate, in facilitating such talks.
E. Consultations between Jordan and Lebanon in same sense.[180]

Thus, the Nixon administration was willing to help set up a Jordan-style situation in Lebanon, in which US allies would deter Syria from intervening in a confrontation between the Lebanese army and the Palestinian militants.

Strikingly, these points do not appear to have been fully conveyed to the Lebanese government. During a conversation with Frangie on July 12, Buffum brought up Abouhamad's request from the previous fall for consultations on measures in the event of a major confrontation with the fedayeen. Frangie said that he would like any such conversation to start with the new foreign minister, Fouad Naffa, and himself and then continue with Naffa. However, since in Buffum's opinion, Frangie did not exude a sense of urgency, he did not go into the talking points.[181] There is no evidence that the United States had any further discussions with the Lebanese over the summer about the possibility of an internal crisis, which suggests that the dialogue effectively ended at that point.

The Nixon administration did increase its military support for the Lebanese army, which was of limited help. After the end of the May fighting, the Lebanese government asked the United States for $45 to $50 million in military equipment, including A-14 Skyhawk planes. However, Lebanese hopes for US financing on concessionary terms were soon disappointed. Grant aid, Military Assistance Program (MAP) aid, and loans of equipment were rejected, one by one.[182] Instead, US aid would likely consist of military credits, which would have to be repaid. This disappointed Lebanese officials, who knew of the massive US assistance to Jordan in the aftermath of the September 1970 crisis.[183] According to Buffum, the Lebanese were "only now facing up to harsh reality that if they want more equipment from us they must pay for it."[184] Although the State Department tried to facilitate the transfer of military equipment from Iran and Jordan, it was unable to quickly provide compensation or replacements to these countries, so the transfers did not occur.[185] NSC staff member William Quandt and Deputy Assistant Secretary of State for Near Eastern Affairs Alfred "Roy" Atherton argued that contingency planning for Lebanon was even more important than planning for broader Arab-Israeli hostilities, because the United States was receiving reports of the possibility of a conflict in Lebanon in the fall.[186] But the limited military assistance suggests that this issue was not a priority for the administration.

The reemergence of the Lebanese internal conflict in 1972 and 1973 had caused US policymakers once again to struggle with the issue of Lebanon. Although the basic structure of the conflict was the same, pitting the Palestinian fedayeen and their local allies against the Lebanese government and security forces, a number of factors had changed, not only in Lebanon but also internationally. US officials understood that the situation in Lebanon was a potential crisis waiting to erupt into a regional or global conflict that could upset the structure of détente that Kissinger and Nixon were so carefully assembling. Still, it took the events of May 1973 to get the United States to finally respond to the Lebanese request for dialogue, and even this came too late. This suggests that Lebanon was a relatively low priority for the United States at the time.

CHAPTER 5

Reckoning Postponed

From the October War to the Civil War

The war that broke out in October 1973 was not the one that the US or Lebanese government expected. If anything, southern Lebanon seemed to be a more likely place for conflict than the Golan Heights and the Sinai Peninsula, both of which had been calm for months. To the great satisfaction of most Lebanese, these few short weeks of fighting were largely limited to these other fronts. But even if the war left Lebanon physically unscathed, both it and the subsequent diplomatic negotiations had a deep impact on the country's internal situation, particularly as it related to the broader Arab-Israeli conflict.

In the period following the October War, as Lebanon entered what seemed to be a permanent state of crisis, US interest in the region seemed greater than ever. Most notably, Secretary of State Henry Kissinger undertook several high-profile shuttle missions to broker agreements between Israel and the Arab states. This provided a chance to address the aspects of the Arab-Israeli conflict that most concerned Lebanon, including the fate of the Palestinians. However, it soon became apparent that Kissinger's step-by-step diplomacy was designed to postpone any discussion of issues related to the Palestinians, thus shutting off the possibility of a regional solution to Lebanon's woes. US policymakers still tried to help the Lebanese government to control internal security, but in the absence of a clear pathway to a resolution of the PLO's grievances, terrorist attacks across the border would continue, sparking Israeli reprisals and calls for the government to defend the country. As hope for resolving the Palestinian issue faded, domestic developments within Lebanon set the stage for the upcoming conflict.

The October War and the Start of Negotiations

On October 6, Egyptian and Syrian troops launched a coordinated attack on the Israeli positions along the Suez Canal and the Golan Heights respectively. Egyptian units broke through the Israeli line relatively quickly; Syrian forces took longer, but eventually pushed Israeli troops off the high ground. Israel struck back, retaking positions in the Golan as well as in the Sinai. By the time a final cease-fire was reached on October 25, the lines of conflict were blurred, with Israeli troops surrounding Egypt's Third Army near the city of Suez and in a position to shell the Syrian capital, Damascus. Although their military losses were great, the Arab countries had achieved a psychological victory, shattering the myth of Israeli military invincibility and allowing for negotiations to ensue regarding a range of grievances.[1]

The implications of the war for Lebanon were evident from the day that the Syrian and Egyptian offensives began. As in 1967, domestic pressures threatened to push the Lebanese government into war. During the 1967 war, Lebanese officials had announced that the country was at war, providing Israel with a pretext to disavow the armistice signed by the two countries in 1949. Similar pressures on the government could force the country to enter the fighting. Unlike in 1967, there was now a massive fedayeen presence in South Lebanon. Should the guerillas launch attacks on Israel, its army might send troops into South Lebanon, occupying territory as it did in the Golan Heights, the Sinai Peninsula, and the West Bank in 1967 (and would later do in Lebanon in 1978 and 1982).

Hoping to prevent the expansion of the war, the US government made a concerted effort to help ensure that Israel did not invade. By October 8, Lebanese officials had made a formal request to the United States to ask Israel not to invade Lebanon. That evening, the Israelis promised to guarantee Lebanon's "sovereignty and independence," if it did not take any military action.[2] Israeli officials wanted to keep their options open in case of attacks from across Lebanese territory, whether from the Syrians or the fedayeen. US diplomats passed on the Israeli message the next day, pointing out that it had a "clear implication that [the] GOL had responsibility on its side [to] prevent military activity against Israel."[3] Once again, the US government sought to foster an unwritten commitment between the two countries.

Despite this warning, Syrian and Palestinian military activities risked dragging Lebanon into the conflict, in some cases with the active complicity of the Lebanese government itself. At several points, Lebanon provided support for Syria that risked violating the laws of neutrality. Soon after the outbreak of hostilities, the Lebanese government put its fuel reserves, as well as its radar stations at Baruk in the Shuf region and Rayak in the Biqa Valley, at the disposal of the Syrians.[4] Israeli warplanes eventually bombed the Baruk station.[5] On October 7, a Syrian fighter plane was allowed to make an emergency landing at an airfield on Lebanese territory near the Syrian border. In an ILMAC meeting, Israeli representatives threatened "grave consequences" if this happened again. US officials in Beirut warned Prime Minister Taqi al-Din Sulh of the risks of providing assistance to Syrian aircraft, while suggesting to Israel "not [to] overreact to this isolated incident."[6] While these actions were technically violations of the country's neutrality, they probably won the Lebanese government some gratitude in Damascus.

The US embassy in Beirut worried that the fedayeen would see the outbreak of war as an opportunity to launch cross-border raids that would drag Lebanon into the war.[7] The guerillas had a number of reasons to participate in the fighting. After all, their raison d'être was that the Arab states had been unable to adequately defend Arab and Palestinian interests. Now that these states had actually launched a war, the Palestinians risked being left out. Indeed, many of the rank and file were clamoring to participate in what seemed like a historic battle. Though many Palestinians in Lebanon went to the front with Israel or were transferred to help Syrian forces, it is unclear whether any raids were launched.[8] The fedayeen did shell Israeli settlements from Lebanese territory, prompting the Israeli army to evince concern to the US defense attaché in Tel Aviv.[9] Lebanese officials told the US ambassador that Prime Minister Sulh had received a commitment from Arafat not to launch raids from Lebanon. The Lebanese army had confiscated a significant amount of material from fedayeen headed to the border.[10] On October 10, the US embassy in Tel Aviv informed the Israelis of Arafat's commitment.[11] However, the Lebanese army could not entirely suppress the Palestinian fire. At one point, Israel's northern sector commander requested permission to send troops into Lebanon, but Minister of Defense Moshe Dayan refused on military grounds, stating that Israel was busy on other fronts.[12]

As in 1967, the US administration was initially concerned about possible attacks by the fedayeen on US interests in Lebanon, including on the estimated five thousand to six thousand US citizens there.[13] Lebanese intelligence sources initially reported threats against US citizens and other foreigners.[14] Soon, calmer assessments of the situation emerged. Nearly a week into the war, the Beirut embassy reported that there seemed to be less visible anti-Americanism than in 1967, or even the previous spring following the Verdun raid.[15] In the meantime, Prime Minister Sulh assured US diplomats that both the Lebanese government and he personally "would spare no effort [to] protect US interests in Lebanon."[16] Even after the news of a US arms resupply to Israel emerged, the Lebanese government emphasized to fedayeen leaders the "need for calm and avoidance [of] attacks on Americans."[17]

The dangers posed by fedayeen activity increased as the Israeli military position improved during the war, since this meant that Israel could now afford to consider launching an attack on another front. On October 16, the Lebanese prime minister, the minister of the interior, and army representatives told Arafat, Saiqa head Zuheir Muhsen, and other fedayeen leaders that they needed to adhere to their promise not to launch attacks from Lebanon.[18] On October 20 and 21, US officials took up the shelling with Lebanese and Israeli officials. Abba Eban told the US ambassador to Israel that the Lebanese government "should consider the lack of a GOI move against the fedayeen to date as good fortune, but they should be warned not to try 'to push their luck.'"[19]

As the war drew to a close, the Lebanese government negotiated with fedayeen leaders for a final "ceasefire." On October 25, a Lebanese official told US deputy chief of mission Houghton that the leaders of Fatah and Saiqa had agreed to stop their attacks if Israel observed the cease-fire and "subsequently (presumably in peace negotiations) publically recognized Palestinian rights and their cause." Other groups soon signed on to this agreement, too.[20] Ambassador Buffum reported that the fedayeen's change in behavior appeared to be in response to pressure from Arab governments.[21] He acknowledged that the May 1973 clashes had "clearly revealed limitations on GOL's ability [to] impose firm control on all fedayeen activities," meaning that the Lebanese government would "require considerable outside support" to impose a cease-fire. The Syrians, the Kuwaitis, and the Saudis had already given assurances they would assist them.[22] For the moment, the Lebanese internal political situation looked stable, but it was unclear how the postwar situation would unfold.

The US diplomatic campaign following the October War would bring about a stark realignment in the international relations of the Middle East. Having ostensibly regained a degree of the dignity lost in 1967, Arab states such as Egypt and Syria were now able to negotiate with Israel, even if this took place indirectly via Kissinger's shuttle diplomacy. The United States reestablished diplomatic relations with Egypt and Syria in 1974, while new, personal relationships would develop between Kissinger and these countries' leaders. Other Arab states, such as Libya and Iraq, as well as a number of Palestinian groups, rejected closer relations with the United States and a compromise with Israel. For the United States, Egypt would come to serve as the new US "moderate" ally in the Middle East, with Jordan and Saudi Arabia playing "supportive roles."[23]

The diplomatic process created after the October War was designed to preserve US dominance in the region. UN Resolution 338 revived the idea of a peace conference in Geneva, in which the Soviet Union and the United States would act as cochairs. However, this was largely for show, to satisfy the Soviet Union's desire to be involved, as well as the Arab states' demand for a comprehensive resolution of all the issues in the Middle East, while allowing Kissinger to broker a series of interim disengagement agreements.

For Lebanon and the Palestinian groups on Lebanese territory, the diplomacy following the war offered both opportunities and challenges. Despite their competing interests, the Lebanese government and many Palestinian leaders had similar though not identical goals for the negotiations, namely, reaching a solution that would allow for the Palestinian refugees and fedayeen to leave Lebanese territory. Negotiations that offered the possibility of addressing these issues thus had the potential to resolve some of the main issues of the Lebanese crisis. By contrast, if the negotiations appeared to exclude the Palestinian issue, they could make the situation in Lebanon even more intractable by providing an incentive for rejectionist groups to take actions to disrupt the negotiations, which could in turn provoke more attacks on Lebanon.

Still, the Lebanese made a conscious decision to remain on the margins of the negotiations. As preparations for the Geneva Conference got under way, the Lebanese government distributed an aide mémoire reserving the right to participate on issues that affected it.[24] Israel argued that Lebanon should receive an invitation to Geneva, though not because it was anxious to negotiate with the Lebanese. In fact, having Lebanon attend would allow Israel to later take the position that new parties (like the PLO) should not be invited after the conference was first convened.[25] Probably for this reason, Lebanese officials soon backed away from their request to participate right away, instead demanding to join only negotiations that concerned the status of a final Lebanese-Israeli border and the issue of Palestinians.[26] By December 12, the Lebanese added the status of Jerusalem to the short list of issues with which they would like to be involved.[27] As Buffum concluded after a meeting with Foreign Minister Fouad Naffa, Lebanese policy was to "support whatever formula other parties concerned accept and which stands some chance of getting the Palestinians off their backs."[28] Lebanese government officials tried to use the negotiations to get a UN force placed along their southern border; however, US officials convinced them to drop the idea.[29]

US officials did not think that Lebanon would have an important role to play in the negotiating process. During discussions about Geneva in early December, Kissinger told Soviet ambassador Dobrynin quite frankly, "We don't give a damn about whether Lebanon comes or not."[30] At this point, it was not even clear whether Israel, Syria, and Egypt would attend the peace conference, much less Lebanon.[31] Still, as a part of the early discussions about Geneva, Kissinger did visit Lebanon during a December trip to the Middle East to muster support for the Geneva Conference, but his visit had few results. Kissinger landed on December 19 at Riyaq air force base instead of the Beirut airport, after the United States received reports of a planned attempt on his life, possibly from Arafat's intelligence chief Ali Hassan Salame.[32] Kissinger understood that his diplomacy had little to offer Lebanon in the short run. In his memoirs, the former secretary of state comments that he did not want to tell Frangie that "he was unlikely to obtain relief from his devouring guests," that is, the PLO.[33] When the two met that afternoon, the conversation fell flat, in large part because there was relatively little of substance to discuss.[34] The visit allowed the Lebanese government to claim that Kissinger had consulted them, but for Kissinger, the stop underlined the country's marginality.

Palestinian groups were split in their response to the ongoing negotiations. Publicly, most fedayeen groups opposed them. However, not all Palestinian leaders rejected a US role in Middle East diplomacy. Yasser Arafat had in fact begun to make clandestine approaches to the United States in the summer of 1973, offering to recognize the principle that Israel would continue to exist and suggesting that the Palestinian problem be resolved within the framework of the Jordanian state, which Kissinger took to mean that they wanted to overthrow King Hussein.[35] While this was far from the vision of Middle East peace held by the US officials, it nonetheless indicated that some Palestinian leaders were open to a negotiated solution and an US role in the peace process. During the October War, Arafat sent several messages to the US government asking for talks, though the Nixon administration seems to have ignored these during the fighting.[36] Although the US government held clandestine meetings in Morocco with Palestinian representatives soon after the war, Kissinger did not seriously consider bringing the PLO into the negotiating process, at least at the time.

Arafat was the one sending out feelers, but he was not the only Palestinian leader struggling to deal with the new reality of Arab-Israeli negotiations.

A deep debate began among Palestinian leaders and intellectuals, not to mention among the refugees themselves, concerning the negotiations. Most remained committed, at least in word, to the idea of a fully liberated Palestine, yet many were coming to terms with the expectation that some Arab and possibly Palestinian territory was likely to be ceded during the negotiations and that control over it would need to go to someone. In February 1974, leaders of Fatah, Saiqa, and the DFLP put forward a suggestion for the PLO to adopt a "phased" or "incremental" strategy of establishing Palestinian control over any "liberated" territory; more radical groups, including George Habbash's PFLP, rejected the idea as opportunistic or even treasonous.[37] Still, the tension between the ideas of total liberation and the realities of incremental liberation—including the likelihood of some compromise with Israel—remained unresolved.

As Kissinger's diplomacy continued without any movement on Palestinian issues, those opposed to negotiations began to see ominous signs in every US move, including in Lebanon. For instance, in February, newly confirmed US ambassador McMurtrie Godley arrived in Lebanon. Sometimes called "Field Marshal Godley" by his peers, the ambassador was known as a strong hands-on leader in his previous posts in the Democratic Republic of Congo and Laos. Several months before, Congress had refused to confirm Godley as assistant secretary of state for Asian affairs because of his personal involvement in US efforts to train militias in Laos during his previous tenure as ambassador there.[38] Some groups interpreted his assignment to Lebanon as a sign of a US intention to force the Lebanese government to clamp down on the Palestinians.[39] The US embassy in Beirut reported that the Soviet Union had been passing on material about Godley to various newspapers and recommended that the State Department bring it up with the Soviet embassy in Washington.[40] On February 9, *al-Muharrir* newspaper ran a front-page article headlined "Nixon Appoints 'Butcher Of Laos And Vietnam' as American Amb[assador] in Beirut."[41]

Rejectionist groups, particularly George Habbash's PFLP and Ahmed Jibril's PFLP-GC, sought to use violence to disrupt the process of negotiations, particularly as states in the region neared agreements that seemed unlikely to help the Palestinians. Sporadic shooting continued across the Lebanese-Israeli border, sparking an occasional Israeli reprisal attack into Lebanese territory. In December, fedayeen cross-border attacks and Israeli reprisals increased, as rejectionist fedayeen groups sought to prevent the Geneva Conference from taking place. By early February, cross-border commando activity appeared to be on the rise again. Two Israelis were killed by shelling in the second week of that month.[42] The State Department instructed the US chargé d'affaires, Bob Houghton, to discuss the shelling with the Lebanese government, while the Israeli government was informed of this demarche.[43] Army chief of staff Kanaan informed Houghton that the government had instructed the army to increase patrols in the south and "to shoot if [the] fedayeen passed beyond certain areas which Kanaan did not define."[44] These activities were reported to Eban, who expressed his appreciation.[45]

In April, a new series of raids into Israel proper began to threaten the negotiations.[46] The primary purpose of these attacks was to challenge the PLO leadership and oppose the peace process.[47] In the first attack, during the night of April 11, three Palestinian fighters from the PFLP-GC infiltrated across the border to the Israeli town of Kiryat Shmona. After entering an apartment complex, they fired at the individuals inside and took hostages. Israeli soldiers stormed the building. When the shooting stopped, eighteen or nineteen Israelis and the three Palestinians were dead.[48] That night, according to the Lebanese G-2, Israeli troops responded by entering South Lebanon, where they destroyed twenty-four houses in six villages, including one with two women still in it, and abducting thirteen Lebanese civilians, which they brought back into Israel.[49] On April 13, Eban publicly denied that Israel's policy was to force the Lebanese to deal with the fedayeen, instead maintaining that Israel's policy was that of "reciprocity." US ambassador Kenneth Keating, however, was not convinced by Eban's speech, arguing that "Israel's real hope is that South Lebanese civilians will force Beirut to control, or arrest, the fedayeen." Israel, he reported to Washington, still compared the situation in Lebanon to that of Jordan.[50] Thus, the same dynamic that had destabilized Lebanon in previous years seemed to be coming into play again.

By this point, the Syrian-Israeli negotiations toward a disengagement agreement were entering a sensitive stage, and Kissinger wanted to do everything possible to keep them on track. The Lebanese government complained to the Security Council about the Israeli attacks, forcing the Nixon administration to decide whether or not to support it. The United States voted for a resolution that condemned Israel for the attacks and demanded that it return the abducted Lebanese civilians, without directly condemning the Palestinian attack that prompted these reprisals.[51] In his memoirs, Kissinger expresses regret at approving this, justifying it as seeming like "at the time a safe middle ground between the various pressures on us."[52] Although the strategy worked and negotiations continued, the attacks had a lasting effect. The US embassy in Beirut noted the "psychological impact" of the Kiryat Shmona raid on the "more moderate" fedayeen, who were coming under increasing pressure from a concerted rejectionist propaganda campaign, backed by Iraq and Libya.[53] The embassy thought that these sorts of spoiling attacks were likely to continue.[54]

During Kissinger's May visit to the Middle East, a second major Palestinian attack threatened to derail negotiations. On May 15, commandos from the PFLP-GC and DFLP infiltrated into the Israeli settlement of Ma'alot, taking eighty-five hostages. Most of these were teenagers who happened to be sleeping overnight in an elementary school. During an Israeli rescue attempt, more than twenty died. DFLP leader Naif Hawatma announced that the goal of the operation was "to abort Kissinger['s] mission."[55] Godley weighed in heavily on the Lebanese government for a statement condemning the massacre, but none was issued.[56] This attack also prompted another series of heavy Israeli retaliations, killing nine Lebanese and forty Palestinians, while wounding up to 260 others.[57] Still, the United States wanted to avoid another bitter Security Council meeting that could disrupt the Middle East negotiations. Nixon sent a message to Frangie on May 17 regretting the "loss of innocent lives" and expressing hope for a break in "this tragic cycle of violence."[58] Frangie decided not to call for a Security Council meeting, telling US embassy officials that this was to help Kissinger's mission.[59] The secretary of state sent a message thanking the Lebanese president for his "courageous statesmanship."[60] The attacks did not prevent the signing of a Syrian-Israeli disengagement agreement, which was finally reached on May 31.

Kissinger's strategy required more than just keeping the PLO out of the negotiations: the agreements that he brokered reflected a desire to get Arab states to control Palestinian groups to the greatest extent possible. As Syria and Israel negotiated a disengagement agreement for the Golan Heights, Asad gave Kissinger a secret oral commitment not to allow Syrian territory to be used by the fedayeen for staging attacks against Israel.[61] Subsequent Israeli announcements that the Syrian government would control the fedayeen aroused consternation in Lebanon, where the government feared that the fedayeen would react violently.[62] Kissinger announced that these stories were speculative.[63] However, the Syrian-Israeli agreement appears to have been real. On May 31, the day the agreement was signed, a US embassy officer in Beirut passed a message to the president's son, Tony Frangie, intended for his father. Although its content has not been declassified, Godley told him of an aspect of the Israeli-Syrian agreement that was "of special importance to Lebanon." Frangie replied that "his father would be very pleased," adding that the Syrian "attitude on [the] fedayeen problem," as described by the ambassador, "fits exactly with what he had been told."[64]

In spite of this agreement, fedayeen attacks on Israel continued in June, in part because the next step in the negotiations planned by US officials was an exploration of an interim agreement between Israel and Jordan, which would have almost certainly addressed the territory of the West Bank, a core interest of the Palestinians. The new Israeli prime minister, Yitzhak Rabin, called the fedayeen attacks from Lebanon the "most immediate and pressing" issue on Israel's agenda.[65] From June 18 to June 20, dozens of Lebanese and Palestinians were killed and injured in Israeli air strikes.[66] On the final day of these raids, fedayeen fired SAM-7 ground-to-air missiles against attacking Israeli planes, embarrassing the Lebanese government and army, which had no weapons of this class.[67] In mid-June, Frangie secretly requested that Assad invite him to Damascus during an upcoming visit by President Nixon, hoping to enhance his stature, as well as to push for a resolution of the Palestinian situation. According to US reports, Asad avoided a reply.[68]

The lack of resistance by the Lebanese army prompted criticism from other Arab states. On June 22, Sadat offered to send troops and equipment to Lebanon, while also sending a letter to Nixon asking him to intervene with Israel to stop its cross-border attacks.[69] At a Cairo meeting of the Arab Defense Council in July, Arab states decided to contribute some forty million Lebanese pounds to construction of underground shelters in the Palestinian refugee camps in Lebanon—shelters that would later protect the PLO during the civil war.[70] Nominally, the relations between the PLO and the Lebanese government remained cordial. On June 30, Prime Minister Sulh received a pledge from a delegation of three Palestinian leaders, including Abu Iyad, to "freeze" all operations from Lebanese territory.[71] Friendly meetings between Lebanese and PLO "moderates" continued throughout the summer, issuing communiques that emphasized the common ground between them. Yet, US officials in Beirut suspected that both sides were "experiencing growing uncertainty" about the future and about what their role in the broader Middle East negotiations would be. The freeze, they thought, was only temporary.[72]

By the summer of 1974, US Middle East diplomacy had offered little of interest to Lebanon. In fact, by moving toward a Middle East settlement that did not take into account the interests of the Palestinians, the disengagement agreements increased the insecurity of all groups in Lebanon. Many Palestinian militias, especially the rejectionist ones, felt they had reason to launch attacks, either to make their presence felt or, even, to derail the negotiations. Israel responded in kind, meaning that the situation in Lebanon would get only worse.

Lebanese Domestic Politics after the October War

In the aftermath of the October War, the structure of conflict that would define the Lebanese civil war began to fall into place. At the beginning of this period, Lebanon's confessional and ideological groups were not yet fully polarized in Christian/rightist and Muslim/leftist wings. Despite its intervention in the May 1973 internal conflict, the army could still play at least the role of an arbiter of internal security. However, over the course of these next few years, two developments began to change that state of affairs. First, the Sunni and Shi'a Muslim communities, as well as a variety of leftist groups, were beginning to develop a common opposition to the Lebanese state, which they increasingly associated with the Christian leadership. Second, as the Lebanese army was discredited, the Lebanese Christian and other militias began to arm themselves. The actions of outside actors, including the United States, exacerbated these trends.

Even prior to the October War, changes were taking place within the Sunni and Shi'a communities, as well as among the Lebanese leftist groups, that resulted in a common opposition to the state, if not alliance with one another. One reason for this was that the Lebanese government remained unable to deal with the country's economic and social problems. During the early 1970s, a variety of social and economic conflicts would break out within Lebanon, including strikes by agricultural and factory workers, protests at the rapid rise in the cost of living and gaps in educational and social services between different regions of the country, and frequent student unrest.[73] Strikes and demonstrations by labor and other groups also contributed to the general sense of unrest. Following the May–June 1973 crisis, Taqi al-Din al-Sulh took over as prime minister on June 14, 1973, appointing a large cabinet to enhance national unity. However, this cabinet was unable to function effectively.[74] Government corruption was seen as endemic. Perhaps most notoriously, the Lebanese postal system almost completely shut down during this time. The fact that the Ministry of Posts was controlled by Tony Frangie, the president's son, was revealing. Public order broke down in parts of the country, particularly in the north.[75]

Challenges to the traditional urban Sunni leadership arose from both within and outside the Sunni community, contributing to the growing political crisis. After Frangie's dismantling of the Deuxième Bureau in 1970–71, the state security apparatus no longer had the resources to control the street thugs that had long played a role in local politics.[76] Palestinian militant groups and certain Arab states began to fund challengers to the traditional leaders, exerting what Kamal Salibi called "a recognized suzerainty over the old-established and emerging Muslim armed gangs, not only in Beirut and its suburbs, but nearly everywhere in the country."[77] The rise of ideological parties, fueled in part by the flow of funds from states such as Libya and Iraq, also undermined the Sunni leadership. Within the Nasserist movement, which had traditionally found its strength in Sunni-majority parts of Beirut, groups loyal to Libya and Iraq split off, forming a new group under Ibrahim Qulaylat.[78] Foreign influences were evident in other ways, too. In Beirut, as public order disintegrated, the streets again became a place for fighting inter-Arab feuds.[79]

A new "Shi'a awakening" within Lebanon also posed a challenge to the state, to the traditional leaders of the Shi'a community, and to other Muslim leaders. The Lebanese Shi'a, many of whom lived in the southern part of the country, had long been marginalized in the country's economic and political life. Fedayeen violence and Israeli reprisals, as well as a search for new economic opportunities, had resulted in an exodus of Shi'a from the southern part of Lebanon to the south of Beirut. This urbanization produced a new solidarity among what had long been a rural and divided group. Inseparable from this new political consciousness was the figure of Musa al-Sadr, a charismatic Shi'a leader of Iranian origin who had assumed the leadership of the Supreme Islamic Shi'ite Council in Lebanon.[80] Through his demands for social and political justice, Sadr posed a challenge, not just to the state but also to Sunni leadership of the Muslim community within Lebanon, as well as to leftist movements, who had often sought supporters among the Shi'a.[81]

In the early 1970s, leftist political parties and groups also played an increasingly important role in the Lebanese political landscape, a phenomenon linked directly to the person of Kamal Jumblatt. Jumblatt, a traditional leader of the Druze community, had long been considered a sort of Saint Jude of leftist groups, whose protests and demonstrations he defended in the national arena. On one hand, he seemed committed to destroying the Lebanese system as it existed, while at the same time, he often played a stabilizing role, trying to keep the demonstrations from turning against the state.[82] Alternating roles as agitator, mediator, and conciliator, he had supporters across the Lebanese communal spectrum and maintained good relations with the fedayeen. In 1970, as interior minister, Jumblatt legalized the status of a host of political parties that had previously been banned. Although these groups had long operated and organized illegally, their legalization marked the beginning of a new period of involvement in public affairs. Some groups, such as the Organization of Communist Action and the LCP, were instrumental in organizing the strikes and uprisings of this period with support from Jumblatt.

Jumblatt's rising importance in Lebanese politics changed the way that governing alliances had traditionally been built. In the past, the Maronite Christian president had usually formed an alliance with a member of the traditional Sunni leadership. From the spring 1973 crisis onward, in part to compensate for his poor relations with Sunni leaders, Frangie began to work closely with Jumblatt, who encouraged him to appoint Amin al-Hafiz as prime minister.[83] Al-Hafiz's government soon fell due to lack of Sunni support, leading to the appointment of Taqi al-Din al-Sulh. In the fall of 1974, Jumblatt again influenced the choice of prime minister, this time imposing his own candidate, Rashid al-Sulh, over the opposition of the Sunni traditional leaders, including Rashid Karame, who had previously worked closely together with Jumblatt.[84] In the meantime, Maronite leaders Gemayel and Chamoun remained close to Frangie, while Karame and Sa'ib Salam joined together with former Hilf member and Maronite Christian Raymond Edde in an alliance known as the Tahaluf, which adopted a strategy of undermining the Frangie government. This caused a political split in the Parliament to develop along largely sectarian lines for reasons that were only partly sectarian in nature.[85] In effect, Jumblatt's relationship with Frangie was the one of the few cross-sectarian links that prevented a polarization between the Christian groups on one hand and the Muslim and leftist groups on the other.

Despite these tensions, there were signs of cooperation and solidarity across the Lebanese political spectrum. The Kataib and other Christian parties took strongly pro-Arab and pro-Palestinian attitudes toward the Middle East negotiations.[86] Even as the tensions between Lebanon and Israel increased, both the Christian parties and the Palestinian groups made efforts to show solidarity. For instance, on April 10, 1974, Pierre Gemayel appeared onstage with Kamal Jumblatt, Saib Salam, Yasser Arafat, and other Lebanese and Palestinian notables, at a ceremony marking the anniversary of the 1973 Israeli raid on Beirut.[87] Meetings continued throughout that year between members of the Kataib and the Syrian Baath party, the Nasserist movements, Imam Musa al-Sadr, the LCP, and especially Kamal Jumblatt.[88] While these meetings were unable to resolve the core issues dividing the country, they would provide important channels for communication after the outbreak of fighting.

The US embassy in Beirut followed closely these shifting alliances but did not necessarily see them as a sign that the country was moving toward a civil war. Following the October War, the US embassy in Beirut reported on the disruptions that were occurring within Lebanon. For instance, in December 1973, a series of demonstrations over the rising cost of living erupted into violence in Tripoli. When protesters began to criticize Frangie, one of his strongmen fired on them. The US embassy reported that Frangie's rivals were highlighting the sectarian element of the conflict to inflame public sentiment.[89] Other such disturbances were reported faithfully by the US embassy over the next year and a half.[90] However, there is no evidence that US officials discussed these incidents with Frangie or other officials, or that the State Department ever responded to these reports. The main interest of the US embassy seems to have been the fedayeen, not the Lebanese social and political movements. In fact, the US embassy had good relations with many of the new Muslim leaders, if not the leftist groups. For instance, US officials had cordial relations with Musa al-Sadr, whom they saw as a relative moderate and potential ally.[91]

In addition to these changes in the Muslim and leftist communities, the buildup of the Maronite militias was of particular importance to the changing political scene in Lebanon. The Christian militias had begun to arm prior to 1973, but in this year, efforts began on a broader scale. Following President Frangie's decision to stop military action against the Palestinians during the May 1973 crisis under pressure from other Arab states, most Maronite Christian leaders saw the army as unable to defend the Lebanese state and the interests of Maronites.[92] Some two months after the conflict, Frangie called a meeting in the presidential palace in Baabda: attendees included Chamoun, Gemayel, army commander Iskandar Ghanim, Head of Internal Security Antoine Dahdah, the DB chief Jules Boustany, and Head of General Security Nabih al-Habr. At this meeting, Frangie, Chamoun, and Gemayel decided to arm their parties. Frangie told the group that it might not be possible for the army to help them. Ghanim stated that the army's DB would take responsibility for this.[93] This collusion between the army and the Christian militias was an important step, since the militias would never have been able to arm to such a degree without assistance from others.

Assistance also came from sources outside Lebanon, including the United States, though there are disputes about how and when assistance occurred. Robert Oakley, who was a political officer at the US embassy in Beirut until 1974, has maintained that the United States provided weapons and money to the Christian parties prior to 1973; however, he claims that the flow of weapons stopped that year, in part because of his recommendation. Oakley also recalled that before he left Lebanon in 1974, he made a point of visiting his friends, telling them, "I hoped that they were not under a mistaken belief that the U.S. would send its military forces into Lebanon to help one faction or another," which he thought "would never occur." However, he maintained that "most of my interlocutors didn't believe me; they were sure that the U.S. would come to Lebanon's aid."[94] Several news articles have also suggested that the United States, through the CIA or Defense Intelligence Agency (DIA), helped arm the Christian militias, though they are vague about how this was allegedly done.[95]

According to a recent account by Lebanese journalist Nicolas Nasif, the United States did covertly help the Christian militias to arm, even after the May 1973 clashes. According to Nasif, at least two arms deals took place following the May 1973 clashes, both of which appear to have been brokered with at least the indirect assistance of the United States, though in one of the cases, it is possible that the United States may not have known which parties would receive the weapons. Following the meeting described above, Boustany spoke to Colonel Forrest Hunt, a military attaché at the US embassy, telling him that the Lebanese wanted closer cooperation with the US intelligence services, including weapons for the Deuxième Bureau. He specified that he needed ten thousand weapons, including guns and mortars. At the beginning of 1974, Washington sent five C-130 planes loaded with rifles and small machine guns to Beirut. Once received, the arms were transferred from the DB to various storage places for the Christian parties, including the residences of some religious men. Soon afterward, the US military attaché told Boustany that he had asked Frangie whether he knew of the request. Frangie said that he had encouraged it, but he thought that the DB had asked for only nine thousand weapons. Some of the rifles were distributed to Christians and Muslims cooperating with the Deuxième Bureau, including the militia of Druze leader Majid Arslan. Most, however, went to the Phalange and Frangie's militia.[96]

Another shipment of weapons was bought by the Lebanese Christian parties directly with the assistance of the United States. It was financed by a wealthy Maronite businessman, Butrus Khoury, and arranged through arms dealer Sarkis Soghanalian, who had previously acted as an agent for weapons sales from the United States to the Lebanese army. Soghanalian purchased the weapons from Bulgaria. These were escorted to Lebanon with assistance from the US Navy, thanks to the intermediary role played by Colonel Hunt. This shipment of five thousand pieces included Kalashnikovs, RPGs, and 82mm mortars. In June 1974, the freighter delivering the weapons landed in the Beirut port, which was the best equipped to handle its size. After an initial unloading supervised by the Deuxième Bureau, the ship moved to Jounieh, north of Beirut, where it was unloaded again. Nasif maintained that this was the only direct shipment of weapons that the Christian parties received before the war. Knowledge of its existence was confined to the DB and the Maronite Christian leadership.[97]

While there is no documentary evidence in US archives that the United States helped with these shipments, State Department officials had heard of similar plans, which gives additional credibility to these accounts. In September 1974, Alexander Raffio, a manager for Fairchild Camera with good contacts among the Lebanese military and intelligence services, told a State Department official that during a visit to Lebanon, he had overheard Christian plans to import fifty thousand (rather than five thousand) Bulgarian manufactured AK-47s via Sarkis Soghanalian to prepare for an offensive by Christian militias to eliminate the fedayeen presence. Raffio noted that Camille Chamoun was a proponent of the project and would stop by the State Department in a few weeks. Though the department officer reported that the plans were "speculative," he noted that the fact that Raffio identified Soghanalian meant that it must be worth checking out.[98] However, there is no available record of any further checks along these lines. Raffio, it should be noted, was a former colleague of Edwin P. Wilson, the notorious former CIA officer and arms trafficker sentenced to prison in 1984. Raffio testified at his trial and reportedly obtained a new identity as part of an agreement with the Justice Department, though not before gaining coauthor credit on a tell-all book about Wilson.[99]

Although Raffio's information can be considered circumstantial evidence at best, others have also confirmed that the US government helped the Lebanese to arm. In an interview with the author, Forrest Hunt confirmed working closely with the Lebanese Deuxième Bureau. He claims that he was not personally involved in the transfer of weapons to militia groups, but that the United States did assist some Lebanese militias prior to the outbreak of the conflict in 1975 by providing weapons, both via the security services and through nongovernmental intermediaries, including Sarkis Soghanalian.[100] Some believe that US allies, including Israel, were supplying weapons to the Christian militias well before this time, but there is no conclusive evidence of it.[101]

The Christian militias were not the only Lebanese groups to arm during this period. By 1969, the LCP was already acquiring weapons and training, including sending some members to Jordan and Syria for instruction.[102] The Nasserist Murabitun was well established by 1973 and claimed to have been the only Lebanese militia that took up arms on behalf of the Palestinians in the May 1973 crisis.[103] Following this crisis, the Lebanese government identified members of the Lebanese Communist Party, the PSP, and other "progressive" militias as having been involved in the fighting.[104] These groups also took steps to increase their arms supplies. A report from the Jordanian intelligence services, given to US officials by the Lebanese, indicated that

Palestinian groups were "smuggling large quantities [of] light and heavy weapons to Lebanese cities and into [the] Shouf area where they will be distributed to leftist groups, including those of Kamal Jumblatt and Najah Wakim (pro-Syrian Nasserist Deputy)." A Lebanese army intelligence report said that Iraq had offered the fedayeen eight thousand weapons, including two thousand Kalashnikov rifles, which were to be split between the Palestinians and various leftist groups.[105] In March 1974, Sadr founded his Movement of the Deprived, pledging to arm and train a militia if the Lebanese government did not pay more attention to Shi'a rights.[106]

Although the US embassy in Beirut was aware of the growing militias, it does not appear to have raised much concern in its reporting. In January 1974, the embassy reported "another disturbing trend—a rapid rise in efforts by Lebanon's multiple 'militia' groups to increase and improve their armaments and training." It noted the possibility of "some accident unleashing, by escalatory chain-reaction, a major confessional armed conflict."[107] However, this comment was buried at the end of a much longer report, which suggests that it may not have been a focus of embassy attention. In October, the embassy acknowledged the growing willingness to use militias to resolve disputes but thought "a new government will change little and [the] country will probably muddle through at least until 1976," when a presidential election offered some hope of change.[108]

Diplomacy on the Rocks

In the final months before the outbreak of conflict, US policymakers at the highest levels paid little attention to what was happening in Lebanon. US Middle East diplomacy continued to focus on Egypt, Syria, and to a lesser extent Jordan, offering little to the Palestinians or the Lebanese government, on whose territory the fedayeen were located. Despite a series of PLO diplomatic successes that raised the level of recognition for the Palestinian cause on the world stage, the Nixon administration did not try to bring the Palestinians into the negotiations. Although US officials continued to mediate between Israel and Lebanon, cross-border violence grew worse, threatening an outbreak of hostilities in southern Lebanon. In this deteriorating atmosphere, a diplomatic incident in October 1974 damaged relations between Frangie and the State Department, preventing any serious communication between the US and Lebanese governments about coordination in the event of a crisis.

Following the signature of the Israeli-Syrian disengagement agreement in May 1974, US Middle East diplomacy seemed stuck. Israel was unlikely to cede any more Egyptian or Syrian territory without significant assurance of their peaceful intentions, such as a commitment to end the "state of belligerency," in effect a pledge to refrain from military action, if not to make peace. Most Arab states refused to provide this, believing that without the threat of force, Israel had little incentive to compromise. For its part, Israel even seemed unwilling to cede the territory it occupied in the West Bank to the Jordanians, much less the Palestinians, whose involvement in the negotiations they rejected a priori. During the summer of 1974, Kissinger attempted to negotiate an interim agreement between Jordan and Israel, which might have facilitated a future role for Jordan in the governance of the West Bank without the involvement of the PLO.[109] However, Kissinger was unable to reconcile the Israeli and Jordanian positions, resulting in his first major failure in Middle East negotiations.

That fall, the PLO managed to score several diplomatic successes that would have a permanent impact on the Arab-Israeli peace negotiations, as well as on the situation in Lebanon. Thanks to assiduous lobbying by the PLO and Arab states over the previous year, the issue of the Palestinians had been put on the agenda of an upcoming UN General Assembly (UNGA) meeting in November. In the meantime, at an Arab League conference in Rabat, the Arab states for the first time officially recognized the PLO as the sole representative of the Palestinian people, undercutting the possibility of Jordan representing the Palestinians in future negotiations, as US officials had previously hoped. Kissinger, who was planning another trip to the region after the UNGA session, made a last minute attempt to influence the outcome of the Arab deliberations, sending a message to Frangie and other Arab leaders that "the US was convinced that Jordan must negotiate regarding the West Bank" and pleading that recognition of the PLO would make US mediation difficult or impossible.[110] Frangie expressed his appreciation for the message but responded that he felt that the PLO should represent Palestinians outside of Jordan.[111] At the UNGA meeting, Frangie delivered a passionate appeal on behalf of the Palestinians, which was followed by Arafat's famous "gun and olive branch" speech before the assembly.

The UNGA meeting was perhaps the last significant moment of cooperation between the Lebanese government and Palestinians prior to the outbreak of the civil war. For many Lebanese, these meetings offered some hope that diplomacy could resolve the internal Lebanese situation.[112] In Lebanon, Godley reported that the meetings had at least temporarily helped to pave over the differences between some groups, though he also predicted that these would likely reappear.[113] However, after the failure of his attempt to broker a Jordanian-Israeli agreement, Kissinger did not try to engage the Palestinians in the negotiations, nor did they make an effort to move toward a more comprehensive solution that could also address the Palestinian question. Instead, he began to pursue negotiations between Egypt and Israel toward a second interim agreement between the two countries, an attempt that finally failed in March 1975.[114]

Even as Palestinian intellectuals and PLO leaders prepared for the UNGA meeting, political crises again threatened Lebanon's political stability. There had long been signs that the Maronite Christians were considering drastic steps to preserve the status quo in the country. Clashes in the summer of 1974 broke out in the Beirut suburb of Dihwana between Christian and Palestinian groups, taking on a sectarian character.[115] The US embassy reported that the events at Dihwana contained "an explosive ingredient" that could impact the situation within Lebanon.[116] However, the situation was resolved soon afterward, with joint committees of Christians and Palestinians manning checkpoints in the area.[117] In September, the growth of the Christian militias sparked a political crisis, as Prime Minister Sulh told Chamoun and Gemayel that they could not keep their training camps open.[118] In response, Jumblatt tried to convince one of his deputies to resign from the cabinet to protest Sulh's inability to control the Christian militias. The dispute between Jumblatt and Gemayel broke out into violence between their supporters in the Metn area near Tarshish, leaving three dead.[119] Lacking support in the Sunni community, Sulh was forced to resign, requiring Frangie to appoint a new prime minister.[120] Frangie soon appointed Rashid al-Sulh, a cousin of Taqi al-Din al-Sulh, widening the split between Jumblatt and the Sunni traditional leaders.[121] In September, journalist Jonathan Randal warned of an impending civil war, as well as clandestine shipments of arms to the Lebanese Christian militias, earning him a six-month expulsion from Lebanon.[122]

In addition to reports from Beirut, numerous individuals warned the United States about the deteriorating situation in Lebanon. On October 9, King Hussein told US ambassador to Jordan Thomas Pickering that Frangie, via the Lebanese ambassador to Jordan, Abd al-Rahman al-Sulh, had sent a message that he feels "alone and embattled" in Lebanon, complaining of Soviet-supported Syrian pressure, Palestinian control, and the governmental crisis, in addition to "general malaise and weakness in Lebanon."[123] On October 14, al-Sulh told Pickering that Hussein had offered general help to Frangie, such as military training. The ambassador claimed to be "a strong and continuing friend of [the] US," who had friends in Beirut who could help in any plan to keep Lebanon "free from Soviet and other malevolent influences," such as Jumblatt and al-Sadr. Pickering passed on his message to Ambassador Godley, who responded that he would be happy to meet with

Sulh, but it is unclear whether or not this meeting happened.[124] Such elliptical exchanges suggest that parties both in Lebanon and throughout the region were already looking to the United States to get involved but that US officials were hesitant to take the initiative.

Unlike during previous Lebanese crises, when the US administration consulted closely with the Lebanese president and Foreign Ministry officials, there is no evidence that the State Department consulted officially with any other country in the region about the situation in Lebanon prior to the outbreak of conflict. Although the US focus on other countries in the region was the primary reason, another was the poor personal relationship between the Lebanese president and US officials, exemplified by a curious diplomatic crisis in November and December 1974. At the Rabat Conference, Frangie had been appointed as the representative of the Arab heads of state to the November UNGA meeting. Upon his arrival at the airport in New York, where he was accompanied by "two former presidents, three former speakers of parliament, and four former prime ministers," the bags of the Lebanese president and his entourage were searched for narcotics, including by drug-sniffing dogs. Frangie took this as a grievous insult. Apparently, the US embassy had received a tip about a plot to smuggle hashish on the plane. Frangie's plane was inspected prior to takeoff and the US embassy sent a cable to the State Department, but apparently this information was not passed on to the relevant authorities in New York.[125] Frangie's pride was deeply wounded, and he bore a grudge that resulted in a virtual stoppage of communications between the Lebanese presidency and the United States for the next few months.

The Ford administration took some steps to alleviate the situation, but Frangie was not satisfied. Two days after the Lebanese president's arrival, Ford issued an invitation to him to visit Washington, but by then it was too late in his stay.[126] Ford also sent a letter to Frangie about the "tradition of close, friendly and constructive ties" between the two countries, which was delivered via the Lebanese foreign minister, along with a note of apology from Ambassador Godley.[127] However, Frangie was upset that Ford's letter did not specifically mention the dogs.[128] In response, he refused to invite Ambassador Godley to attend the Lebanese Independence Day celebration. This prompted the US ambassador to return to Washington.[129] The diplomatic feud continued, as Frangie threatened to not invite a US representative to the president's New Year's Eve party. US chargé Houghton made it clear to his Lebanese interlocutors that this diplomatic slight could not occur without serious repercussions for the relations between the two countries.[130] Foreign Minister Philippe Taqla made numerous efforts to resolve the dispute, even threatening at one point to resign if a solution could not be reached.[131] Finally, Kissinger agreed that Godley could be out of the country on New Year's Eve if the Lebanese guaranteed that this would solve the problem; otherwise he would be withdrawn indefinitely.[132] This appears to have resolved the situation. Frangie sent a warm Christmas message to President Ford, and Ford responded. This smoothed over relations and allowed Godley to attend the celebration.[133]

It is difficult to judge how much this episode truly damaged Lebanese-US relations, less than half a year away from the outbreak of civil war. At the very least, it illustrates the distance between Frangie and the new Ford administration at the time. Godley's personal relations with Frangie suffered, as did his impression of the Lebanese president. Godley's early cables had described Frangie as a moderate, strong leader; now the ambassador called the president "well-intentioned but . . . basically a simple stubborn mountaineer leader with li[m]ited intel[l]ectual horizons and educational background. Pride and personal dignity are of paramount importance to him and his fellow mountaineers and he feels that his p[r]ide and dignity have been cha[ll]enged."[134] One imagines that Frangie may have had some strong words about Godley and the United States, too. In any case, these poor personal relations may have also prevented consultations between the United States and Lebanon as happened before the conflicts in 1969, 1970, and 1973. There is no indication that Godley met with Frangie between the New Year's Eve party and the April outbreak of conflict, a far cry from the frequent consultations between Porter and Helou.

Still, US cooperation with the Lebanese government continued at other levels. For instance, the Ford administration attempted to shore up the Lebanese government through military and diplomatic assistance, though neither did much to alleviate the situation. To demonstrate to the public that they were doing something about the Israeli threat in South Lebanon, the Lebanese officials had ordered US-made TOW antitank missile launchers the previous year. As the violence along the border intensified over the summer of 1974, Lebanese officials wanted the United States to expedite their delivery; the United States agreed to provide two immediately.[135] Lebanon again consulted with Iran about the possibility of providing US-made weapons, but Iranian officials decided against it.[136] In late December, Kanaan pleaded for the delivery of more antiaircraft and antitank weapons. Not having these weapons, he claimed, would risk internal chaos. The US defense attaché countered that the Lebanese government had not accepted US military credits for 1973 and 1974. Kanaan complained that the Lebanese could not accept the prices or delivery times that the United States had offered.[137] The

Ford administration agreed to send a few more TOW and other missiles, though they warned that the delivery would fall short of "Lebanese hopes and expectations." The US embassy argued for more aid, even if it required shifting the weapons from elsewhere.[138]

There are questions about what effect the diplomatic stalemate had on the Lebanese Christian parties' attitude toward the Palestinians. Some, such as Fred Khouri, have speculated that Washington's failure to address the Palestinian question may have contributed to the willingness of Lebanese Christian groups to challenge the Palestinian militias, thereby taking matters into their own hands.[139] If this was the case, there is no evidence that they talked about it with US officials in Washington or Beirut. In the summer of 1973, as we saw earlier, Frangie had already warned the militias that they would have to rely on themselves. In fact, Christian leaders still hoped for help from the Western countries, whether via arms shipments or through diplomatic measures to address the Palestinian question, but they could not be certain that they could rely on it. However, former Phalange party official Karim Pakradouni recalled to this author that prior to the outbreak of the civil war, Camille Chamoun and likely Pierre Gemayel believed that the United States would intervene to protect Lebanon.[140] On the balance of this evidence, the most plausible interpretation is that these Christian leaders hoped for and believed that Washington would take steps to help them, though they also recognized that there was a possibility that this would not happen.

At the end of the year, the security situation in Lebanon improved slightly, at least in the short term. On December 5, Rashid al-Sulh won a vote of confidence in the cabinet, ending the political crisis that had been ongoing since September 25.[141] His government then tried to reassert control over security, at least in the cities, if not in South Lebanon. In early January 1975, the army launched operations in downtown Tripoli, taking a number of prisoners. However, as the US embassy observed, the Tripoli issue was not the country's most serious security problem, which was rather the "fedayeen presence and activity, home-grown 'militia' gangs, and unrestrained trigger-happiness of most of this country's male citizens."[142] On January 10, reports surfaced of weapons reaching the Lebanese port of Aquamarina, destined for delivery to Christian militias. Pierre Gemayel denied any knowledge of the shipments, but said if it were true, he approved.[143] Also that month, following a particularly devastating raid in South Lebanon by Israel, Gemayel submitted a memorandum to President Frangie that called for a general referendum on the presence of Palestinian commandos in Lebanon.[144]

By early 1975, US officials had grown concerned about Lebanon, particularly the fighting in the south. In early January, Frangie and Asad met in the mountain town of Chtaura, in part to discuss the tense situation in the south. At this meeting, Asad offered to station Saiqa troops in southern Lebanon to protect it against Israeli attacks. In response to this announcement, Israel's defense minister, Shimon Peres, warned that Israel would not remain "indifferent" to the presence of foreign forces. Foreign Minister Allon told the US ambassador that this warning was designed in part to help Frangie resist the Syrian requests.[145] CIA and NSC officials warned that as the fighting in the South got worse, it could interfere with the US negotiating strategy in the Arab-Israeli conflict.[146] Joseph Sisco, now undersecretary of state for political affairs, asked his successor, Assistant Secretary of State for Near Eastern Affairs Alfred Atherton, to take the lead to examine what the US government could do about the situation in South Lebanon and later requested a study on the possibility of stationing UN forces there.[147] The US embassy in Beirut, on the other hand, highlighted the threat of an internal conflict, warning that the Lebanese government faced either a confrontation with the fedayeen or continued, wider-ranging reprisals from Israel, either of which "could place unbearable strains on this country's ability to maintain domestic order and perhaps even to survive as an independent, sovereign state."[148] By early February, Robert Oakley noted that the fighting constituted a "very real threat," though he recognized that the issue was not Kissinger's "top priority."[149] However, neither the State Department nor the US embassy report noted the significance of trends other than the violence in the south, in particular the rise of the Lebanese militias.

At the end of February and beginning of March, clashes during a strike in Sidon produced a state of tension that would last until the outbreak of the civil war on April 13. Weinberger called it the "socio-economic trigger" of the hostilities in Lebanon.[150] The mostly Muslim fishermen of the southern Lebanese town of Sidon were angered when the government granted exclusive fishing rights along the coastline to a company known as Proteine. Although the contract had been authorized by the cabinet of the Sunni prime minister, Camille Chamoun was the chairman of Proteine's board, a fact that inflamed local leftist (and mostly Muslim) groups.[151] Over the opposition of the prime minister, the Lebanese government decided to send the army into Sidon to control the protesters, a decision that was followed by a number of violent incidents. On February 26, a Lebanese army corporal was killed and two soldiers were wounded when dynamite was thrown at their jeep during a demonstration.[152] The responsibility for these attacks remains unclear. Between February 28 and March 1, at least fourteen civilians and five soldiers were killed in fighting around the port.[153] The wounded included Maruf Saad, a prominent local politician and former leader of the "Popular Resistance" in Sidon, who later passed away from his wounds.[154]

The US embassy in Beirut followed these events closely, particularly as concerned the involvement of foreign powers. There have been different interpretations of the role of Palestinian and other Arab influences in the Sidon crisis. Salibi saw the strike to be completely unrelated to the commandos.[155] Deeb and Azzim suggest that the crisis was largely inspired by Syria, while el-Khazen has called it a "Palestinian show of force."[156] Godley reported that information from "other channels," probably a reference to intelligence sources, indicated that the Syrian government played a largely restrained role in these events and had counseled Saiqa to withdraw from the Sidon area and to "avoid trouble with the Lebanese army." However, he also noted that Saiqa leaders "were not overly careful to comply with these instructions." Lebanese military leaders, particularly Kanaan, insisted that Saiqa forces took part in the demonstrations.[157] Foreign Minister Taqla called the Syrian government's conduct "constructive," noting that Saiqa had been told to cooperate with the authorities.[158]

Whether or not these events were deliberate instigations, they helped bring about a full alignment of many Muslim and leftist groups against the government and the army leadership. Because the army had ignored the prime minister's instructions not to intervene, Sunni leaders now demanded the reorganization of the army leadership into a council whose membership was divided between Christians and Muslims.[159] From this point onward, the Sunni leadership distrusted the army, making it nearly impossible for the army to be used in domestic confrontations.[160] An important conflict resolution mechanism in Lebanon had effectively been taken out of play.

Still, there is little evidence that US policymakers or intelligence organizations seriously considered the possibility of a renewed internal conflict in Lebanon along the lines of previous years. From Beirut, Ambassador Godley described the situation as "probably one of more serious upsurges of confessional feeling in recent years."[161] In Washington, however, US policymakers concentrated on the broader negotiating strategy in the Middle East, which had run into an impasse after the United States had been unable to broker a third disengagement agreement between Israel and Egypt. Paradoxically, despite the worsening situation in Lebanon, US policymakers seemed less interested in Lebanon during this period than at any point during the previous four and a half years. The outbreak of conflict in April, however, would eventually force the United States to reconsider its level of involvement in the Lebanese internal situation.

CHAPTER 6

Disturbing Potential

The United States and the Renewed Conflict

Although the Ford administration understood that one consequence of its diplomacy after the October War would be that Lebanon would continue to experience instability, there is little evidence that they expected a full scale civil war to break out. Once it did, how did US policymakers react? During the first eight months following the outbreak of conflict, the US government remained distant from events in Lebanon. Some, including Henry Kissinger, have implied that the United States was distracted at the time by the collapse of the South Vietnamese government and a reassessment of US Middle East policy.[1] Jonathan Randal goes further, claiming that Kissinger "indeed forgot" about the country's problems.[2] Although that is part of the story, the reasons go beyond it.

The initial aloofness of US policymakers from the Lebanese conflict was driven by their understanding of broader US interests in the region. US diplomacy in the Arab-Israeli conflict, which was entering an increasingly delicate phase, required maintaining good relations with all the key players in the Arab-Israeli conflict. The State Department worried that any action on Lebanon might draw the United States into the middle of local and regional conflicts being played out in that country. However, in the fall, as conflict threatened to spread beyond Lebanon's borders, the United States undertook diplomatic consultations in an attempt to contain it, though by this point their attempts were too little too late.

The Outbreak of Conflict

While some details of the events that mark the beginning of the Lebanese Civil War remain murky, the basic outlines of the first month of fighting are clear enough.[3] On April 13, 1975, a carload of Palestinians shot at Phalange leader Pierre Gemayel as he was dedicating a church in the Beirut district of Ayn al-Rummana, killing several bodyguards and bystanders. Later that afternoon, a group of gunmen from the Phalange party opened fire on a busload of Palestinian militiamen passing through that area, killing all of its passengers. The next morning, the headquarters of the Phalange party near Martyr's Square was hit by three rocket-propelled grenades (RPGs). Following these initial incidents, sporadic fighting broke out throughout Beirut, developing into a political crisis that focused on two issues: demands for internal reforms and the future of the fedayeen in Lebanon. On April 26, leftist and Palestinian leaders issued a statement calling on Arab leaders to isolate the Phalange as a political party, which had the effect of mobilizing Christian opinion in favor of the Phalange. Jumblatt refused to allow any of his supporters to serve in a government with members of the Phalange. The government's two Kataib ministers resigned on May 7, followed by four others on May 12. Prime Minister Sulh accused the Kataib of a massacre and, in a resignation speech before the parliament on May 15, written with leftist leaders, called for a restructuring of the Lebanese confessional system.[4]

There are no available documentary records that adequately explain the strategies of the various militias at the onset of the conflict. As Farid el-Khazen has maintained, many of the details of the Ayn al-Rummana confrontation seem suspicious, from the route that the bus took on April 13 to the strange police reports that were filed about the incident.[5] Another account claims that it was an "open secret that Gemayyel had long been planning an all-out offensive against armed Palestinian commandos," but that Chamoun and Edde had refused to join him in this plan.[6] Moreover, during the first month of fighting, each side appears to have engaged in provocations. Much of the early combat took the form of shelling, which, in an urban environment, was bound to result in extensive damage and civilian casualties. Snipers began to operate in numerous areas, targeting Christian and other quarters of town. Many shops were bombed, looted, or both. Each side blamed the other for these acts of chaos.[7] Yet, even as the fighting spread, negotiations continued throughout, involving the Lebanese government, the political parties/militias, and Palestinian leaders, not to mention Arab countries and the Arab League, suggesting that all sides were at least somewhat interested in reestablishing peace, even if each group wanted it on its own terms.

Considering that the fighting marked the beginning of a fifteen-year civil war, it is perhaps difficult to understand why the United States did not immediately take some sort of action on Lebanon. Yet at the time, top US officials were occupied by a host of other issues. The structure of détente that Kissinger had spent the previous six years building now seemed under threat from both within and without. At the beginning of 1975, members of Congress and the US foreign policy establishment increasingly criticized the Ford administration over trade policy and secret negotiations toward a second Strategic Arms Limitation Treaty (SALT II) with the Soviet Union.[8] On April 30, the last US officials evacuated the US embassy in Saigon by helicopter, marking the fall of South Vietnam and the failure of several decades of US policy toward Southeast Asia. In Angola, a civil war was heating up, leading the United States to consider taking measures to counteract what it saw as the spread of Soviet influence. Finally, over the course of April, US officials ostensibly began a "reassessment" of their Middle East policy following the failure of attempts to negotiate a second interim disengagement agreement between Egypt and Israel. By May, Kissinger was in the middle of, as Jüssi Hanhimäki has called it, his "worst hour."[9]

It was in the context of the Middle East reassessment that US officials first discussed the fighting in Lebanon at the highest level. On April 14, Kissinger and Ford greeted the US ambassadors to Israel, Egypt, Jordan, and Syria at a long-planned meeting to discuss US policy on the Arab-Israeli conflict. During the meeting, Ford asked what the significance was of the current internal dispute in Lebanon. Kissinger stated that he thought the Lebanese were trying to assert some control over "Fatahland," as the southern Arqub region was sometimes called.[10] This was entirely incorrect. Unlike in May 1973, the Lebanese army and security forces had not (yet) joined in the conflict. Nor was the fighting taking place in the south. Kissinger's slip may have been minor, but it illustrates the low priority that Lebanon had assumed in his Middle East considerations. Indeed, the fact that the US ambassador to Lebanon had not even been invited to this meeting suggests that the country had become peripheral to US Middle East strategy.

Kissinger's misunderstanding was not the fault of the US embassy in Beirut. Despite the embassy's complacent message of the previous October, expecting Lebanon to "muddle through" until 1976, Ambassador Godley's first cables recognized the "disturbing potential" of the events, including the seriousness of the break between Gemayel and Jumblatt, the pillars behind the Sulh government. The embassy also presciently noted that the events in Sidon less than two months earlier meant the "likely neutralization of [the] army and security forces" and the "possibility that they will not be directed to act decisively in current crisis."[11] Indeed, soon thereafter, a conflict developed between President Frangie and Prime Minister Sulh concerning the use of the army, which had posed two conditions for its intervention: proclamation of martial law and authorization for its commander to make decisions without interference from any source.[12] Whether Kissinger just did not read the cables or whether his staff failed to warn him of the seriousness of the crisis is unclear; what is obvious is that the warnings fell by the wayside.

Still, although distraction and ignorance partially explain US inattention to Lebanese affairs, they are not enough. Even if Kissinger had been paying closer attention, it is unlikely that the United States would have taken a more active role there. US domestic concerns militated against any military action, even if it had been considered. The so-called Vietnam Syndrome reduced the willingness of the United States to deploy troops abroad. Heightened congressional scrutiny of US foreign policy in the aftermath of the Watergate scandal and revelations about alleged US misdeeds in Chile and other countries reduced the US willingness to employ covert actions, such as the provision of weapons.[13] Although the Ford administration funded several groups in the Angolan civil war from the summer of 1975, by December, Congress had cut off those funds.[14] In such an atmosphere, assistance to the Lebanese Christian militias was riskier than it had been several years earlier.

Moreover, US involvement would have risked upsetting the administration's broader goals for the region. Prior to the October War, US contingency planning vis-à-vis Lebanon had emphasized support for the Lebanese government against the Palestinians and their external supporters, particularly Syria, Egypt, and the Soviet Union. Since then, America's relations with Egypt and Syria had changed drastically. Kissinger now sought to help these countries achieve mutually acceptable agreements with Israel, which required maintaining good relations with them. At the same time, Egypt and Syria could ill afford to be seen as compromising the interests of the Palestinians and their fellow Arabs. Thus, the Ford administration needed to avoid the appearance of working against the interests of any Arab parties to the conflict, including the Palestinians. Of course, this image of impartiality was an illusion. In Kissinger's worldview, the Palestinians (not unlike the Lebanese) were at best a sideshow to be ignored to the extent possible.

Finally, the dynamic of the early fighting may have discouraged US involvement. In the early months, and indeed throughout the war, the violence took a cycle of fighting and cease-fires that repeatedly raised hopes that the situation could be contained. For instance, on April 17, after the first of dozens of cease-fires between the parties, Godley closed his report to the State Department by writing, "Insha-llah [*sic*] (God willing), this will be our last regular sitrep on [the] [P]halange/Palestin[i]an crisis."[15] As the political crisis persisted, the prognoses from the US embassy would become increasingly pessimistic. Still, at least at the beginning of the conflict, a major confrontation between the government and the Palestinians along the lines of May 1973 seemed unlikely. Instead, a permanent state of unrest ensued, lacking flash points that might prompt other countries such as Syria to intervene militarily. This in turn seemed to relieve the need for immediate US action.

From the beginning of the conflict, many parties in Lebanon sought political, military, and financial support from outside the country. As in previous crises, the Arab countries played a more important role than the United States. As in 1973, the Palestinians and leftists tried to involve other Arab states on their behalf. Arafat sent a cable to Arab leaders asking for their intervention.[16] In a heated meeting between Suleiman Frangie and Arab ambassadors, the Lebanese president accused them of intervention in Lebanese internal affairs through their media campaigns.[17] The Lebanese government sent representatives to seek Asad's help in influencing the leftists and Palestinians.[18] From the US point of view, Syria seemed to be playing a calming role, dispatching a special envoy to the scene to tell Saiqa and others "to cool it." Within two days of the outbreak of fighting, Arab League secretary General Mahmud Riad also arrived in Beirut to mediate.[19]

The available evidence suggests that at the beginning of the conflict, the Lebanese government did not try to involve the United States in the conflict. As previously discussed, relations between the Lebanese government and US diplomats had deteriorated over the previous two years, and the impact of the dog–sniffing incident of the previous November may have further contributed to President Frangie's unwillingness to undertake security consultations with the United States. Moreover, at the time of the outbreak of hostilities, Frangie was in the hospital recovering from gallbladder surgery less than two days before. On April 14, US ambassador Godley visited the president at the hospital to deliver a get-well message from President Ford.[20] It is unclear whether Godley talked to Frangie, but in the reception room, he ran into Foreign Minister Taqla, who asked for his opinion on the situation. Godley responded that "we and other friends of Lebanon considered it extremely grave for in all honesty we did not see that the [country] today had a government." Taqla expressed his concern about the potential for an Israeli invasion in South Lebanon, but made no request for US support as had Abouhamad in 1972 and Tony Frangie in 1973.[21]

Perhaps surprisingly, there is no evidence that key Maronite leaders asked US diplomats directly for support, as had happened in so many cases previously. Some private individuals affiliated with the Maronite cause requested US assistance, but their entreaties appear to have been rebuffed. In fact, US diplomats tried to convince their contacts that the United States would not intervene on their behalf. On April 28, two Maronite interlocutors informed Godley that the Phalange had received what they called "modest support" from the Lebanese army during the recent fighting. They then implied that help should also come from "other friends." Godley rejected this, saying that "the greatest error [the] Kataeb [sic] could currently make would be to count on external assistance" and urging them to make every effort to solve the issues by negotiations.[22] The State Department approved the embassy's line, noting, "We want to avoid encouraging Christian extremists or giving the impression (which of course would be totally false) that we in any way supported them in recent fighting or would do so in the future."[23]

The Christian militias asked other governments for help, too. Several scholars have claimed that contacts with Israel began immediately after the war began in April 1975 and that they were a "constant phenomenon" throughout the war, whether between lower level envoys or at the ministerial level, including in Paris and Rome.[24] Over the next year, the Christian militias also received military aid from Jordan and European countries, though it is unclear exactly when this began. A US Defense Intelligence Agency report indicated that in June 1975 the Phalange had received money from Iran. Jordan and "Jordanian Christian groups" had "reportedly" provided the group with training, weapons, and supplies. In addition, Israel had "reportedly" delivered 81mm mortars to the group in May. The DIA assessed the reports of foreign assistance as credible, particularly from Israel.[25] However, with the exception of the Iranian money, the use of the word "reportedly" suggests that the agency was less than 100 percent certain that this had been provided.

Although the Ford administration did not directly support the Christian militias at the beginning of the conflict, Palestinian and leftist groups suspected that the United States was secretly doing so. In April 1975, the Yugoslav ambassador to Syria informed Godley that the head of the PLO Foreign Affairs Bureau, Faruq Qaddumi, had told him that he (Qaddumi) and Arafat were convinced that the Phalangists had staged the recent confrontation with the PLO with "prior knowledge" and backing of the US embassy in Beirut. The ambassador said he wanted the United States to know this not because the accusation was valid, but because it demonstrated the PLO's hostility to the United States. Nor were the Palestinians the only ones with suspicions. Syrian foreign minister Abd al-Halim Khaddam also remarked to the US ambassador that he suspected US involvement.[26] Still, many scholars believe that the PLO, and particularly Fatah leader Yasser Arafat, was relatively cautious at the beginning of the Lebanese conflict.[27] In the early days of fighting, the Phalange fought against units of the Rejection Front, the DFLP, and Saiqa, rather than Fatah.[28] Arafat's reluctance to enter the fighting may well have been a reflection of his hope to participate in the negotiations over the Arab-Israeli conflict. For the fighting parties, the connection between the regional situation and the events in Lebanon seemed obvious.

The Military Cabinet and Syrian Mediation

Although the United States was inclined to keep its distance from the conflict, the increasing involvement of other countries in Lebanon over the next month began to provide reasons to pay attention. Following Sulh's resignation, the logical choice for the next prime minister was Rashid Karame. However, Frangie and Chamoun both opposed the nomination of their old rival.[29] Instead, on May 23, Frangie announced the formation of a cabinet of military officers headed by a retired Sunni general, Nur al-Din al-Rifai.[30] The formation of the military government surprised most Lebanese observers. Only the Phalangists and Chamoun's National Liberal Party approved of this step, which ran counter to the opposition of the Muslim and leftist parties to the use of the army in the conflict. Syria opposed this new military government, sending Foreign Minister Khaddam to Beirut to mediate between the factions. By May 26, due to broad rejection from many quarters and the resumption of the worst fighting to date, the military government resigned, forcing Frangie to nominate Karame as prime minister. Khaddam's visit also brought about a cease-fire, though Lebanese army sources told the United States that the Syrians had conducted a massive resupply effort to their fedayeen allies and possibly to Lebanese leftist groups, too.[31]

The potential involvement of Syria, and thus also of Israel, in the Lebanese conflict now demanded US attention. A CIA report warned of the possibility of a civil war that could jeopardize prospects for a Middle East settlement. The report concluded that if the Lebanese army threatened the destruction or expulsion of the fedayeen from Lebanon, the Syrians would likely intervene. The most likely outcome of a new regime, it asserted, would be a leftist, Muslim-dominated government more sympathetic to the Palestinians and radical Arab states. It also suggested that in the event of an Israeli military intervention, Israel would likely occupy at least part of Lebanon on a long-term basis.[32] As if to reaffirm this danger, during Khaddam's visit, Israel launched a series of reprisal attacks on Lebanon, which sparked confrontations with the Lebanese army. On May 25, seven Lebanese soldiers were killed in fighting with the Israelis. Godley commented that the incident "could not r[e]p[ea]t not have happened at a worse time," since due to internal pressures, the military government basically had no choice but to confront the IDF.[33] Israel requested that US diplomats explain to the Lebanese that they had targeted the fedayeen, but the State Department refused to get involved, suggesting that Israel use UNTSO instead to get the message to the Lebanese.[34]

There was a gap between the positions of US diplomats in the region and Secretary of State Henry Kissinger on the implications of Syrian mediation in the conflict. Political reporting from Beirut and Damascus suggested that Syrian diplomacy was constructive and intended to establish order in Lebanon, albeit on Syrian terms. In Damascus, Asad's adviser Adib Daoudi explained to Ambassador Richard Murphy that the Syrian initiative sought to avoid a repetition of the May 1973 conflict and that Syria had not considered direct military intervention, which would have probably produced an Israeli counteraction. Daoudi also indicated that Syrian support for the Palestinians was not unconditional, hinting that Syria had an interest in maintaining a balance between the two sides.[35] Godley agreed that the Syrians were helping the situation in Lebanon, noting reports that Khaddam had taken a harsh line with Arafat for not cooperating with the Lebanese government or controlling his followers and rivals.[36] Over the summer, Syrian mediation played a key role in efforts to form a cabinet, which succeeded on June 30.[37] Kissinger, however, took another tack on the Syrian mediation, warning publicly against any outside military intervention in Lebanon via leaks to the media that were attributed to a "high ranking [US] official."[38] Inquiring about these reports, Godley countered that "Syrian actions here, i.e. Khaddam's visit, etc., were helpful in cooling [the] situation."[39] Kissinger's remarks may have been off-the-cuff, but they reflected his instinct, expressed consistently over the next year, that a Syrian intervention had to be prevented at all costs.

Over the summer, a growing inter-Arab rivalry began to manifest itself in regard to the Lebanese conflict, reflecting the regional and international tensions over the possibility of another separate disengagement agreement between Egypt and Israel, brokered by the United States. Arab mediators and agents from many different countries worked independently in Lebanon, with little obvious coordination between them. As Khaddam pursued his mediation in Lebanon on June 17, the Egyptian ambassador returned from Cairo bringing messages from Sadat for Frangie, Arafat, Jumblatt, and possibly others.[40] That same day, Sadat was quoted in *al-Nahar* newspaper as stating that the "Soviets and Libyans [are] waging warfare against him in Lebanon and elsewhere." The US embassy heard that Egypt had once again begun to fund Sunni street groups in Lebanon, which they had not done since the time of Nasser' death, probably as a counterweight to Libyan, Iraqi, and other influences.[41] Elias Sarkis, the governor of the Lebanese Central Bank and former presidential candidate, told a US official that he had information from private banks that some $35 million had been transferred into Lebanon from Libya during May, and that funds continued to come in at about $1 million per day. "Important" amounts of Saudi and Iraqi funds also continued to arrive.[42] Syria began to grow closer to Jordan as part of an "Eastern Front" strategy in a reaction to the increasing likelihood of a second disengagement agreement on the Sinai; eventually, this cooperation would be extended to Lebanon, but it was not yet there at the time.

Although the US embassy in Beirut had reported faithfully on this internationalization of the conflict, its staff remained distant from Lebanese political developments. Following the hospital visit in April, Godley did not see Frangie again until June 13, when the ambassador accompanied former senator J. William Fulbright on a visit to the president's summer residence in Ehdin. During this meeting, Godley was "shocked by [the] appearance of [the] President whom I have not seen for about three months." During the meeting, Frangie was "not at all alert," lacked any sense of humor, and "at times . . . stared into the distance." Godley blamed it on the surgery and overwork.[43] In a second meeting on June 16, Frangie seemed "more alert." He did not request assistance from the United States.[44] Still, Godley reported his impression that "Lebanon's problems totally surpass his intellect and he has nothing constructive to contribute to their solution at this time. . . . He struck me as more and more a small time Christian leader and not the President of all the Lebanese."[45] Throughout the fall, Godley's reports would increasingly portray the Maronite leaders, particularly Frangie and Chamoun, as stubborn and unwilling to compromise.

Over the summer, the Lebanese military began to request aid from the United States, but there is none was provided. In his capacity as minister of the interior, Camille Chamoun requested military assistance from the United States for the internal security forces, including armored cars and personnel carriers. He portrayed the conflict in the context of the Cold War, claiming that the Soviet embassy was supporting the "Communists and leftists," while the Lebanese government had no support in what Chamoun called "the final battle with the Left." Godley responded that he thought that grant assistance was unlikely. Chamoun told him that he understood, but thought "it was inconceivable that Lebanon's old good friend the U.S. could [let] the GOL down at this crucial moment." The US ambassador, however, thought that the "solution lies within Lebanese capability and should not r[e]p[ea]t not involve U.S. generosity."[46] Godley's opposition reflected his understanding that the internal security forces were not viewed as neutral parties in the conflict, and that providing assistance was likely to prolong the conflict.

Whether or not the United States government assisted in the flow of weapons to the Christian militias, this activity was associated with the United States. Arms dealer Sarkis Soghanalian, whom Godley described as the "principal munitions procurer" for Chamoun and Gemayel, invoked the name of the United States in his work, much to the chagrin of the US diplomats in Beirut. On July 8, a Boeing 707 owned by Soghanalian's company, United Trade International, landed and "began off-loading unmarked olive drab footlocker size cases into olive drab trucks." Soghanalian apparently told a local Pan Am employee that the US embassy had approved the use of Pan Am equipment and that all documentation should be sent to the embassy. Godley called presidential adviser Dib to tell him that the shipment was "none of my business," but that it was "my business that certain individuals might [be] trying to embroil this mission in internal Lebanese political-military machinations" and that he "wished in strongest terms to disassociate my government with this matter and to be sure that no responsible Lebanese . . . might try to implicate us." US intelligence indicated that the shipment included AK-47s purchased in Warsaw and shipped via Madrid, intended for the Phalange.[47] Whatever the attitude of US intelligence services toward these shipments, the State Department opposed them.

During the previous crises in Lebanon between 1969 and 1973, US diplomats had actively sought out their allies in the region to find ways to calm the situation in Lebanon. Now, that dynamic appeared to have been reversed. Partially in reaction to apparent US passivity, conservative states across the region took the initiative to discuss the Lebanese crisis with US officials. In June 1975, Iranian minister of court Asadollah Alam told the US deputy chief of mission in Tehran that the Lebanese ambassador to Iran and Chamoun ally Khalil al-Khalil had asked for assistance for his National Liberal Party (NLP) militia. Alam told al-Khalil that the Shah doubted that much could be done and "certainly does not want to get involved in a losing game," asking "whether any other country was doing anything to help out," in particular the United States.[48] Godley commented that the US embassy in Beirut did not consider the situation hopeless and suggested that the shah might counsel restraint in Baghdad which, along with Tripoli, continued to "add fuel to the flames."[49] Consultations between the United States and Iran continued during the summer, and, as previously mentioned, a Defense Intelligence Agency report suggested that Iran did provide weapons to the Christian militias.[50] In Jordan, the Lebanese ambassador told US ambassador Pickering that Prime Minister Rifai had offered help to Lebanon, saying that the Lebanese military had been training in Jordan for some time. However, he did not provide any details about what kind of assistance this entailed.[51] Godley responded that he could not see anything that Jordan could do for the Lebanese.[52] During previous crises, Jordan's primary role had been to deter Syria, though it had provided some material assistance to the Lebanese government in 1973. Now, Syria no longer needed to be deterred, nor would Asad's new friend Hussein have been likely to do this, even if the US had wanted it.[53] In short, these discussions led nowhere. Despite a superficial calm reigning in Lebanon throughout the summer, the threat of renewed conflict was never far from the surface.

Sinai II and the Resumption of Violence in Lebanon

There has been significant speculation about the coincidence in timing of the resumption of violence in Lebanon and the signature of the Sinai II Agreement between Israel and Egypt. The so-called Fourth Round of fighting in Lebanon broke out on August 28, following a fight over a game of pinball in the town of Zahle in the Biqa Valley.[54] Meanwhile, after a summer of Kissinger's shuttles between Cairo and Jerusalem, Egyptian and Israeli representatives signed a second disengagement agreement on September 4.[55] For many within Lebanon and across the Middle East, the timing of the two incidents seemed suspicious, since the fighting in Lebanon provided a convenient outlet for the tensions generated by the Sinai II Agreement. The conflict between Egypt and Syria deepened, producing strange sets of new regional bedfellows as Syria grew closer to Jordan and other moderate states while Egypt worked together with Libya, even as the two clashed over numerous other issues. Just how related were these incidents?

On one hand, Lebanon had its own dynamics that were largely separate from regional politics. As Lebanese historian Kamal Salibi observed, "There were enough reasons to explain the resumption of the hostilities at the purely domestic level."[56] In simplest terms, the military situation worsened, while the political deadlock continued. Throughout the summer, the militias had continued to arm and train. The existence of a Shi'a militia, Amal, run by Musa al-Sadr, was revealed after an accident in the Biqa Valley killed dozens of young men training with the PLO on the use of land mines.[57] Tensions were also on the rise as the possibility of compromise on political issues remained elusive. Hardly any communication took place between President Frangie, who had returned to his summer home in the mountain town of Ehdin, and Prime Minister Karame, who had remained in Beirut.[58] On August 18, a member of the staff of the Sunni Mufti published an article stating that Muslim acquiescence to living in a non-Islamic state was already a concession on their part, meaning that they would not compromise further in their demands for political reform. The same day, the Lebanese National Movement published a political program of "Five Demands," including the abolition of confessionalism, electoral reform, and the reorganization of the government, the administration, and the army. This broad program was seen by the Christian forces as a provocation.[59]

Even if the main causes of the renewed violence were domestic, international factors associated with the Sinai II Agreement contributed to its spread. On August 29, Israel began launching air raids that US officials thought were intended to preempt Palestinian raids triggered by the Sinai II Agreement.[60] Among the Palestinians, the Fatah faction under Yasser Arafat and his allies, excluded from the peace negotiations, saw little reason to support Sinai II, but they did not yet take an active role in the fighting. Palestinian rejectionist organizations, however, played an increasingly provocative role in Lebanon, whether hoping that the violence could undermine the agreement or simply viewing a victory as necessary to prevent their own liquidation. On September 9, PFLP leader George Habbash publicly rejected neutrality in the Lebanese crisis, claiming that the conflict pitted 4 percent of the population against 96 percent.[61] In addition, the dispute between Syria and Egypt over Sinai II gave each party an incentive to thwart the other's objectives in Lebanon. Their row worsened as Khaddam visited Beirut from September 19 to September 25, where the Syrians sponsored the creation of a "Committee of National Dialogue" that included Gemayel, Jumblatt, and other important leaders. Although the formation of this commission was accompanied by a cease-fire, the international tensions around the country continued. On September 26, Sadat's adviser and *al-Ahram* newspaper board chair Ihsan Abd al-Qaddus wrote an article blaming Syria's "surrender to stalemates" for "intra-Arab fighting" such as was occurring in Lebanon.[62] Khaddam struck back, calling Lebanon's problems a "side effect of Sinai II."[63] The Committee of National Dialogue's efforts soon reached a stalemate, as Jumblatt demanded that the committee's discussions be on the basis of the Five Demands, most of which were unacceptable to the Christian parties.[64]

This virulent Syrian-Egyptian split went beyond the intentions of Kissinger and other US policymakers. US officials may have wanted to divide the Arab states to a certain extent, but they did not anticipate the level of animosity that developed. Kissinger had aimed to pull apart the Egyptian-Syrian alliance so that step-by-step interim agreements between Israel and other Arab states would be possible; this required breaking the Arab consensus on a need for a comprehensive solution. But since another Egyptian-Israeli agreement would reduce the incentive for Israel to reach agreements with Syria, Jordan, and the Palestinians, these groups could be expected to resist it. Although US policymakers were aware of this, they may have underestimated the Syrian reaction. By August, US officials noted signs that Damascus had accepted that another interim agreement was likely.[65] Perhaps this was wishful thinking, but in any case, there were limits to how far Kissinger wanted to push the Arab states apart. The secretary of state in fact needed to preserve a degree of Arab unity to prevent other Arab states from turning against Egypt, undermining that country's ability to adhere to the separate agreements that it signed. In his memoirs, Kissinger admits that during the final negotiations for Sinai II, Ford promised Prime Minister Rabin not to force Israel to make any "major decisions" prior to 1977.[66] Despite this promise, the United States would make an effort to get Israel to conduct negotiations toward another agreement with Syria or to make other concessions during the next six months, viewing a stalemate in the negotiations as a recipe for disaster.

Syria and Jordan's common opposition to Sinai II established a foundation for a closer relationship that also could potentially concern Lebanon and the PLO. As the two countries grew closer, Jordan began to see an alliance with Syria as an opportunity to replace the PLO leadership. On September 19, King Hussein told visiting Ambassador Godley that "he hopes soon to obtain Syrian President Assad's [sic] assistance in [an] effort to bring about a more moderate and responsible PLO leadership which would contribut[e] to stability in Lebanon," and he "inquired whether I thought President Frangieh [sic] and GOL would welcome such action on their part."[67] A few weeks later, Godley responded that he had "no quarrel should [a] close relationship develop with Syria, Jordan and Lebanon, for this would be in my view a factor for stability" in Lebanon.[68] At this point, however, Syria continued to generally support the position of the PLO and the Left in Lebanon, even though its primary goal was to obtain a cease-fire.

The severity of the Syrian–Egyptian split posed a dilemma for US poli-cymakers: Should they try to mediate a dispute between the conflicting re-gional powers in order to stop the violence in Lebanon? Doing so posed a risk of being seen as supporting either Syria or Egypt. The United States had no desire to upset Egypt, which had just signed a second disengagement with Israel that was strongly opposed by much of the Arab world. Neither did the United States want to give Syria another reason to distance itself. Most US officials thought that the Syrian mediation was generally constructive.[69]

After the fighting in the Biqa broke out, some Christian groups pursued a military strategy that deliberately sought to force outside intervention in the conflict, whether from the Lebanese army and security forces or from international sources. The Phalange militia began to shell the downtown Bei-rut souk area, in part to force the intervention of the army in the capital.[70] Around the same time, the Maronite camp proposed an "internationaliza-tion" of the crisis.[71] However, they refused an Arab military role in Leba-non.[72] Initially, no Christian leaders asked the United States to intervene in Lebanon, and in fact, Godley left Lebanon on a short trip from Septem-ber 13. While he was gone, on September 18, Interior Minister Chamoun called to tell the US chargé that he had had the agreement of the president and a number of government ministers that if Karame did not broker an agreement to the conflict by that evening, Chamoun would send in the army the next day.[73] Worried that the Interior Minister and militia leader might interpret these exchanges with the United States as assent in these plans to use the army, the State Department quickly responded with instructions for the chargé not to contact Lebanese leaders in Godley's absence, since "any initiative—even though designed merely to elicit information—could be mis-construed or misused to allege U.S. involvement or support."[74]

More and more Lebanese began to urge the US government to do some-thing. On September 22, Ghassan Tueini, the Harvard-educated editor of *al-Nahar* newspaper then serving as petroleum minister, invited Godley to his home and asked whether the United States would consider military in-tervention in Lebanon. Godley responded that "I though[t] he knew my country sufficiently well at this time to [be] able to answer that question him-self." Tueini also asked for a statement in support of Lebanon's territorial integrity, but Godley responded that every message he had given to Frangie from Nixon and Ford had already contained such a statement.[75] After re-ceiving Tueini's message, the State Department replied that they would be willing to provide yet another such statement, if the Lebanese government asked.[76] Godley, however, recommended against it, arguing that even a statement in support of Lebanese stability "would encourage Christian stubbornness and brinksmanship," and "would be interpreted as a threat by the Syrians and [the] Lebanese Moslem extremists." The ambassador felt that "Christian right[-]wing activism bears more than 50 percent of responsibility for Round 4." The "specter of US intervention," he wrote, "plays both [a] positive and negative role in [the] present situation. It tends to moderate the demands of the Moslem left but also encourages the Christian extremists. Public statements cannot significantly modify this specter."[77]

Godley reiterated US neutrality in private conversations with Christian leaders, hoping to convince them that the United States was unlikely to intervene. In a conversation with the new Maronite patriarch Khreish, the ambassador was impressed by the leader's moderation and realism about the undesirability of a US intervention. When the patriarch asked whether the Palestinian problem "would be solved at Lebanese expense," Godley called this "malicious gossip," but also warned that if no solution was found, "the Palestinians could well take over a portion of the country. This would be regrettable, but I did not think anyone should assume we would use force to maintain the status quo."[78]

As the violence worsened, US policymakers began to fear that the situation in Lebanon could deteriorate to a point at which its interests in the Middle East would be affected. In discussions with US embassy staff, Syrian officials such as army chief of staff Hikmat Shihabi seemed increasingly negative about the outcome of their mediation.[79] In Amman, King Hussein, who claimed to have sat in on a briefing from Shihabi and several telephone conversations between Khaddam and Asad, told Pickering that "Syria will pull out if the Lebanese do not shape up their own government."[80] If Syria ceased its mediation, the situation within Lebanon could deteriorate even further, with unpredictable consequences for the United States and the region.

Other countries asked the United States to consider becoming more involved, each for its own reasons. Israel was concerned about the possible collapse of the Christian forces. On September 20, Defense Minister Shimon Peres asked Kissinger whether the United States could "assist moderate elements" in Lebanon, a reference to the Maronite parties. The notes of this meeting indicate only that the "discussion was inconclusive."[81] Four days later, Yigal Allon, now foreign minister, asked Kissinger whether the United States could do anything to keep Lebanon from becoming "moslemized." Kissinger prevaricated, expressing "uncertainty about what we could usefully do."[82] Israel clearly wanted the United States to provide arms or money to the Christian forces, but there is no evidence that the Ford administration did so. French officials also sought cooperation with the United States. In a September 27 meeting with Kissinger, French foreign minister Jean Sauvagnargues argued that the Syrians should be allowed to use force in Lebanon if necessary, asking whether Israel would intervene if Syrians sent just a couple of battalions into the country. Kissinger responded that he thought that they would. Sauvagnargues protested that a Syrian intervention would "not affect the security of Israel."[83] Over the next nine months, Sauvagnargues would advocate for Syrian military action in Lebanon on several other occasions, but the secretary of state would resist his arguments each time.

At the UN on September 30, Kissinger met with Foreign Minister Taqla in what was described as a "very useful and friendly meeting." After discussing the US strategy for negotiations, Taqla indicated that what was needed in Lebanon was a solution that produced a redistribution of power while preserving Lebanon as a unitary state. The two agreed to issue a statement of support for Lebanon after the meeting, ignoring Godley's advice that such a statement would discourage Frangie from compromising. Kissinger told Taqla "in strictest confidence" that Allon had promised that if Syria did not intervene, the Israelis would not either.[84] Soon afterward, a State Department representative announced US "support for [the] independence and integrity of Lebanon." Doubtless, the secretary was pleased to encounter an Arab representative that displayed a friendly attitude toward his actions. He would remember Taqla over the course of the fall. The Lebanese army commander, Hanna Said, also made a pitch for US involvement in the conflict, suggesting to Godley that Kuwait, Saudi Arabia, and Egypt could put pressure on Syria to not allow the flow of arms into Lebanon to continue.[85]

Other Lebanese wanted the United States to go even further. Lebanon's former foreign minister, Khalil Abouhamad, suggested that the US government "help those elements of the Lebanese population which seek to preserve Lebanon's pro-Western liberal society"—a clear reference to the Christian forces. However, the US embassy in Beirut remained opposed to this.[86] Following up on his previous cables, Ambassador Godley argued that many parties in Lebanon, including both Christians and Muslims, hoped for or at least expected some sort of US intervention. This included Gemayel and Chamoun, who may have believed that US assistance was coming. Godley thus continued to recommend getting the message to Christians that they must make concessions.[87]

In early October, the violence in Lebanon reached its worst point yet. As the military situation grew worse, the United States conducted a formal reevaluation its policy toward the conflict in Lebanon. WSAG meetings on Lebanon were held on Friday, October 10, and then the following Monday.

The Ford administration had by then grown concerned about the possibility that Syria would deploy troops to Lebanon, thus sparking an Israeli counter-intervention. This, rather than the death and destruction in Lebanon itself, prompted the increased US concern. At the WSAG meeting on October 10, Kissinger argued that "the principle United States concern is not the resolution of the Lebanese internal problems per se, but the prevention of outside intervention (by Syria and Israel in particular) that would be likely to lead to wider Middle East war."[88] He asked that a working group be formed over the weekend to deal with both the internal situation and the possibility of Syrian intervention. In the meantime, he would get in touch with Foreign Minister Taqla.[89]

At the October 13 meeting, WSAG members discussed ways to intervene in the conflict short of using military force. Prior to the meeting, NSC staff members had drafted an options paper on engagement in Lebanon, which outlined two possible strategies. The first emphasized "constructive political intervention," urging the Christians toward compromise and the Israelis away from support for the Christians. A second possible strategy, clearly disfavored, was entitled "Try to Put the Christians Back on Top," in which the United States would support a "reassertion of traditional Christian dominance." This included finding "indirect ways" of getting arms to the Phalange, offering "substantial amounts of grant military equipment (MAP) quickly to the Lebanese government, with the expectation that it would then be available for use against the Moslems," and warning Syria about the US "inability to restrain Israel in the event the situation in Lebanon went too far." However, it warned, this risked exacerbating the situation in Lebanon and harming US relations with other states.[90] At the meeting, Kissinger joked that "the bureaus always give me two choices: what the bureau wants or all-out nuclear war," but despite his irritation with the options, he did not argue, as he had in 1969, that the United States should directly support the Christian groups.[91]

The meeting also considered the trickier question of how to deal with a potential Israeli-Syrian clash over Lebanon. A joint intelligence report by the CIA, DIA, and State Department's Bureau of Intelligence and Research argued that although Tel Aviv saw certain advantages in continued fighting (such as distracting the fedayeen), Israel might tolerate a Syrian military intervention under certain conditions.[92] At the time, however, top US policymakers did not proceed on this assumption. Another options paper discussed strategies in the case of a Syrian and Israeli intervention, concluding that it would be best to simply prevent such interventions from occurring in the first place.[93] For Kissinger, it was important to "get a specific answer on what the Israeli judgment is of a tolerable level of Syrian activity."[94]

Following these deliberations, the State Department began a diplomatic campaign with three basic components. First, it wanted to give encouragement to the Lebanese government, to urge Saudi Arabia and Kuwait to counsel restraint to the Palestinians, and to discuss the situation with the French.[95] However, these contacts proved relatively fruitless. The Saudis were pessimistic about their ability to influence the situation, while the Kuwaitis responded in generalities, avoiding comment on the US suggestion that they contact the Palestinians directly to urge moderation.[96] A French official in Paris told US ambassador Kenneth Rush that the French would talk to the various Arab parties and the Maronite patriarch, who would visit Paris soon. He then asked about the US reaction to a possible international intervention with US, Soviet, and French soldiers. Rush recalled the negative US reaction to the possible stationing of Soviet soldiers in Egypt during the Yom Kippur War.[97] Clearly, the United States wanted to avoid a joint mission with the Soviets, but it was also unlikely that the United States would have intervened in Lebanon under any circumstances.

Second, and more importantly, the State Department began a dialogue with Israel and Syria concerning Lebanon. In the case of Israel, officials sought to discourage the possibility of an Israeli military intervention and Israeli support for the Christian groups. On October 11, the State Department instructed Ambassador to Israel Malcolm Toon to discuss the situation in Lebanon with his host government, including to ask "whether or not there is a point at which the Christian community, by taking too rigid a position against Moslem demands for a greater share of power, may bring to a head the crisis we all hope to avoid and may itself be the principal loser."[98] Foreign Minister Allon claimed to agree with much of the message's strategic appraisal, but stated that Israel would continue to warn against military intervention by other powers, namely, Syria, claiming that their warnings had been effective. Allon also asked if the United States could provide some support to the Maronites, but denied that Israel was in touch with them.[99] Whether this is true or not is unclear; probably it was not. On October 22, Allon told Toon that the Israeli reaction to a Syrian intervention would "depend on the circumstances," including the nature of the intervention and its size, geographical area, and intention. However, according to the Foreign Minister, any Israeli reaction to a Syrian intervention would only take place after approval by the cabinet and consultations with the United States.[100] A later chronology of events referred to this statement as an Israeli "commitment" not to intervene in Lebanon until its government had consulted with the United States.[101]

Meanwhile, instructions were issued on October 14 for Murphy to begin a "serious and confidential exchange" with the Syrians, assuring them that the US government did not "support [the] hard-line Christian position." The United States, he was to say, was willing to see a shift in the division of power in the country, and also that "Syrian views are likely to be close to ours on major elements of [a] desirable outcome in Lebanon." However, though the United States had counseled Israel with restraint, the Jewish state might retaliate to the introduction of foreign forces no matter what the US reaction was.[102] This was intended as a subtle warning to the Syrian leader not to intervene. In Damascus, Asad "appeared happy with idea of conducting this dialog[ue]," and seemed interested in the fact that Israel might intervene no matter what the United States said, asking whether "this was our conclusion after consultations with [the] Israelis." Murphy replied that "it was simply [a] matter of our independent best judgment."[103] Although the conversation ended here, this exchange can be seen a precursor to the US-Syrian dialogue over intervention that would develop in March of the next year.

Third, the United States tried to support Arab diplomacy in regards to Lebanon, though it did so cautiously. On October 13, the Arab League announced that a foreign ministers' meeting would be held in Cairo to discuss the situation in Lebanon, though Syria and some other parties refused to participate.[104] Under consideration was the possibility of creating a pan-Arab force for Lebanon, which the Lebanese Christian groups, Israel, and Syria all opposed, though for different reasons. The Christian groups and Israel were suspicious about the intentions of Arab troops in Lebanon, while Syria resisted any initiative that would reduce its margin of maneuver in Lebanon, particularly if it was proposed by Egypt. In messages that it sent to Cairo and Jidda, the State Department underlined that the Ford administration was not committed to the Christian position, though they pointed out the possibility of an Israeli military reaction to the deployment of an inter-Arab military force in Lebanon.[105] Still, most Arab governments, including Saudi Arabia and Egypt, believed that an outside intervention was necessary to stop the fighting.[106] In Egypt, Foreign Minister Ismael Fahmy suggested that the United States do whatever it could to "weaken Syrian capability to aggravate [the] situation," such as "breaking [the] newly-forged Syrian-Jordanian Common Front."[107] In a message to Egypt and Saudi Arabia, the State Department for a time suggested that Israel might accept an Arab League force in Lebanon, if it was "clearly for non-military purposes" and "accepted by [the] principal elements, including [the] Christians, in Lebanon."[108] Kissinger, however, was skeptical, telling Ford that he doubted "the Israelis will stand still for" an Arab force.[109]

The United States was not the only country encouraging Israel to accept a more significant Syrian role in Lebanon. According to a transcript provided to the United States, probably by Israel, on October 17, King Hussein assured Rabin that Syria was "trying to play the role of moderation" in Lebanon. The Syrian leadership, Hussein told the Israeli prime minister, hoped that Lebanon would not be dismantled.[110] There is no indication that Hussein was arguing for a direct Syrian military intervention at the time, but he would progressively become a stronger advocate for a Syrian role in Lebanon over the next six months. At this time, his entreaties had little impact on the Israeli attitude.

As fighting continued, the conflict of interests between the United States and Israel over Lebanon became more perceptible. In late October, the US Department of Defense reported that the Lebanese Christians had obtained "large quantities" of M-16 rifles, probably from the Israelis.[111] According to reports by the US defense attaché in Beirut, at least seventy-six hundred M-16s had been included in shipments of weapons to Lebanese Christians, some of which were US government property that had been shipped to Israel.[112] On October 31, Kissinger confronted an Israeli official for the first time about Israeli aid to the Maronites. After a discussion of Sadat's visit, Israeli ambassador Simcha Dinitz asked Kissinger for his thoughts on the situation in Lebanon, to which Kissinger responded, "I think you're arming the Maronites and the Libyans are arming the Moslems." Dinitz denied this. While Kissinger stepped out to take a phone call, Dinitz asked Atherton whether Kissinger was serious about the weapons. Atherton replied affirmatively.[113] In this conversation, Kissinger neither encouraged nor discouraged Israeli aid, but his silence on this matter may have been interpreted as assent.

Syrian officials stayed suspicious of US intentions in Lebanon, partially as a result of the Sinai II Agreement, though they remained open to dialogue. In an October 22 meeting between Murphy and Shihabi, in which the US ambassador sought Syrian assistance to obtain the release of two US Information Service employees that had been kidnapped in Beirut, the general noted that although common ground existed between the US and Syrian positions, the Lebanese crisis served to distract attention and criticism from Sinai II, which worked to US advantage. Murphy responded that the US government was not worried about "durability" of the Sinai II Agreement. Shihabi warned the ambassador not to "think that if the Lebanese situation continues or even if it worsens, this will mean trouble for Syria." Shihabi offered to host the ambassador at his apartment the next week in a more

leisurely setting, which led Murphy to think he "may have a mandate to explore our thinking."[114] There are no records of whether they met again at
that time.

On the ground in Lebanon, the US embassy remained disengaged from
the situation, which continued to deteriorate. In late October, battles broke
out in downtown Beirut and spread throughout the city, including along what
would become known as the Front des Grands Hôtels, in which many high-
end stores and hotels in the downtown area were repeatedly shelled and
looted, often changing hands between the various militias. These included
the twenty-eight-story, still unfinished Rizk Tower and the recently opened
Holiday Inn.[115] On October 21, things were so bad that when Godley visited Foreign Minister Taqla in his temporary offices at the Ministry of Education, the only refreshment that the foreign minister could offer him was
Turkish coffee out of a thermos. Taqla told him that no one had been in the
Foreign Office for weeks and that he and Karame were considering resigning. Godley encouraged him to remain in office, while mediation continued.
Taqla asked for US assistance, but admitted that he had no concrete ideas
about what kind of help the United States could provide.[116] Godley also suggested twice to Chamoun that he visit Damascus as part of an effort to broker a solution to the crisis, but the Christian leader did not make the trip.[117]

In November, the Lebanese leader who seemed to be working the most
to broker compromise was Prime Minister Rashid Karame. After repeatedly
attempting to get the Lebanese Parliament to meet to discuss the crisis, on
October 28, Karame went to the Serail, or Lebanese seat of government,
and announced the formation of a so-called Security Board composed of
prominent members that were to meet to discuss the situation.[118] Through
his efforts, as well as via contacts with Palestinian and Syrian leaders, a new
"Higher Coordination Committee" was formed and empowered to investigate acts of violence, ultimately slowing the fighting.[119] On November 5,
Kissinger sent a message to Karame praising his efforts but did not send a
similar message to Frangie, the head of state, a measure that was intended as
"implicit discouragement for the uncompromising attitudes of some Christian leaders."[120] Frangie was duly offended, but the gesture had no impact
on his negotiating position.

Following these efforts, US initiatives basically ground to a halt. At the
end of October, Sisco lamented to Kissinger, "We just cannot seem to influence the situation. I don't think we have the capacity."[121] Occasional messages of encouragement and disapproval seemed to be the only initiatives
the Ford administration was willing and able to undertake. Other Western
countries undertook high-profile mediation efforts, with little success. From

November 9, an envoy from the Vatican spent a week in Lebanon meeting with various parties. This was followed by a mission from a French special envoy, Maurice Couve de Murville, who arrived on November 20. After eleven days in Beirut, de Murville visited Damascus from December 1 to December 3. This mission resulted in an invitation from Asad to Pierre Gemayel to come to Damascus, a seeming success.[122] Gemayel left on his trip on December 6, but on this day, four Christians were found murdered in the Metn, following which Christians in Beirut and elsewhere went on a rampage, killing at least seventy Muslims. This in turn sparked an offensive of Sunni forces in Beirut that became known as the Fifth Round. The violence ended only under Syrian and PLO pressure on December 15.[123] However, Gemayel's meetings with Asad resulted in an agreement between the party and the Syrians that would lay the basis for a possible resolution of the conflict, as the Kataib agreed not to get involved in schemes to partition the country, while both sides pledged to support the Lebanese authorities and avoid fighting.[124] Thus, even amid horrible violence, progress was being made behind the scenes.

The January Cease-Fire

Still, the fighting was far from over. At the end of 1975 and beginning of 1976, the Lebanese crisis reached its worst point yet. From the perspective of the Christian militias, the Palestinian refugee camps at Tal al-Zaatar, Jisr al-Basha, and other locations posed a threat to links between East Beirut and the Christian populations in Mount Lebanon.[125] In mid-December, the Christian militias thus began to eliminate pockets of Palestinian and leftist forces in Mount Lebanon and other areas under their control. On January 4, Maronite forces launched a siege on several Palestinian camps in the Beirut area, marking the start of the Sixth Round of conflict, in which the bulk of the PLO forces entered the war for the first time.[126] The army intervened openly for the first time on January 7 in support of the Maronite forces, then again on January 17, when the air force, against the orders of Prime Minister Karame, attacked Palestinian forces laying siege to the Christian village of Damour, near Camille Chamoun's residence.[127] Fearing a descent into chaos, on January 22, Syria sent Palestine Liberation Army units under their control into Lebanon, which led to a halt in the fighting that would allow space for negotiations. During this period, again, the Ford administration closely followed the developments in the crisis, but its actions remained restrained.

In preparation for an upcoming meeting of the UN Security Council on the Arab-Israeli conflict, Roy Atherton planned to visit the Middle East in mid-December, providing an opportunity to consult about Lebanon. During this trip, NSC staffer Robert Oakley in Washington and Ambassador Godley in Beirut each urged their superiors to make a major effort with the Vatican, France, Egypt, and Saudi Arabia, as well as resume discussions with Shihabi. Godley in particular was concerned about Sadat, who continued to issue warnings about outside interference in Lebanon.[128] Urging caution, US ambassador Hermann Eilts in Cairo pointed out that there was no evidence that Sadat was interfering with Syrian mediation.[129] Godley countered that Sadat's recent statements had been interpreted as interference and maintained that the Christians were unlikely to compromise as long as "hope for Egypt, Saudi, Iranian and other conservative initiatives exists."[130] Sisco decided to be cautious, expressing hesitation about Syria's long-term objectives vis-à-vis Lebanon. He instructed Atherton to limit his conversations to general discussions of the Lebanese situation.[131] His trip thus produced little new.

In the meantime, Syria upped its mediation efforts in Lebanon through several efforts. In late December, Saudi king Khalid visited Damascus. After three days, Asad, Khalid, and Arafat announced the so-called Damascus Accord, which contained three principles: (1) Saudi support for Syrian efforts to settle the Lebanese crisis, (2) Saudi agreement to help persuade Arab countries and other parties to work for a settlement, and (3) following the settlement of the crisis, holding a mini-summit in Riyadh with Khalid, Sadat, and Asad, which would then expand to include Hussein and Arafat.[132] In addition, Syrian officials had been conducting a dialogue with the Kataib. Finally, since November, Syria had been discussing a possible peace agreement through a back-channel connection with Frangie's adviser, Lucien Dahdah, in Paris. Negotiations over a number of weeks led to a draft agreement on internal reforms in Lebanon, though some issues remained to be settled.[133]

Many of the Lebanese Christian leaders hoped that the United States would guarantee the implementation of a final settlement of the conflict. On December 30, Dahdah told a US embassy officer that he and the Syrians had agreed on a set of principles for resolving the conflict: Frangie would remain in office until the end of his term, Syria would try to get the so-called Muslim factions to agree to Karame as their representative, and a two-man "plenipotentiary meeting" would work out a deal on issues of "Lebanese sovereignty, distribution of gov[ernmen]t jobs, powers of [the] Pri[m]e Min[ister] and Parliamentary reform." The Syrians offered to guarantee this agreement alone, though the Christians wanted a "co-guarantor," preferably the United States.[134] While the lack of a second guarantor was not the only stumbling block to the agreement, it probably contributed to its failure. In January, Dahdah reiterated that the Christians refused to accept a Syrian guarantee alone for any agreement.[135]

By the second week of January, the increasing possibility of a Syrian intervention meant that the United States could no longer ignore the situation in Lebanon, which again threatened to draw in Israel. In an interview with a Kuwaiti newspaper on January 8, Khaddam threatened that Lebanon would return to Syria if it fell apart. In response, Israeli defense minister Shimon Peres warned publicly that Syrian intervention in Lebanon could not leave Israel indifferent.[136] A State Department spokesman reaffirmed US opposition to any intervention in Lebanon, mentioning both Syria and Israel by name.[137] However, US officials had few ideas about what they could do. At a staff meeting on January 12, the State Department's only idea was another concerted effort with some European countries, Syria, and Israel. At the same time, Atherton suggested that "we have to think very seriously whether the lesser evil might not be some Syrian action before we just write it off as a possibility." Kissinger agreed that this might be the case and requested an options paper on this subject, though he appeared ambivalent: "I don't understand all the profundities involved here; but since the worst thing that can happen is a Syrian intervention matched by an Israeli intervention, why should we then try [that]?"[138] By January 13, the NEA section of the State Department had concluded that the US government should not encourage a Syrian intervention, because of the likelihood of an Israeli counteraction.[139] They instead proposed a strategy in which the United States would ask the Vatican, the United Kingdom, and France to join in an appeal to stop the fighting, while also connecting to the UN and local groups, and arguing for food shipments to the besieged Palestinian camp at Tal al-Zaatar.[140] Kissinger, revealing his priorities, noted that the State Department would definitely want to check with Sadat before doing anything.[141]

One action that the Ford administration did take at the time concerned the flow of arms to combatants. Some foreign leaders, including Prince Hassan of Jordan, had urged that the United States consider supplying arms to the Christian militias. In response to a request from Kissinger, Atherton drafted a memo arguing that supporting the Christians, whether through arms or otherwise, would signal that the US government was writing off a political solution. According to the memo, the United States had received no direct requests for arms from the Phalange or the National Liberal Party. There had been a number of requests from "individual army leaders through somewhat indirect channels for large amounts of equipment, some of it heavy equipment," such as tanks and self-propelled artillery. The State Department had responded that these requests should come from the government, rather than directly from the military. The memo made clear that "to supply arms to the army was to provide them to a mainly Christian force that might ultimately use them in the Christian cause." However, it noted that if the US government did decide to send the Christian militias weapons, the army could be a "useful channel."[142] This was reminiscent of US considerations in previous Lebanese crises in 1969 and 1973.

Now, the State Department began to consult with some governments in an apparent attempt to create an arms embargo on Lebanon. US diplomats encouraged Syria to reduce the flow of arms to Muslim combatants and also made overtures to Western European countries, particularly Belgium, but also West Germany, France, Italy, and Spain, which the United States believed served as production sites and transit points for arms destined for Lebanon, primarily to the Christian militias.[143] The European governments claimed that they would not license arms exports to the Lebanese, but most maintained that they were unable to prevent the illegal transfer of arms. French and British officials saw the transfer of arms as a "symptom rather than a cause of the conflict."[144] While the US campaign seemed on the surface to be a sensible measure, it ignored one significant source of weapons: Israel. Though the United States had long suspected that Israel was supplying weapons to the Christian forces, by now, US officials had received confirmation of this. In a December 30 meeting, Dahdah told a US embassy officer that "various organizations of the Christian right had been approached by Israeli sources during the past few weeks for the purpose of rendering assistance." In his opinion, "it was to the credit of the Lebanese Christians that most (but only most) of the Israeli offers had been rejected."[145] In late January, Rabin admitted to Kissinger that the Israelis had sent two shipments of weapons to Chamoun, though he did not say when this occurred.[146] On the whole, however, the Israeli appraisal of the Christian forces was that they were "not well organized and, moreover, lacked courage."[147] Still, the flow of Israeli arms continued. The fact that Israel was not included in the US campaign suggests that the US intent to limit the flow of weapons to the Christian militias was limited.

It was at this point that the PLO for the first time began openly intervening in the conflict. The Palestinian militias had been seen as supporting the Lebanese Left since the fighting began in April. Units of the PFLP and other groups had been participating in the fighting for some time. Some PLO fighters had been involved in the confrontations in the center of Beirut since at least October. However, at least nominally, the PLO, as an umbrella organization, had remained somewhat distant, trying to preserve a veneer of neutrality.[148] Now that the camps were being targeted, the PLO cast aside its pretense, launching a limited offensive by the Palestine Liberation Army on January 6 that would spread in scope over the next few weeks.[149]

After a temporary improvement in the security situation, the conflict in Lebanon worsened again. On January 17, the Lebanese army carried out air strikes against the fedayeen in violation of Karame's orders not to attack, prompting the prime minister to resign.[150] Even worse, over the next two days, Syria deployed two battalions of Palestine Liberation Army forces under its control into Lebanon.[151] Israeli officials warned their US counterparts that Syrian troops could "overrun the Christians."[152] The State Department disputed this, but promised to express concern to the Syrian and other governments.[153] Jordan also sent a flurry of messages to the Ford administration, probably concerning the situation in Lebanon, but their content remains classified.[154] Adding to the dangers, US and British intelligence agencies both reported that Egypt had contingency plans to send troops to Lebanon if the situation continued to deteriorate, which would have likely provoked a clash with Syria, though US and UK officials expressed skepticism that such a risky action would actually be implemented.[155] In response, on January 17, the State Department and CIA representatives proposed a new international initiative led by the French, possibly involving the UN secretary general.[156] On January 19, the State Department authorized US ambassador Godley to remind Karame of the US message of November 6 and to encourage him to remain in office.[157] However, it had little to offer him except moral support.

The United States finally contacted the French on January 20 to suggest that they develop a common initiative, spearheaded publicly by the French and supported by the United States behind the scenes through their contacts with Egypt, Israel, Saudi Arabia, and other countries.[158] Foreign Minister Sauvagnargues told Rush that they had had a similar idea, and had contacted Karame and Frangie, but the Lebanese had discouraged the idea of a Security Council meeting. The Lebanese foreign minister had suggested French, US, and Soviet tripartite mediation, but the French government "rejected this as totally unrealistic." French diplomats had proposed a UN meeting on January 19, but the Syrians responded negatively. The French therefore wanted to wait to see how the Syrian mediation went before launching another move.[159] On January 21, French officials announced publicly that they were willing to undertake a mediation if the Syrian effort failed, which the US embassy in Paris thought was "an excellent beginning and is certainly as much as we could have hoped for as an initial French response."[160] In the meantime, however, a meeting of State Department and intelligence officials back in Washington expressed doubts of any chance of successful negotiations unless one of the parties changed their strategy, which was unlikely to happen while the Christians were enjoying military success.[161]

Before any such international intervention took form, Syria's indirect military intervention via the PLA forced the Christian groups to agree to a halt in the fighting. Around the time this was announced, US ambassador Murphy received instructions to warn Shihabi that the United States doubted it could prevent an Israeli reaction in the event of overt Syrian military intervention.[162] However, Murphy received the message just after the departures of Shihabi, Khaddam, and Syrian Air Force chief Naji Jamil to Beirut on January 21.[163] The State Department instructed Murphy to raise the issue of the PLA forces with the Syrians anyway, since they had gone on record with Hussein and the Israelis that Murphy had been instructed to convey their concern and wanted to establish their position as firmly opposing the deployment of Syrian troops in Lebanon.[164]

For the first time since the summer, a tenuous calm held in Lebanon, but the Ford administration had done little to bring it about. In the early stages of the fighting, the State Department sought to remain as distant as possible from the developments in that country. However, this strategy was not sustainable. Particularly after the resumption of hostilities in Lebanon at the end of August 1975 and the signing of the Sinai II Agreement, Egyptian-Syrian tension deepened and the possibility of a regional war involving Syria and Israel increased, threatening US negotiating strategy in the Middle East. For the first time, the United States took some tentative steps to engage in a dialogue with the international actors whose interests fueled the flames of the conflict in Lebanon. Over the next few months, as the conflict worsened and other external actors stepped in, the United States would again perceive a need to become more active to prevent a regional war.

CHAPTER 7

Reluctant Interveners

The Red Line Agreement and Brown's Mediation

The events of the first half of 1976 are at the heart of the historical debate over the US role in the Lebanon crisis. In January, the United States and other countries did their utmost to prevent an overt Syrian military intervention out of concern that Israel would launch a counterinvasion that could result in a region-wide war that would wreck the ongoing Arab-Israeli peace negotiations. In June, Syrian troops in regular army uniforms marched into Lebanon with little international outcry, including from the United States and Israel. How can this change be explained?

One explanation has come to dominate accounts of these events. Between March and June, in a series of secret negotiations conducted via third parties, Syria and Israel allegedly came to an unwritten, informal understanding about Lebanon, often known as the "Red Line Agreement," which defined the scope of the Syrian intervention in Lebanon. Several works, including the memoirs of Henry Kissinger, have established that between March and June, the State Department played a role in communicating between Syria and Israel regarding the possibility of a Syrian military intervention in Lebanon. These communications even included discussions of specific details such as the geographic location of forces, the number of troops, and the types of armament they could employ. However, a number of aspects of the US role are in dispute, including exactly what the agreement was and what attitude the United States took toward the possibility of a Syrian intervention.

First, scholars disagree about whether the agreement was a straightforward authorization of the Syrian intervention, a set of vague understandings, or a formal set of conditions that was passed on. Initially, some interpreted the US role during this period as a straightforward "green light" authorizing Syrian intervention.[1] Other accounts have emphasized that the so-called agreement was vague and unclear.[2] Participants in these events have provided descriptions of the so-called agreement in technical language that conceals as much as it reveals. For Israeli scholar Yair Evron, it was a "deterrence dialogue," while Kissinger calls it a "careful minuet" between the two countries.[3] Syrian officials, for their part, have long denied that any sort of understanding was reached with Israel or the United States concerning their intervention in Lebanon.[4]

Second, beyond simply what transpired in these discussions, it is unclear whether the United States supported or opposed an understanding that would facilitate a Syrian intervention in Lebanon. Some accounts seem to suggest that Kissinger deliberately sought to encourage a Syrian intervention.[5] In his memoirs, Kissinger never states whether or not he encouraged a Syrian intervention, but rather maintains only that the United States preferred a "political solution" sponsored by Syria without a Syrian military intervention.[6] Recently, drawing on newly declassified US documents, Michael Kerr has argued that "Kissinger came to view a Syrian solution to the war for Lebanon as a price worth paying for limiting Soviet influence in the Middle East and drawing Asad into an Arab-Israeli peace process."[7]

This author argued in his doctoral dissertation, and David Wight has maintained in a more recent article, that the Ford administration, in particular Kissinger, was much more hesitant about a Syrian intervention than is commonly known.[8] As Wight correctly argues, the United States "did not accept a Syrian occupation of Lebanon until just before or just after Syria commenced its full scale intervention."[9] However, Wight's account leaves out important aspects of the internal debate within the Ford administration, three of which are worth noting here. His article does not mention that many Ford administration officials argued in favor of a Syrian military intervention in Lebanon. He also misses the story of how a potential reassessment of US relations with the Palestinians shaped considerations about Lebanon. And finally, while partially true, his claim that Kissinger "sought to support the Lebanese Christians" takes the former secretary of state too closely at his word.[10] While US officials did not want the Lebanese Christian parties to lose, neither did they seek to provide them with any direct support, or even the impression of having US support, because they in fact wanted the Maronite groups to reach a compromise with their opponents.

In short, although from March to June 1976 the United States played a role in passing messages between Syria and Israel, US officials actively sought to discourage a Syrian intervention throughout this period. In March, the United States was so hesitant about such an intervention that Kissinger sent retired US diplomat Dean Brown to Lebanon in an attempt at mediation. Although this helped to temporarily calm the situation, violence soon broke out again. Up until the moment of the Syrian intervention, US leaders thought that the Israelis were likely to forcefully oppose any Syrian deployment to Lebanon. There was thus no green or even yellow light from the United States to Syria to intervene. Moreover, the red lines given by Israel were not nearly as clear as many have assumed. Although the US role in influencing events in Lebanon was important, the Red Line Agreement is a historical red herring.

The Constitutional Document and Shifting Alignments

The indirect Syrian military intervention in January 1976 produced a ceasefire that allowed negotiations to take place, albeit under Syrian auspices. Syrian mediation picked up where it left off in December via discussions with Frangie and Dahdah.[11] On February 7, Frangie and Karame visited Damascus. Their trip resulted in the so-called Constitutional Document, which proposed a set of seventeen changes to the Lebanese Constitution.[12] Most importantly, the distribution of seats in the parliament would be changed from a six-to-five Christian-to-Muslim ratio to an even distribution, while preserving the Christian presidency, the Sunni prime ministership, and the Shi'a speaker of parliament. Moreover, confessionalism would be abolished in the distribution of civil service posts, except at the senior level.[13] As part of this agreement, Syria would guarantee the implementation of the 1969 Cairo Agreement requiring the Palestinian militias to cooperate with the Lebanese authorities.[14] Although US officials did not want to get involved in the negotiations, they signaled to the Lebanese that they supported the process. US chargé d'affaires George Lambrakis, who had arrived in Lebanon the previous summer, met separately with both Karame and Frangie to convey US approval of the accord.[15]

However, this Syrian mediation contained the roots of its own failure. Many Lebanese opposed an agreement that was imposed from outside. With the exception of Frangie, Karame, and Shi'a leader Kamal al-Asad, nearly all important Lebanese leaders had some degree of concern about the agreement, though the Christian leaders (except Raymond Edde) appeared to support it more than did the Lebanese Left.[16] After remaining silent for more than a week, Jumblatt publicly signaled his rejection of the document.[17] For the Muslim and leftist leaders, it simply contained too few concessions.

Now, for the first time since the beginning of the conflict, a split began to develop between Syria and its allies in Lebanon. With Jumblatt's rejection, the Lebanese National Movement was officially opposed to Syria's Lebanon policy. A divide was also beginning to open between Syria and the PLO, whose movement Syria was increasingly trying to control through its support to the Saiqa organization.[18] Key Palestinian leaders suspected Asad of reaching an agreement with the United States and Israel that would have Syria control the PLO in exchange for some sort of concession.[19] Following the signing of the Constitutional Document, Jordanian leaders told their US counterparts that the Syrians had informed them of their determination to enforce the Cairo Agreement, including removing most of the heavy weapons from the Fatah-controlled camps in Lebanon.[20] The shift in alliances was reinforced by personal relationships between members of the Lebanese Christian leadership and the Syrian regime. In February, according to CIA reports, Rifaat al-Asad, the brother of the Syrian president, cut off the flow of Syrian arms to Lebanese leftists as a favor to his business partner, Tony Frangie, the son of the Lebanese president.[21]

Egypt and Israel, each for its own reasons, opposed the increased Syrian involvement in Lebanon. To many US officials, Egyptian policy toward Lebanon appeared to be almost entirely focused on undermining Syrian interests. During the January fighting, Sadat had sent a brigade of the so-called Ayn al-Jalut forces, a part of the Palestine Liberation Army, from Egypt to Lebanon to fight on behalf of the Palestinians and leftists.[22] Implicitly, however, this was also a move against the Syrians, whose disputes with the PLO were growing.[23] The head of Egyptian military intelligence even told US embassy officials that Arafat had requested this after the Syrians had sent in another Palestinian unit under their own control.[24] Just a few days after the Syrian deployment of troops, however, Foreign Minister Fahmy suggested to US ambassador Eilts that the "USG should support Christians with arms and ammunition," stating that this could be done from Brussels or Paris. Eilts thought that Egyptian resentment of Syria was so intense that they would actually welcome an Israeli military intervention against Syria in Lebanon.[25] Sensing the depths of the animosity, the State Department hesitated to get involved in the dispute between the two countries, despite pleas from the US embassy in Beirut to mediate for the sake of Lebanon.[26]

Israel opposed the growing Syrian role in Lebanon, primarily due to its concerns about having a hostile state on its northern border. According to Kissinger's memoirs, on January 28, during a visit to the White House, Rabin warned Ford that if uniformed Syrian troops entered Lebanon, Israel would occupy the country up to the Litani River.[27] The available archival records of their conversations do not contain any such threat; however, they do reveal that Kissinger cautioned Rabin against intervention, stating that "if there is another war [in the region], you will face the most massive political pressures you have ever faced, however it starts." Kissinger then asked Rabin for his vision of a solution to the Lebanon crisis. The Israeli prime minister responded by arguing for a de facto partition of Lebanon, stating that the Christians should try to bring about a "population centration" to separate the Christians from the rest of the population, though he thought the Syrians would not allow any formal partition to occur.[28] Whether or not Rabin's comments reflected Israeli discussions with the Christians is unclear, but they certainly reflected the thinking of many Christian factions. Kissinger offered no endorsement of the idea of partition, which the United States had consistently opposed over the previous months.

The split between Syria and the Palestinians contributed to the collapse of the Lebanese army, which would reignite the conflict in Lebanon. Over the previous year, the army's neutrality had been drawn into question by its actions during the strike at Sidon, rumors of its role in the arming and training of the Christian militias, and finally its participation in fighting in January. Now, following the January cease-fire, the army fragmented into several groups.[29] On March 11, Brigadier General Abd al-Aziz Ahdab staged a "coup" on television in which he demanded Frangie's resignation. Arafat's intelligence chief Ali Hassan Salame helped arrange this affair.[30] However, the Palestinian leaders were divided about whether to expand the coup any further. Arafat warned that this could trigger an Israeli intervention.[31] Some remnants of the army declared their loyalty to Frangie, while a few forces remained at their posts.[32] Ahdab's movement, unlike previous attempts at rebellion, appeared to have some popular support, since his demands, particularly for Frangie's retirement, mirrored those of a broad portion of the Lebanese political spectrum. In fact, by March 13, two-thirds of the deputies in the Lebanese parliament had signed a petition requesting Frangie's resignation, which the president refused. He had support from the Christian militias and was determined to remain in office.[33]

As the Constitutional Document's success appeared increasingly in doubt, the parties again prepared for war. On March 17, the Palestinians and leftists decided to launch an offensive against Christian positions in the Mount Lebanon area.[34] By that point, any hope of implementing the Constitutional Document without additional force was effectively gone. A remarkable reversal of roles had taken place, as Syria now supported the Christian forces against the coalition of Muslim, leftist, and Palestinian groups. This change would eventually bring a reconsideration of regional attitudes toward a possible Syrian intervention.

The Non-Negotiation of the Red Line

It was at this point that the infamous "negotiations" began between Syrian and US officials in Damascus, allegedly leading to an "agreement" authorizing a limited Syrian intervention in Lebanon. Kissinger's memoirs recount that on March 13, Syrian chief of staff Hikmat Shihabi told US ambassador Richard Murphy that he "despaired of solving the Lebanese crisis short of introducing regular Syrian forces," suggesting that Israel might accept this with or without a formal agreement. Kissinger assumed that it was "impossible that Shihabi was acting on his own"; thus, he concluded, it was likely that "Asad was testing our reactions via his trusted associate."[35] Murphy's report of the conversation, however, casts some doubt on this interpretation. In what the US ambassador described as a "conversation of unrelieved gloom," Shihabi mused about everything from setting up "duplicate arrangements existing on the Golan" in Lebanon—essentially deploying Syrian forces throughout Lebanon, possibly up to the Israeli border—to annexation of the country, and even getting rid of the entire Lebanese leadership. Murphy suggested that Shihabi was an "exhausted and thoroughly fed up chief of staff who may not have been considering fully what he was saying."[36] This argues against Kissinger's assertion that the Syrian general was exploring on Asad's behalf. Kissinger claims that he told Murphy to continue exploring the topic, while warning Syria not to use "Syrian regular forces," in which event the United States would guarantee that Israel would not intervene.[37] There are no available documents in the US archives that confirm that these instructions were issued. Indeed, in a March 15 discussion with Murphy, Asad "gave no hint that [the] introduction of Syrian regulars was high on his list of options," and the ambassador did not request this, either.[38]

Still, US officials remained conflicted about the possibility of Syrian intervention. US intelligence reports now suggested that should Asad's Lebanon policy fail, he faced the possibility of overthrow from within Syria, which would bring about an even more radical government in that country, possibly led by other military officers.[39] On the other hand, Kissinger remained convinced that if Syria intervened with any forces at all, Israel would launch a counter-intervention. Israeli officials had in fact repeatedly told this to their US counterparts. In a March 15 telephone conversation, Ambassador Dinitz, back in Israel, told Kissinger that the introduction of Syrian regular forces would "logistically change the situation"—a vague response that suggested counter-intervention.[40] In a meeting two hours later, the secretary of state instructed Atherton to warn the Israelis against this, though he was sure that Israel would respond militarily to a Syrian intervention. Atherton stated that he thought they might under certain circumstances, but Kissinger sharply disagreed: "Allon is a fool. . . . No, I'm afraid that we could never exert enough influence to stop Israel."[41] Despite the risk of an Israeli counter-intervention, Syria still deployed around a thousand Syrian regular troops disguised as PLA forces, with tank support, to prevent Muslim and leftist forces from attacking Christian positions.[42] On March 18, Asad told Murphy that Frangie had asked for the Syrian intervention.[43] However, these forces failed to stop the fighting, prompting the possibility of a larger Syrian intervention.

Syrian officials then began a dialogue with the United States concerning the possibility of intervention in Lebanon. At noon on March 23, while Murphy was back in Washington for consultations, Minister of Foreign Affairs Khaddam summoned US chargé Robert Pelletreau to inform him that Frangie had requested a Syrian intervention. However, before they sent in troops, they "wished to have 'approval of several countries whose agreement we believe is necessary.'" Khaddam could not comment on the size of the force, since the decision had not yet been taken, though they would "view positively any proposal advanced by US." Khaddam thought that it would take about a week to get a "political solution."[44] As a delaying tactic, Kissinger sought to draw out the dialogue with the foreign minister, sending a message that warned against an intervention. The message stated that the US's "independent judgment" was that if Syria sent in "regular forces," Israel would "occupy substantial parts of Southern Lebanon and perhaps elsewhere." In addition, it asked about the size, location, mission, and duration of the force, the guarantees for the "independence and integrity of Lebanon," and for Syria's views on the possibility of "an inter-Arab force, in which Syria would play [a] leading role, or UN forces."[45] This is far short of the guarantee of no intervention in the case of non-regular forces that Kissinger claimed in his memoirs to have given. Khaddam said that he would transmit the message to Asad and contact the US embassy if there were a reply.[46]

In the meantime, Kissinger continued to consult with Israeli officials about whether or not they would accept the Syrian intervention under any conditions. On the evening of March 24, Dinitz presented US officials with a document indicating three conditions under which Israel would oppose Syrian military actions in Lebanon: (1) "open and declared Syrian military entrance into Lebanon"; (2) the entry of forces above brigade size, including those already present; and (3) the introduction of weapons along the coast. Furthermore, moving troops or equipment more than ten kilometers south of the Beirut-Damascus axis would nullify this agreement.[47] Kissinger later told his colleagues that Dinitz informed him privately that if Syria intervened, the "Israelis would then quietly take over strategic points in Southern Lebanon and in effect hold them hostage till the Syrians leave," using the opportunity to "go in and clean up Fatahland."[48] For the first time, Israel had implicitly suggested that it might accept a Syrian intervention under some circumstances, though these were so limited as to make it practically impossible. US officials struggled to figure out what the Israelis meant by the term "brigade," which the US embassy in Damascus translated as *liwaa*, an ambiguous term in the Syrian army. Since the US estimate was that between one and two thousand Syrian troops were already in Lebanon in Palestinian uniforms, they might well have been close to or at the brigade-level limit already.[49]

The communications between Syria and the United States were supplemented by messages sent via Jordan. On March 24, Pickering was instructed to ask Hussein to warn Asad about the risks of putting regular forces into Lebanon.[50] Hussein maintained that he knew nothing about Syrian intentions but changed his line later that day, even sending Kissinger a written message proclaiming that Asad had little choice but to intervene and asking for help in restraining Israel. In his message, the king noted that he was not specifically arguing for an intervention, but rather pleading for US understanding.[51] Kissinger responded that "it is not clear to us that all the alternatives except introduction of [a] Syrian military forces have been exhausted."[52] The next morning, after Pickering delivered Kissinger's response, Prime Minister Rifai linked the situation with Hussein's planned visit to Washington from March 29 to April 2, stating that if the US government thought the chance of an Israeli intervention was high, he could not leave the country.[53] This was clearly intended to put pressure on the United States to support the Syrian policy.

Syrian officials began to offer more details about the shape of an intervention, probably in hope that it would produce a US green light. Later on

March 25, Khaddam summoned Pelletreau to tell him that Syrian forces would move into Beirut, the Biqa Valley, and parts of the mountains, with a goal of guaranteeing Lebanese independence. No troops would be stationed in South Lebanon. He avoided specifying how many troops would be sent in, but claimed that it would not be a "large force." It would be withdrawn after "a political solution" was reached, and "when Lebanese establishments can exercise their responsibilities," possibly after several months. Finally, the foreign minister stated that the Syrians were unhappy with the US attitude on this issue.[54] Kissinger promptly relayed these points to Dinitz in Israel by telephone.[55] In the meantime, the State Department promised an answer within a week, while warning against intervention based on "reliable information that this could lead to serious consequences."[56]

At a March 26 meeting of Kissinger, Murphy, and the NEA department, US officials hammered out a response to the Syrian initiative: The United States, it read, had so far successfully argued against Israeli military action in Lebanon. In the process, they had "gained a certain understanding" of circumstances in which Israel might react militarily to a Syrian intervention. These included the open declaration of a military move by Syria, the commitment of more than a brigade of forces, or the use of heavy weapons. In addition, it would be more dangerous if troops were sent "south of the Damascus-Beirut axis." The message asked the Syrians to provide as many details as possible, including the time frame of the intervention. Finally, the message suggested speaking with Lebanese leaders to bring about an end to the fighting, or even to arrange a Security Council meeting.[57] Considering how often Kissinger had opposed UNSC meetings on the Middle East, on the grounds that it would involve the Soviets, this suggests that the United States wanted very much to prevent a Syrian intervention. Pelletreau gave the message to Khaddam the next day.[58]

On March 27, Asad met with Jumblatt, but the meeting did not go well, again increasing the likelihood of a Syrian intervention. In the meantime, Kissinger instructed Ambassador Pickering to convey to King Hussein the limits that the Israelis had communicated to him.[59] After receiving the message, Hussein called Asad. The Syrian leader told him that Jumblatt had refused to compromise. Thus, he would now send in a division of troops to Lebanon, promising that they would stay out of the south. According to Hussein, Asad asked the king to request "full US support in keeping [the] Israelis out." Rifai thought Syrian forces would focus on "establishing a Syrian corridor from [the] border into Beirut," thus staying out of the south.[60] The State Department warned that this might trigger an Israeli reaction and asked for up to a day to get a response.[61] Having returned to the embassy to send a report to the State Department, Pickering woke Hussein up in the night to deliver the response. The king called Asad right away in the ambassador's presence. Asad told Hussein that he would see Arafat that day and "try to separate Arafat from Jumblatt," by which he meant reaching a separate agreement to keep the Palestinian forces from supporting the leftist offensive. Hussein offered an endorsement of Asad, telling Pickering that US officials could "associate him in any way you believe useful in your approaches to Israelis."[62] The king continued to pass similar messages while en route to the United States, including while visiting Spain, where he discussed the situation by telephone with Asad, who told him that he wanted to put in a division of troops for three or four weeks.[63] Possibly at the request of the Syrians, French officials in Washington also asked the United States to stop opposing a "limited" Syrian intervention, suggesting that some sort of international guarantees be issued via the UN Security Council. Initially, US officials seemed open to this possibility but soon rejected the idea after it remained clear that Israel would not accept international guarantees.[64]

In the meantime, Kissinger made efforts to preempt an Israeli counterintervention in the event that Syrians sent more troops into Lebanon. On the evening of March 27, Kissinger made repeated phone calls to Ambassador Dinitz, who was on a return trip to Israel, warning that the Syrians wanted to send in troops.[65] In one call, Kissinger warned Dinitz about the possibility of a "more radical Lebanon and a radicalized Syria" if the PLO won and Asad was overthrown, asking for a new analysis of a Syrian move "no later than first thing in the morning. A considerate analysis of the problem. Not just 3 _____ [sic] in the form of ultimatums."[66] The next afternoon, when Dinitz called back with no new information, Kissinger responded irritably: "We flood you with information and you flood us with ultimatums." It was a "hell of a way to conduct business."[67] Finally, the Israelis gave Kissinger talking points, intended only for him, stating that they intended to supply the Christians with enough arms to continue to resist Jumblatt, and that if Syria actually entered Lebanon, they would eventually reach an agreement with the PLO and leftists that would be supported by the Soviets. Kissinger now indicated that he tended to agree and promised to try to prevent a Syrian intervention.[68]

Even though the risk of a Syrian-Israeli conflict over Lebanon loomed larger than ever before, Egypt's opposition to Syrian policy remained intense. US officials were getting intelligence that Egypt was ready to send additional Palestinian forces to Lebanon. The State Department still sought to avoid giving Egyptian officials the impression that it was supporting Syria or acting in defense of Israeli interests.[69] On March 24, Eilts passed on a message that the United States had warned Syria not to intervene. Fahmy noted that there was a "widespread impression that USG supports Asad's role in Lebanon and has given [the] Syrians carte blanche." Egypt, he boasted, had deployed the rest of the Ayn al-Jalut brigade, part of which had been sent in January, to Lebanon in support of the PLO. The Egyptians wanted the US government to tell the Syrians and the Jordanians not to intervene, while urging Frangie to resign and the French to launch a mediation mission.[70] The Saudis, for their part, told the United States that one of their ministers had told Asad not to send in troops but instead to work on calming the leftists. Asad had assured the minister that he would not intervene, even though the Lebanese president had requested this.[71] Fahmy was informed of the list of Israeli conditions that the State Department had passed to the Syrians, but not that the Israelis had told the Syrians that a limited, unannounced mission might be acceptable. Eilts worried that the United States risked angering the Egyptians, suggesting that it was best to tell them and the Saudis the "whole story." The State Department authorized this later that night.[72]

The US embassy in Beirut struggled to figure out a course of action. Ambassador Godley had left his post in mid-January after discovering that he had contracted throat cancer, and he had still not been replaced. Now, the State Department wanted to keep embassy staff in Lebanon on a tight leash, both because the Christian groups were seeking a more active US role and because some in Washington harbored doubts about whether the embassy was accurately portraying the US position to local leaders. Christian leaders, including Charles Malik and Camille Chamoun, had been calling the US embassy to ask for a US intervention.[73] On March 24, Malik sent messages via the US embassy to contacts in Washington, including Vice President Rockefeller and Senators Humphrey and Sparkman, pleading that "the danger of a leftist takeover is clear and present" unless the United States got involved; he specified that this did not have to mean landing marines, but that the United States needed to work with European countries and Syria.[74] Three days later, the former foreign minister warned the embassy that the leftists could be in the Christian stronghold of Jounieh, just a few miles from Beirut, within twenty-four hours.[75] Back in Washington, the State Department was left unclear on what the actual military balance was.[76]

On March 28, the State Department instructed Chargé Lambrakis or the economic counselor, Robert Waring, to convey to Jumblatt, Chamoun, and Karame a list of talking points outlining US opposition to partition and support for Syrian diplomatic efforts, though not military ones. The goal, the cable specified, was to convey US concern about the Christian military position without raising expectations of a US military intervention. Lambrakis was to report any other communications he felt he "should be authorized to make."[77] US officials in Beirut went slightly beyond this mandate. On March 28, just before they received the message from the State Department, Lambrakis and Waring had a forty-five-minute meeting with Jumblatt upon his return from Damascus, during which Lambrakis asked him for a "precise formulation" of his demands.[78] From Washington's perspective, this request for information in itself indicated US interest in his suggestions. On March 29, the State Department instructed Lambrakis to stick to a "limited approach."[79] The US talking points elicited little new from the Lebanese parties.[80]

Lacking reliable information on the situation, with no political solution in sight and a Syrian intervention seemingly imminent, Kissinger decided that sending a US envoy to Lebanon was the best chance they had of containing the Lebanese situation. The idea of a US mission to the Middle East had been on Kissinger's mind for several weeks. In a March 15 conversation with Ford, Kissinger suggested that he might even need to go to the Middle East himself to prevent a larger war from breaking out over Lebanon.[81] After considering various possibilities, Kissinger finally chose Dean Brown, US ambassador to Jordan during the Jordanian Civil War in September 1970, who was serving as the president of the Middle East Institute in Washington. Still, Kissinger remained unsure that the mission could prevent a Syrian intervention.[82] In case the situation deteriorated even further, the United States deployed some ships from the Sixth Fleet even closer to the Lebanese coast, both for a possible evacuation of US citizens and to deter the Soviet Union from any possibility of intervention.

Up until the launching of the Brown mission, the so-called Red Line Agreement had involved no agreement whatsoever. Although several specific conditions were passed from Israel to the United States to Syria, Syria never agreed to respect them. In fact, during this period, Syria deployed more forces covertly, ignoring the red line about the number of Syrian troops that Israel would tolerate in Lebanon. That said, Asad almost certainly took US signals into account in his considerations about whether or not to send in troops. This was most strongly demonstrated by his requests for a US green light, delivered via Jordan as well as through France in its discussion of international guarantees.

The Brown Mission and the PLO

Brown's mission to Lebanon would mark the first time since 1958 that a US mediator would get involved in the fine details of Lebanese politics, something that US policymakers had long been resisting. Neither Kissinger nor Brown had definite ideas about what the approach would entail, though Kissinger provided a set of guidelines at a staff meeting on March 30:

> What we need precisely is, first, an exact assessment of the situation. Second, we want to be helpful to encourage a cease-fire. Third, we want to see an outcome something like the Syrian solution at the end of January. Fourth, we want to get in some contact with the PLO. . . . We've got to try to split off Jumblatt from the PLO. They've got to be made to understand that the PLO will be the principal victim of Israeli intervention. Fifth, we cannot break the back of the Christians. They must not collapse on us. Sixth, we've got to keep the Syrians out. Seven, the Syrians must get the impression that we're working like hell to get an agreement along their lines. . . . I'm in favor of support for the Christians. You know I'm doing nothing to prevent the Israelis helping the Christians. The stronger they are, the better.[83]

The most sensitive part of the mission was whether or not Brown should contact the PLO. In his memoirs, Kissinger qualifies his instructions on this point as subject to approval from Washington, which he claims was never actually requested.[84] His claim stretches the truth, as we will see. In any case, these instructions suggest that Kissinger was unwilling to sanction a Syrian intervention but was hesitant about contacting the PLO.

The possibility of contacts with the PLO had great implications for broader US policy in the region. Two potential scenarios regarding Lebanon and the PLO seemed plausible. First, Syria might intervene militarily in Lebanon against the leftists and the Palestinians. If this did not provoke an Israeli counterreaction, it could weaken the PLO or leave it under Syrian control. This in turn could make it easier for the United States to broker a solution to the Palestinian issue as part of a broader Arab-Israeli agreement, as King Hussein had suggested the previous fall. During the US-Jordanian discussions in late March, Prime Minister Rifai again argued that a Syrian military intervention might have the potential to reconfigure the PLO in a way that was more favorable to the United States, Jordan, and Syria.[85] On March 24, Kissinger told Ford that that it would be good, though risky, if "Syria could go in quickly and clean it [Lebanon] out," since "they would leave the PLO in the same condition as in Jordan." If an intervention did occur, Kissinger said, the United States would have to put massive pressure on the Israelis.[86] The secretary of state also had other reservations about Syrian intervention. At a cabinet meeting in April, Ford recalled Hussein's position that "Jordan had eliminated the radicals in 1970 and Syria has an excellent opportunity to finish the job now." Kissinger, however, quickly added, "For a year or two, this would be a good thing. . . . But later you would get too much Syrian influence and then we would have to contend with a massive problem."[87] He might have added that such a scenario would endanger the US embassy in Lebanon, which by that point was under the guard of the PLO, as well as infuriate Egypt and other Arab friends of the United States in the Middle East.

US mediation in Lebanon allowed for a second scenario: cooperation between the United States and the PLO. State Department and US intelligence reports recognized the relatively moderate role that Arafat's forces had played in Lebanon. In early November 1975, US ambassador Godley argued that "a more forthcoming attitude on the part of the USG" toward the Palestinians could help Arafat and other "moderate" Palestinians resist pressures from more extremist elements to join the fighting.[88] Joseph Sisco seemed to agree with this logic, noting in a memo for his files that "as we begin to make accommodating noises towards Arafat and the PLO, probably in a [*sic*] direct proportion, they'll be able to refrain from feeling forced to back the extremists. The point is that we can't save Lebanon overnight by an about-face on the PLO (which we are not about to do in any case), *BUT,* if we begin to move towards dealing with them and accepting talks with them, it will have a moderating influence on the whole Lebanese scene."[89] This did not necessarily mean a quid pro quo connecting an Arab-Israeli settlement and the situation in Lebanon. Even limited contacts concerning Lebanon alone would serve as a tacit recognition of the PLO, which some within the organization would consider a benefit. Now, as Dean Brown's plane carried him across the Atlantic toward the Middle East, US prestige had been invested in finding a solution to the Lebanese imbroglio, and contact with the PLO would have been highly desirable.

Indeed, the Ford administration had already received numerous signs that the PLO was ready to work with US diplomats in Lebanon. Since at least the previous fall, the US embassy had secretly begun to cooperate more closely with the Palestinian forces in West Beirut, where the embassy was located. These measures had their origins in the CIA contacts with Fatah intelligence chief Ali Hassan Salame that began in the early 1970s and aimed at bringing about cooperation between the United States and the PLO.[90] Although these contacts had failed to develop into an open relationship, once the conflict in Lebanon broke out, discussions began between the US embassy, the American University of Beirut (located adjacent to the US embassy), and the PLO regarding security issues.[91] By the spring of 1976, PLO forces had already helped several times in obtaining the release of captured

US civilians and government representatives, including an army officer and two USIA representatives; in both cases, the United States had sent words of thanks to Arafat and Fatah leaders indirectly, via other Arab leaders.[92] Although these communications were limited, had they been revealed publicly, it would have been damaging for the administration, which could have been accused of cooperating with terrorists. In order to allow US officials an element of deniability, the embassy was officially guarded by officers of Lieutenant Ahmed al-Khatib's Lebanese Arab Army, which had split off from the main army in January.[93] In fact, this unit was fully under the control of the Palestinian forces, probably Fatah's Force 17, which was under Salame's command.[94] By protecting the embassy, PLO leaders hoped to send a signal to the United States that they were capable of behaving "responsibly" and thereby deserved a place in the negotiations.

Whatever strategy the United States pursued, it needed to avoid antagonizing Syria, Egypt, or Israel. Asad remained irritated at the US refusal to endorse a Syrian intervention. According to Hussein, who was visiting the United States at the time, Jumblatt had told Asad that he had the support of the United States to continue fighting. Kissinger instructed Murphy to tell Asad that this was a "malicious, cynical lie."[95] Kissinger also sent a back-channel message (probably via the CIA) to Brown at the Beirut embassy, emphasizing that the king's report about Jumblatt "reinforces my view which I expressed to you yesterday that you must make it categorically clear to Jumblatt and other leftists that we not only strongly favor an immediate ceasefire but that we will get such a ceasefire one way or another. You should be tough and brutal on this and leave them with no uncertainty. You are authorized to use [the] usual channel to get this message to the PLO."[96] Similarly, supporting Syria too openly would have risked antagonizing Egypt and Israel. US diplomats were treading a fine line between these parties.

Brown's first actions on the ground were to meet with the various Lebanese sides, as well as to get a sense of the balance of forces. He soon concluded that the Christian military position was better than expected.[97] US officials wanted to avoid giving the Christian militias any hope that the United States would provide them with weapons directly. At the beginning of March, the State Department refused to let Bashir Gemayel meet with Robert Oakley in Washington because they were worried that he would request weapons.[98] However, at least the highest echelon of US officials knew that Israel was providing the Christians with weapons, and even encouraged this. On April 3, a few days after Brown's arrival, Kissinger told Dinitz that he would like them to supply the Christians with arms. This is the first time that the secretary of state is documented as approving this.[99] Over the next month, Israeli officials kept Kissinger informed about the meetings that they were holding with Christian leaders, including representatives of Gemayel and Chamoun, and provided extensive information about the types and quantities of weapons that they were supplying.[100] One account of this period portrays Dean Brown as telling the Christian leaders that the United States wanted them to be "strong" so that they could negotiate, which they eventually understood to mean that they should accept weapons from Israel.[101] From the records of Kissinger's instructions and Brown's conversations, there is no evidence that Brown hinted at this possibility. At this time, US officials did not discuss the US-Israeli understanding with Lebanese Christian leaders. Indeed, several weeks later, Frangie's adviser, Dahdah, commented to Brown that Israelis had told the Maronite middlemen not to inform US officials, though he believed that the United States already knew. Dahdah also maintained that he had told the Syrians personally about the deliveries of weapons from Israel, but was told that "it made no repeat no difference to them."[102] Brown did not confirm or deny it.

During these early meetings, Brown decided that the main issues to be negotiated were a cease-fire, Frangie's resignation from office, and the election of a new president.[103] The Christian leaders' attitude toward Syria appeared to be ambivalent. On one hand, they complained that the United States was holding up a Syrian military intervention. On the other hand, they clearly did not trust their easterly neighbor, repeating their demands for an outside guarantor, other than Syria, for any agreement. Frangie indicated privately that he would be willing to resign if an amendment to the constitution was passed to allow an earlier election.[104] Brown also met with Jumblatt, who outlined his social program, warning that he could again use force if there was no reform.[105] That evening, reflecting on the visits, Brown reported that he thought it was best to hold off a Syrian intervention, since it would take responsibility out of Lebanese hands. Nor was he convinced that the Syrians really had the ability to intervene "quickly and efficiently."[106] The next day, Jumblatt's deputies offered to extend a cease-fire if Frangie resigned and a new president was elected.[107]

After these initial consultations, Brown wrote to the State Department with his ideas. In a first cable, the US envoy proposed to support a constitutional amendment that would allow for Frangie's resignation and a new election, while advocating a plan to constitute a new Lebanese security force, along with a possible US role in the economic reconstruction of Lebanon.[108] However, in a message intended only for Kissinger and his close advisers, Brown painted a more pessimistic picture. The Lebanese, he felt, would be unable to resolve the situation on their own. Barring this, there were only two options for resolving the situation: either the United States could put pressure on Israel to allow the Syrians to intervene, or he could be authorized to talk to the PLO. Brown, who had served as ambassador to Jordan during the 1970 Jordanian Civil War, and had argued for US pressure on the Lebanese government to crack down on the Palestinians in May 1973, noted the irony of this proposition, writing, "You know from my history how I never thought I'd put myself in a position where I would talk to Arafat." In any such approach, he would talk directly with Arafat, rather than other Palestinian leaders. Through intermediaries, the Palestinian leader had said that he would refuse a clandestine meeting, though he would accept that the discussion be limited to the situation in Lebanon only and not touch on broader Middle East issues. If such a meeting took place, Brown wanted to recognize the constructive role that Arafat was playing in Lebanon, while reinforcing his commitment to the idea of reconstituting a security force.[109] Kissinger responded to the first cable, agreeing that Brown should meet the Christians to propose his ideas about security and reconstruction.[110] There is no available record of the response to the second cable, but one assumes that it was negative, since no such meeting took place.

The Christian reaction to Brown's ideas was largely favorable, though the parties seemed divided on key issues. On April 5, Brown met again with Christian leaders Gemayel, Chamoun, and Frangie in Jounieh to put forward his ideas for a joint security force with the Palestinians, Saiqa, and the army, as well as for an international consortium to rebuild the Lebanese economy and security forces. Gemayel was the most supportive, offering to contribute units from the Phalange to the joint security force. Frangie was skeptical about Brown's idea, but he was willing to have Maronite forces committed to the force. In his mind, the primary question was how to get the Syrians to go along with this proposal. Chamoun, after hearing Brown's points, privately confided that he felt that the Syrians were intent on establishing a state in Lebanon that was "100 percent hostile to Israel," but that the "Maronites would never fight the Israelis," since they had "good relations with Israel." He then advocated a confederational state with "one flag . . . but separate rights." Brown told him that his idea was unworkable because it amounted to partition and that the Christians would have to find another way to guarantee their security.[111]

Among Muslim, leftist, and Palestinian groups, Brown's ideas met mixed reactions. Prime Minister Karame seemed positive about Brown's presence in Lebanon, though he wanted a Syrian military intervention to stop the fighting, calling this a "must."[112] Kamal Jumblatt personally appeared optimistic about Brown's mission. In a well-publicized meeting on April 8, Jumblatt reacted positively to Brown's security plan, promising to respond through an intermediary. However, he insisted that he could not accept the idea of Syrian military pressure on Lebanon.[113] The US diplomat had received several reports from friends of Shafiq al-Hut, the head of the PLO office in Beirut, that contrary to its public statements, the PLO was not hostile toward Brown's mission. Al-Hut was reportedly trying to encourage Arafat to stop making anti-US statements such as "We will sink [the] Sixth Fleet in Lebanon."[114] In their cables, Brown and other US diplomats repeatedly argued in favor of talking to Arafat. Echoing Ambassador Godley's message the previous fall, Brown praised the PLO leader's moderation, arguing that discussion of the Lebanese situation "could allay his suspicions of USG intentions here and strengthen his resolve to behave constructively."[115] Kissinger, however, still refused to authorize this. Unsurprisingly, rejectionist Palestinian and leftist parties denounced Brown's mission.[116]

Syrian leaders were wary of Brown's mission, reflecting a deeper mistrust of US policy in the region. Although they were informed about both the US plans to bring about a cease-fire and the possibility of US contacts with the PLO, they did not express an opinion about these ideas immediately.[117] As Ambassador Murphy noted, Asad could not reject US contacts with the PLO, which had long been an Arab demand, but he did not want to strengthen an organization and leadership with whom he was coming into deeper conflict.[118] Through its contacts in Lebanon and the region, the State Department received contradictory signs about the Syrian attitude toward the US idea of a joint force.[119]

While these contacts were taking place, on April 7, the US National Security Council met to discuss Brown's mission. By this time, the differences of views within the administration about Syrian intervention had become clearer. Many, including Robert Oakley and National Security Advisor Brent Scowcroft, had begun to argue that a tacit US acceptance of a Syrian force in Lebanon was necessary to stop the fighting. This in turn would protect broader US interests, including continuing the peace process.[120] Yet, Kissinger argued against tacit acceptance, which he felt could provoke a counter-intervention that would end with Israel in South Lebanon, leaving Syria with a "dominant position in an arc stretching from Lebanon through Jordan," which would "pose a major radical threat, in line with its past tradition." However, if there were a war, Kissinger argued that the United States should "overpower it quickly and use it as the point of departure to solve the whole Middle East problem." Echoing what he had told Dean Brown previously, the secretary of state told the group that the United States might have to contact the Palestinians, though this would not change the US position on the PLO's role in the Middle East negotiations.[121] There is no evidence that any official other than Kissinger opposed a Syrian military intervention to the same degree. The fact that Kissinger was willing to consider contacting the PLO as part of a plan to keep the peace in Lebanon suggests that the secretary of state was deeply committed to preventing a Syrian intervention.

On April 10, without consulting the Ford administration, Syria sent in another group of PLA troops in order to force a meeting of the Lebanese Parliament to pass a constitutional amendment on early elections, and possibly as a show of defiance to the United States. After the deployment, Asad's assistant gave Murphy a response to Dean Brown's proposals: Syria did not believe that a joint force would be "practical," but they would respond to any requests from the new Lebanese president. Asad, he said, had no objection to US contacts with the PLO.[122] The deployment of troops forced Kissinger to scramble to make sure that Israel would not react militarily. In a message sent to Tel Aviv, Kissinger referred to this movement of "700 to 2,000 . . . lightly armed" troops as a "show of force."[123] However, Israel still wanted to send a warning to Syria, and perhaps to the United States as well. In Tel Aviv, Allon told US ambassador Toon that this intervention was "of a different magnitude" than the others, though they "were not at the 'red line.'"[124] On April 13, Kissinger asked Murphy to tell Shihabi or his adviser Adib Daoudi that "[the] Israeli government has informed us today that it considers the Syrian actions had gone right to the line past which Israel would have had to take measures of its own."[125] On April 19, Asad replied through his adviser that Syria rejected the message, which he claimed contained an ultimatum. The situation in Lebanon, he said, was an internal Arab matter. Daoudi added that although he was not under instructions to say so, he felt that US officials should view his message as directed toward Israel, and asked that the United States pass it on to them.[126] There is no indication that the United States did so, but this suggests how sensitive were the Syrians regarding external pressure.

Despite their concern about increased military action, US policymakers supported Syria's efforts to achieve a diplomatic solution. The feud between Syria and Jumblatt continued, but Kissinger felt that Brown should stay out of it, since there were many layers to the dispute that US diplomats did not understand.[127] Clearly frustrated, Brown thought that there were "definite limits" on how long he should remain in Lebanon.[128] There was little he could do to help reconcile the positions of the two sides concerning the internal reforms. After a visit to Jounieh on April 13, Brown thought he had convinced Chamoun that his partition proposals would create nonviable states without any solid industrial or financial base.[129] Frangie seemed surprised by Brown's report of Syria's negative attitude toward the US security proposals, saying that when he had spoken with Asad, the Syrian president had been "much less negative." Frangie told Brown that he intended to propose a consortium in which Syria, other Arab states, and Western countries could fund reconstruction in Lebanon.[130] So as not to undercut the Syrians or the new government, the State Department suggested that, in the future, Brown limit what he told the Lebanese about US discussions in Damascus and instructed him to tell Frangie that the United States did not oppose his plan in principle, but wanted to see what the new government would propose.[131]

Although Brown's initial mediation may have produced few results, some of his ideas ended up being put into place via an unlikely source. Following a breakdown of security on April 14, Arafat proposed his own peace plan that closely mirrored Brown's suggestions, a move that transformed him from protagonist to mediator. In a cable to the State Department, Brown joked that he felt "mugged."[132] Arafat's plan called for the parties to agree on a successor for Frangie, establish a mixed commission for security, and abandon the seventeen-point Baabda Declaration, possibly with increased concessions to Jumblatt.[133] Arafat traveled to Syria, where agreement on the so-called Damascus Accord was announced on April 16. Jumblatt agreed to its terms the next day.[134] Palestinian rejectionists and some leftist leaders condemned the agreement, with George Habbash and George Hawi both calling it a US-Syrian plot.[135] But although the US government certainly approved of the plan, there was no active coordination between the two sides.

As negotiations about the implementation of the Damascus Accord continued, the Christian groups became increasingly nervous about the plan, which gave the Palestinians a role in Lebanese security. Frangie now announced new conditions for his resignation. Brown still felt that the United States should push them toward supporting the agreement, as well as recognizing that the Palestinians were inevitably going to be a part of any agreement.[136] Brown also suggested that US officials be blunter in encouraging Frangie to resign, perhaps via a note from Ford to Frangie about the need for a transition.[137] Though no presidential message was sent, Kissinger agreed that Brown should tell the Christian leaders that the delay was against their interests. He also approved Brown's line on the Palestinians, though he said that it should be "soft-pedaled" as Brown's own personal thoughts.[138] At the same time, Brown asked to be recalled briefly until after the elections, when he would return to Lebanon.[139] Plans were made for Brown to meet Kissinger in London, then to proceed back to Washington to see the president, after which he would return to Lebanon. Before leaving Lebanon on April 23, Brown also met with Jumblatt and Frangie separately. In this meeting, after a significant amount of protest, the Lebanese president finally agreed to sign the constitutional amendment the next day, though he insisted that his resignation would be contingent on the security situation.[140] Frangie indeed signed the amendment on April 24, setting the stage for an election in early May. If Brown really was the one to convince Frangie to sign the agreement, it was probably his greatest contribution to a potential resolution of the Lebanese crisis.

Back in Washington, top US officials continued to discuss the threat of a regional war stemming from Lebanon. During the month of April, the US Navy had moved ships from the Sixth Fleet closer to the country. This sparked a series of exchanges with the Soviet Union, in which US officials claimed (only partially telling the truth) that the movement was to assist in a possible evacuation.[141] Now, US officials began drawing contingency plans for the deployment of peacekeeping troops in various parts of Lebanon and its environs, including between the fighting parties in Beirut, as well as along the Litani River and the old UN line in the Golan Heights, to prevent or stop Syrian-Israeli confrontations. The latter two locations were considered the most likely. One official even suggested that the State Department start discussions with Sadat about the possibility of sending in troops, but Kissinger prevaricated.[142] These plans were never implemented, but the fact that they were even discussed indicates the depth of concern with which the Ford administration viewed the situation in Lebanon.

Thus far, Brown's mission had arguably achieved some significant short-term gains, avoiding another outbreak of fighting and opening a path to a resolution of the conflict through Frangie's resignation and new elections. In London, Brown told Kissinger that the one thing he could have done differently was to see Arafat the first week, though he understood the secretary's problem with this. Kissinger suggested sending Arafat a private message noting that they had noticed his conduct. However, he insisted that there be no cable traffic. Brown offered to carry the message himself and to use Ghassan Tueini as a contact, but Kissinger wanted to send it through the CIA.[143] Back in Washington, a draft message to Arafat was composed. Its content was vanilla and vague, praising Arafat's "constructive role" in the fighting and suggesting that "possibilities for a more formal dialogue could develop without prejudice to any other issues."[144] It is unclear whether this message was ever sent. In any case, the fact that Brown did not meet with Arafat passed up a potential opportunity to split him away from Jumblatt,

FIGURE 7. An undated photo of US envoy L. Dean Brown (bottom, third from left) in Lebanon with members of the Lebanese Arab Army. NARA II, RG 59, Central Photographic Assignment Files, VS 967-77, April/May 1976.

although it would have required a change in US Middle East policy, and the United States would have paid a price in terms of its relationship with Israel. Several years later, Brown suggested that the decision had to do with Kissinger's concern about the US presidential election that fall.[145]

From Election to Intervention

In Lebanon, once Frangie had signed the constitutional amendment, attention was focused on the presidential election. In conversations with Lebanese notables, embassy officials claimed to be neutral regarding candidates, but this was somewhat misleading. There were two main front runners: Elias Sarkis, supported by Syria, and Raymond Edde, supported by the Palestinians and the Left. US officials were disinclined toward Edde, in part because he had frequently made allegations that there was a conspiracy between the US and Syrian leaders concerning Lebanon.[146] For Brown himself, however, this was not the deciding factor. Edde, he thought, "would probably be the better man in normal times," and both candidates were "devoted to a liberal style economy and Western style democracy." However, Sarkis would likely better serve US interests, because he "hold[s] his peace and does not make enemies unnecessarily." Furthermore, a "close, easy[,] discreet cooperation, as could exist between us and Sarkis, would be difficult in the case of Edde."[147] Even if the United States leaned toward Sarkis, however, it is unclear whether they took any measures to support him. Brown felt that the US embassy should stay out of the election campaign, such as it was, unless the political process broke down, in which case he felt it might be considered.[148]

In early May, Brown returned to a relative calm in Lebanon, but violence threatened to break out again. The envoy did not immediately visit Jounieh, to avoid the appearance of collusion with the Christian groups.[149] As increasing violence appeared to prevent the parliament from meeting, Brown decided to reach out to Lebanese leaders.[150] On May 4, Brown met with Karame, though little came out of the meeting.[151] That evening, Brown also had a "long talk" with Jumblatt, telling him that his demands for an "immediate and total withdrawal of Syrians as [a] pre-condition for elections were non-starters."[152] Jumblatt later acknowledged that Brown convinced him to call for a cease-fire on the eve of the presidential election.[153]

The Christian leaders continued to push for a Syrian military intervention. On May 6, the day before the election, in a private meeting with Brown, Frangie insisted that "unless the United States withdrew its objections to Syrian intervention, the only solution was partition." Brown argued against both intervention and partition.[154] In a subsequent meeting, the Christian leaders expressed "general dissatisfaction that [US officials] had no specific plan and were allegedly blocking Syria from providing the security needed for the country's continued existence." After presentations from Chamoun and Gemayel, Father Charbel Qassis, head of the Order of Maronite Monks, noting that he was "speaking in the name of the Church," said that perhaps Lebanon had chosen the wrong friends, since "it was better to be a live Communist than a dead Democrat."[155] During the visit, a Phalangist delegation returned from Damascus, where Asad had told them that he could not send in troops because "he was prevented from doing so by the Americans." Asad had also let the delegation "read transcripts of all recent conversations with [Ambassador] Murphy, including one paper that he identified as an official note from USG."[156]

Sarkis won the election by a comfortable margin, but his victory resolved little. The election took place in a temporary parliament building under shelling from leftist and some rejectionist Palestinian troops.[157] Other Palestinian forces aligned with Arafat supported the elections, helping some Western diplomats reach the meeting place and refusing to shell the parliament building.[158] According to el-Khazen, the Palestinian leader had decided to accept Sarkis's election to avoid further angering Damascus.[159] Soon after the election, Frangie declared that he would not resign because of the security situation, leaving Lebanon with two elected presidents. Just before leaving Beirut, Brown suggested that if Frangie had not resigned by the following week, he begin a campaign to pressure him to resign, but this did not happen.[160] Although its candidate had won the election, Syria remained discontent about the situation. On the evening of the election, around midnight Damascus time, President Asad himself placed a call to the White House, asking to speak with President Ford. Ford was not in the White House, so the call was never put through, and Asad said that he would try again. NSC staffers speculated that the phone call likely related to Lebanon.[161]

By the time Brown left on May 11, US diplomacy on the ground was virtually at a standstill. Newly arrived US ambassador Francis Meloy endorsed Brown's earlier proposal that the United States suggest to Frangie that he resign, perhaps in a parallel initiative with the French.[162] In the meantime, Meloy did not present his credentials to Sarkis, in order to avoid offending Frangie.[163] Sarkis told another US diplomat, Robert Waring, that if the efforts to bring the parties together failed, he might have to invite in foreign troops that "at least in the first instance" meant Syrian, in which case "he would have to call upon the United States for assistance in making this possible."[164] The State Department's response on May 20 underlined that the United States would not be able to "make it possible" for Syrian troops to enter.[165] Even at this late date, the United States was refusing to help facilitate a Syrian intervention.

Some Arab and European countries tried to mediate during this period, but their efforts had little effect. Even prior to the election, the State Department had encouraged the Saudis to mediate in Lebanon.[166] Crown Prince Fahd responded that he planned to consult Arab parties including Egypt, Syria, Jordan, and the Palestinians about the idea. If they agreed, the Saudis would then issue a call to Lebanese factions.[167] Following the election, Fahd offered to mediate after Frangie steps down, urging US diplomats to push him to do so.[168] Frangie did not, and Saudi mediation never took place. Instead, Libya took a central role, as Prime Minister Abd al-Salam Jalud arrived in Lebanon on May 17 to act as a mediator. This, in turn had the effect of causing the Maronites to rally around Frangie, who was increasingly looking to Europe for assistance. In mid-May, Lucien Dahdah took a secret mission to Paris to discuss the situation with French leaders.[169] In fact, the

French thought poorly of Frangie. During a visit to Washington on May 18, French president Valery Giscard d'Estaing called him "a very foolish man who has done harm." But, according to Giscard, the French were considering sending a few thousand troops to intervene. Kissinger suggested that they be sure that their intervention would not simply allow more Syrian troops to be deployed. The French promised to consult with the United States before making any decisions. However, on May 23, Giscard publicly proposed this idea without notifying US officials.[170] US inquiries in Paris seemed to suggest that his suggestion was off-the-cuff and not coordinated with the Middle East department at the Quai d'Orsay.[171] At any rate, the idea was received poorly. European countries, presumably including France, may have also provided new weapons shipments to the Christian factions, increasing their confidence.[172] By then, the tensions were so great that no outside power had enough credibility with all sides to effectively mediate.

The overt Syrian military intervention came during the night of May 31, 1976, but the much-feared Israeli response did not come. Had some party given assurances to the Syrian president that his intervention would not provoke an Israeli counter-intervention? Although US attitudes toward a Syrian intervention were beginning to shift during May, there is no evidence that US diplomats passed on any assurances about this to Asad. Syrian officials remained convinced that the United States remained opposed to a Syrian intervention in Lebanon. On May 16, Asad told visiting Phalange official Karim Pakradouni that the US government was trying to "mess up my plans" (*brouiller mon jeu*) by opposing a Syrian intervention, but he would "mess up theirs."[173] Several months later, Kissinger told US ambassadors to the Middle East that Israel would not have launched a counter-intervention even if the Syrians had gone in with full force in June. However, he continued, the United States had not given Syria a signal about this, in part because they had not received any new signals from Israel.[174] There is little reason to doubt this claim.

A more convincing theory is that King Hussein was the key broker of Israeli assurances to Asad. As we have seen, Hussein had repeatedly advocated for a Syrian military intervention to officials in Washington, as well as directly to the Israeli leadership in October 1975. In April 1976, Hussein secretly visited the Israeli ambassador in London to argue Asad's case for military intervention. According to Evron, this culminated in an Israeli assurance to Syria, via Hussein, that Israel trusted the king and would follow events with an "open mind."[175] Even this, however, is far from consent to intervene, and there are no available records of any further contact between the Israelis and the Jordanians. Syrian foreign minister Khaddam visited Amman

on May 25, which one writer has speculated may have been to request assurances of US and Israeli neutrality.[176] In an interview, however, Khaddam
told this author that Syria did not have any party's permission before entering Lebanon.[177] After the intervention, Kissinger later speculated with British, French, and German foreign ministers about Hussein's role, telling them
that "the Israelis may be in contact with the Syrians through Jordan—but
certainly not through us. I wonder, quite honestly. Because the Israelis did
the exact opposite of what they told us."[178] Whether Kissinger was being
honest, or whether he knew more than he said, is unclear. The Jordanian
possibility thus seems more likely than the US one, but there is no documentary evidence to prove either at this time.

Regardless, the "Red Line Agreement" between Syria and Israel is a myth
that covers up a complex set of interactions. There is no concrete evidence
of a "green light," or even a "yellow" one, from either Israel or the United
States, prior to the Syrian intervention in June 1976. In March 1976, the
Syrians essentially asked the US government for these assurances, both via
the discussions with Khaddam and through Jordan and France. But none was
delivered, meaning that it is incorrect to interpret these communications as
an authorization or endorsement of Syrian intervention. Although Henry
Kissinger realized the potential of a Syrian intervention to weaken the PLO,
he firmly believed that Israel would respond militarily to a Syrian intervention. He also realized that he might not be able to prevent such a clash from
occurring, and thus was ready to try to prevent an Israeli counterreaction to
keep the Lebanese conflict from spreading. The fact that no such clash occurred, however, can at best be partially attributed to the United States.

CHAPTER 8

Taking Its Course

The Syrian Intervention and Its Limits

In the night between May 31 and June 1, 1976, some eight thousand Syrian troops, accompanied by heavy armor, crossed the border into Lebanon in the northern province of 'Akkar and in the Biqa' Valley in the east.[1] Fighters on all sides, not to mention the public, held their breath as they waited to figure out what the Syrians were up to, and how the world would react. The government in Damascus remained silent about its intentions. Syrian radio announced that the troops were being sent on behalf of Christian villages near the border region, but it said nothing about their further plans. Israeli authorities similarly remained silent. Beginning on June 6, two columns of forces began advancing toward Beirut and Sidon, marking the beginning of an overt Syrian military presence in Lebanon that would last until 2006.

Most importantly from the US perspective, the feared Israeli counter-intervention did not occur, signaling the Jewish state's tolerance of Syrian actions. Israel's tacit acceptance meant that the worst fear of the Ford administration, that an international war over Lebanon would destroy the peace process, had passed. However, the events posed a new set of challenges and opportunities for the United States. Arab opposition to the Syrian inter-vention threatened to harm the US relationship with Egypt and, to a lesser extent, with Saudi Arabia. US officials would also have to address a host of other issues, including the assassination of two US officials in Beirut and a subsequent evacuation of US nationals, all of which diminished the US role in Lebanon.

Moreover, the civil war in Lebanon remained directly connected to Arab-Israeli conflict. Although it reduced pressure on the United States to produce forward movement in the Arab-Israeli negotiations, the problem of what to do next remained as salient as it had been since the signing of the Sinai II Agreement. In addition to preserving its relations with Syria, Egypt, and Jordan, the United States had to decide how to treat the PLO, and Palestinian issues more broadly. At this time, the majority of US diplomats involved in Middle East issues recommended that the United States begin a dialogue with the PLO, yet Kissinger remained resistant to the idea, worrying about angering the Israeli government and fearing the domestic fallout during an election year. With Syria beating up Palestinian forces in Lebanon, the secretary's hope was that a weakened PLO might be more amenable to compromise, or perhaps even under the control of the Syrians, by the time negotiations resumed in earnest after the US presidential elections that fall.

For the most part, the Syrian intervention unfolded under its own dynamics, with little US involvement. In at least three ways, however, the United States attempted to influence the course of events in Lebanon to advance its interests there. First, following the assassination of the two US officials, Kissinger authorized limited contacts with PLO representatives in order to help facilitate an evacuation of US officials. Second, over time, Kissinger and the State Department offered mild encouragement for the Syrian military offensive in order to control the violence in Lebanon and to potentially shape the course of the Arab-Israeli conflict. The fact that the Syrian actions infuriated the Soviet Union was also a bonus. Finally, after a ceasefire was reached in October 1976, Kissinger tried to mediate once again between Israel and Syria along the lines of the previous March, now regarding the dispersal of Syrian forces in South Lebanon. These negotiations would have enormous implications for the future of Lebanon, as well as for the political landscape of the Middle East.

Reacting to the Syrian Intervention

For US policymakers, the most important consideration regarding the Syrian intervention remained how it would affect their Middle East negotiating strategy, which seemed frozen. Having been offered little more than a vague promise of another future interim agreement in exchange for their relative silence in the run-up to Sinai II, Syrian leaders were dubious about US willingness or ability to obtain concessions from Israel regarding the issues most important to Syria: the status of the Golan Heights and the fate of the Palestinians. In early 1976, Egypt and Israel approved a general idea of pursuing a round of interim settlements for a minor Israeli withdrawal on all three fronts—Egyptian, Syrian, and Jordanian. As part of this, on May 15, the United States presented Syria a proposal in which Israel would abandon some settlements on the Golan Heights in exchange for an end to the state of belligerency with Israel. According to Kissinger, Syria never responded.[2] In May, Syria agreed to the renewal of the mandate of the UN disengagement force on the Golan Heights separating Israeli and Syrian troops without receiving any major concessions from Israel. The renewal was taken as a sign that Syria wanted to maintain the peace on the Golan while it was occupied with Lebanon. For the moment, Lebanon seemed to have relieved the need to move forward with an Arab-Israeli negotiation.

Still, it remained important to prevent any event that might inhibit the possibility of future movement. As before, after the Syrian intervention, the first US goal was to ensure that Israel did not launch a counter-intervention. During a staff meeting on June 1, after Kissinger heard that Israel had announced that it would not intervene at that time, he responded, "Well then, we have no reason to do anything."[3] Israeli public rhetoric continued to indicate that they would tolerate the intervention. On June 2, Israeli defense minister Shimon Peres made a public statement that the Israeli reaction to a Syrian intervention would depend on (1) which side the Syrians supported, (2) the size of the force, and (3) whether the intervention extended to the south.[4] This was a partial reiteration of the Red Line principles. Unlike in March, however, Israel did not try to transfer a message to the Syrians via the United States, nor were US diplomats instructed to ask Israeli officials for their reaction.

Even if Israeli leaders were content, the Ford administration still had to deal with the broader regional reaction to the Syrian intervention. Only King Hussein of Jordan and the Shah of Iran, two of the most conservative leaders in the region, asked the United States to support Asad.[5] The Jordanians were far from happy, though. On June 1, Prime Minister Rifai took a bitter tone when he told the US deputy chief of mission in Amman that he was glad that the Syrians had made this move, and they should have done so earlier when they were "restrained" by the United States.[6] King Hussein, who was in touch with Asad, told visiting US envoy Dean Brown that "while Syrian intervention had thus far been limited to responding to appeals of besieged villages, he thought it would go further." In the king's view, "only fast and, if necessary, brutal occupation and disarming of combatant[s] could solve [the] Lebanese problem."[7]

The intervention threatened to harm the US relationship with Egypt, whose government suspected that Kissinger supported the Syrian intervention. On June 3, in Cairo, Egyptian foreign minister Fahmy showed the US chargé d'affaires a copy of a *New York Times* article that suggested the US government tacitly supported the Syrian actions. The chargé denied that this was US policy. Fahmy wanted the State Department to request that the French call for a Security Council meeting to bring about a French military deployment to Lebanon, possibly alongside a small Arab security force.[8] That day, France offered the use of French troops as peacekeepers to Khaddam in Paris, but the Syrian foreign minister rejected this offer.[9] Out of concern for the Egyptians' sensitivities, Kissinger instructed the US embassy in Beirut to inform key Lebanese political leaders that the intervention still contained the risk of provoking a counter-intervention from Israel.[10]

Initially, US officials wanted to remain active diplomatically within Lebanon. Though they had no specific plan for mediation, Kissinger and Meloy hoped to find ways of "discreetly pushing Frangie to step down at [an] auspicious moment."[11] Yet the lack of security in Beirut kept Meloy from contacting key Lebanese, particularly Christian leaders, who were mostly located across the Green Line, the heavily fortified battle front separating West and East Beirut. At the time of the Syrian intervention, Meloy had still not yet presented his credentials to either of the Lebanese presidents. US diplomats stayed in contact with Lebanese leaders through the embassy's economic counselor, Robert Waring. This included Sarkis and Jumblatt, both of whom thought Kissinger had given Syria a green light to intervene. As Syrian armor rolled across the border, Jumblatt told Waring that he wanted another country, such as the United States or France, to mediate between the parties, rather than Syria. He now conceded that his opposition to a French security force the previous month had been hasty.[12] In meetings on June 4 and June 5, Sarkis requested to be briefed on Syrian intentions, leaving Waring with the impression that the newly elected president had not known about the Syrian plans in advance.[13]

The Syrian intervention soon encountered both military and political obstacles. On June 6, Syrian troops began to advance along two axes, in the Metn area and farther south toward Sidon. Once in the city, thirteen Syrian tanks were destroyed in clashes with Palestinian forces.[14] Meanwhile, Syrian troops blockaded West Beirut, where PLO forces began to decimate Syrian-controlled Saiqa troops. Asad sent a letter to Arafat threatening to send more troops into Lebanon if he did not cooperate, while Arafat responded that he would ease up on West Beirut if the Syrians would withdraw their forces.[15] In the meantime, outside pressure on Syria increased. Iraq moved troops to the Syrian border, while the Soviet Union delivered warnings to their Syrian allies. On June 8, the Arab League Council adopted a seven-point resolution calling for a cease-fire and a dispatch of a diplomatic commission, as well as a "symbolic Arab security force" to replace the Syrian forces.[16] While this resolution represented a setback for Syria, it did not require them to withdraw their forces immediately.

To avoid giving the impression of inactivity, the United States sought to help with the Arab League effort. On June 10, the State Department instructed the Cairo embassy to ask the Egyptians what it could do. Fahmy asked the US government to urge restraint on Asad.[17] Fahmy boasted of Egyptian efforts to contain Syria, claiming that Sadat was behind Arafat's response to Asad's letter and that Egypt had suggested to Saddam Hussein that Iraq send units to the Syrian border. Fahmy suggested that the State Department (1) tell Frangie that he should resign, (2) calm Christian fears about the idea of an Arab League force, (3) stop inflating Syrian prestige, and (4) warn the Israelis against an intervention that would "set the area on fire," as well as tell them that they should have confidence in the Arab League force, which would be headed by an Egyptian officer.[18] The next day, Sadat told Eilts that Arafat had requested the demarche that Fahmy had made.[19] If Sadat's claim is to be believed, even the Palestinian leader saw the United States as key to obtaining Syrian withdrawal from Lebanon.

In the meantime, Syria wanted approval from the United States to continue their intervention, or at least US assistance in restraining Israel. However, they did not contact the US government directly. The US embassy in Damascus' contacts with high-level Syrian leaders were reduced to a bare trickle for several months.[20] This reflected a variety of factors, including Assad's frustration with the Ford administration's failure to help Syria in Lebanon or the broader Arab-Israeli conflict, as well as, paradoxically, the regime's concern about being seen as too close to the United States. US communications with Jordan were also hampered at this time, as the Jordanian government (bemoaning what it saw as a lack of US support) was considering purchases of Soviet military equipment. In early June, Kissinger was so irritated with King Hussein that he told the embassy in Amman that the United States "will not, for the time being, continue to consult with the Jordanians on Lebanon simply as a gesture of friendship."[21]

Despite the attempt at tough talk, Kissinger found plenty of reasons to continue the dialogue with Jordan over Lebanon. Shortly after the Arab League meeting, Asad sent a message to the United States through King

Hussein. Though the telegram that actually contains this message remains classified in the US archives, several days later, Kissinger acknowledged "the King's comment" that Asad wanted a "green light" from the US government, but that the US "position cannot basically change." The secretary took credit for "encouraging" Israeli restraint, but warned that the risks of an Israeli response would increase if there was "substantial movement" south of the Beirut-Damascus axis or if "sizeable military elements of the radical Arab states" were included in a joint force in Lebanon.[22] A few days later, Hussein gave US officials an even more dire warning. Asad, he said, was concerned about the possibility of a Cuban military intervention in Lebanon.[23] This suggestion, which recalled the recent deployment of Cuban troops in Angola, seems especially designed to raise US fears.

The dialogue with Jordan began to reflect the implications of the conflict for the future of the region. On June 11, Prime Minister Rifai gave Pickering points that he said the United States "should feel free to pass on to [the] Israelis," including that Asad would not move his forces south or deploy additional forces to Lebanon, that radical states such as Libya would not be allowed to "get anywhere" in Lebanon, that Asad intended to "'chew [the PLO] up' to the point they will [no] longer be a real factor for Syria," and that the Syrians wanted only a cease-fire that preserved Lebanon as an independent, stable state. Jordan, Rifai continued, hoped that the United States would do whatever it could to restrain the Israelis. He also seemed concerned about the impact of a regime change in Syria, which would almost certainly be more anti-Jordanian, and possibly even pro-Iraqi.[24] It is likely that Asad intended the Jordanians to pass on this message, which essentially made the argument that Syria's actions in Lebanon were good for Israel, since they would tame the Palestinians and prevent the radicals from taking over. The State Department appears to have passed this message on to Foreign Minister Allon.[25]

The Israeli government, however, refused to believe these messages. Although they were tolerating the Syrian intervention, they opposed a deployment of an Arab League force in Lebanon. On June 14, Dinitz told Kissinger that "if the Syrians folded and gave way to an inter-Arab force, Lebanon would become a radical and leftist-oriented country," which would be the "worst contingency."[26] This may have reflected in part Lebanese Christian opposition to an Arab League force. The State Department passed on Israeli concerns to their Arab friends, telling the Egyptians about the Israeli reaction and the Saudis about the Lebanese Christian one. However, both Egyptian and Saudi leaders dismissed US concerns.[27] The Ford administration made an effort to convince the Israelis that the Syrian-Jordanian messages should be taken seriously. In Washington, Kissinger told an Israeli official that one of Asad's goals in Lebanon may have been "to remove the incubus of the PLO from his negotiating flexibility and get Jordan back in a West Bank negotiation—a Jordan more under Syrian influence."[28] But the Israeli government seemed to have an unrealistic sense of what was possible. On June 17, Israeli ambassador Dinitz gave Kissinger a suggestion from Rabin that the Ford administration "see Syria's isolation [from other Arab countries] as an opportunity (1) to crush the PLO as both a political and military force, and (2) to fashion a coalition of Syria, Egypt, and Saudi Arabia." Kissinger agreed that this would be a good outcome and said that he had told this to a cabinet meeting that morning.[29] In fact, the secretary had told the cabinet that this was unlikely to occur.[30] Syria's intervention, he thought, was only designed to tame the PLO or, at most, put them under Syrian authority, and would not result in a complete realignment such as Dinitz suggested. Still, even if they disagreed over long-term strategy, Kissinger and Israeli leaders agreed that the Syrian military intervention against the PLO had thus far served their interests.

Indeed, there were already signs that Syrian-Palestinian reconciliation was possible. As the Syrian-Christian offensive continued, Arafat began to look for ways to end the conflict. On June 22, he sent three of his advisers,

FIGURE 8.   President Gerald R. Ford and Secretary of State Henry Kissinger join the Meloy and Waring families for the arrival ceremony of the remains of Ambassador to Lebanon Francis E. Meloy Jr. and Economic Counselor Robert O. Waring, who were assassinated by terrorists in Beirut on June 16. Also present are L. Dean Brown, special emissary to Lebanon, and Secretary of the Senate Francis Valeo. Courtesy of the Ford Library.

including Mahmud Abbas, to Damascus to meet Asad, apparently striking a tentative deal for a cease-fire. That same day, Chamoun's NLP launched a siege of the Palestinian refugee camps of Jisr al-Basha and Tal al-Zaatar in East Beirut, while the next day, the main electrical cable to Beirut was cut. Both of these actions had a large psychological effect on the capital.[31] Following the siege, Arafat and other PLO officials broke off the negotiations, though it is unclear whether this was because they were displeased with concessions by Palestinian representatives in Damascus, shocked by the events in Beirut, or simply hoped to get better terms from the Syrians.[32] On June 29, an agreement between Syrian and PLO representatives halted the Syrian offensive, though not the siege of Tal al-Zaatar. Soon thereafter, in early July, thirteen hundred Saudi and Sudanese troops arrived in Lebanon to join the Arab League force, but even this failed to stop the violence.[33]

Assassinations and Evacuations

While the State Department was working to keep the fighting from spreading, the assassination of two US diplomats in Lebanon crippled what little US influence remained in that country. In mid-June, Kissinger urged US ambassador Francis Meloy to present his credentials to Sarkis as soon as possible, since his lack of accreditation was limiting the US ability to contact the parties there.[34] On June 16, while crossing the Green Line to meet with Sarkis, a leftist group kidnapped Meloy, his economic counselor Robert Waring, and their driver. The two officers were killed, and their bodies were dumped in an abandoned lot. In his memoirs, Kissinger stated that he felt personally responsible for the death of the US diplomats. Although he had ordered the ambassador to get more active, Kissinger alone cannot be blamed for the incident. Meloy himself apparently refused a military escort on the trip.[35]

Most accounts suggest that the murder was committed by a Lebanese faction affiliated with the PFLP. According to Abu Iyad, the killers were from a previously unknown group, the Arab Socialist Action Party, funded by Iraq, which hoped to spark a US invasion of Lebanon that would produce a Vietnam-like situation in the country. Yezid Sayigh called the group the PFLP's "sister" Lebanese party.[36] At a meeting with Kissinger on June 18, the Israeli ambassador provided what he called "admittedly sketchy" information that the "so-called Arab Socialist Labor Party" was behind the killing. He called this group a Lebanese leftist pro-Iraqi faction connected with the PFLP. Kissinger noted that this was similar to information that the United States had.[37] Since the Arabic words for "action" and "labor" are the same (*amal*), this supports Abou Iyad's account. Jumblatt later told US officials that to the best of his knowledge, Wadi Haddad, a Palestinian leader who headed an offshoot group of the PFLP, had ordered the killings.[38] In 1983, eight men were arrested in connection with the murders.[39]

The investigation of the murders posed a challenge for US officials, since there was no way that they could collect information without the cooperation of the PLO, which they could not directly contact. The State Department therefore instructed its diplomats to ask Saudi, Egyptian, and Lebanese officials to urge the Palestinians to give the US government information. These officials promised to do their best, though some suggested that they would be better off just contacting PLO officials directly, rather than via their security officers. Talcott Seelye, who had been sent to Lebanon as an interim ambassador, agreed that this would be useful. However, he requested authorization before doing so to be sure that these fell under the rubric of "security matters."[40] No answer came at first from Washington. In a security meeting on July 12, PLO security officials told their US counterparts that the organization wanted to exchange information about the murders, telling them that two groups had been arrested: one responsible for the kidnapping, the other for the assassinations.[41] That same day, Kissinger indicated that he would prefer "for the time being" to keep contacts in the Egyptian and Saudi channels, rather than discussing it directly.[42] To a certain extent, Kissinger prioritized minimizing contacts with Palestinians over the chance of finding out information regarding the murder of the US diplomats.

After the murders of Meloy and Waring, the US embassy conducted an evacuation of US diplomats and nationals on June 20. Initially, the embassy hoped to transport these individuals via a convoy from Beirut to Damascus, a complicated mission that involved crossing the Green Line into East Beirut, as well as numerous checkpoints in the mountains. To arrange this, the State Department communicated with the PLO via British, French, Tunisian, and Egyptian diplomats, as well as through low-level contacts through the embassy's security officer. The day before the evacuation, however, the State Department judged it too dangerous to travel along this route and decided to send in the US Navy ship USS *Spiegel Grove* to evacuate them through the Bain Militaire in Beirut.[43] In recognition of their assistance, Ford praised the Palestinians publicly, while the State Department sent messages of thanks via several diplomatic channels, including via Egypt.[44] The Egyptian ambassador to Lebanon passed this message to PLO Executive Committee member Abu Lutf, who responded that the Palestinians were only doing their duty.[45] In the meantime, from Beirut, Seelye again urged Washington to allow the US embassy to build closer ties with the Palestinians, such as creating a "direct consular contact" with the PLO, like the British had done.[46] Washington again refused. Seelye then recommended that the embassy be taken down altogether and all US citizens evacuated.[47] The State Department did not do so, but the embassy conducted a second evacuation on July 27. Prior to the second evacuation, a US representative held meetings directly with PLO director of political affairs Abu Jaafar.[48]

The assassinations largely put an end to US efforts to bring about a political solution in Lebanon through direct contacts with actors on the ground. US embassy officers specifically told their contacts that Ambassador Seelye intended to maintain a lower profile than Brown.[49] Still, Kissinger hoped that Seelye would be "less active than Brown and more active than Meloy."[50] To avoid having to regularly travel across the Green Line, Seelye wanted to station an officer on the Christian side, but this never happened.[51] The State Department also refused to grant permission to visit the Maronite area, due to safety concerns and a desire to avoid the impression that the United States was cooperating with Syria and the Maronites.[52] This meant that there was no direct contact between the US embassy, located in the western part of the city, and East Beirut for the rest of the summer. By the end of July, only thirteen staff members remained in the embassy, and they did not have contact with most factions.[53] Seelye tried to make the argument that for his own security, he be authorized to contact the PLO during his time there. However, Kissinger agreed only to allow a US security officer to contact his counterpart in the PLO—no political contacts were authorized.[54]

Over the next few months, the Syrian and Christian forces sought to eliminate pockets of resistance within the territory that they held, particularly Tal al-Zaatar and Jisr al-Basha, two neighboring refugee camps in East Beirut.[55] Not all of the Christian forces agreed with this. Colonel Fouad Lahoud, a leading NLP member, even criticized the plan, telling US embassy officers that Chamoun and Kataib leaders were "playing general," ignoring the likelihood of retaliation elsewhere and attempting to further their goal of partition by creating a Christian enclave.[56] Throughout the siege, a popular rumor presented the action as a US response to the assassination of their ambassador.[57] In fact, the United States made diplomatic representations to Syria and the Christian parties about the fate of the individuals within the Palestinian camps. On July 1, the State Department cabled Murphy in Damascus, asking him to pass word to the Syrians that the attacks on the camps ruled out political progress, threatened "a spiral of atrocities and counter-atrocities," and "would appear to be related to the goal of partition."[58] Daoudi promised to seek Asad's assessment, making a personal comment that "he was very pessimistic about [the] prospects of an early peace in

Lebanon."[59] But this was not a priority for Kissinger. After hearing that a message to the Christians had not yet been delivered, he suggested holding up the message to the Syrians, lamenting, "I don't see what we are gaining" by talking to the Syrians about Tal al-Zaatar and worrying that the Syrians would see this as intervention.[60]

There is no record of a Syrian response to the US demarche. In early July, the smaller Jisr al-Basha camp fell, followed by Tal al-Zaatar in August. The fall of each camp was accompanied by massacres, despite efforts to allow the evacuation of the wounded. At least fifteen hundred civilians were killed indiscriminately on the final day of the siege of Tal al-Zaatar, while observers from the Syrian army looked on, making it one of the greatest tragedies of the entire war.[61]

The New US-Syrian Dialogue

Though the US embassy in Beirut was cut off from events on the ground, US officials outside the country still remained active in the diplomatic sphere, particularly regarding the Syrian role in Lebanon. In late summer, two factors prompted a new dialogue between the United States and Syria: increasing Soviet opposition to the Syrian intervention and concern about the future of the peace process. US officials had not anticipated the possibility of a conflict between the Soviets and the Syrians over Lebanon. Unbeknownst to US officials, Syria did not give the Soviet Union any advance notice of their intention to invade.[62] Just two days after the Syrian military intervention, the chairman of the Soviet Council of Ministers, Alexei Kosygin, visited Damascus. The contents of the discussions during this trip remain unknown, and a relatively bland statement was issued by the parties on June 4.[63] However, on June 9, as the Syrians pushed toward Beirut, the Soviet Union publicly condemned all "foreign intervention" in the conflict.[64] Taking this as at least partially aimed at the United States, US policymakers exchanged oral messages with the Soviets, but their tone remained muted by Cold War standards.[65]

By mid-July, the Syrian-Soviet confrontation had worsened, prompting Asad to reach out to the United States and the conservative countries in the Middle East for support. On July 17, King Hussein told Ambassador Pickering that Asad had asked him to get in touch with Iranian, Saudi, and US leaders to ask for help against the Soviets. Pickering asked whether the Soviets had threatened to stop arms and economic aid to Syria. Hussein responded that he thought "such a step was implied not specifically threatened." The king hoped that there would be a discreet way to get Asad's views to the Israe-lis.[66] Considering that the United States had previously considered Syria one of the closest Soviet allies in the region, these efforts seemed like a complete turnaround. The State Department responded to Hussein that it had no information about this but was interested in maintaining Syria's ability to have "an independent national policy."[67] Hussein called Asad right away and conveyed the message. The Syrian leader was appreciative.[68]

For the United States, the Soviet role initially seemed more of a threat than an opportunity. On July 19, Kissinger told President Ford he felt that "the Soviets may be going for broke," since they might see themselves as closed out of the Middle East if the PLO was destroyed. Kissinger suggested moving the US Sixth Fleet to within twenty-four hours travel time from Lebanon, as a warning, and asked for permission to recall Ambassador Mur-phy to Washington for consultations about the situation. He would also talk to Dinitz about the Israeli reaction. Ford readily agreed to all of these sug-gestions.[69] Soon, the split between the Soviets and the Syrians spilled out in the open once again. On July 20, *Le Monde* published a letter allegedly writ-ten by Brezhnev, exhorting Asad to stop operations "against the resistance and the Lebanese national movement." The letter appeared to be so blunt that many, including Murphy, initially doubted its authenticity.[70] That same day, Asad delivered a lengthy speech at Damascus University that outlined Syria's policy toward Lebanon, even praising Brown's mission.[71]

In the meantime, the Ford administration grew concerned about a pos-sibility of military supply, either directly from the Soviet Union or via one of the Arab states, to the Palestinians and leftists, who had constructed sev-eral large airfields in the south of Lebanon to receive supplies. Throughout the summer, Syrian, Jordanian, and other officials repeatedly emphasized their concerns about these airfields to the United States, one of which was alleg-edly two kilometers long and capable of handling large military transport planes, including Soviet Antonov cargo aircraft.[72] While it seems unlikely that the Soviet Union itself would have delivered weapons directly to the Palestinians, other countries such as Iraq or even Egypt could have done so on their behalf.

At that point, US officials saw a chance to undermine the Soviet position in the region by providing intelligence to Syria about flows of Soviet and other weapons into Lebanon. In his memoirs, Kissinger implies that this was a US idea.[73] In fact, Syrian officials specifically requested this from the United States. On July 20, in response to questions from the State Department, Syr-ian officials affirmed that the Soviets were pressuring them.[74] Before return-ing to Washington, Murphy met with Khaddam, who confirmed that the text of the *Le Monde* article was authentic. Khaddam also confirmed that there had been an attack on a Lebanese gunboat looking into Soviet arms deliveries in Tripoli. When asked for evidence of Soviet activities, the Syrian vice president said simply that he assumed the United States had more information than Syria did and asked for intelligence reports.[75] King Hussein later passed on a Syrian request for intelligence about a Soviet ship unloading weapons in Sidon.[76] In response to these requests, Kissinger authorized Murphy to give Asad information concerning Soviet arms shipments to the PLO via other Arab states such as Libya, with the exception of information concerning Egypt, a US ally.[77] Murphy finally met with Khaddam on August 3 to do so. During the presentation, Khaddam praised the US information as "extremely precise."[78]

Although the US cooperation with Syria was directed against the Soviets, the United States had to proceed cautiously to avoid alienating other Arab and regional governments. As Kissinger's instructions about intelligence sharing had shown, the secretary wanted to preserve US relations with Egyptian leaders, who remained livid about Syrian policy in Lebanon. The State Department therefore sent word to Sadat of the Jordanian approach regarding Syria's predicament, noting that the United States was helping Syria maintain "an independent national policy free of Soviet pressure."[79] It instructed the US embassies in Saudi Arabia and Iran to tell their countries' leaders that any support they could give to Syria would be helpful.[80] The State Department also sent a message to Israeli leaders about the Soviet-Syrian split, seeking to justify their increasing support for the Syrian intervention.[81] The Israelis responded that Asad might be exaggerating the Soviet threat, believing that the Soviets had learned from their previous experiences with Egypt about "heavy-handed diplomacy" (a clear reference to the Egyptian expulsion of Soviet combat troops in 1972) and would not punish Syria. The Syrian leader, they thought, might be "preparing the ground" for an invasion of South Lebanon.[82] None of these parties were informed about the US provision of intelligence information to Syria.

At the end of July, the situation in Lebanon seemed to be heating up. In part due to new Syrian military pressure, the PLO signed a second agreement with Syria in Damascus on July 29.[83] The threat of fighting remained, however, and a new risk of a conflict between the Arab states seemed to be present. According to Jordanian officials, Sadat had sent a confidant, Ashraf Marwan, to three states in the Gulf "seeking opinions on the possibility of and reactions to open Egyptian intervention" in Lebanon. Saudi Arabia rejected this, sending a message via their intelligence director Kamal Adham in response to Marwan.[84] US officials also suspected that Eastern Bloc intervention was possible. In a July 31 meeting with Ford and Murphy, Kissinger discussed Israeli reports that East Europeans may be introduced into Lebanon, in which case the administration "would have to do something—or else unleash the Israelis." Kissinger suggested that "if there is a Congressional investigation [into Lebanon], we are in trouble. We will just have to say it was self-defense."[85]

In June, the fighting in Lebanon and the lack of movement in Arab-Israeli negotiations prompted a new debate within the State Department over the future of US policy toward the Arab-Israeli conflict, particularly the Palestinian issue. There had long been advocates of engagement with the PLO in the State Department, though their advocacy was limited. For instance, no US policymaker disagreed with the premise that the Syrian intervention, the weakening of the PLO, and the possibility of its subjugation to Syrian control benefited US policy in the Middle East, at least in the short term. However, they had different ideas about whether, alongside these developments, US diplomats should talk to the Palestinians. In a June 22 meeting in Paris, Kissinger disagreed with his Middle East ambassadors on whether the State Department should begin discussions with the PLO.[86] The secretary of state pleaded that "solely domestic" reasons were enough not to talk to them, since "no Arab can keep his mouth shut." Once word of the talks leaked, "the Israelis will beat us all over the head. It's after all, only four months" until the US presidential election.[87] Following the meeting, US ambassadors to the Middle East disputed openly over cable traffic whether or not the United States should use negotiations with the Palestinians over Lebanon as a pivot to begin taking a US position in favor of a separate Palestinian state in the West Bank.[88] These exchanges were no doubt exasperating to the secretary of state, who, for seven and a half years, had argued consistently against measures that would benefit the Palestinians at the expense of Israel.

These issues came to a head in August, when Kissinger traveled to Iran for a visit. On August 7, Kissinger met with most of the Middle East ambassadors at the US embassy in Tehran. He later wrote that he "knew there was some restiveness in the ranks about my attitude toward the PLO." He first met with Talcott Seelye, who he referred to as "the principal advocate of the PLO-first strategy in the State Department," telling him that he thought that negotiating with the PLO would cost the United States "all our leverage over them."[89] At the subsequent meeting with the other ambassadors, Kissinger maintained, "If at some stage we wanted to move for a Sinai III for Egypt, Sadat would not be able to do it if he had to contend with the PLO. We are not considering that idea for now but it could happen."[90] Thus, Kissinger wanted to keep his options open. At the meeting, the group agreed on a set of talking points to deliver to Middle Eastern leaders about US strategy. These talking points remain classified, but they included a point about eventually bringing the PLO into the dialogue on the Middle East.[91] Although Kissinger opposed US contacts with the PLO, he also wanted to maintain a maximum degree of flexibility for the future evolution of US mediation.

In advance of this meeting, Kissinger sent a set of talking points to Damascus, as well as a personal message for Asad, inviting him to consult with the US government if he felt that his policy was threatened by the Soviet Union. Murphy met privately with Asad, who was vacationing in the Latakia area. According to Kissinger's memoirs, the Syrian leader answered in broad philosophical terms, warning about the threat of "total revolution" in the Arab world, probably referring to the PLO, leftists, and the Soviet Union. The United States, Saudi Arabia, and the Gulf states, among others, had "had a vital stake in insuring that elements dedicated to revolution did not succeed."[92] Kissinger's message also urged Asad to continue his offensive in Lebanon. Murphy reported that Asad had "smiled broadly" as he read the secretary's message that "there is no reward for losing in moderation and no substitute in some situation[s] for a military victory."[93] Over the next few months, Asad appears to have taken Kissinger's hint that Syria should seek a military victory, though another Syrian offensive would not be launched until September. It was also during this conversation that Asad, for the first time, personally confirmed that Hussein had been accurately transmitting messages from him.[94]

In the meantime, Israel continued to supply the Christian forces with weapons and appears to have even sunk a ship attempting to resupply the Palestinian and leftist forces. Israeli officials continued to argue for the effective partition of Lebanon. In a meeting with Ambassador Toon on August 13, Allon pushed the case for "the need for cantonalization" in Lebanon. Toon reiterated US opposition to this, saying that the State Department might soon try to get back in touch with the Christians, but this did not represent a change in their policy. Toon then said that "speaking personally" he "hoped that none of the arms which were being supplied to the Christians were of U.S. origins," to which Allon responded that they were "sending all sorts of weapons from a number of different sources but none of it is of U.S. origin." Publicly, "Israel will continue to deny that it is supplying weapons," being "very much aware of Washington's sensitivities."[95] Soon thereafter, the Soviets protested to the State Department that Israel was directly intervening in Lebanon, complaining about the sinking of supply ships and the veritable blockade and saying that it was difficult to imagine that this was done without the approval of Washington.[96] Kissinger responded that Israel had told them that it was only taking "precautionary measures" to protect their coast from infiltration and terrorism.[97]

In mid-August, the State Department decided to send a diplomatic mission to Jounieh, the Christian enclave north of Beirut, to meet with the Christians, their first attempt to do so since the Meloy/Waring assassination. Led by former deputy chief of mission Bob Houghton and State Department officer David Mack, this initiative aimed to get a sense of the Christian forces' goals and their views of the future.[98] The trip was widely seen as an expression of US concern about moves toward partition.[99] The two first traveled to Cyprus, from where they embarked by ship to Jounieh. Frangie, who had still not officially resigned, seemed upset by the US distance from the problems in Lebanon. He decried the fact that Meloy had intended to see Sarkis before him. Former ambassador Buffum, he claimed, had promised that the United States "would empty its military stores in the case of aggression."[100] The Christian leaders now hoped to eliminate Palestinian political influence in Lebanon through the application of the Cairo Agreement on terms favorable to them. Frangie himself advocated the departure of all Palestinians that arrived in Lebanon after 1969.[101] After a trip back to Nicosia for consultations, Houghton and Mack returned to Jounieh with instructions to inform the Christian leaders that the US government supported a negotiated solution but would not provide weapons to them or establish a separate presence in Jounieh, which they felt would give the impression of supporting partition.[102] The Christian leaders received this news with mixed emotions. Frangie maintained that they did not expect military support at that time, but Chamoun pleaded for weapons so that they could achieve a military victory.[103] The envoys, of course, had no power to make such a promise, and there is no sign that this was seriously considered back in Washington.

The Second Syrian Military Offensive and the End of the Conflict

From August until October, the fighting in Lebanon continued under the influence of local and regional dynamics, with little interference from the United States. The upcoming end of Frangie's term in office on September 23 provided an opportunity for the parties in Lebanon to reach a political agreement. However, Christian forces insisted that the Palestinians abandon their positions in the Upper Metn as part of any peace deal. In spite of numerous meetings between the sides, no solution was reached. The Syrians supported the Christian demands for a Palestinian retreat before any discussions of a peace settlement took place.[104] Following the failure of the negotiations, Syria publicly accused Sadat of undermining the talks.[105] Two days after a September 26 attack by Palestinian terrorist Abu Nidal on the Semiramis Hotel in Damascus, the Syrians launched a second military offensive in Lebanon over Sarkis's objections, aimed at dislodging the Palestinians and leftists in the Metn area.[106] Following this, the PLO presented a draft working paper that proposed talks followed by an "orderly PLO withdraw[a]l" from the Metn, followed by implementation of the Cairo Agreement. This was initially ratified at a meeting at Chtaura. However, following the meeting, the Syrians requested a two-day break, and in the meantime decided that they could implement their demands by force. Terrorist attacks by Abu Nidal in Rome and Islamabad on October 11 also provided excuses to launch offensives, which ended in a cease-fire under Arab pressure on October 14 and 15.[107]

Syrian-US cooperation continued throughout this period, but it soon became apparent that the US government could offer only limited assistance. Hussein told Pickering that on August 20, Asad had told him that he had received a second letter from the Soviets about Syrian actions in Lebanon. Although the Syrians had not indicated that the Soviets had cut off military supplies, they were "making serious threats . . . which migh[t] possibly include such a step."[108] Soon, the dispute again became public.[109] On September 11, the Soviet Union requested that Syria withdraw its troops from Lebanon.[110] Murphy was instructed to see Asad to share US impressions from Houghton/Mack trip and to ask for Syrian suggestions for a public statement around the time of Sarkis's inauguration, or other measures.[111] Asad noted that Syria did "not intend to occupy Beirut and we have no plans for a military victory"—despite Kissinger's earlier hints that this might be desirable. In response to the US offer of diplomatic assistance, Asad stated that he would have to think about it.[112] On September 17, Khaddam passed on Asad's message that a US statement should express "support for Lebanese territorial integrity and cohesion," "opposition to partition," and an appeal to strengthen Sarkis as "the legitimate leader of Lebanon." Khaddam also asked US officials to request that the Gulf states renew their financial assistance to Syria, indicating that "material pressure" from the Soviets had increased.[113] On September 21, Murphy told Khaddam that his suggestions would be included in the US public statement on Lebanon, while the United States would address the cutoff of aid for Syria with appropriate ministers in the upcoming UN General Assembly.[114] Khaddam was "very pleased" and agreed that this issue must be held "in close[s]t confidence."[115] However, US initiatives had little impact on the Gulf states, disappointing the Syrians. In early October, Hussein passed word to Pickering that Asad doubted the value of US support and suspected that the US was secretly encouraging the Egyptians to attack the Syrians publicly.[116]

Still, Asad conveyed one final request to the United States via Jordan for support against the Soviets. On October 12, King Hussein passed on a message from Asad to Kissinger and Ford, arguing that Syria was being pushed around by the Soviet Union the way that Egypt once had been. Four days earlier, Khaddam had visited King Hussein to say that the Soviets had cut off spare parts, supplies, and new weapons; cancelled repair and maintenance arrangements of important military equipment; and removed some military advisers. In the meantime, next door in Iraq, terrorists such as Carlos the Jackal, the Baader-Meinhof Group, Wadi Haddad of the PFLP, and others were conspiring to cause trouble for Syria. Asad wanted help, and the king suggested that the State Department ask Saudi Arabia and Iran to assist Syria, as well as provide US economic assistance. Ambassador Pickering interpreted this to mean that the Syrian government seemed ready to alter its position in regional affairs as Sadat had from 1973 to 1975.[117]

A few days later, now ex-prime minister Rifai told Pickering that Asad was disappointed with the United States, since America's allies, Egypt and Saudi Arabia, still opposed his actions in Lebanon. The United States, Rifai maintained, did not understand that "if Syria withdrew in Lebanon [sic] tomorrow it could have 3,000 tanks and another 1,000 aircraft from the Soviet Union." Asad, he said, wanted confirmation that he could rely on the United States and follow in Sadat's path.[118] In Damascus, Murphy thought that Hussein's message sounded "more alarmist" than messages that he had gotten in Damascus and noted there was at least some evidence that a Syrian-Soviet military relationship continued. Still, he recommended that the US government take some steps to show support for Syrian policy in Lebanon, such as authorizing him to discuss with the Syrians the provision of food aid for refugees and the needy in Lebanon.[119]

On October 17, the State Department responded to Hussein that it was considering ways of providing "tangible support" to Syria but had not received any communication directly from the Syrians. Pickering was instructed not to mention the possibility of military aid if Hussein did not bring it up.[120] When the ambassador delivered the message, Hussein did not give a comment, but he seemed "visibly concerned" that Asad had not contacted the US government.[121] There is no evidence that Asad tried to send Kissinger another such message, either directly or via Hussein, nor did the State De-

partment make the offer of direct food assistance to Asad. Thus, an opportunity may well have been missed to deepen the cooperation with the Syrian
regime.

By this point, negotiations for an end to the conflict had once again
resumed. From October 16 to October 21, six Arab leaders met at a mini-
summit in Riyadh, where a Syrian-Egyptian reconciliation over Lebanon
finally took place under Saudi auspices. Prior to the conference, Sadat
hoped to reduce Syrian influence in Lebanon by replacing the Syrian forces
with an Arab League force under the command of an Arab League general.
Asad, by contrast, wanted to obtain retroactive Arab approval for Syrian actions, as well as aid for the reconstruction of the country, without ceding
military control over the forces in Lebanon. King Hussein, who did not
attend the conference but received regular updates, told Pickering that the
Saudis and Kuwaitis were ready to exert "heavy financial pressure" on Asad to
come to terms with the Egyptian position on Lebanon, which he thought
might undo "everything which Syria has tried to accomplish up until now."[122]
Arafat and Sarkis were invited to the conference, but Jumblatt and the Christian leaders were not, leaving some afraid that Maronite parties would be left
out. To prevent the interests of the Christian forces from being ignored,
which would leave them completely dependent on Israel, Hussein decided to
provide them with four hundred tons of weapons and ammunition from Jordanian stocks.[123]

One key to Syria's strategy was the new Lebanese president, Elias Sarkis,
who did not have his own military force and would be reliant on Syrian
forces for support. At the mini-summit, Sarkis proposed four measures: a ces-
sation of hostilities, the PLO's respect for the Cairo Agreement and Lebanese sovereignty, the deployment of an inter-Arab force, and Arab financial
aid for reconstruction. Of these, the notion of a common Arab force was
the most controversial. Sarkis, supported by Syria, asked for it to be under
his authority, while Sadat wanted it to be under the Arab League. Thanks to
mediation by Crown Prince Fahd of Saudi Arabia, Sadat ended up supporting the idea of an Arab force under the command of Sarkis, thereby recon-
ciling his differences over Lebanon with Asad.[124] The Syrian leader knew
that other Arab states would not be willing to provide more than token numbers of troops, thus making Syria's own forces the largest component of any
joint force, even as they enjoyed the Arab stamp of legitimacy. The Riyadh
Agreement produced a cease-fire in Lebanon on October 21, allegedly the
fifty-seventh since the fighting began in April 1975.[125] In Cairo a few days
later, an Arab League summit officially created the Arab Deterrent Force
(ADF). US diplomats expressed their support for these agreements to the

Arab states, while urging them to "allay Christian anxiety that their legitimate concerns will not be respected."[126]

Soon thereafter, US chargé George Lane visited East Beirut from November 5 to November 9 to meet with the Christian leaders. Lane brought a message of reconciliation: he was to express sympathy for the Christian leaders' concerns, to note that the United States did "not want to see the Christians absorbed into Moslem society or dominated by it," and to tell them that the US government had "encouraged outside support for the Christians in order to prevent this."[127] This language conveyed more open support than the State Department had previously given to the Christian leaders, in part because its leaders no longer felt the need to pressure them to compromise. President Sarkis told Lane that the United States could best help him by encouraging Arab states to continue their cooperation.[128] Chamoun welcomed the US message, stating that he had not previously heard such a strong statement of support from the United States. The former Lebanese president then stressed his support for Israel, saying that "the existence of Israel is essential for the safety of Lebanon; I insist on this point." He also insisted that the bulk of the Palestinians must leave Lebanon. Asking rhetorically what the US government would have done with such a large "foreign refugee population" on its own territory, he answered his own question: "You would have killed more of them than we have and you would have been right."[129] Gemayel seemed to take a more moderate position, but he also wanted to see the departure of the Palestinians.[130] Maronite clergymen asked whether the United States would provide guarantees for the withdrawal of the ADF, by which they meant the Syrian army, and for the continued existence of the Christian community in Lebanon. Father Qassis wondered whether UN troops could be stationed along Lebanon's southern border.[131] Neither an outside guarantee nor the possibility of deploying UN troops was seriously considered by the US government at the time, but Lebanon's south did concern US policymakers, who were already shifting their attention in that direction.

Red Line Redux?

Although the Riyadh and Cairo conferences marked an end to the fighting, the future problems of Lebanon were already beginning to manifest themselves, especially in the south of the country. During the conflict, many of the fedayeen in South Lebanon had left to fight elsewhere, either against the Christian militias or the Syrian army. Now that the fighting had ended, the

Palestinian groups began to move forces back to the south, where they would be in a position to threaten Israel, which could in turn cause Israeli retaliations that would begin the civil strife anew in Lebanon. Once again, Lebanese internal stability and broader regional peace seemed to depend on South Lebanon. The two Arab summits had nominally reaffirmed the validity of the Cairo Agreement, which sanctioned the presence of fedayeen in the Arqub region, but they had also demanded that all militias surrender their heavy weapons. The implementation of this was left to the Quadripartite Committee of Syria, Egypt, Saudi Arabia, and Kuwait, as well as the ADF, which would have to actually collect the weapons.[132] However, Israel refused to allow Syria, whose troops constituted the bulk of the ADF, to deploy to the south of Lebanon, fearing the presence of Syrian troops along their northern border.[133] Without troops in South Lebanon, the ADF would be unable to confirm that the Palestinians had surrendered their weapons. In turn, the Lebanese Christian forces could claim that their opponents were not complying with the agreement, providing an excuse for them not to disarm. As in March, the United States attempted to help Israel and Syria communicate, but this time Kissinger pushed Israel, albeit unsuccessfully, to adjust its demands in regard to the most important of the "red lines": the southern limit on the deployment of Syrian troops.

Israel had its own ideas for the future of South Lebanon. In the summer of 1976, the Israeli government had begun what it called its "Good Neighbor" or "Good Fence" policy, which opened up its border to certain Christian villages for trade, humanitarian relief, and military assistance. The State Department had been aware of these developments, and while it did not support them, Kissinger had not strenuously protested. For instance, in a conversation in July, an Israeli official in Washington told Kissinger and Atherton that he thought that these activities would help Israel's international image. The secretary of state countered that he thought it was a "grandstand play" that was "helpful for your domestic propaganda," but he did not suggest that the Israelis discontinue their policy.[134] In 1975 and 1976, a few Palestinian attacks into Israel and reprisal raids occurred, but the Palestinians were primarily preoccupied with the fighting in Lebanon itself. By that fall, Israel was pursuing a strategy of creating a "security belt" of Christian villages along its border with Lebanon, working closely with Major Saad Haddad, a Lebanese Greek Orthodox Christian who had rebelled from the army to align himself with the Jewish state against the Palestinian militias. Haddad would later turn the forces under his command into the South Lebanon Army (SLA), which cooperated with Israel against the Palestinian and leftist militias.[135]

Soon after the signature of the Riyadh Agreement, Syrian officials began to discuss the situation in the south of Lebanon with US embassy officials. They did not directly ask for any assistance, but the content of the discussions suggests that they continued to see the US government as a channel of information to Israel. Asad's political adviser Daoudi expressed his concern about the possibility of the cease-fire breaking down over the events in South Lebanon.[136] In a meeting on October 28, Khaddam expressed Syrian determination to keep the border quiet, though he did not specify how this was to be accomplished.[137] Two days later, Kissinger instructed Murphy to see Khaddam and express concern about the movement of Palestinian forces into the south of Lebanon, and to ask whether he had any ideas about what the US government could do.[138] Khaddam, however, did not provide a response.[139]

As it became clear that controlling South Lebanon would be crucial to the implementation of peace, the State Department began to consult with Israel. On November 1, Dinitz told Kissinger that Israel would not tolerate a PLO presence in the south similar to the one prior to the civil war.[140] On November 8, the Israeli chargé in Washington told Kissinger that although there was a "vacuum" in South Lebanon, the current situation "should be maintained without the entrance of Syrian, inter-Arab and terrorist forces." He asked the secretary of state to bring this to Syria's attention. Kissinger responded that the US government had told the Syrians of "Israeli sensitivities," but he reiterated the US belief that the PLO would return if a vacuum remained. Thus, the United States did not object to Sarkis's sending in security forces, and the only one available was the ADF, which was mostly Syrian.[141]

The Israeli government rejected this idea out of hand. Allon argued in a somewhat contradictory manner that the Syrians through "their control of the situation in Beirut and most of the country can keep peace and order along the Israeli border without their direct presence in South Lebanon." Until then, control should remain in the hands of the "villagers" in the south, whom Israel was arming and equipping through their "good fence." The foreign minister outlined his prescription for Syrian action: "Syria should not give Israel any surprises; it should let Israel know through us [the United States] what it plans to do and how it plans to control the area"; however, South Lebanon "should remain purely Lebanese."[142] In the meantime, Israeli troops began to provide artillery support to militias in South Lebanon fighting PLO and leftist forces near the town of Bint Jbeil.[143] Although US officials in Damascus continued to discuss the situation with Asad and Khaddam, they do not appear to have conveyed the Israeli view at this time, probably because they understood that it would likely be negatively received by Syria.[144]

Around this time, US-Israeli relations were soured by several other issues. After a near comeback in the polls, President Ford lost the presidential election to Jimmy Carter on November 2. Although foreign policy was not the only issue in the election, many in the press criticized Ford's association with Kissinger. Although much of the criticism related to negotiations over the Panama Canal and détente, Kissinger was sometimes portrayed as an anti-Israel albatross around the president's neck, warding away Jewish voters.[145] Following the elections, the United States and Israel clashed over the Israeli settlements that were being constructed in the Gaza Strip and the West Bank. On November 11, the United States voted for UN Security Council Resolution 446, which stated that "the policy and practices of Israel in establishing settlements in the Palestinian and other Arab territories occupied since 1967 have no legal validity and constitute a serious obstruction to achieving a comprehensive, just and lasting peace in the Middle East." Allon called the statement a "great disappointment" and an "unfriendly act."[146] While it is difficult to draw a direct connection between these issues and the Israeli position regarding the south of Lebanon, it probably reduced the receptivity of Israel to US initiatives.

Underlining the dangers of the situation, on November 21, for the first time in several months, fedayeen groups launched rocket attacks from Lebanese territory, hitting the Israeli settlement of Nahariya, some six miles south of the border.[147] Following the rocket attacks, Ambassador Murphy finally discussed the situation in the south of Lebanon with the Syrians, who questioned Israeli motives. On November 22, Shihabi argued that the basic question was "whether Israeli concern was a short-term one about stability along the border, or a longer term one of building up their political gains achieved by the 'good fence' policy." Shihabi told Murphy that Syria planned to conduct a "country-wide disarmament of Lebanon and Palestinians" after it had finished its "deployment to Tyre and other areas where a Syrian presence may be required to establish security."[148] The next day, Syrian foreign minister Khaddam reiterated Shihabi's message, stating that they might send perhaps a hundred troops to Tyre to establish control there. This, he said, would pose no threat to Israel whatsoever.[149] While Shihabi and Khaddam did not ask that this information be passed on to the Israelis, neither did they warn against it. As was the case the previous March, these two leaders appear to have seen a possible role for the United States in facilitating Syrian entry into the south of Lebanon.

The State Department tried to convince Israel to agree to allow the Syrian force to move to Tyre and Nabitiyya. Kissinger brought up the subject with Dinitz on November 23, telling him that US officials in Damascus had talked to Shihabi, who said that the Syrians wanted to deploy troops to Tyre. Fudging the truth somewhat, he claimed that the Syrians were "not opposed to open fences as long as the peace process continues" and that they were opposed to fedayeen raids.[150] In fact, no Syrian had said that they were "not opposed to open fences," but since Shihabi and Khaddam had stated that they did not want a conflict in the south of Lebanon, they were not likely to oppose Israeli policy by force. Kissinger then pointed out the contradiction in the Israeli approach: they wanted Syria to control the Palestinians in the south but would not allow them to deploy troops there. At first, Dinitz seemed to agree, stating that they could pursue an agreement with Sarkis for these assurances.[151] However, the next day, the Israeli chargé conveyed a message from Rabin asking that the United States "strongly urge [the] Syrians not to move into Tyre." Kissinger protested this, warning that "in view of Khaddam's categorical assurance that Syria has no plans or authority to establish itself in South Lebanon, a unilateral Israeli move would not be understood." If Rabin agreed, then they would go back to the Syrians to reiterate the importance of going no farther south and using a minimum number of forces in Tyre and Nabitiyya.[152] However, the Israelis never gave their consent. In fact, on November 28, the Israeli cabinet issued a statement opposing further southern deployment of Syrian troops.[153]

In the meantime, the US government made it clear to Syrian and Lebanese officials that it could not guarantee a positive Israeli reaction to their deployment in South Lebanon. On November 25, Kissinger instructed Murphy to tell Khaddam that "the best method to end concern about Southern Lebanon is to help Sarkis rapidly form a Lebanese military force," and that "any further southward movement of Syrian forces would bring a serious risk of destabilizing the delicate situation in the South."[154] Khaddam argued that "the Israelis wish not only to manufacture a crisis but to see the fighting continue," as well as "to cover up their own practices in the Occupied Territories and 'to prepare the ground vis-à-vis Washington to keep your President-elect from following the activist policy in the Middle East along the lines pursued by President Ford.'"[155]

The State Department also delivered this message to Sarkis. On November 23, the State Department instructed Lane to tell Sarkis that a "reinforced" Palestinian presence in South Lebanon would be a problem for Israel but that US officials were in touch with Syria and Israel and prepared to play "a helpful role."[156] Sarkis responded that it was impossible at the moment to use a Lebanese force to restore security.[157] The State Department then instructed Lane to ask Sarkis whether the Christian force along the border could be built up into one throughout the southern region.[158] However, the Lebanese president felt that the Christian forces in the South were militarily too weak, and their use would be politically too divisive, since they were identified with the Christians and accused of cooperating with Israel. The ADF would have to be sent into South Lebanon, but it needed Syrian troops.[159] In the meantime, Lebanese newspapers maintained that the United States had again transferred a warning from Israel to Syria and Lebanon.[160] Still, Sarkis clearly wanted some sort of assurance from the United States, calling Lane on December 3 to ask whether he had any news for him and asking him to call as soon as he did, regardless of the hour.[161]

Ultimately, the United States government bowed to the Israeli viewpoint on this issue, though not without trying again to change their minds. In a December 1 meeting, State Department official Lawrence Eagleburger told Ambassador Dinitz that the US government had reached some "tentative conclusions," including that the "only feasible and effective security force" that Sarkis could use was the ADF force, and that it could not "second guess" the Lebanese president's refusal to use Christian forces. Thus, the State Department could not understand Israel's opposition to the deployment of ADF forces in Tyre and Nabitiyya, and thought it was unrealistic to expect "any sweeping gesture against the Palestinians."[162] On December 4, in another meeting with Dinitz, Kissinger tried one last time to encourage Israel to allow Syrian troops to enter the south. Dinitz disagreed, stating that Israel "consider[ed] prevention of Syrian entry into Southern Lebanon to be the first and overriding priority," while "preventing terrorist activity in Southern Lebanon must be secondary to this."[163]

On December 5, Kissinger instructed Murphy to tell Syrian and Lebanese officials that the State Department had conveyed Sarkis's position to the Israelis. Although the United States disagreed, the Israelis were not likely to change their position, which meant that they assumed the "southward movement of Arab security force elements would bring the risk of destabilization."[164] In the meantime, Syrian vice president Khaddam had been wounded in an assassination attempt. Another official received the message in Khaddam's absence, promising to convey the points to Asad. Murphy, he said, would be informed if there was any comment.[165] None came.

Sarkis himself was distressed by the Israeli refusal to authorize the use of Syrian troops. After hearing the message, the Lebanese leader fumed, asking "How do you expect me to establish security in Lebanon if I do not control Tyre?" He added that if he could not stop the flow of weapons to the Palestinians, he would not be able to do so to the Christians, since he would be seen as taking sides against them. Sarkis said that he would send a force to

Tyre "tomorrow" if Israel agreed.[166] US officials continued to discuss the subject with Israel, but no further movement was produced.[167]

A primary reason for the lack of movement was that the Ford administration was on its way out of office. The electoral defeat dampened what might have otherwise been seen as a case of relative success for Kissinger's foreign policy. The secretary of state had not welcomed the violence in Lebanon, but he endeavored to shape the course that it eventually took. It left the PLO in a relatively weakened state, while enhancing the position of Syria. It had also opened a wide rift between Syria and the Soviet Union, leaving the former isolated in the Middle East and the latter estranged from the Arab-Israeli conflict. Had Kissinger remained in office, he might have tried to partner more closely with the Asad regime in order to broker another disengagement agreement between Syria and Israel, building on the relations that had been built between the United States and Syria over the previous three years.

As it was, despite the peace agreement, the prospects for Lebanon were far from good. Signs of many future problems in Lebanon were becoming apparent, and not just along the southern border with Israel. In the final weeks of the Ford presidency, Lebanese Christian leaders began to contact the United States regarding tensions that were developing between the Christians and the Syrians.[168] However, there was little that the Ford administration could or would do at this point. A new era of conflict in Lebanon awaited the incoming Carter administration, which would be no more successful than its predecessors in addressing the problems of Lebanon.

Epilogue
The Cycle Continues

As outlined in the introduction, US Lebanon policy was always subordinated to the country's goals in the Cold War and the Arab-Israeli conflict. Most of the time, the Arab-Israeli conflict was the primary factor. After 1967, some, including many State Department officials, believed that the spreading radicalism was a manifestation of tensions directly related to the Arab-Israeli conflict, which the United States was helping prolong through its support for Israel. These individuals felt that the United States should pressure Israel in order to resolve the tensions and relieve pressure on the United States' moderate allies. Others, particularly Henry Kissinger, argued repeatedly that the turmoil within the moderate states did not justify taking steps in the Middle East conflict that would sacrifice the security of Israel for the sake of the United Arab Republic and Syria. Nixon was convinced enough of the danger to the moderate states to allow the State Department to launch its diplomatic plans, though, like Kissinger, he did not want to press Israel for the sake of Egypt and Syria, which appeared to be openly espousing anti-Americanism sentiments and fueling unrest across the region. After the 1973 war, US policy changed drastically, and Kissinger began to work with Egyptian and even Syrian leaders to take steps toward resolving the Middle East conflict.

This might well have had a salutary effect on Lebanon, but the US government chose to ignore one of the issues at the core of the conflict: the status of the Palestinians. The primary factor enabling this policy was the relative stability of Jordan and Lebanon at the time, as King Hussein and President Suleiman Frangie exerted relative control over the Palestinians in their respective countries, at least until the war broke out in Lebanon. Several times between 1973 and 1976, the State Department leadership would consider again the possibility of changing its attitude toward the Palestinians, but a change never came to pass, primarily because Kissinger refused to consider it. In fact, by 1976, Kissinger was almost single-handedly preventing the United States from engaging with the PLO. The secretary of state may have intended the question of the Palestinians to be addressed at a later date, when it could more easily be dealt with, but this was not a message that Palestinian leaders could accept. Their isolation drove them to take measures to disrupt the Middle East negotiations, which in turn had repercussions for Lebanon.

Although the US government was not ready to address the cause of the disease, they were willing to take steps to deal with its symptoms, including the violence in Lebanon. In this area, US-Lebanese bilateral relations were more important in influencing the course of events in Lebanon than has previously been thought, though there were definite limits on the US ability to affect the situation. During the crises of 1969 and 1970, the Lebanese government repeatedly looked to the United States for assistance. Throughout the last two years of Helou's term in office, the Lebanese president maintained a dialogue with US officials concerning Lebanon's internal security situation, both directly and via intermediaries. However, several factors prevented the United States from providing effective assistance. Most important among these was the worsening of the Arab-Israeli conflict and the decline of US status in the region, which made any open association with the United States a potential liability. Military assistance from the United States was complicated by the fact that many within Lebanon suspected (correctly) that the aid was primarily intended to be used against the fedayeen. That said, had the United States been more generous, the Lebanese probably would have accepted it. However, military aid could only have a limited degree of impact on the situation. In the crises of 1969, 1973, and 1975, the strength of the army was not a decisive factor in the conflict; rather, the army was unable to control the fedayeen due to political factors. Because of its internal political structure, there was never any real hope that Lebanon would be able to act as a policeman in the same way that Jordan had, cracking down on the fedayeen militarily.

The US reaction to the outbreak of the civil war in April 1975 demonstrated how much US-Lebanese relations had changed over the years. In each of the significant crises in 1969, 1970, and 1973, the United States held high-level meetings that considered possible reactions to the situation in Lebanon. Following the outbreak of the civil war, no such meetings were held until long after the fighting broke out. By 1975, the increased scrutiny of Congress and domestic backlash about US intervention elsewhere had undermined the administration's ability to meddle in conflict zones around the world, whether through direct military intervention or through indirect methods such as the provision of weapons. In any case, by this point, there was not much of a Lebanese government left for the United States to partner with. The US government no longer had a real dialogue with Lebanese officials, as the power had shifted to the militias, with whom the United States did not initially maintain a dialogue for fear of being seen as supportive of their aims. Although the United States made occasional shows of support for what remained of the Lebanese government, until March 1976, the Ford administration tried to avoid becoming involved in the details of the conflict. Only the threat of Syrian intervention in March 1976 led the United States to increase its involvement in Lebanon. Throughout the spring and summer of 1976, Kissinger and US diplomats tried to help create conditions for peace in Lebanon, until the assassination of the US ambassador limited their ability to help the parties communicate. At the end of 1976, Kissinger tried to facilitate the entrance of Syrian troops into the south of Lebanon in order to control the Palestinians, but Israel would not allow it. Ultimately, the United States decided not to force them to do so, thereby setting up the wicked game for the next round.

In the years that followed, Lebanon remained a deadly battleground. After the Carter administration took office, the situation in the country deteriorated once again. Following the election of Menachim Begin as prime minister in June 1977, Israel developed an even more aggressive policy of reprisals toward Lebanon, while also drawing closer to the Maronite Christians. After an attack on a school bus in 1978, Israel launched a full scale invasion of South Lebanon. The Carter administration helped bring about a withdrawal of Israeli troops by supporting a UN resolution that established a UN force in South Lebanon, an interim measure that remains there today. The Israeli invasion also expanded the "good fence" into an official "security belt" in South Lebanon.[1] Israel invaded again in 1982, expelling the PLO from the region but at the same time bringing about a new militia in the south, Hizbullah, which would be just as anti-Israeli as the fedayeen, but if anything, better armed and organized. Israel withdrew most of its troops over the course of 1985, with the exception of some in the southern security zone to support the SLA, but the fighting in the rest of the country did not stop. Only in 1991 did the Lebanese Civil War finally draw to a close, though the fighting in the south would continue until the withdrawal of the remaining Israeli troops in 2000. In 2006, Israel once again invaded South Lebanon, resulting in over a thousand Lebanese and 150 Israeli deaths, and the threat of resumed violence still remains today. Clearly, Lebanon has yet to escape from the vicious cycle.

Throughout this latter period, subsequent US administrations watched the situation in Lebanon closely, vacillating between support for and mild opposition to Israel's actions. Again, government spokespersons paid lip service to preserving Lebanese sovereignty, but most US officials had accepted that it was largely a necessary fiction, no matter who was in office. In some cases, such as in 1978, the Carter administration made a serious push to force Israel to evacuate. In other cases, as in 1982, the Reagan administration offered relatively weak resistance to Israeli actions, being content to allow Israel to push its agenda forward under the guise of neutrality, even as the United States offered military and diplomatic support. Hoping to facilitate the expulsion of the PLO, President Reagan even agreed to the deployment of a few thousand marines to Lebanon as peacekeepers that year. After a suicide bomber killed more than 241 of these servicemen, domestic support for the peacekeepers declined, and the Reagan administration withdrew the troops within six months. Tending its wounds, the United States would no longer consider sending troops to Lebanon, but the country remained a hub for US covert action, including the trading of arms for hostages and other operations. More recently, US officials have continued to play an important role in the country's politics, advocating for the country's participation in the International Criminal Tribunal established after the 2005 assassination of Prime Minister Rafiq Hariri, as well as for the disarmament of Hizbullah's armed wing.

Understanding the US role is essential to understanding the evolution of the conflict in Lebanon, not because the United States strongly supported one party or another, but simply because it had the power to do so. Even if the *intent* of the Nixon and Ford administrations to destroy Lebanon is largely absent from the historical record, so too is evidence of a deep will to keep Lebanon out of the cross fire by addressing the real problems that faced the Middle East, particularly the Palestinian issue. Whatever the goals of US policymakers, local actors considered the United States a major factor in their own courses of action, for the simple reason that they believed that the US government had the power to hurt them or help them. It was this very nature of these power relations that made the US sphere of intervention so important in the struggles that have defined Lebanon's recent history.

NOTES

AAD	Access to Archival Databases, US National Archives and Records Administration, available at aad.archives.gov
CF	Central Files
CF	Country File
CMP	Charles Malik Papers, Library of Congress, Washington, DC
CREST	CIA Records Search Tool, US National Archives and Records Administration, College Park, MD
DNSA	Digital National Security Archive, National Security Archive, Washington, DC
FAOH	Foreign Affairs Oral History Collection of the Association for Diplomatic Studies and Training, Frontline Diplomacy, available online at memory.loc.gov
FBIS	Foreign Broadcast Information Service (FBIS), microfilmed records, LOC
FOIA	Freedom of Information Act
FRUS	Foreign Relations of the United States
GRFL	Gerald R. Ford Presidential Library, Ann Arbor, MI
GRFL-KTF	Kissinger Trip Files, GRFL
GRFL-PCF-MESA	Presidential Country Files, Middle East and South Asia, GRFL
KLF	Kissinger Lot Files, RG 59, NARA
LBJL	Lyndon B. Johnson Presidential Library, Austin, TX
LBJL-NSF	National Security File, LBJL
LBJL-NSF-CF-SC	Country Files, Files of the Special Committee of the NSC, LBJL
LOC	Library of Congress, Washington, DC
MESA	Country Files, Middle East and South Asia
NARA	National Archives and Records Administration, College Park, MD

NPM	Nixon Presidential Materials, currently at the Richard Nixon Presidential Library, Yorba Linda, CA
NPM-NSC-CF	National Security Council, Central File, NPM
NSF	National Security File
RAC	Remote Archive Capture
RG	Record Group, National Archives and Records Administration, College Park, MD
RLF	Rogers Lot Files, RG 59, NARA
RRIAIA	Records Relating to Israel and Arab-Israel Affairs, 1951–76, RG 59, NARA
RRIJLS	Records Relating to Iraq, Jordan, Lebanon, and Syria, 1966–72, RG 59, NARA
SLF	Joseph J. Sisco Lot Files, RG 59, NARA
UNBIS	United Nations Bibliographic Information System

Introduction. "This Is the American Policy"

1. See video of Nasrallah's remarks at "Words of Sayyid Hassan Nasrallah on Martyr's Day" [Kalimat as-Sayid Hasan Nasr Allah fi Yawm al-Shahid], Nov. 11, 2010, 9:45, http://www.youtu.be/qVB4BfJMjtQ.

2. See *Beirut Observer* [online], Nov. 12, 2010.

3. *Al-Manar* [online], "Salim Nassar to As-Safir: I Wrote Kissinger's Letter Based on Direct Sources," Nov. 13, 2010; *As-Safir*, Nov. 13, 2010; *Al-Nahar*, Nov. 20, 2010.

4. Some Western sources have also made this argument. See, e.g., Dilip Hiro, *Lebanon: Fire and Embers: A History of the Lebanese Civil War* (New York: St. Martin's Press, 1992), 20.

5. The Two Years' War is sometimes called the "Lebanese Civil War," a term that can also refer to the conflict throughout the entire fifteen-year period of war in Lebanon (1975–90).

6. Casualty figures discussed in Michael Johnson, *Class and Client in Beirut: The Sunni Muslim Community and the Lebanese State, 1840–1985* (London: Ithaca Press, 1986), 190.

7. E.g., Edward Azar and Kate Shnayerson, "United States-Lebanese Relations: A Pocketful of Paradoxes," in *The Emergence of a New Lebanon: Fantasy or Reality?*, ed. Edward Azar (New York: Praeger, 1984), 220.

8. Erika Alin, "U.S. Policy and Military Intervention in the 1958 Lebanon Crisis," in *The Middle East and the United States: A Historical and Political Reassessment*, ed. David W. Lesch (Boulder, CO: Westview Press, 1996), 147–48; Salim Yaqub, *Containing Arab Nationalism: The Eisenhower Doctrine and the Middle East* (Chapel Hill: University of North Carolina Press, 2004), 7.

9. See Ussama Makdisi, *Artillery of Heaven: American Missionaries and the Failed Conversion of the Middle East* (Ithaca, NY: Cornell University Press, 2008).

10. On Britain, see Peter L. Hahn, *Caught in the Middle East: U.S. Policy toward the Arab-Israeli Conflict, 1945–61* (Chapel Hill: University of North Carolina Press, 2004), 23.

11. See ibid., 152; Yaqub, *Containing Arab Nationalism*, 38–39.

12. See, e.g., Daniel Yergin, *The Prize: The Epic Quest for Oil, Money and Power* (New York: Simon and Schuster, 1991), 395–96.

13. Irene Gendzier, *Notes from the Minefield*, 2nd ed. (New York: Columbia University Press, 2006), 66.

14. Douglas Little, *American Orientalism: The United States and the Middle East since 1945* (Chapel Hill: University of North Carolina Press, 2002), 58; Fawaz A. Gerges, "Lebanon," in *The Cold War and the Middle East*, ed. Yezid Sayigh and Avi Shlaim (Oxford: Oxford University Press, 1997), 92; Rafael Kandiyoti, *Pipelines: Flowing Oil and Crude Politics* (London: I.B. Tauris, 2008), 69–70.

15. Hahn, *Caught in the Middle East*, 71–75.

16. Warren Bass, *Support Any Friend: Kennedy's Middle East and the Making of the U.S.-Israel Alliance* (Oxford: Oxford University Press, 2003), 2–3.

17. Fawaz A. Gerges, "The 1967 Arab-Israeli War: U.S. Actions and Arab Perceptions," in *The Middle East and the United States: A Historical Reassessment*, ed. David Lesch (Boulder, CO: Westview Press, 1996), 285–313.

18. William B. Quandt, *Peace Process: American Diplomacy and the Arab-Israeli Conflict since 1967*, 3rd ed. (Washington, DC: Brookings Institution Press, 2005), 13–15.

19. Though the outbreak of the Lebanese Civil War is briefly mentioned in the second edition of Quandt's *Peace Process*, it does not appear in the third. Kissinger's memoirs provide few details on US-Lebanon policy before 1975. Henry Alfred Kissinger, *White House Years* (Boston: Little, Brown and Company, 1979), 373. Nor is it mentioned in Kenneth Stein, *Heroic Diplomacy* (New York: Routledge, 1999). On the comparable neglect of Jordan, see Clea Lutz Bunch, "Strike at Samu: Jordan, Israel, the United States, and the Origins of the Six-Day War," *Diplomatic History* 32, no. 1 (2008): 57.

20. Many recent works on the Israeli-Arab conflict concentrate on these countries. See, e.g., Salim Yaqub, "The Nixon Administration and the Arab-Israeli Conflict, 1969–73," in *The Cold War in the Middle East: Regional Conflict and the Superpowers 1967–73*, ed. Nigel Ashton (London: Routledge, 2007), 227–48; Craig A. Daigle, "The Limits of Détente: The United States, the Soviet Union, and the Arab-Israeli Conflict, 1969–1973" (PhD diss., George Washington University, 2008).

21. James Stocker, "Diplomacy as Counter-Revolution? The 'Moderate States', the Fedayeen and State Department Initiatives towards the Arab-Israeli Conflict, 1969–1970," *Cold War History* 12, no. 3 (2012): 407–28.

22. For a collection of such accounts, see Nabil Khalifi, *Lebanon in Kissinger's Strategy: A Political and Geostrategic Comparison (Lubnán fī strátíjiyyat kísinjar: muqáriba siyásiyya wa-jiyyú-strátíjiyya)* (Biblos, Lebanon: Biblos Center for Studies and Research, 2008), 8. See also Roger Azzim, *Liban: l'instruction d'un crime* (Coudray-Macouard, France: Cheminements, 2005).

23. Joseph Chami, *Le mémorial de la guerre* (Beirut: Sharikat ash-sharq al-awsaṭ li-tazwíʿ al-maṭbuʿat, 2003), 74; Tracy Chamoun, *Au nom de mon père* (Paris: Edition Jean-Claude Lattès, 1992), 49. See also Theodor Hanf, *Coexistence in Wartime Lebanon* (London: Center for Lebanese Studies, I.B. Tauris, 1993), 376–78.

24. Shafiq al-Ḥút, the former head of the PLO office in Beirut, argues that, in 1975, "the Kissinger Plot succeeded in igniting the fire of struggle in Lebanon" (*najaḥat muʾámarat kísinjar fī ʾish ʿál nár al-fitna fī lubnán*) to eliminate the PLO.

Shafiq al-Ḥút, *Between the Nation and Exile (Bayna al-waṭan w-al-munfá: min yáfá bad'a al-mashwár)* (Beirut: Riyáḍ al-rís l-il-katab w-al-nashar, 2007), 190.

25. See, for instance, Paul Salem "Superpowers and Small States: American-Lebanese Relations in Perspective," *Cahiers de la Méditerranée* 44 (1992), 135–64.

26. See, e.g., Karim Pakradouni, *The Curse of the Nation: From the Lebanon War to the Gulf War (La'na al-waṭan: min ḥarb lubnán ila ḥarb al-khalíj)* (Beirut: 'Abr ash-sharq l-al-munshawarat, 1991), 64.

27. Jonathan Randal, *Going All the Way: Christian Warlords, Israeli Adventurers, and the War in Lebanon* (New York: Viking Press, 1983), 171. See also Library of Congress, Foreign Affairs Oral History Project [FAOH] Interview, David Korn, Dec. 11, 1990; Henry Alfred Kissinger, *Years of Renewal* (New York: Simon and Schuster, 1999), 1024.

28. Jüssi Hanhimäki, *The Flawed Architect: Henry Kissinger and American Foreign Policy* (Oxford: Oxford University Press, 2004), xviii.

29. Fawwaz Traboulsi, *A History of Modern Lebanon* (London: Pluto Press, 2007), 106.

30. See, e.g., George Corm, *Le liban contemporain: Histoire et société*, 2nd ed. (Paris: Ed. La Découverte, 2005), 181; Oren Barak, "Towards a Representative Military? The Transformation of the Lebanese Officer Corps," *Middle East Journal* 60, no. 1 (2006): 89.

31. See, e.g., Muhsin Ibráhím, *The War and the Experiment of the Lebanese National Movement (Al-harb wa tajribat al-harakat al–waṭaniyyat al-lubnániyya)* (Beirut: Bayrút al-Masá', 1983). See also Hanf, *Coexistence in Wartime Lebanon*, 381–82.

32. Traboulsi, *A History of Modern Lebanon*, 155.

33. Farid el-Khazen, *The Breakdown of the State in Lebanon, 1967–1976* (London: I.B. Tauris, 2000), 250ff, esp. 259. See also Michael Hudson, "The Breakdown of Democracy in Lebanon," *Journal of International Affairs* 38 (1985): 277.

34. Joseph Abou Khalil, *Les Maronites dans la guerre au Liban: Récit Autobiographique* (Paris-Beirut: Edifra, 1992), 18.

35. On the intrastate security dilemma, see Paul Roe, "The Intrastate Security Dilemma: Ethnic Conflict as a 'Tragedy'?," *Journal of Peace Research* 36, no. 2 (1999), 183–202.

36. Michael Hudson, "The Palestinian Factor in the Lebanese Civil War," *Middle East Journal* 23, no. 3 (1978): 265.

37. al-Ḥút, *Between the Nation and Exile*, 191.

38. Michael Johnson, *All Honourable Men: The Social Origins of War in Lebanon* (Oxford; London: Centre for Lebanese Studies, I.B. Tauris, 2001), 6.

39. Reuven Avi-Ran, *The Syrian Involvement in Lebanon since 1975* (Boulder, CO: Westview Press, 1991), 7; Patrick Seale, *Asad: The Struggle for the Middle East*, rev. ed. (Berkeley: University of California Press, 1995), 184.

40. Hussein Sirriyeh, "Lebanon, Dimensions of Conflict," *Adelphi Paper No. 243* (1989): 38.

41. These two are not necessarily the same. Daniel Pipes, *Greater Syria: The History of an Ambition* (New York: Oxford University Press, 1990).

42. Samir Kassir, *La guerre du Liban: de la dissension nationale au conflit régional (1975–1982)* (Paris; Beirut: Karthala; CERMOC, 1994), 194. See also Adeed Dawisha,

"The Motives of Syria's Involvement in Lebanon," *Middle East Journal* 38, no. 2 (1984): 231; Seale, *Asad: The Struggle for the Middle East*, 349–50.

43. Zeev Maoz, "Evaluating Israel's Strategy of Low-Intensity Warfare, 1949–2006," *Security Studies* 16, no. 3 (2007): 320.

44. Barry M. Blechman, "The Impact of Israel's Reprisals on Behavior of the Bordering Arab Nations Directed at Israel," *Journal of Conflict Resolution* 16, no. 2 (1972): 156–59.

45. For instance, Clea Bunch argues that one such reprisal, in 1966 at Samu in Jordan, helped bring about a temporary reorientation of Jordanian foreign policy toward Egypt at a critical point prior to the 1967 War. Bunch, "Strike at Samu," 56.

46. John L. Nelson, "Political Integration in Lebanon" (PhD diss., University of Chicago, 1976), 183.

47. Johnson provides an analysis of these trends. Johnson, *Class and Client in Beirut*, 170–74.

48. Frederic Hof, *Galilee Divided: The Israel-Lebanon Frontier, 1916–1984* (Boulder, CO: Westview Press, 1985), 2.

49. Kirsten E. Schulze, *Israel's Covert Diplomacy in Lebanon* (Houndmilles, UK: Macmillan Press, 1998), 2.

50. Nasser M. Kalawoun, *The Struggle for Lebanon: A Modern History of Lebanese-Egyptian Relations* (London: I.B. Tauris, 2000), 1.

51. See, e.g., Abbas Samii, "The Shah's Lebanon Policy: The Role of SAVAK," *Middle Eastern Studies* 33, no. 1 (1997): 66–91.

52. Stocker, "Diplomacy as Counter-Revolution," 409.

53. Rashid Khalidi, *Sowing Crisis: The Cold War and American Dominance in the Middle East* (Boston: Beacon Press, 2009), 134.

54. Ibid., 197; George Basil Lambrakis, "Perception and Misperception in Policymaking: The U.S. Relationship with Modern Lebanon, 1943–1976" (PhD diss., George Washington University, 1989), abstract; Robert Stookey, "The United States," in *Lebanon in Crisis: Participants and Issues*, ed. P. Edward Haley and Lewis Snider (Syracuse, NY: Syracuse University Press, 1979), 234; Randal, *Going All the Way*, 169; Bassam Abdel Kader Namani, "Confessionalism in Lebanon, 1920–1976: The Interplay of Domestic, Regional, and International Politics" (PhD diss., Columbia University, 1982), 323–24. See also FAOH interview, Talcott Seelye; author interview, Karim Pakradouni.

55. Marwan Buheiry, "The US and the Arab-Israeli Conflict in 1975," in *The Formation and Perception of the Modern Arab World: Studies by Marwan R. Buheiry*, ed. Lawrence Conrad (Princeton: Darwin Press, 1990), 438.

56. See, e.g., Azar and Shnayerson, "United States-Lebanese Relations: A Pocketful of Paradoxes," 248; Kissinger, *Years of Renewal*, 1025; Stookey, "The United States," 234.

57. E.g., Seale, *Asad: The Struggle for the Middle East*, 278.

58. Walid Khalidi, *Conflict and Violence in Lebanon: Confrontation in the Middle East* (Cambridge, MA: Harvard University Press, 1979), 87.

59. Kissinger, *Years of Renewal*, 1020.

60. See, e.g., FAOH interview, Talcott Seelye; Wilbur Crane Eveland, *Ropes of Sand: America's Failure in the Middle East* (London: W. W. Norton, 1980), 341; Randal,

Going All the Way, 172–74; Yezid Sayigh, *Armed Struggle and the Search for State: The Palestinian National Movement, 1949–1993* (Oxford: Clarendon Press, 1997), 361.

61. Kissinger, *Years of Renewal*, 1042.

62. Khalidi, *Conflict and Violence in Lebanon*, 88.

1. Sparks in the Tinderbox

1. See, e.g., Salim Yaqub, *Containing Arab Nationalism: The Eisenhower Doctrine and the Middle East* (Chapel Hill: University of North Carolina Press, 2004), 206–7.

2. Robert Murphy, *Diplomat among Warriors* (New York: Doubleday, 1964), 396–409.

3. On Chehab's economic program, see Michael Hudson, *The Precarious Republic: Political Modernization in Lebanon* (Boulder, CO: Westview Press, 1985).

4. See, e.g., Kamal Salibi, *Crossroads to Civil War: Lebanon 1958–1976* (Delmar, NY: Caravan Books, 1976), 3–4.

5. William Harris, *The New Face of Lebanon: History's Revenge* (Princeton, NJ: Markus Wiener Publishers, 2006), 145.

6. Salibi, *Crossroads to Civil War*, 22.

7. Fawaz A. Gerges, *The Superpowers and the Middle East: Regional and International Politics, 1955–1967* (Boulder, CO: Westview Press, 1994), particularly chapters 5 and 6.

8. Nasser M. Kalawoun, *The Struggle for Lebanon: A Modern History of Lebanese-Egyptian Relations* (London: I.B. Tauris, 2000), 18–20, 24–26, 104–10.

9. Nigel Ashton, *King Hussein of Jordan: A Political Life* (New Haven, CT: Yale University Press, 2008), 100.

10. Charles Helou, *Mémoires*, vol. 2 (Beirut: An-Nahar), 19–20.

11. Even during the 1958 uprising, the tiny LCP supported, but was not included in, the United Front of groups that opposed President Camille Chamoun. Tareq Ismael and Jacqueline Ismael, *The Communist Movement in Syria and Lebanon* (Gainsville: University Press of Florida, 1998), 53–54.

12. On Jumblatt, see Farid al-Khazen, "Kamal Jumblatt, the Uncrowned Druze Prince of the Left," *Middle Eastern Studies* 24, no. 2 (1988), 178–205; Yusri Hazran, "Lebanon's Revolutionary Era: Kamal Junblat, The Druze Community and the Lebanon State, 1949 to 1977," *Muslim World* 100, no. 1 (2010), 157–76.

13. See, e.g., Júrj al-Baṭal, "Reading the Life Story of a Communist Leader (Qirá'a fi síra qá'id shiyú'í)," in *George Hawi: Positions of the Leader and Testimonies of Comrades (Jurj ḥáwí: muwáqif al-qá'id wa shahádát al-rifáq)* (Beirut: Dar al-Nahár, 2005), 48–49. Kamal Jumblatt was a veteran in such affairs, having chaired the Afro-Asian People's Conference in 1960 and represented Lebanon at the Congress of Afro-Asian Solidarity in 1966.

14. Ismael and Ismael, *The Communist Movement in Syria and Lebanon*, 71.

15. Yezid Sayigh, "Reconstructing the Paradox: The Arab Nationalist Movement, Armed Struggle, and Palestine, 1951–1966," *Middle East Journal* 45, no. 4 (1991): 621–22. See also Basil Raouf al-Kubaisi, "The Arab Nationalist Movement, 1951–1971: From Pressure Group to Socialist Party" (PhD diss., American University, 1971); Muhammad Jamál Bárút, *Movement of Arab Nationalists: Origins, Development, Fates*

(*Ḥarakat al-Qawmīyīn al-'Arab: al-nash'ah, al-taṭawwur, al-maṣā'ir*) (Damascus: al-Markaz al-'Arabī lil-Dirāsāt al-Istirātījīyah, 1997).

16. Ismael and Ismael, *The Communist Movement in Syria and Lebanon*, 71. Of these parties, the LCP and SSNP were officially banned. See ibid., 81. The Lebanese Ba'th party, which had Iraq and Syrian branches, merely lacked a licensed status. Asad Abukhalil, "Syria and the Shiites: al-Asad's Policy in Lebanon," *Third World Quarterly* 12, no. 2 (1990): 4. The same can be said for the Arab nationalist movement, which was not embodied by a single party, at the time, but found expression in groups such as the Organization of Lebanese Socialists and Socialist Lebanon.

17. Helena Cobban, *The Palestinian Liberation Organisation: People, Power and Politics* (Cambridge: Cambridge University Press, 1984), 47.

18. FRUS, 1964–8, Vol. XVIII, Doc. 248.

19. Niqúlá Náṣif, *The Deuxième Bureau: Ruling in the Shadow (Al-maktab al-thání: ḥákim fi-l-ẓul)* (Beirut: Dár mukhtárát, 2007), 225–28.

20. Theodor Hanf, *Coexistence in Wartime Lebanon* (London: Center for Lebanese Studies, I.B. Tauris, 1993), 122.

21. See, e.g., FAOH Interview, David E. Zweifel; Armin H. Meyer, *Quiet Diplomacy: From Cairo to Tokyo in the Twilight of Imperialism* (New York: iUniverse, Inc., 2003), 111.

22. Yaqub, *Containing Arab Nationalism*, 237–67.

23. See, inter alia, Gerges, *The Superpowers and the Middle East*, 14.

24. Warren Bass, *Support Any Friend: Kennedy's Middle East and the Making of the U.S.-Israel Alliance* (Oxford: Oxford University Press, 2003), 65, 87.

25. Gerges, *The Superpowers and the Middle East*, 167.

26. Yaqub, *Containing Arab Nationalism*, 39–43.

27. Douglas Little, "The Making of a Special Relationship: The United States and Israel, 1957–1968," *International Journal of Middle East Studies* 25, no. 4 (1993): 568.

28. FRUS, 1961–3, Vol. XVIII, Doc. 102.

29. Meyer, *Quiet Diplomacy*, 112.

30. For a summary, see Douglas Little, "His Finest Hour? Eisenhower, Lebanon, and the 1958 Middle East Crisis," *Diplomatic History* 20, no. 1 (1996): 35–36.

31. RG 59, CF 1964–6, Box 2432, POL 14, A-250, Sep. 30, 1964.

32. Ibid., Box 1657, DEF 12 LEB; Ibid., State to Lebanon, Number unclear [x00064], Jul. 1, 1964; Memo, Davies to Talbot, Jul. 4, 1964.

33. Ibid., A-607, Feb. 24, 1964. A-711, Mar. 27, 1964.

34. Ibid., Box 1656, DEF LEB, Beirut 5455, Nov. 6, 1965.

35. Ibid., Box 1657, DEF 12 LEB, Beirut 3639, Jan. 6, 1966.

36. See, e.g., RG 59, CF 1964–6, DEF LEB, Box 1656, Beirut A-1056, Jun. 16, 1966; RG 59, CF 1967–9, Box 1573, DEF 12–5 LEB A-993, May 8, 1967.

37. FRUS, 1964–8, Vol. XVIII, Doc. 210.

38. Ibid., Doc. 248.

39. See FAOH interviews with Dwight Porter, James Bishop.

40. RG 59, CF 1964–66, Box 2434, POL 15-1, Beirut A-242, Sep. 30, 1965.

41. Ibid., Airgram A-258, Oct. 11, 1965.

42. During Meyer's term as ambassador (1961–66), visits took place about twice a year. Meyer, *Quiet Diplomacy*, 120.

43. See, e.g., RG 59, CF 1964–6, Box 1657, DEF 17-1 LEB, Beirut, Feb. 2, 1966.

44. Lyndon B. Johnson Library [LBJL], National Security File [NSF], Country File, Box 149, Lebanon, Vol. I, Beirut 4293, May 5, 1966.

45. RG 59, CF 1964–6, Box 1758, DEF 19-8, Beirut 1244, Jun. 7, 1966.

46. Ibid., Box 1657, DEF 17-1 LEB, Airgram Beirut A-1084, Jun. 24, 1966. On the Skyhawk sale, see Zach Levey, "The United States' Skyhawk Sale to Israel, 1966: Strategic Exigencies of an Arms Deal," *Diplomatic History* 28, no. 2 (2004), 255–76.

47. RG 59, CF 1964–6, Box 1657, DEF 17-1 LEB, Beirut A-463, Dec. 2, 1966.

48. RG 59, CF 67–9, Box 2304, POL 7 LEB, Beirut A-643, Jan. 25, 1967.

49. Ibid., Beirut 8143, Mar. 9, 1967; Beirut 9198, Mar. 10, 1967.

50. FRUS, 1964–1968, Vol. XVIII, Doc. 409; RG 59, CF 67–9, Box 1573, Beirut A-1037, DEF LEB-US, Beirut 9274, Apr. 12, 1967.

51. *Al-Nahar*, Apr. 19, 1967.

52. Yosef Govrin, *Israeli-Soviet Relations, 1953–67: From Confrontation to Disruption* (New York: Frank Cass, 1998), 305.

53. RG 59, CF 67–9, Box 1573, DEF LEB-US, Beirut A-1037, May 19, 1967.

54. For balanced reinterpretations of the goals of these states, see the chapters in William Roger Louis and Avi Shlaim, *The 1967 Arab-Israeli War: Origins and Consequences* (New York: Cambridge University Press, 2012).

55. For a discussion of Palestinian goals prior to the 1967 war, see Yezid Sayigh, *Armed Struggle and the Search for State: The Palestinian National Movement, 1949–1993* (Oxford: Clarendon Press, 1997), 139–42. See, e.g., Ray Vicker, "Crisis Crux: Palestinian Refugees," *Wall Street Journal*, Jun. 2, 1967.

56. For an argument that the Soviet Union and Arab countries sought to provoke a war, see Isabella Ginor and Gideon Remez, *Foxbats over Dimona: The Soviets' Nuclear Gamble in the Six Day War* (New Haven, CT: Yale University Press, 2007), 7.

57. Avi Shlaim, *The Iron Wall: Israel and the Arab World* (New York: W. W. Norton, 2001), 240–41.

58. See William B. Quandt, *Peace Process: American Diplomacy and the Arab-Israeli Conflict since 1967*, 3rd ed. (Washington, DC: Brookings Institution Press, 2005), 40–41.

59. Little, "The Making of a Special Relationship," 578.

60. FRUS, 1964–8, Vol. XIX, Doc. 114.

61. See Quandt, *Peace Process*, 43; Michael Oren, *Six Days of War: June 1967 and the Making of the Modern Middle East* (New York: Random House, 2002), 234; Elie Podeh, " 'The Big Lie': Inventing the Myth of British-US Involvement in the 1967 War," *Review of International Affairs* 2, no. 1 (2002): 1–23.

62. Oren, *Six Days of War*, 242.

63. LBJL-NSF-CF, Box 113, Middle East Crisis Sandstorm/Whirlwind [1 of 2], Beirut 11282, Jun. 6, 1967.

64. *New York Times*, Jun. 21, 1967; Jun. 22, 1967.

65. RG 59, CF 67–9, Box 2306, POL 23–8, Beirut 11252, Jun. 6, 1967.

66. Ibid., DEF 12 LEB, Beirut A-1455, Nov. 15, 1968; see also *New York Times*, Jun. 7, 1967.

67. FAOH interview, Dwight Porter.

68. The Phalange militia allegedly also cordoned off the Jewish sector of Beirut against the possibility of attacks until the Lebanese security forces arrived. RG 59, CF 67–9, Box 2304, POL 13, Beirut A-1417, Oct. 21, 1968.

69. LBJL-NSFCF, Files of the Special Committee of the NSC [LBJL-NSF-CF-SC], Box 113, "Lebanon," Beirut 21A, Jun. 30, 1967.

70. RG 59, CF 67–69, Box 2304, POL 12 LEB, Beirut 11663, No Subject, Jun. 22, 1967.

71. LBJL-NSF-CF-SC, Box 5, "Lebanon," Beirut 61, No Subject, Jul. 5, 1967. For an NLP request in July, see RG 59, CF 67–69, Box 2304, POL 12 LEB, Beirut A-27, Jul. 12, 1967.

72. RG 59, CF 67–9, Box 2304, POL 13-3, Beirut A-12, Jul. 7, 1967.

73. LBJL-NSF-CF-SC, Box 5, Lebanon, Telegram, Beirut 308, Jul. 13, 1967.

74. Ibid., Beirut 693, Jul. 21, 1967.

75. Ibid., Beirut A-55, "Arab Boycott Ford, R.C.A, Coca Cola," Jul. 21, 1967.

76. Ibid., Beirut 721, Jul. 28, 1967.

77. Ibid., Beirut 880, Aug. 3, 1967.

78. See Ashton, *King Hussein*, 121–22.

79. Quandt, *Peace Process*, 45.

80. FRUS, 1964–8, Vol. XIX, Doc. 237.

81. FRUS, 1964–8, Vol. XIX, Doc. 311.

82. FRUS, 1964–8, Vol. XIX, Doc. 310; Doc. 330 (footnote).

83. RG 59, CF 67–69, Box 2307, POL LEB-US, State 12993, Jul. 23, 1967.

84. Lambrakis, "Perception and Misperception," 136–37.

85. RG 59, CF 1967–9, E 2 LEB, Box 1613, A-218, Sep. 13, 1967.

86. Hussein's comments in Ashton, *King Hussein*, 129.

87. Kalawoun, *The Struggle for Lebanon*, 137.

88. Ihsan Hijazi, "War Shakes Beirut's Economy," *New York Times*, Jan. 15, 1968.

89. Quandt, *Peace Process*, 47.

90. Little, "The Making of a Special Relationship," 579.

91. LBJL-NSF-CF, Middle East, Box 148, Vol. V, Memo, Helms to President, Dec. 7, 1967.

92. RG 59, CF 67–9, Box 1573, DEF 1–6 LEB, Beirut 6500, Feb. 9, 1968.

93. CREST #CIA-RDP79-00927A006300050003-7, CIA, Weekly Summary—Special Report, "Lebanon Faces Crucial Elections," Mar. 8, 1968; RG 59, CF 67–9, Box 2304, POL 14, "Ex-President Chamoun's Request for U.S. Support in the Lebanese Elections," Feb. 14, 1968. Frangie also urged the US to be ready to intervene. RG 59, CF 67–9, Box 2304, Beirut 7344, "Lebanese Elections," Mar. 12, 1968.

94. RG 59, CF 67–69, Box 2305, POL 15-1 LEB, Beirut 6838, Feb 21, 1968.

95. Ibid., POL 14 LEB, State 130370, Mar. 14, 1968.

96. On the strikes in spring, see Betty S. Anderson, "Voices of Protest: Arab Nationalism and the Palestinian Revolution at the American University of Beirut," *Comparative Studies of South Asia, Africa and the Middle East* 28, no. 3 (2008): 261–80; Makram Rabah, *A Campus at War: Student Politics at the American University of Beirut 1967–1975* (Beirut: Dar Nelson, 2009).

97. Ismael and Ismael, *The Communist Movement in Syria and Lebanon*, 95–96; Sayigh, "Reconstructing the Paradox," 628; Al-Kubaisi, "The Arab Nationalist Movement," 99.

98. See Ashton, *King Hussein*, 138–39.

99. NARA, Records Relating to Iraq, Jordan, Lebanon and Syria, 1966–72 [RRI-JLS], Box 1, "Letters from Posts, Lebanon, 1968," Letter, Official-Informal, Mak to Houghton, Mar. 14, 1968.

100. Sayigh, *Armed Struggle*, 188.

101. Ibid.

102. FBIS, May 13, 1968, citing Beirut Domestic Service, May 12.

103. FBIS, May 14, 1968, citing Damascus MENA.

104. FRUS, 1964–8, Vol. XIX, Doc. 174.

105. RRIAIA, Box 2, "Briefing Papers, 1968 (1 of 3)," memo, Battle to Atherton, "Your Meeting with Ambassador Rabin," May 17, 1968.

106. FRUS, 1964–8, Vol. XIX, Doc. 192. See also Lambrakis, "Perception and Misperception," 140.

107. FBIS, Damascus MENA, Aug. 6, 1968.

108. Samir Ishaq was the Phalange representative. RG 59, CF 67–9, Box 2304, POL 13, A-1417, "The Phalange Party," Oct. 21, 1968.

109. RRIJLS, Box 1, "Memcons—Misc.," Memcon, Talhouk and Porter, Oct. 22, 1968.

110. Sayigh, *Armed Struggle*, 189.

111. RG 59, CF 1967–9, Box 2306, POL 23 LEB, Beirut 11090, Jul. 17, 1968. See also US Foreign Broadcast Information Service, Daily Reports: Middle East & Africa [FBIS], July 18, 1968, citing Damascus Middle East News Agency [MENA], July 17.

112. See, e.g., Katzenbach's comments in LBJL, NSF, Box 2, NSC Meeting Minutes, Feb. 26, 1968.

113. LBJL-NSF-CF, Middle East, Box 103, Middle East, Vol. I, Rostow to LBJ, Mar. 30, 1968; Memo, "Next Step with Israel-Jordan," Mar. 29, 1968.

114. Avi Shlaim, *Lion of Jordan: The Life of King Hussein in War and Peace* (New York: Vintage Books, 2009), 286–88.

115. LBJL, LBJ Confidential File, Box 6, Note, Rostow to LBJ, May 23, 1968; Letter, Rusk to LBJ, May 23, 1968; LBJL, NSF, CF, Box 103, Middle East [3 of 3], Vol. II, Memo, E. Rostow, No Subject, Jun. 25, 1968.

116. *New York Times*, Oct. 20, 1968.

117. FBIS, Nov 15, 1968, citing MENA reports.

118. *New York Times*, Nov. 15, 1968; FBIS, Nov 15, 1968, citing MENA reports; Paul Chamberlin, "Preparing for Dawn: The United States and the Global Politics of Palestinian Resistance, 1967–1975" (PhD diss., Ohio State University, 2009), 67.

119. RG 59, CF 67–9, Box 2406, POL 23–8 LEB, State 270894, "Lebanese Internal Defense Capabilities," Nov. 13, 1968.

120. LBJL, NSF, Country File, Middle East, Box 103, Middle East, [1 of 3], Vol. II, Memo, Rostow to LBJ, "Recent Steps in the Mid-East," Nov. 15, 1968.

121. See Salibi, *Crossroads to Civil War*, 18.

122. Nāṣif, *The Deuxième Bureau*, 175–78; Sámí al-Khaṭíb, *In the Eye of the Event: Forty-Five Years for Lebanon (Fi 'ayn al-hadath: khamza wa 'arb'ayn 'ám l-'ajal lubnán)*, vol. 1 (Beirut: Ciel, 2009), 196–97. See also Wade Goria, *Sovereignty and Leadership in Lebanon, 1943–1976* (New York: Ithaca Press, 1985), 96.

123. FBIS, Jan. 16, *Al-Nahar*, Jan. 12, 1969.

124. FBIS, Jan. 14, 1969, citing Cairo MENA, Jan. 13.

125. FBIS, Jan. 14, 1969, citing Cairo MENA, Jan. 13.

126. RRIJLS, Box 3, Memos with NEA, Memo, Seelye to Hart, Dec. 30, 1968; Box 5, "Pol-2 Gen. Reports & Stats. Lebanon," Memo, Jan. 8, 1969.

127. LBJL, NSF, Country File, Middle East, Box 103, Middle East, [1 of 3], Vol. II, No Author [NSC], Point Paper, Political-Military Situation in Middle East, Jan. 9, 1969.

128. Peter Groses, "Johnson Aide Says Israel Disrupts Effort for Peace," *New York Times*, Dec. 30, 1968.

129. LBJL, Confidential File, Box 9, CO 126, Memo, Goldstein to President, Jan. 2, 1969.

130. UNBIS Documents, Letter, S/8945, "Letter Dated 29 December 1968 from the Permanent Representative of Lebanon Addressed to the President of the Security Council," Dec. 29, 1968.

131. Nixon Presidential Materials, NSC Country Files [henceforth NPM-NSC-CF], Box 604, "Israel Vol. I [1 of 2]," Tel Aviv 81, Jan. 2, 1969.

132. RRIJLS, Box 3, memos within NEA, Hart to Seelye, Dec. 30, 1968.

133. NPM-NSC-CF, Box 604, "Israel Vol. I [1 of 2]," "Arab Sabotage and Terrorism against Israel," Dec. 20, 1968. Transferred under cover on Jan. 2, 1969.

134. NPM-NSC-CF, Box 647, "Middle East Negotiations State Outgoing 1969" [2 of 2], State 1428, "Special Summary Number 240," Jan. 5, 1969.

135. Ibid., State 2784, "Special Summary No. 6," Jan. 8, 1969.

136. NPM-NSC-CF, Box 604, "Israel Vol. I [1 of 2]," Tel Aviv 67, Jan. 6, 1969.

137. Ibid., "Israel Vol. I [1 of 2]," Tel Aviv 68, Jan. 2, 1969.

138. NPM-NSC-CF, Box 647, "Middle East Negotiations State Outgoing 1969" [2 of 2], State 2017, Jan. 7, 1969.

139. NPM-NSC-CF, Box 620, "Lebanon Vol. 1, Jan 69–31 Jan 70 [3 of 3]," State 2768, Jan. 8, 1969.

140. RG 59, CF 1967–9, Box 2403, POL 2 LEB, Beirut 163, Jan. 7, 1969.

141. NPM-NSC-CF, Box 647, "Middle East Negotiations State Outgoing 1969" [2 of 2], State 2784, Jan. 8, 1969; Box 604, "Israel Vol. I [1 of 2]," Tel Aviv 316, Jan. 27, 1969.

142. RRIJLS, Box 5, "Pol-2 Gen. Reports & Stats. Lebanon," Letter, Official-Informal, Seelye to Porter, Jan. 9, 1969.

143. Mahmoud Riad, *The Struggle for Peace in the Middle East* (London: Quartet Books, 1981), 91.

2. Compromise in Cairo

1. See, e.g., Kamal Salibi, *Crossroads to Civil War: Lebanon 1958–1976* (Delmar, NY: Caravan Books, 1976).

2. Charles Helou, *Mémoires*, vol. 2 (Beirut: An-Nahar), 146.

3. FAOH, Holsey G. Handeyside.

4. On the differences between Kissinger and the State Department, see, inter alia, William B. Quandt, *Peace Process: American Diplomacy and the Arab-Israeli Conflict since 1967*, 3rd ed. (Washington, DC: Brookings Institution Press, 2005), 61–62; Jüssi

Hanhimäki, *The Flawed Architect: Henry Kissinger and American Foreign Policy* (Oxford: Oxford University Press, 2004), 94–98.

5. See James Stocker, "Diplomacy as Counter-Revolution? The 'Moderate States,' the Fedayeen and State Department Initiatives towards the Arab-Israeli Conflict, 1969–1970," *Cold War History* 12, no. 3 (2012), 407–28, esp. 413.

6. Wade Goria, *Sovereignty and Leadership in Lebanon, 1943–1976* (New York: Ithaca Press, 1985), 98.

7. NPM-NSC-CF, Box 620, Lebanon Vol. 1[3 of 3], Beirut 733, Jan. 23, 1969.

8. Ibid., State 4211, "Lebanese Views Re ILMAC and Israeli-Lebanese Border Problems," Jan. 10, 1969.

9. RG 59, RRIAIA, Box 22, "POL 32-1 Israel/Lebanon 1969," Memo, Atherton to Sisco, "Lebanese Approach to British on Reviving ILMAC," Mar. 31, 1969.

10. NPM-NSC-CF, Box 620, Lebanon Vol. 1[2 of 3], Beirut 1325, Feb. 11, 1969.

11. Ibid., Beirut 1632, Feb. 20, 1969.

12. NPM-NSC-CF, Box 620, Lebanon Vol. 1[3 of 3], State 44798, Mar. 23, 1969.

13. Niqúlá Náṣif, *The Deuxième Bureau: Ruling in the Shadow (Al-maktab al-tháni: ḥákim fi-l-ẓul)* (Beirut: Dár mukhtárát, 2007), 281.

14. Sámí al-Khaṭíb, *In the Eye of the Event: Forty-Five Years for Lebanon (Fi 'ayn al-hadath: khamza wa 'arb'ayn 'ám l-'ajal lubnán),* vol. 1 (Beirut: Ciel, 2009), 1, 207–8.

15. Goria, *Sovereignty and Leadership in Lebanon,* 118.

16. NPM-NSC-CF, Box 620, Lebanon Vol. 1[2 of 3], Beirut 888, Jan. 28, 1969.

17. Reference to a request in January by Gemayel's militia is made in an April telegram, but there are no details here. NPM-NSC-CF, Box 620, Lebanon Vol. 1[3 of 3], State 67131, Apr. 30, 1969.

18. NPM-NSC-CF, Box 620, Lebanon Vol. 1[2 of 3], Beirut 888, Jan. 28, 1969.

19. Ibid., Beirut 2931, "Increased Fedayeen Presence in Lebanon," Apr. 8, 1969.

20. See, e.g., Helou, *Mémoires,* 2, 206.

21. NPM-NSC-CF, Box 620, Lebanon Vol. 1[2 of 3], Beirut 2931, Apr. 8, 1969.

22. Ibid., Beirut 3178, Apr. 16, 1969.

23. Farid el-Khazen, *The Breakdown of the State in Lebanon, 1967–1976* (London: I.B. Tauris, 2000), 144.

24. Ibid.

25. Júrj al-Baṭal, "Reading the Life Story of a Communist Leader (Qirá'a fi síra qá'id shiyú'í)," in *George Hawi: Positions of the Leader and Testimonies of Comrades (Jurj ḥáwí: muwáqif al-qá'id wa shahádát al-rifáq)* (Beirut: Dar al-Nahár, 2005), 63–64.

26. NPM-NSC-CF, Box 620, Lebanon Vol. 1[2 of 3], Beirut 3178, "GOL's Policy on Fedayeen Intervention," Apr. 16, 1969.

27. Ibid., Beirut 3253, Apr. 18, 1969.

28. Ibid., Beirut 3178, Apr. 16, 1969. See also RRIJLS, Box 5, "Pol-7 Visits and Meetings, Lebanon, 1969," Briefing Memorandum, Seelye to Sisco, "Your Meeting with Ambassador Kabbani," Apr. 25, 1969.

29. NPM-NSC-CF, Box 620, Lebanon Vol. 1[2 of 3], Beirut 2931, Apr. 8, 1969.

30. RRIJLS, Box 5, "Pol 13-10 Fedayeen, 1969," Memo, Yosef Ben-Aharon, Bryan Bass, Apr. 16, 1969.

31. FRUS, 1969–76, Vol. XXIV, Doc. 7.

32. RRIJLS, Box 5, "Pol-2 Gen. Reports & Stats. Lebanon," Letter, Seelye to Porter, May 2, 1969; RG 59, Sisco Lot Files [SLF], Box 17, Draft Cable, May 8, 1969; NPM-NSC-CF, Box 620, Lebanon Vol. 1[2 of 3], Beirut 3465, Apr. 26, 1969.

33. NPM-NSC-CF, Box 620, Lebanon Vol. 1[2 of 3], Beirut 2931, Apr. 8, 1969.

34. RG 59, CF 67–69, "POL 17 LEB-US," Box 2307, Beirut 3410, Apr. 23, 1969.

35. FRUS, 1969–76, Vol. XXIV, Doc. 3.

36. RRIJLS, Box 5, Pol-1 General Policy, Background, 1968–1969, Memo, Country Policy Appraisal [Draft, sent Dec. 30, 1968].

37. Ibid., Memo, Seelye to Sisco, "Contingency Planning for Lebanon," Apr. 28, 1969.

38. NPM-NSC-CF, Box 620, Lebanon Vol. 1[2 of 3], Beirut 3678, May 3, 1969.

39. NPM-NSC-CF, Box 620, Lebanon Vol. 1[3 of 3], Draft Cable, May 6, 1969.

40. RRIJLS, Box 5, "Pol-2 Gen. Reports & Stats. Lebanon," Letter, Seelye to Porter, May 8, 1969.

41. NPM-NSC-CF, Box 620, Lebanon Vol. 1[3 of 3], State 70266, May 6, 1969.

42. NPM-NSC-CF, Box 620, Lebanon Vol. 1[2 of 3], Beirut 3824, No subject, May 8, 1969.

43. Ibid., Beirut 3881, May 9, 1969.

44. NPM-NSC-CF, Box 620, Lebanon Vol. 1[3 of 3], State 66691, Apr. 29, 1969.

45. NPM-NSC-CF, Box 620, Lebanon Vol. 1[2 of 3], Beirut 3881, May 9, 1969.

46. Ibid., Beirut 3868, May 9, 1969; Beirut 4270, May 23, 1969.

47. NPM-NSC-CF, Box 620, Lebanon Vol. 1[2 of 3], Beirut 3545, Apr. 29, 1969.

48. NPM-NSC-CF, Box 620, Lebanon Vol. 1[3 of 3], State 67131, Apr. 30, 1969.

49. RG 59, CF 67–69, "POL 15 LEB," Box 2305, "Views of Ex-President Camille Chamoun," May 1, 1969.

50. RG 59, CF 67–69, "POL 17 LEB-US," Box 2307, State 68459, May 2, 1969.

51. NPM-NSC-CF, Box 620, Lebanon Vol. 1[3 of 3], State 68447, May 1, 1969.

52. NPM-NSC-CF, Box 620, Lebanon Vol. 1[2 of 3], Beirut 3659, May 2, 1969.

53. NPM-NSC-CF, Box 620, Lebanon Vol. 1[3 of 3], State 69429, May 3, 1969.

54. Ibid., State 75036, May 12, 1969.

55. NPM-NSC-CF, Box 620, Lebanon Vol. 1[2 of 3], Beirut 4375, May 28, 1969.

56. el-Khazen, *The Breakdown*, 146–47.

57. Nāṣif, *The Deuxième Bureau*, 278.

58. NPM-NSC-CF, Box 620, Lebanon Vol. 1[2 of 3], Beirut 4035, May 15, 1969.

59. Helou, *Mémoires*, 2, 172–73.

60. el-Khazen, *The Breakdown*, 156, citing 1997 article by Boustany in *As-Safir*.

61. al-Khaṭīb, *In the Eye of the Event*, 1, 215–16.

62. RRIJLS, Box 5, "Pol-2 Gen. Reports & Stats. Lebanon," Letter, Seelye to Porter, Jun. 13, 1969.

63. NPM-NSC-CF, Box 620, Lebanon Vol. 1[2 of 3], Beirut 5469, Jun. 30, 1969.

64. Ibid., Beirut 5470, Jun. 30, 1969.

65. RG 59, CF 67–69, "POL 12 LEB," Box 2305, Airgram A-282, "Views of ex-President Camille Chamoun on Lebanese Crisis," Jul. 3, 1969.

66. RG 59, "POL 12 LEB," Box 2305, Airgram A-301, "Phalangist Request for Arms," Jul. 15, 1969.

67. RG 59, CF 67–69, "POL 2 LEB," Box 2304, Airgram, A-324, "The Dilemma of the Pro-West Lebanese," Aug. 1, 1969.

68. RRIJLS, "Pol-2 General Reports and Statistics, Misc., 1969," Box 5, Memo, Seelye to Davies, "Miscellaneous Items," Aug. 1, 1969.

69. NPM-NSC-CF, Box 624, "Middle East—General Vol. 1 (February–September 69) [3 of 3], Memo, Saunders to Kissinger, "President's Tuesday Briefing," May 5, 1969.

70. *New York Times*, Aug. 11, 1969.

71. SLF, Box 27, "Memoranda for the NSC (folder 1)," NSC Interdepartmental Group for Near East and South Asia, "Contingency Study of Resumption of Arab-Israeli Hostilities," Aug. 8, 1969.

72. SLF, Box 17, "JJS Chron File—9-12/1969," Memo for the President, "Next Steps on the Middle East," Sep. 4, 1969. See also Quandt, *Peace Process*, 66.

73. NPM-NSC-CF, Box 620, Lebanon Vol. 1[2 of 3], Beirut 6806, Aug. 15, 1969.

74. NPM-NSC-CF, Box 604, Israel Vol. II [2 of 3], Tel Aviv 3175, Aug. 19, 1969.

75. RRIJLS, Box 5, "Pol-2 Gen. Reports & Stats. Lebanon," Letter, Seelye to Houghton, Aug. 22, 1969.

76. NPM-NSC-CF, Box 604, Israel Vol. II [2 of 3], State 146323, Aug. 29, 1969.

77. RRIJLS, Box 5, "Pol-7 Visits and Meetings, Lebanon, 1969," Memo, Seelye to Sisco, "Ambassador Kabbani's Call on You at 3:00 p.m. Wednesday September 17, 1969," Sep. 16, 1969.

78. RG 59, CF 67–69, "POL 23 LEB," Box 2306, Beirut 7419, Sep. 6, 1969.

79. On these points, see Abbas Samii, "The Shah's Lebanon Policy: The Role of SAVAK," *Middle Eastern Studies* 33, no. 1 (1997): 66–91.

80. RG 59, CF 67–69, "POL LEB-A," Box 2307, State 159222, Sep. 18, 1969.

81. RG 59, CF 67–69, "POL 23 LEB," Box 2306, Tehran 3800, Sep. 22, 1969.

82. NPM-NSC-CF, Box 620, Lebanon Vol. 1[3 of 3], State 152733, Sep. 10, 1969.

83. NPM-NSC-CF, Box 620, Lebanon Vol. 1[2 of 3], Beirut 7563, Sep. 11, 1969.

84. Ibid., Beirut 7577, Sep. 12, 1969.

85. RG 59, CF 67–69, "POL 23 LEB," Box 2306, State 157557, Sep. 17, 1969.

86. NPM-NSC-CF, Box 620, Lebanon Vol.1[3 of 3], Beirut 7992, Sep. 24, 1969. On September 30, Khoury told Porter that Helou had received a similar message from Eban via the Vatican, and that Israel had not contacted them through other channels, such as at the border. Ibid., Beirut 8074, Sep. 30, 1969.

87. NPM-NSC-CF, Box 620, Lebanon Vol. 1[3 of 3], Beirut 8008, Sep. 26, 1969.

88. Salibi, *Crossroads to Civil War*, 41–42.

89. RRIJLS, Box 5, "Pol-2 Gen. Reports & Stats. Lebanon," Letter, Seelye to Porter, Oct. 17, 1969.

90. Ibid., Letter, Seelye to Porter, Sep. 18, 1969.

91. Ibid., Letter, Seelye to Porter, Oct. 10, 1969.

92. See its mention in Jewish Telegraph Agency, Online Archive, "United States Urges Avoidance of Any Assault on Territorial Integrity of Lebanon," October 15, 1969, available at http://archive.jta.org.

93. Ibid., Letter, Seelye to Porter, Oct. 17, 1969.

94. Cited in Helou, *Mémoires*, 2, 215–16.

95. RG 59, CF 1966–69, POL 23 LEB, Box 2306, Beirut 8640, "Pres Helou's Reaction to Sisco Statement on Lebanon," Oct. 17, 1969.

96. See, e.g., *Al-Nahar*, Oct. 1, 1969. See al-Khaṭib, *In the Eye of the Event*, 1, 221.

97. Victor Cherkashin and Gregory Feifer, *Spy Handler: Memoir of a KGB Officer* (New York: Basic Books, 2005), 96–98.

98. See Stocker, "Diplomacy as Counter-Revolution," 414.

99. Goria, *Sovereignty and Leadership in Lebanon*, 107.

100. el-Khazen, *The Breakdown*, 148.

101. NPM-NSC-CF, Box 620, Lebanon Vol. 1[1 of 3], Memo, Kissinger to Nixon, "Reflections on Lebanon," No date, [circa Oct. 28, 1969].

102. The cable for this, probably State 180291, was not found in the State Department Central Files, but its content can be inferred from several responses that are there. See, e.g., Beirut 8846 (below).

103. NPM-NSC-CF, Box 620, Lebanon Vol. 1[2 of 3], Beirut 8846, Oct. 24, 1969.

104. Ibid., State 180949, Oct. 24, 1969.

105. NPM-NSC-CF, Box 620, Lebanon Vol. 1[3 of 3], State 180293, Oct. 24, 1969; State 180294, Oct. 24, 1969; State 181404, Oct. 25, 1969; State 182820, Oct. 29, 1969.

106. NPM-NSC-CF, Box 620, Lebanon Vol. 1[3 of 3], State 180289, Oct. 24, 1969; NPM-NSC-CF, Box 604, Israel Vol. II [2 of 3], Tel Aviv 4035, "Lebanon," Oct. 24, 1969.

107. NPM-NSC-CF, Box 604, Israel Vol. I [1 of 2]," State 180300, Oct. 24, 1969.

108. NPM-NSC-CF, Box 620, Lebanon Vol. 1[1 of 3], Memo, Rogers to Nixon, Oct. 27, 1969.

109. Ibid., Beirut 9027, Oct. 30, 1969; State 183705, Oct. 30, 1969.

110. el-Khazen, *The Breakdown*, 164.

111. NPM-NSC-CF, Box 620, Lebanon Vol. 1[2 of 3], Beirut 8845, Oct. 24, 1969.

112. Ibid., Beirut 8921, Oct. 27, 1969.

113. NPM-NSC-CF, Box 620, Lebanon Vol. 1[1 of 3], Memo, Rogers to Nixon, "Crisis in Lebanon," Oct. 27, 1969.

114. DNSA, Kissinger Telcons, Sisco and Kissinger, Oct. 25, 1969.

115. NPM-NSC-CF, Box 620, Lebanon Vol. 1[1 of 3], Memo, Rogers to Nixon, "Crisis in Lebanon," Oct. 27, 1969.

116. DNSA, Kissinger Telcons, Kissinger, Nixon, Oct. 25, 1969.

117. NPM-NSC-CF, Box 620, Lebanon Vol. 1[1 of 3], Memo, Saunders to Kissinger, "Statement on Lebanon," Oct. 27, 1969.

118. NPM, Kissinger Telcons, Box 2, "Telephone Conversations—Chron File, 10," Joe Sisco, Oct. 28, 1969, 3:55 p.m.

119. NPM-NSC-CF, Box 651, "Middle East (Vol. II) [1 of 2]," State 185136, Nov. 1, 1969.

120. NPM-NSC-CF, Box 620, Lebanon Vol. 1[2 of 3], Beirut 8921, Oct. 27, 1969.

121. NPM-NSC-CF, Box 620, Lebanon Vol. 1[1 of 3], Memo, Rogers to Nixon, "Crisis in Lebanon," Oct. 29, 1969; *Al-Nahar*, Oct. 28, 1969.

122. NPM-NSC-CF, Box 620, Lebanon Vol. 1[3 of 3], State 182970, Oct. 29, 1969.

123. NPM-NSC-CF, Box 620, Lebanon Vol. 1[1 of 3], Beirut 8977, Oct. 28, 1969.

124. Ibid., Beirut 8981, Oct. 28, 1969.

125. See *Al-Nahar*, Oct. 28, 1969.

126. Helou, *Mémoires*, 2, 261–62. Cited in el-Khazen, *The Breakdown*, 158.

127. Only the Phalange is referred to in the minutes of this meeting, but the aid may well have been intended for delivery to other militias, too.

128. RRIJLS, Box 5, "Pol-2 Gen. Reports & Stats. Lebanon," Status Report, DCM to Ambassador, Sep. 20, 1969; RG 59, CF 67–69, "POL LEB," Box 2304, Memcon, Seelye and Tabourian, Sep. 30, 1969.

129. FRUS, 1969–1976, Vol. XXIII, Doc. 60.

130. NPM, HAK Telcons, "Telecons [*sic*]: Kissinger and the President," Oct. 31, 1969, 9:40 a.m.

131. NPM-NSC-CF, Box 620, Lebanon Vol. 1[1 of 3], Memo, To the Secretary of Defense, "Lebanon," Nov. 4, 1969.

132. NPM-NSC-CF, Box 620, Lebanon Vol. 1[1 of 3], Memo, Rogers to Nixon, "Crisis in Lebanon," Oct. 23, 1969; Rogers to Nixon, "Crisis in Lebanon," Oct. 25, 1969; State 181399, Oct. 25, 1969; Beirut 8893, Oct. 25, 1969.

133. Ibid., Memo, Rogers to Nixon, "Crisis in Lebanon," Oct. 27, 1969.

134. NPM-NSC-CF, Box 620, Lebanon Vol. 1[1 of 3], Saunders to Kissinger, Memo, "Memo for the President on Lebanon," Oct. 28, 1969.

135. NPM-NSC-CF, Box 334, "Items to Discuss with the President, 8/13/9–12/30/69 [2 of 3]," Memo, Haig to Kissinger, "Items to Discuss with the President, October 29, 1969," Oct. 29, 1969.

136. NPM-NSC-CF, Box 620, Lebanon Vol. 1[1 of 3], Memo, Rogers to Nixon, "Crisis in Lebanon," Oct. 27, 1969.

137. FRUS, 1969–1976, Vol. XXIII, Doc. 60.

138. NPM-NSC-CF, Box 620, Lebanon Vol. 1[3 of 3], Beirut 9054, Oct. 31, 1969.

139. RG 59, CF 67–69, "POL 23 LEB," Box 2306, London 8961, Nov. 1, 1969.

140. NPM-NSC-CF, Box 620, Lebanon Vol. 1[3 of 3], Beirut 9083, Nov. 1, 1969.

141. NPM-NSC-CF, Box 620, Lebanon Vol. 1[1 of 3], Intelligence Note, Denney to Rogers, Oct. 27, 1969.

142. NPM-NSC-CF, Box 613, "Israel Vol. II 6/1/69–To–30 Nov 69," Amman 5217, Oct. 28, 1969.

143. NPM-NSC-CF, Box 620, Lebanon Vol. 1[1 of 3], Beirut 8981, Oct. 28, 1969.

144. NPM-NSC-CF, Box 620, Lebanon Vol. 1[3 of 3], Beirut 9054, Oct. 31, 1969; Beirut 9081, Nov. 1, 1969.

145. For the text, see "Towards Lebanese National Reconciliation: Reference Texts," in *Reference Texts* (Geneva: Centre for the Democratic Control of Armed Forces [DCAF], 2009).

146. In NPM-NSC-CF, Box 620, Lebanon Vol. 1[3 of 3], Beirut 9245, Nov. 6, 1969.

147. Ibid., Beirut 9244, Nov. 6, 1969.

148. Ibid., State 189505, Nov. 8, 1969.

149. Ibid., Beirut 9244, Nov. 6, 1969.

150. NPM-NSC-CF, Box 624, "Middle East—General Vol. II (Oct 69–Jan 70) [1 of 2], Memo, Kissinger to Nixon, "New Soviet Doctrine on the Middle East," Nov. 10, 1969.

151. SLF, Box 17, "JJS Chron File—9-12/1969," Draft Telegram, No Subject, No date [November 1969]. Later sent as State 187681.

152. Ibid., Memo, Secretary to President, "Four Power Talks on the Middle East," Nov. 18, 1969.

3. From Cairo to Amman

1. NPM-NSC-CF, Box 620, Lebanon Vol. 1[3 of 3], Beirut 9560, Nov. 18, 1969.

2. Ibid., Beirut 4280, Jan. 10, 1970.

3. Ibid., Memo, Saunders to Kissinger, "Rifles for Lebanon," Nov. 24, 1969; Kissinger to President, "Arms for the Lebanese Government," Nov. 28, 1969.

4. NPM-NSC-CF, Box 620, Lebanon Vol. 1[3 of 3], State 205505, Dec. 11, 1969.

5. USAID Greenbook.

6. NPM-NSC-CF, Box 620, Lebanon Vol. 1[3 of 3], Beirut 4280, Jan. 10, 1970.

7. NPM-NSC-CF, Box 620, Lebanon Vol. 1[1 of 3], Beirut 802, Jan. 29, 1970.

8. NPM-NSC-CF, Box 621, Lebanon Vol. II [2 of 2], Beirut 1372, Feb. 20, 1970.

9. NPM-NSC-CF, Box 620, Lebanon Vol. 1[3 of 3], Beirut 9568, Nov. 19, 1969. On Soghanalian's role in arming the Christian militias, see "Merchants of Death" (CBS News, Discovery Channel, 1999), 2:00.

10. NPM-NSC-CF, Box 620, Lebanon Vol. 1[3 of 3], State 197912, Nov. 25, 1969.

11. NPM-NSC-CF, Box 621, Lebanon Vol. II, Beirut 1726, Mar. 4, 1970.

12. Ibid., Beirut 1869, Mar. 10, 1970.

13. Ibid., Beirut 1989, Mar. 13, 1970.

14. Ibid., Memo, Haig to Kissinger, No subject, Mar. 16, 1970.

15. Ibid., Beirut 2944, Apr. 15, 1970.

16. RG 59, CF 67–69, POL 23 LEB," Box 2306, Beirut 9634, Nov. 20, 1969.

17. FRUS, 1969–76, Vol. XXIII, Doc. 68.

18. FOIA Request #NW 33645, RG 59, Central Files, 1967–9, POL LEB 23–8, Memo, Sisco to Secretary, "Crisis in Lebanon," Dec. 9, 1969.

19. NPM-NSC-CF, Box 620, Lebanon Vol. 1[1 of 3], Airgram, Beirut A-514, "Phalange Request for Arms," Nov. 26, 1969.

20. Ibid., Beirut 9738, Nov. 25, 1969.

21. NPM-NSC-CF, Box 620, Lebanon Vol. 1[1 of 3], Airgram, Beirut A-502, "Uneasiness among Armenian Community in Lebanon (Need for Arms)," Nov. 20, 1969; Beirut A-501, "Request for Arms by Druze Deputy of Aley, Sheikh Fadlallah Talhouk," Nov. 20, 1969.

22. RG 59, CF 67–69, POL LEB, Box 2304, Airgram, A-537, "Tour d'horizon with the French Ambassador," Dec. 11, 1969.

23. RG 59, CF 67–69, POL 15-1 LEB, Box 2305, Airgram, Beirut A-554, "December 12 Meeting with President Helou," Dec. 23, 1969.

24. NPM-NSC-CF, Box 620, Folder 6, POL 23-3 LEB, Airgram, A-55, Jan. 28, 1970.

25. NPM-NSC-CF, Box 621, Lebanon Vol. II[2 of 2], Beirut 1104, Feb. 9, 1970.

26. Ibid., Beirut 1350, Feb. 20, 1970.

27. Ibid., Beirut 2959, Apr. 15, 1970.

28. A survey by *al-Nahar* maintained that 52 percent of the public thought that Lebanon's stability required a strong government, a strengthened army, and the president remaining in office without resigning. *Al-Nahar*, Nov. 17.

29. el-Khazen, *The Breakdown*, 164.

30. Niqúlá Náṣíf, *The Deuxième Bureau: Ruling in the Shadow (Al-maktab al-tháni: hákim fi-l-ẓul)* (Beirut: Dár mukhtárát, 2007), 305.

31. *Al-Nahar*, Nov. 26, 1969.

32. Rex Brynen, *Sanctuary and Survival: The PLO in Lebanon* (Boulder, CO: Westview Press, 1990), 54.

33. Yezid Sayigh, *Armed Struggle and the Search for State: The Palestinian National Movement, 1949–1993* (Oxford: Clarendon Press, 1997), 193.

34. NPM-NSC-CF, Box 620, Lebanon Vol. 1[1 of 3], Beirut 10209, Dec. 13, 1969.

35. Sámí al-Khaṭíb, *In the Eye of the Event: Forty-Five Years for Lebanon (Fi ʿayn al-hadath: khamza wa ʾarbʾayn ʿám l-ʾajal lubnán)*, vol. 1 (Beirut: Ciel, 2009), 1, 269.

36. *Al-Nahar*, Dec. 17, 1969.

37. William B. Quandt, *Peace Process: American Diplomacy and the Arab-Israeli Conflict since 1967*, 3rd ed. (Washington, DC: Brookings Institution Press, 2005), 68.

38. FRUS, 1969–76, Vol. XXIV, Doc. 18.

39. FRUS, 1969–76, Vol. XXIV, Doc. 17. See also Beirut 4280, above.

40. *Al-Nahar*, Dec. 24, 1969; el-Khazen, *The Breakdown*, 189.

41. *Al-Nahar*, Jan. 3, 1970.

42. *Al-Nahar*, Jan. 5, 1970. These were identified as twenty-two civilians from Kfarkila.

43. NPM-NSC-CF, Box 620, Lebanon Vol. 1[1 of 3], Beirut 258, Jan. 10, 1970.

44. NPM-NSC-CF, Box 620, Lebanon Vol. 1[3 of 3], State 5147, Jan. 13, 1970; State 7920, Jan. 17, 1970.

45. RG 59, CF 70–73, Box 2050, POL 27 ARAB-ISR 1/16/70, Tel Aviv 270, Jan. 17, 1970.

46. NPM-NSC-CF, Box 620, Lebanon Vol. 1[1 of 3], Beirut 258, Jan. 10, 1970; Beirut 261, Jan. 11, 1970. In a later telegram, Khoury said that Abba Eban had tried to relay a message to Helou from a "Greek Catholic bishop [name unspecified]." NPM-NSC-CF, Box 621, Lebanon Vol. II, Beirut 4518, Jun. 8, 1970. It is unclear whether these references are to the same individual, though it is likely. At this time, Christian clergy with permits were allowed to cross the border between Israel and Lebanon. *New York Times*, Aug. 9, 1968.

47. NPM-NSC-CF, Box 620, Lebanon Vol. 1[1 of 3], Beirut 261, Jan. 11, 1970. Helou also said that there was a fourth point that he would not make, which was that "a threatened Lebanon has the power to hurt Israel more than any Arab state has done to date." His reasoning was that "if Israel should decide [to] destroy Lebanon he would convoke leaders [of] all Lebanon's Christian communities and have

them use their maximum influence in all the Christian capitals of the world to turn sentiment against Israel."

48. Ibid., Beirut 258, Jan. 10, 1970.

49. *Al-Nahar*, Jan. 21, 1970.

50. James Feron, *New York Times*, "Likelihood of Action," Mar. 1, 1970; James Feron, *New York Times*, "Israel Asks West," Mar. 5, 1970.

51. NPM-NSC-CF, Box 621, Lebanon Vol. II [2 of 2], State 38852, Mar. 3, 1970.

52. Ibid., Beirut 1725, Mar. 4, 1970.

53. Frederic Hof, *Galilee Divided: The Israel-Lebanon Frontier, 1916–1984* (Boulder, CO: Westview Press, 1985), 73. See also Schmidt, Dana Adams, *New York Times*, "Threat to Beirut Reported," Mar. 7, 1970, 1.

54. NPM-NSC-CF, Box 606, "Israel Vol. IV [2 of 3]," State 32998, Mar. 6, 1970.

55. *Al-Nahar*, Mar. 7, 1969, 1–2.

56. NPM-NSC-CF, Box 621, Lebanon Vol. II, Beirut 1839, No Subject, Mar. 9, 1970.

57. *New York Times*, "Israel Fortifying Her Settlements at Lebanese Line," Mar. 11, 1970, 1.

58. In NPM-NSC-CF, Box 621, Lebanon Vol. II, Beirut 1875, Mar. 10, 1970; NPM-NSC-CF, Box 606, "Israel Vol. IV," Tel Aviv 1168, May 12, 1970.

59. NPM-NSC-CF, Box 606, "Israel Vol. IV," Tel Aviv 1168, May 12, 1970; Tel Aviv 1463, Mar. 20, 1970.

60. *New York Times*, "Beirut Adopts Plan to Avoid Clashes with Commandos," Mar. 21, 1970, 4.

61. *New York Times*, "Lebanese and Commando Leaders Appeal for Restraint," Mar. 27, 1970, 9.

62. Kamal Salibi, *Crossroads to Civil War: Lebanon 1958–1976* (Delmar, NY: Caravan Books, 1976), 45.

63. Dana Adams Schmidt, "Gunfire Spreads to Central Beirut," *New York Times*, Mar. 28, 1970, 7.

64. FAOH Interview, Robert Oakley.

65. NPM-NSC-CF, Box 621, Lebanon Vol. II, Beirut 2344, No Subject, Mar. 25, 1970.

66. Brynen, *Sanctuary and Survival*, 58; Shafiq al-Ḥút, *Between the Nation and Exile (Bayna al-waṭan w-al-munfá: min yáfá bad'a al-mashwár)* (Beirut: Riyáḍ al-rís l-il-katab w-al-nashar, 2007), 167.

67. RRIJLS, Box 8, "POL 12-10, Fedayeen Correspondence," Seelye to Sisco, "Summary Report of Internal Disturbances in Lebanon," Apr. 1, 1970. See also Goria, *Sovereignty and Leadership in Lebanon*, 119.

68. Wade Goria, *Sovereignty and Leadership in Lebanon, 1943–1976* (New York: Ithaca Press, 1985), 118.

69. NPM-NSC-CF, Box 621, Lebanon Vol. II, Beirut 2456, Mar. 27, 1970.

70. *New York Times*, "U.S. Property Hit, Arabs in Beirut Say," Mar. 30, 1970, 11.

71. NPM, Presidential Daily Diary, Apr. 16, 1970.

72. See NPM-NSC-CF, Box 601, Iran Vol. 1[3 of 3], State 59088, Apr. 21, 1970; NPM-NSC-CF, Box 621, Lebanon Vol. II[2 of 2], Beirut 7246, Aug. 31, 1970.

73. NPM-NSC-CF, Box 621, Lebanon Vol. II, State 136003, Aug. 20, 1970; Draft Message, "President's Reply to Message from Patriarch Meouchi," Aug. 13, 1970.

74. RRIJLS, Box 8, "Pol-1 General Policy; Background," Memo, "Answers to Possible Questions Posed by Symington Subcommittee," Undated [prob. May 1970]; NPM-NSC-CF, Box 621, Lebanon Vol. II [2 of 2], State 49939, Apr. 6, 1970.

75. *LA Times*, Apr. 19, 1970.

76. RRIJLS, Box 8, "Pol-1 General Policy; Background," Letter, Official-Informal, Seelye to Porter, May 19, 1970. On the role of the 40 Committee, see Jüssi Hanhimäki, *The Flawed Architect: Henry Kissinger and American Foreign Policy* (Oxford: Oxford University Press, 2004), 24.

77. Farid el-Khazen, *The Breakdown of the State in Lebanon, 1967–1976* (London: I.B. Tauris, 2000), 188–91.

78. *New York Times*, May 13, 1970.

79. See James Stocker, "Diplomacy as Counter-Revolution? The 'Moderate States,' the Fedayeen and State Department Initiatives towards the Arab-Israeli Conflict, 1969–1970," *Cold War History* 12, no. 3 (2012), 418–20.

80. Sam Pope Brewer, *New York Times*, "U.N. Asks Israelis to Leave Lebanon," May 13, 1970, 1; RG 59, RRIAIA, Box 20, "POL 17 Diplomatic and Consular Rep. (Amb. Rabin, etc.) 1970," State 79531, May 23, 1970.

81. NPM-NSC-CF, Box 621, Lebanon Vol. II, Beirut 4029, May 24, 1970.

82. RG 59, RRIAIA, Box 20, "POL 17 Diplomatic and Consular Rep. (Amb. Rabin, etc.) 1970," State 79567, May 24, 1970; Tel Aviv 2650, May 25, 1970.

83. NPM-NSC-CF, Box 607, "Israel Vol. V [2 of 3]," Tel Aviv 2676/1, May 25, 1970; State 80447, May 26, 1970.

84. NPM-NSC-CF, Box 621, Lebanon Vol. II, Beirut 4113, May 26, 1970.

85. Ibid., Beirut 4238, Jun. 1, 1970.

86. Ibid., State 84071, Jun. 2, 1970.

87. Ibid., Beirut 4311, Jun. 2, 1970; NPM-NSC-CF, Box 607, "Israel Vol. V [2 of 3]," Tel Aviv 2784, Jun. 2, 1970.

88. NPM-NSC-CF, Box 621, Lebanon Vol. II, Beirut 4351, Jun. 3, 1970.

89. NPM-NSC-CF, Box 607, "Israel Vol. V [2 of 3]," Tel Aviv 2810, Jun. 2, 1970.

90. Ibid., Tel Aviv 2837, Jun. 3, 1970; Tel Aviv 2838, Jun. 3, 1970.

91. NPM-NSC-CF, Box 621, Lebanon Vol. II, Beirut 4608, Jun. 10, 1970.

92. Ibid., Beirut 4518, Jun. 8, 1970.

93. Ibid., Beirut 4525, Jun. 8, 1970.

94. Kamal Salibi, *The Modern History of Jordan* (London: I.B. Tauris, 1993), 233.

95. NPM-NSC-CF, Box 621, Lebanon Vol. II, Beirut 4775, Jun. 13, 1970.

96. NPM-NSC-CF, Box 607, "Israel Vol. V [2 of 3]," State 91817, Jun. 12, 1970.

97. Ibid., Tel Aviv 3060, Jun. 13, 1970.

98. Ibid., Tel Aviv 3063, Jun. 13, 1970.

99. NPM-NSC-CF, Box 621, Lebanon Vol. II, Beirut 4771, Jun. 13, 1970.

100. NPM-NSC-CF, Box 621, Lebanon Vol. II, Beirut 4775, Jun. 13, 1970.

101. Ibid., Beirut 4859, Jun. 15, 1969.

102. NPM-NSC-CF, Box 607, "Israel Vol. V [2 of 3]," Tel Aviv 3116, Jun. 16, 1970.

103. Ibid., Beirut 4775, Jun. 13, 1970.

104. Ibid., Beirut 4912, Jun. 16, 1970.

105. Ibid.

106. DNSA, Kissinger Telcons, Sisco, Kissinger, Jun. 13, 1970; Rogers, Kissinger, Jun. 17, 1970.

107. Henry Alfred Kissinger, *White House Years* (Boston: Little, Brown and Company, 1979), 596–97.

108. Ibid., 597.

109. FRUS, 1969–1976, XXIV, Doc. 26.

110. NPM, NSC Institutional Files, Box H-078, "WSAG Meeting, Lebanon and Jordan, 6/22/70," Memo, Saunders and Kennedy to Kissinger, "WSAG on Lebanon and Jordan," Jun. 20, 1970.

111. See Quandt, *Peace Process*, 77.

112. NPM, NSC Institutional Files, Box H-078, "WSAG Meeting, Lebanon and Jordan, 6/22/70," Memo, "U.S. Intervention in Lebanon against Aggression," Jun. 20, 1970.

113. Ibid., Memo, "Summary of Conclusions," Jun. 22, 1970.

114. SLF, Box 17, "JJS Chron 9-12/1969," Letter, Sisco to Porter, Jun. 12, 1970.

115. NPM-NSC-CF, Box 621, Lebanon Vol. II, Beirut 4017, No Subject, May 22, 1970.

116. Ibid., Beirut 4990, No Subject, Jun. 18, 1970.

117. Ibid., Beirut 5168, No Subject, Jun. 23, 1970.

118. Ibid., Beirut 5562, No Subject, Jul. 6, 1970.

119. SLF, Box 25, "Middle East 1973 and Earlier," Sisco to Porter, "WASAG [*sic*] Meeting on Lebanon and Middle East at 3:00 P.M. Tuesday, May 15," May 14, 1973.

120. el-Khazen, *The Breakdown*, 193.

121. Quandt, *Peace Process*, 73–74.

122. See, e.g., Michael Johnson, *Class and Client in Beirut: The Sunni Muslim Community and the Lebanese State, 1840–1985* (London: Ithaca Press, 1986), 155; el-Khazen, *The Breakdown*, 193.

123. Salibi, *Crossroads to Civil War*, 46–47.

124. *Al-Nahar*, Jul. 5, 1970.

125. NPM-NSC-CF, Box 621, Folder 1, Report, Malik to Nixon, Jul. 13–20, 1970.

126. RG 59, CF 70–73, Box 2446, "POL 14 LEB," Airgram, Beirut A-326, "Opposition of Maronite Patriarch Meouchi to Presidential Candidacy of Fuad Chehab," Jul. 31, 1970.

127. Ibid., Airgram, Beirut A-328, "Lebanese Elections—Hajj Hussein Oueini," Aug. 3, 1970.

128. Bassám al-Jisr, *Fouad Chehab (Fu'ád shiháb)* (Beirut: Fouad Chehab Foundation (Mu'ásasat fu'ád shiháb), 1998).

129. Násif, *The Deuxième Bureau*, 339.

130. Ibid., 357.

131. RG 59, CF 70–73, POL 7 LEB, Box 2446, Airgram, Beirut A-276, "Lebanese Parliamentary Speaker to Visit USSR," Jun. 19, 1970; RG 59, CF 70–73, POL 14 LEB, Box 2446, Airgram, Beirut A-316, "Tidbits on the Lebanese Elections," Jul. 15, 1970.

132. NPM-NSC-CF, Box 621, Lebanon Vol. II, Beirut 5477, Jul. 1, 1970.

133. Ibid., Airgram A-311, "Soviets Offer Support to Michel Khoury for Presidential Elections," Jul. 17, 1970.

134. RG 59, CF 70–73, POL LEB-USSR, Airgram, Beirut A-300, "Recent Evidence of Increasing Soviet Influence in Lebanese Affairs," Jul. 7, 1970.

135. "The War of Lebanon (Ḥarb lubnán)," (Al-Jazíra, 2001), Episode 5, 27:00–29:00.

136. See Náṣíf, The Deuxième Bureau, 368–76.

137. RG 59, CF 70–73, POL 15-1 LEB, Box 2447, Airgram Beirut A-354, "First Post-Election Meeting with President-Elect Frangié," Aug. 28, 1970. See also Beirut 7245.

138. NPM-NSC-CF, Box 620, Lebanon Vol. II, Beirut 7245, Aug. 31, 1970.

139. NPM-NSC-CF, Box 621, Lebanon Vol. II, Beirut 7246, Aug. 31, 1970.

140. RRIJLS, Box 10, FT-11-2, Letter, Sep. 9, 1970.

141. al-Khaṭíb, In the Eye of the Event, 1, 284–87.

142. Mahmoud Riad, The Struggle for Peace in the Middle East (London: Quartet Books, 1981), 160.

143. FRUS, 1969–76, Vol. XXIV, Doc. 214. See also NPM, NSC Institutional Files, Box H-077, "WSAG & SRG Meeting, Middle East, Cambodia, 9/10/70," Memo, "WSAG/SRG Meeting on the Middle East—Thursday, September 10," Sep. 10, 1970; FRUS, 1969–76, Vol. XXIV, Doc. 222.

144. For more on US actions, see Quandt, Peace Process, 79–83.

145. NPM, NSC Institutional Files, Box H-071, "WSAG, Middle East, 9/24/70," Beirut 8054, No Subject, Sep. 22, 1970.

146. Ibid., Memo, "Talking Points, WSAG—Jordan," Sep. 24, 1970 [Inst2, 384]; Beirut 8054, No Subject, Sep. 22, 1970.

147. FRUS, 1969–76, Vol. XXIV, Doc 326.

148. RG 59, CF 70–73, Box 2447, "POL 23 LEB," State 158523, Sep. 25, 1970.

149. Ibid., Beirut 8246, Sep. 26, 1970.

150. NPM-NSC-CF, Box 621, Lebanon Vol. II, State 159037, Sep. 26, 1970.

151. Ibid., Beirut 8325, Sep. 28, 1970.

152. Ibid., Beirut 8341, Sep. 28, 1970.

153. Ibid., Beirut 7637, Sep. 11, 1970.

154. Ibid., Beirut 8555, Oct. 3, 1970.

155. Ibid., Beirut 11019, Dec. 30, 1970.

4. Plus ça change

1. NPM-NSC-CF, Box 621, "Lebanon Vol. II, 1 Feb 70–31 Dec 70," Beirut 9895, Nov. 17, 1970.

2. NPM-NSC-CF, Box 621, Lebanon Vol. III[2 of 3], Beirut 11020, Dec. 30, 1970.

3. Farid el-Khazen, The Breakdown of the State in Lebanon, 1967–1976 (London: I.B. Tauris, 2000), 194.

4. See, e.g., NPM-NSC-CF, Box 621, Lebanon Vol. III[3 of 3], State 166080, Sep. 9, 1971.

5. NPM-NSC-CF, Box 608, Israel Vol. VI, Tel Aviv 88, Jan. 7, 1971; State 3133, Jan. 8, 1971; Bassam Abdel Kader Namani, "Confessionalism in Lebanon, 1920–1976: The Interplay of Domestic, Regional, and International Politics" (PhD diss., Columbia University, 1982), 304.

6. William B. Quandt, *Peace Process: American Diplomacy and the Arab-Israeli Conflict since 1967*, 3rd ed. (Washington, DC: Brookings Institution Press, 2005), 91–92.

7. Yezid Sayigh, *Armed Struggle and the Search for State: The Palestinian National Movement, 1949–1993* (Oxford: Clarendon Press, 1997), 303–6.

8. Ibid., 306.

9. Ibid.

10. *New York Times*, Feb. 25, 1972.

11. *New York Times*, Feb. 24, 1972.

12. *Al-Nahar*, Feb. 29, 1972.

13. RG 59, CF 70–73, Box 2044, POL 13-1 ARAB, Beirut 2535, Mar. 8, 1972.

14. RG 59, CF 70–73, Box 2447, "POL 15-1 LEB," Beirut 2636, Mar. 10, 1972.

15. RG 59, CF 70–73, Box 2388, POL ISR-LEB, Beirut 2704, Mar. 13, 1972.

16. RG 59, CF 70–73, Box 2044, POL 13-10 ARAB, Beirut 2535, Mar. 8, 1972.

17. Ibid., State 40356, Mar. 9, 1972.

18. *Al-Nahar*, Jun. 1, 1972.

19. NPM-NSC-CF, Box 609, Israel Vol. X, Tel Aviv 3455, Jun. 2, 1972.

20. RRIAIA, Box 4, "Briefing Papers, 1972," Memo, Davies to Acting Secretary, May 31, 1972; CF 1970–73, Box 2044, "6-2-73 Pol 13-10 Arab," State 102019, Jun. 8, 1972.

21. Wade Goria, *Sovereignty and Leadership in Lebanon, 1943–1976* (New York: Ithaca Press, 1985), 137.

22. NPM-NSC-CF, Box 609, Israel Vol. X, Memo, Acting Secretary to Nixon, Jun. 2, 1972.

23. RG 59, CF 1970–73, Box 2044, "6-2-73 Pol 13-10 Arab," Beirut 6045, Jun. 3, 1972.

24. Ibid., Beirut 6213, Jun. 7, 1972; Beirut 7157, Jun. 29, 1972.

25. NPM-NSC-CF, Box 609, Israel Vol. X, State 97086, Jun. 1, 1972.

26. Ibid., Tel Aviv 3541, Jun. 2, 1972.

27. Ibid., State 97628, Jun. 2, 1972; State 99067, Jun. 6, 1972; Tel Aviv 3621, Jun. 6, 1972.

28. Ibid., Memo, Acting Secretary to Nixon, Jun. 2, 1972.

29. NPM-NSC-CF, Box 621, Lebanon Vol. III[1 of 3], Memo, Saunders for Kissinger, Jun. 8, 1972. Italicized text was underlined in the original document.

30. NPM-NSC-CF, Box 609, Israel Vol. X, Memo, Situation Room to Kissinger, Jun. 21, 1972; *Al-Nahar*, Jun. 24, 1972.

31. NPM-NSC-CF, Box 621, Lebanon Vol. III[2 of 3], Beirut 7197, Jun. 30, 1972.

32. Ibid., Beirut 7385, Jul. 6, 1972.

33. NPM, Haig Chronological Files, Box 998, "Haig Telcons 1972 [1 of 2]," Telcon, Nixon/Haig, 10:35 p.m., Sep. 5, 1972.

34. FRUS, 1969–1976, Vol. E-1, Doc. 91.

35. See ibid., Docs. 93 and 94; NPM, Haig Chronological Files, "Haig Memcons [Jan–Dec 1972] [2 of 3]," Memo, Haig to Files, Sep. 11, 1972.

36. *New York Times*, Sep. 9, 1972, 1.

37. NPM-NSC-CF, Box 134, "Rabin—1972—Vol. 3," Memo, Haig to Nixon, Sep. 9, 1972; *New York Times*, Sep. 11, 1972; NPM-NSC-CF, Box 621, Lebanon Vol. III[3 of 3], Memo, Sep. 12, 1972.

38. DNSA, KA08619, Sep. 16, 1972. On the deaths of the soldiers, see RG 59, CF 1970–73, Box 2044, "POL 13-10 ARAB, 1/1/72," Tel Aviv 6209, Sep. 23, 1972.

39. NPM-NSC-CF, Box 609, Israel Vol. X, Beirut 9869, Sep. 16, 1972.

40. Ibid., Tel Aviv 6062, Sep. 16, 1972; Beirut 9873, Sep. 16, 1972.

41. RG 59, CF 70–73, Box 2044, POL 13-10 ARAB, Beirut 10343, Sep. 27, 1972.

42. NPM-NSC-SF, Box 1169, File 1, Memo, "President's Wednesday Briefing," Sep. 19, 1972.

43. NPM-NSC-CF, Box 621, Lebanon Vol. III[3 of 3], Memo, "President's Saturday Briefing," Sep. 15, 1972.

44. Ibid., Beirut 9831, Sep. 15, 1972.

45. NPM-NSC-SF, Box 1169, File 1, Tel Aviv 6173, Sep. 21, 1972.

46. NPM-NSC-CF, Box 621, Lebanon Vol. III[2 of 3], Beirut 10478, Sep. 29, 1972.

47. NPM-NSC-CF, Box 658, "NODIS/CEDAR/DOUBLE PLUS [Jan 73–Apr 73]," Memo, Sisco to Kissinger, Oct. 3, 1972.

48. NPM-NSC-CF, Box 658, "NODIS/CEDAR/PLUS, Vol. V [Jan 1972–31 Dec 72], [1 of 2]," Memo, Rogers to Nixon, Nov. 30, 1972; See also NPM-NSC-CF, Box 658, "NODIS/CEDAR/PLUS, Vol. V [Jan 1972–31 Dec 72], [2 of 2]," Beirut 11400, Oct. 21, 1972.

49. NPM-NSC-CF, Box 658, "NODIS/CEDAR/PLUS, Vol. V [Jan 1972–31 Dec 72], [1 of 2]," Memo, Nov. 30, 1972.

50. RLF, Box 2, Letter, Official-Informal, Oakley to Atherton, Oct. 10, 1972.

51. Frederic Hof, *Galilee Divided: The Israel-Lebanon Frontier, 1916–1984* (Boulder, CO: Westview Press, 1985), 73–74. For the US reaction, see James Stocker, "The Limits of Intervention: US-Lebanese Relations and the Collapse of the Lebanese State, 1969–1976" (PhD diss., Graduate Institute of International and Development Studies, 2010), 223–24.

52. NPM-NSC-CF, Box 658, "NODIS/CEDAR/PLUS, Vol. V [Jan 1972–31 Dec 72], [1 of 2]," Memo, Rogers to Nixon, Nov. 30, 1972. See also ibid., "NODIS/CEDAR/PLUS, Vol. V [Jan 1972–31 Dec 72], [2 of 2]," Beirut 11400, No Subject, Oct. 21, 1972.

53. NPM-NSC-CF, Box 658, "NODIS/CEDAR/PLUS, Vol. V [Jan 1972–31 Dec 72], [1 of 2]," Memo, Haig to Kissinger, No date [probably Nov./Dec. 1972].

54. RG 59, CF 70–73, Box 2448, "POL LEB-US," State 191665, Oct. 20, 1972; State 192672, Oct. 20, 1972.

55. Ibid., State 202283, Nov. 2, 1972.

56. RG 59, CF 70–73, Box 2045, POL 13-10 ARAB 10-1-72, Tel Aviv 6502, Oct. 4, 1972.

57. NPM-NSC-CF, Box 658, "NODIS/CEDAR/PLUS, Vol. V [Jan 1972–31 Dec 72], [2 of 2]," Beirut 11405, Oct. 21, 1972.

58. RG 59, CF 70–73, Box 2388, POL ISR-LEB, Jerusulem 1030, Dec. 28, 1972.

59. NPM-NSC-CF, Box 610, Israel Vol. 11, October 71–Feb. 1973 [2 of 3], Jerusalem 112, Feb. 5, 1973.

60. For a copy of the Israeli draft proposal, see NPM-NSC-CF, Box 621, Lebanon Vol. III[2 of 3], Beirut 1433, Feb. 7, 1973.

61. Ibid., Lebanon Vol. III[2 of 3], Beirut 1433, Feb. 7, 1973.

62. "Israeli Tells of Planned Arab Attacks," *Chicago Tribune*, Feb. 22, 1973.

63. "Israeli Raids Reopen Refugee Debate," *Washington Post*, Feb. 22, 1973.

64. NPM-NSC-CF, Box 621, Lebanon Vol. III[3 of 3], State 33714, Feb. 23, 1973; Beirut 2093, Feb. 23, 1973; State 33714, Feb. 23, 1973.

65. Paul Chamberlin, *The Global Offensive: The United States, the Palestine Liberation Organization, and the Making of the Post-Cold War Order* (Oxford: Oxford University Press, 2012), 187–90.

66. NPM-NSC-CF, Box 621, Lebanon Vol. III[2 of 3], Beirut 2155, Feb. 23, 1973; "Arabs Fail to Ask Meeting of U.N. Council," *Los Angeles Times*, Feb. 22, 1973.

67. Ibid., Lebanon Vol. III[3 of 3], State 41111, Mar. 6, 1973.

68. On the Khartoum attacks, see David Korn, *Assassination in Khartoum* (Bloomington: Indiana University Press, 1993). See also Aaron Klein, *Striking Back: The 1972 Munich Olympics Massacre and Israel's Deadly Response* (New York: Random House, 2007), 148–51. For a view that casts doubt on Arafat's role, see Chamberlin, *The Global Offensive*, 191–92.

69. CREST #CIA-RDP79B00380R000500060008-7, Memo, CIA Operations Center.

70. For a discussion, see Douglas Little et al., "Roundtable Discussion of Paul Chamberlin's *The Global Offensive*," *H-Diplo Roundtable Review* 15, no. 20 (2014).

71. AAD, Delhi 3040, Mar. 16, 1973.

72. See, e.g., NPM-NSC-CF, Box 621, Lebanon Vol. III[2 of 3], Beirut 4659, Apr. 20, 1973.

73. NPM, NSC, Saunders Files, Box 1171, "Middle East—Jarring Talks—March 1–31, 1973 [1 of 2], Memo, Saunders and Kennedy to Kissinger, Mar. 3, 1973.

74. NPM-NSC-CF, Box 621, Lebanon Vol. III[3 of 3], Beirut 3632, Mar. 30, 1973; Beirut 3707, Apr. 7, 1973; State 41440, Mar. 7, 1973.

75. NPM-NSC-CF, Box 618, "Jordan Vol. IX, Jan 73–Oct 73" [2 of 3], Amman 2400, Mar. 7, 1972.

76. NPM-NSC-CF, Box 621, Lebanon Vol. III[2 of 3], Beirut 2983, Mar. 15, 1973; NPM-NSC-CF, Box 620, "Kuwait Vol. I, Jan 20, 1969–Jun 30, 1974 [1 of 2]," Kuwait 810, Mar. 17, 1973.

77. DNSA, TE00259, Apr. 2, 1973.

78. AAD, State 52984, Mar. 22, 1973.

79. RG 59, CF 70–73, Box 2406, POL 13-10 ARAB 4-1-73, Beirut 4101, Apr. 9, 1973.

80. AAD, State 44576, Mar. 10, 1973.

81. AAD, Vienna 2065, Mar. 14, 1975.

82. NPM-NSC-CF, Box 621, Lebanon Vol. III[2 of 3], Beirut 3245, Mar. 21, 1973.

83. NPM, NSC Saunders Files, Box 1171, "Middle East—Jarring Talks, January 1–31, 1972," State 12943, January 23, 1973; Memo, Saunders to Kissinger, "Middle East Policy—Getting a Hold on Decision-Making," Jan. 24, 1973.

84. Henry Alfred Kissinger, *Years of Upheaval* (Boston: Little, Brown and Company, 1982), 207.

85. Ibid., 211–12, 24–25.

86. Kissinger implies that Nixon's comment was "prophetic" of the interstate war that fall, but it could be interpreted either way. Ibid.

87. See Klein, *Striking Back*, 157–70.

88. el-Khazen, *The Breakdown*, 205.

89. Goria, *Sovereignty and Leadership in Lebanon*, 143.

90. NPM, Kissinger Telcons, Box 19, "Telephone Conversations—Chron File, 1973 7–11 Apr," Apr. 10, 1973, 6:00 p.m.

91. NPM-NSC-SF, Box 1171, "Middle East—Jarring Talks—April 1–30, 1973 [1 of 2]," State 70173, Apr. 14, 1973.

92. NA, CREST #CIA-RDP79T00975A024200060003-4, Central Intelligence Bulletin, Apr. 12, 1973.

93. AAD, State 70179, Apr. 14, 1976.

94. NA, CREST #CIA-RDP79T00975A024200080002-3, Central Intelligence Bulletin, Apr. 14, 1973.

95. FAOH Interview, Robert Oakley; AAD, USUN 1339, Apr. 13, 1973.

96. NPM-NSC-CF, Box 130, "Middle East Sensitive, 1971–74," Memo, Saunders, Apr. 30, 1973; Memo, CIA to Kissinger, "Soviet Anti-U.S. Campaign in the Middle East," May 2, 1973.

97. NPM-NSC-SF, Box 1171, "Middle East—Jarring Talks—April 1–30, 1973 [1 of 2]," State 70173, Apr. 14, 1973; AAD, State 68250, Apr. 12, 1973.

98. AAD, State 69439, Apr. 13, 1973.

99. AAD, State 79359, Apr. 27, 1973.

100. Kamal Salibi, *Crossroads to Civil War: Lebanon 1958–1976* (Delmar, NY: Caravan Books, 1976), 66–67; Salibi, *Crossroads to Civil War*, 66–67; el-Khazen, *The Breakdown*, 205.

101. Goria, *Sovereignty and Leadership in Lebanon*, 143.

102. Meir Zamir, "The Lebanese Presidential Elections of 1970 and Their Impact on the Civil War of 1975–1976," *Middle Eastern Studies* 16, no. 1 (1980): 65.

103. Goria, *Sovereignty and Leadership in Lebanon*, 143; el-Khazen, *The Breakdown*, 206.

104. NPM-NSC-CF, Box 621, Lebanon Vol. III[2 of 3], Beirut 4659, Apr. 20, 1973.

105. NPM-NSC-SF, Box 1171, "Middle East—Jarring Talks—April 1–30, 1973 [1 of 2]," No Number, "Communication From Secretary to Foreign Minister," Apr. 14, 1973.

106. AAD, Tel Aviv 3026, Apr. 17, 1973.

107. AAD, Beirut 4307, Apr. 13, 1973.

108. NPM-NSC-SF, Files, Box 1171, Memo, Saunders to Kissinger, Apr. 19, 1973; Nixon to Kissinger, Apr. 19, 1973.

109. See UNSC Resolution 332, Apr. 21, 1973.

110. DNSA, TE00259, Apr. 11, 1973.

111. DNSA, TE00259, Draft Telegram, No date [April 1973].

112. el-Khazen, *The Breakdown*, 206.

113. See AAD, Beirut 5021, May 2, 1973; Tony Walker and Andrew Gowers, *Arafat: The Biography* (London: Virgin Books, 2003), 141.

114. NA, CREST #CIA-RDP79T00975A024400010001-9, Central Intelligence Bulletin, May 3, 1973.

115. NPM-NSC-CF, Box 621, Lebanon Vol. III[2 of 3], Beirut 5136, May 5, 1973.

116. Sayigh, *Armed Struggle*, 315.

117. This interpretation runs somewhat counter to that of Farid el-Khazen, who notes that Arab governments were "unanimous in their condemnation of the Lebanese government." See el-Khazen, *The Breakdown*, 206–14, esp. 207.

118. AAD, Beirut 5065, May 3, 1973; Cairo 1320, May 4, 1973.

119. Mahmoud Riad, *The Struggle for Peace in the Middle East* (London: Quartet Books, 1981), 235.

120. NA, CREST #CIA-RDP79T00975A024400070001-3, Central Intelligence Bulletin, May 10, 1973.

121. el-Khazen, *The Breakdown*, 207.

122. RG 59, CF 70–73, "POL 23–8 LEB," Box 2447, Amman 2490, May 8, 1973.

123. NPM-NSC-CF, Box 621, Lebanon Vol. III[2 of 3], Beirut 5251, May 9, 1973.

124. RG 59, CF 70–73, "POL 23–8 LEB," Box 2447, Amman 2518, May 10, 1973.

125. NPM-NSC-CF, Box 137, "Jordan/Rifai, January 3–Oct. 11, 1973 [2 of 2]," Memo, Scowcroft to [Name Redacted], May 18, 1973; FRUS, 1969–1976, Vol. XXV, Doc. 62.

126. AAD, Tel Aviv 3673, May 10, 1973.

127. FRUS, 1969–1976, Vol. XXV, Doc. 64.

128. AAD, State 83810, May 3, 1973.

129. AAD, Beirut 5066, May 3, 1973.

130. NPM-NSC-CF, Box 621, Lebanon Vol. III[1 of 3], Memo, Saunders and Quandt for Kissinger, May 1, 1973.

131. Ibid., Memo, Saunders to Scowcroft, May 3, 197.

132. Jüssi Hanhimäki, *The Flawed Architect: Henry Kissinger and American Foreign Policy* (Oxford: Oxford University Press, 2004), 277–78.

133. AAD, State 90031, May 11, 1973.

134. AAD, Beirut 5438, May 12, 1973.

135. NPM-NSC-CF, Box 621, Lebanon Vol. III[2 of 3], Beirut 5324, May 10, 1973.

136. RG 59, CF 70–73, Box 2448, "POL LEB-US," State 89738, May 10, 1973.

137. AAD, Beirut 5412, May 11, 1973.

138. AAD, Paris 13058, May 11, 1973; State 89678, May 10, 1973.

139. AAD, State 100616, May 24, 1976.

140. RG 59, CF 70–73, Box 2447, "POL 23–8 LEB," State 9253 (repeating Beirut 5588), May 15, 1973.

141. Ibid., Memo, Porter to Eliot, May 15, 1973.

142. SLF, Box 25, "Middle East 1973 and Earlier," Sisco to Porter, May 14, 1973.

143. NPM-NSC-SF, Box 1172, File 1, "Middle East—Jarring Talks—May 1–31, 1973 [1 of 3]," Memo, Saunders and Kennedy to Kissinger, May 14, 1973.

144. Ibid., Memo, "Analytical Summary of Contingency Plans," May 14, 1973.

145. FRUS, 1969–1976, Vol. XXV, Doc. 57.

146. NPM-NSC-CF, Box 621, Folder: "Lebanon Vol. III, Jan 71–Oct 73" [3 of 3], State 94202, May 17, 1973.

147. el-Khazen, *The Breakdown*, 210.

148. NPM-NSC-SF, Box 1172, "Middle East—Jarring Talks—May 1–31, 1973 [1 of 3]," Memo, Quandt, May 19, 1973.

149. AAD, Beirut 5755, May 18, 1973.

150. RG 59, CF 70–73, "POL 23–8 LEB," Box 2447, Memo, Dib, Rush et al., Jun. 8, 1973.

151. NPM-NSC-CF, Box 137, "Jordan/Rifai, January 3–Oct. 11, 1973 [2 of 2]," Memo, Scowcroft to [Name Redacted], No Subject, May 18, 1973.

152. RG 59, CF 70–73, "POL 23–8 LEB," Box 2447, Amman 2670, May 18, 1973.

153. AAD, State 96645, May 19, 1973.

154. AAD, Tehran 3453, May 19, 1973; State 96645, May 19, 1973.

155. RG 59, CF 70–73, Box 2407, Jun.1, 1973, Beirut 6565, Jun. 5, 1973; Beirut 7043, Jun. 14, 1973. On the Syrian attitude during this period, see el-Khazen, *The Breakdown*, 211–14.

156. Goria, *Sovereignty and Leadership in Lebanon*, 145.

157. Michael Hudson, "The Palestinian Factor in the Lebanese Civil War," *Middle East Journal* 23, no. 3 (1978): 266.

158. Rex Brynen, *Sanctuary and Survival: The PLO in Lebanon* (Boulder, CO: Westview Press, 1990), 72–73.

159. On the formation of the center, see Sayigh, *Armed Struggle*, 205.

160. RLF, Box 3, PLO Planning Center, Beirut, Report No. 43.

161. Axel von Frohn, "Hilfe vom Roten Prinzen," *Der Spiegel*, Sep. 8, 2001; See also Kai Bird, *The Good Spy: The Life and Death of Robert Ames* (New York: Crown Publishers, 2014), Kindle edition, 2319–46.

162. CIA, Helms Collection, Aimes to Helms, "Contacts with Fatah Leadership," Jul. 18, 1973.

163. Ibid.

164. "Sadat Confidant Suggests Limited War," *Sun*, Mar. 25, 1972.

165. CIA, Helms Collection, Aimes to Helms, "Contacts with Fatah Leadership," Jul. 18, 1973.

166. Stein, *Heroic Diplomacy*, 68. See also Guy Laron and Zach Levey, "The Nixon Administration," *Passport: The Society for Historians of American Foreign Relations Review*, Sept. 2013, p. 55.

167. SLF, Box 25, Middle East 1973 and Earlier, Memorandum to the President, Rogers, "Next Steps on the Middle East," No date [Early May 1973].

168. Hanhimäki, *The Flawed Architect*, 291–94.

169. NPM-NSC-CF, Box 621, Lebanon Vol. III[3 of 3], State 117944, Jun. 15, 1973.

170. AAD, State 119401, Jun. 19, 1973.

171. NPM-NSC-CF, Box 621, Lebanon Vol. III[2 of 3], Beirut 7363, Jun. 21, 1973.

172. Ibid., Beirut 8165, Jul. 11, 1973.

173. Ibid., Beirut 7203, Jun. 18, 1973.

174. RG 59, CF 70–73, "POL LEB-US," Box 2448, Action Memo, Sisco to Rogers, Jun. 21, 1972.

175. AAD, State 128591, Jun. 29, 1973.

176. Library of Congress, Charles Malik Papers, General Correspondence, Box 5, Folder 6, Letter, Malik to William Baroody Jr., Sep. 6, 1973.

177. SLF, Box 25, "Middle East, 1973 and Before," Memo, Thornton to Porter, Jun. 13, 1973.

178. NPM-NSC-CF, Box 621, Lebanon Vol. III[1 of 3], Memo, State for Kissinger, Jun. 28, 1973.

179. Ibid., Memo, Saunders and Quandt for Kissinger, Jun. 28, 1973.

180. NPM-NSC-CF, Box 621, Lebanon Vol. III[3 of 3], State 132168, Jul. 6, 1973.

181. Ibid., [2 of 3], Beirut 8277, Jul. 13, 1973; Beirut 8278, Jul. 13, 1973.

182. Ibid., [1 of 3], Telegram, No Number, Jun. 22, 1973; Memo, Saunders for Kissinger, Jun. 28, 1973; State 109631, Jun. 7, 1973; State 109667, Jun. 7, 1973.

183. Ibid. [2 of 3], Beirut 6899, Jun. 12, 1973.

184. AAD, Beirut 8948, Jul. 31, 1973.

185. See AAD, Tehran 3453, May 19, 1973; State 101446, May 25, 1973; Tehran 3713, May 29, 1973; State 104372, May 31, 1973; Tehran 4476, Jun. 25, 1973; Tehran 5417, Aug. 1, 1973; Tehran 6827, Sep. 25, 1973.

186. NPM-NSC-SF, Box 1172, "Middle East—Jarring Talks—August 1–31, 1973," Memo, Quandt to Day, Aug. 6, 1973.

5. Reckoning Postponed

1. William Cleveland and Martin Bunton, *A History of the Modern Middle East*, 4th ed. (Philadelphia: Westview Press, 2009), 375–77.

2. Henry Alfred Kissinger, *Crisis: The Anatomy of Two Major Foreign Policy Crises* (New York: Simon & Schuster, 2003), 117–18, 143.

3. DNSA, Kissinger Telcons, Sisco and Kissinger, October 8, 1973, 7:20 p.m.; NPM-NSC-CF, Box 621, Lebanon Vol. III[3 of 3], State 199794, Oct. 9, 1973; Beirut 11946, Oct. 9, 1973.

4. Kamal Salibi, *Crossroads to Civil War: Lebanon 1958–1976* (Delmar, NY: Caravan Books, 1976), 72; Wade Goria, *Sovereignty and Leadership in Lebanon, 1943–1976* (New York: Ithaca Press, 1985), 160.

5. AAD, Tel Aviv 7939, Oct. 10, 1973.

6. AAD, Beirut 11884, Oct. 7, 1973; State 199724, Oct. 8, 1973; Tel Aviv 7810, Oct. 7, 1973.

7. NPM-NSC-CF, Box 621, Lebanon Vol. III[2 of 3], Beirut 11877, Oct. 6, 1973.

8. Abu Iyad later maintained that the fedayeen did launch raids, but the author found no other record that any occurred. Abou Iyad and Eric Rouleau, *My Home, My Land: A Narrative of the Palestinian Struggle* (New York: Times Books, 1981), 126.

Yezid Sayigh also maintains that some raids occurred, though he only provides statistics that prove that settlements were shelled. Yezid Sayigh, *Armed Struggle and the Search for State: The Palestinian National Movement, 1949–1993* (Oxford: Clarendon Press, 1997), 331–32.

9. NPM, NSC Saunders Files, Box 1173, 1973 Middle East War File 2—October 7, 1973, Tel Aviv 7866, Oct. 8, 1973.

10. Ibid., Beirut 11966, "Lebanese Involvement in Hostilities," Oct. 9, 1973.

11. AAD, Tel Aviv 7939, Oct. 10, 1973.

12. Abraham Rabinovich, *The Yom Kippur War: The Epic Encounter that Transformed the Middle East* (New York: Schocken Books, 2004), 336.

13. AAD, Beirut 12321, Oct. 20, 1976.

14. NPM, NSC Saunders Files, Box 1173, 1973 Middle East War File 4—October 7, 1973 [2 of 2], Beirut 11930, Oct. 9, 1973.

15. NPM-NSC-CF, Box 621, Lebanon Vol. III[2 of 3], Beirut 12020, Oct. 11, 1973; Box 647, Middle East (General) Vol. 9 [1 of 2], Memo, Quandt to Kissinger, "Middle Eastern Issues," Oct. 9, 1973.

16. AAD, Beirut 12183, Oct. 16, 1973.

17. AAD, Beirut 12215, Oct. 17, 1973.

18. AAD, Beirut 12215, Oct. 17, 1973.

19. AAD, Beirut 12321, Oct. 20, 1976; NPM, NSC Saunders Files, Box 1175, 1973 Middle East War File 16—October 21, 1973, Tel Aviv 8441, Oct. 21, 1973. See also AAD, Tel Aviv 8578, Oct. 24, 1973.

20. NPM-NSC-CF, Box 621, Lebanon Vol. III[2 of 3], Beirut 12470, Oct. 25, 1973; Beirut 12479, Oct. 25, 1973.

21. Ibid., Beirut 12488, Oct. 26, 1973.

22. AAD, Beirut 12488, Oct. 26, 1973.

23. William B. Quandt, *Peace Process: American Diplomacy and the Arab-Israeli Conflict since 1967*, 3rd ed. (Washington, DC: Brookings Institution Press, 2005), 133.

24. NPM, NSC Saunders Files, Box 1175, 1973 Middle East War File 18—October 23, 1973, Beirut 12357, Oct. 23, 1973; AAD, Beirut 12587, Oct. 31, 1973.

25. NPM, NSC Saunders Files, Box 1179, 1973 Middle East War File 16—October 21, 1973, Tel Aviv 9699, Oct. 31, 1973.

26. Ibid., Middle East, 1973 Peace Negotiations [2 of 2], Beirut 12979, Nov. 11, 1973.

27. Ibid., M.E.—1973 Peace Negotiations, December 6–12 [1 of 3], Beirut 14145, Dec. 12, 1973.

28. Ibid., Middle East, 1973 Peace Negotiations, Nov 16–Nov 20, 1973, Beirut 13354, Nov. 20, 1973.

29. See, e.g., AAD, State 219383, Nov. 10, 1973; AAD, Peking 1382, Nov. 10, 1973; NPM-NSC-CF, Box 621, Lebanon Vol. III[3 of 3], State 222716, Nov. 11, 1973.

30. DNSA, Kissinger Telcons, Dobrynin and Kissinger, Dec. 5, 1973.

31. Quandt, *Peace Process*, 140–41.

32. David Ignatius, *Wall Street Journal*, "Mideast Intrigue," Feb. 10, 1983; Kai Bird, *The Good Spy: The Life and Death of Robert Ames* (New York: Crown Publishers, 2014), Kindle edition, 2566.

33. Henry Alfred Kissinger, *Years of Upheaval* (Boston: Little, Brown and Company, 1982), 788.

34. NPM, NSC Presidential/HAK Memcons, Box 1027, December 1973 Memcons, Kissinger, Frangie, al-Solh et al., Dec. 16, 1973.

35. Kissinger, *Years of Upheaval*, 626.

36. Ibid., 503, 627. See also NPM, HAK Office Files, Country Files, Box 137, Palestinians [July 73–July 74]," No Subject, Oct. 13, 1973.

37. See Muhammad Muslih, "A Study of PLO Peace Initiatives, 1974–1988", in *The PLO and Israel: From Armed Conflict to Political Solution, 1964–1994*, ed. Avraham Sela and Moshe Ma'oz, 38–39 (New York: St. Martin's Press, 1997); Sayigh, *Armed Struggle*, 333–39; Paul Chamberlin, *The Global Offensive: The United States, the Palestine Liberation Organization, and the Making of the Post-Cold War Order* (Oxford: Oxford University Press, 2012), 229–30.

38. *New York Times*, "McMurtrie Godley, 82, Envoy to Laos during Vietnam War," Nov. 10, 1999.

39. Michael Hudson, "The Palestinian Factor in the Lebanese Civil War," *Middle East Journal* 23, no. 3 (1978): 266.

40. AAD, Beirut 622, Jan. 17, 1974.

41. AAD, Beirut 1756, Feb. 12, 1974.

42. NPM-NSC-CF, Box 611, Israel Vol. 14 [1 of 2], Tel Aviv 780, Feb. 11, 1974.

43. NPM-NSC-CF, Box 622, Lebanon Vol. IV, State 27852, Feb. 11, 1974.

44. AAD, Beirut 1816, Feb. 13, 1974.

45. NPM-NSC-CF, Box 611, Israel Vol. 14 [1 of 2], Tel Aviv 843, Feb. 13, 1974.

46. Kiryat Shamona on April 11, Maalot on May 15, and Shamir on June 13, a seaborne raid on Naharya on June 24. Frederic Hof, *Galilee Divided: The Israel-Lebanon Frontier, 1916–1984* (Boulder, CO: Westview Press, 1985), 75.

47. Sayigh, *Armed Struggle*, 339.

48. Ibid.; Chamberlin, *The Global Offensive*, 235–36.

49. AAD, Beirut 4345, Apr. 13, 1974; Beirut 4348, Apr. 13, 1974.

50. NPM-NSC-CF, Box 611, Israel Vol. 14 [1 of 2], Tel Aviv 2185, Apr. 13, 1974.

51. UNSC Resolution 347 (1974), Apr. 24, 1974, available at daccess-dds-ny.un.org.

52. Kissinger, *Years of Upheaval*, 1049.

53. AAD, Beirut 4426, Apr. 16, 1974.

54. AAD, Beirut 4624, Apr. 19, 1974.

55. Quoted in Farid el-Khazen, *The Breakdown of the State in Lebanon, 1967–1976* (London: I.B. Tauris, 2000), 223. See also Sayigh, *Armed Struggle*, 341.

56. NPM-NSC-CF, Box 622, Lebanon Vol. IV, Beirut 5541, May 16, 1974.

57. AAD, Beirut 5599, May 17, 1974.

58. NPM-NSC-CF, Box 622, Lebanon Vol. IV, State 103059, May 17, 1974.

59. AAD, Beirut 5610, May 18, 1974.

60. AAD, Jerusalem 949, May 17, 1974; NPM-NSC-CF, Box 622, Lebanon Vol. IV, Beirut 5627, May 18, 1974; NPM-NSC-CF, Box 611, Israel Vol. 15 [1 of 2], Jerusalem 1067, May 23, 1974.

61. Quandt, *Peace Process*, 151.

62. NPM-NSC-CF, Box 622, Lebanon Vol. IV, Beirut 5944, May 29, 1974.

63. NPM-NSC-CF, Box 611, Israel Vol. 16 [2 of 2], Jerusalem 1183, May 29, 1974.

64. NPM-NSC-CF, Box 622, Lebanon Vol. IV, Beirut 6055, May 31, 1974.

65. NPM-NSC-CF, Box 135, Dinitz, July 1–Dec 31, 1974, Memo, Nixon, Rabin et al., Jun. 17, 1974.

66. AAD, Beirut 6941, Jun. 19, 1974; Beirut 7016, Jun. 21, 1974.

67. AAD, Beirut 7015, Jun. 20, 1974; Beirut 7083, Jun. 21, 1974; Beirut 7430, Jun. 28, 1974.

68. NPM-NSC-CF, Box 622, Folder 1, "Lebanese President's Desire to Meet with President Nixon," Jun. 14, 1974.

69. NPM-NSC-CF, Box 622, Lebanon Vol. IV, Beirut 7349, Jun. 27, 1974; *Al-Nahar*, Jun. 22, 1974.

70. el-Khazen, *The Breakdown*, 224.

71. AAD, State 14250, Jul. 2, 1974.

72. AAD, Beirut 8265, Jul. 17, 1975.

73. See Fawwaz Traboulsi, *A History of Modern Lebanon* (London: Pluto Press, 2007), 138–55. For an opposing view that downplays the importance of these factors, see el-Khazen, *The Breakdown*, 250–63.

74. Goria, *Sovereignty and Leadership in Lebanon*, 157–58.

75. Salibi, *Crossroads to Civil War*, 91.

76. Michael Johnson, *Class and Client in Beirut: The Sunni Muslim Community and the Lebanese State, 1840–1985* (London: Ithaca Press, 1986), 142–43, 178.

77. Salibi, *Crossroads to Civil War*, 55.

78. Johnson, *Class and Client in Beirut*, 178–79.

79. Ibid., 181.

80. For more on Sadr, see Goria, *Sovereignty and Leadership in Lebanon*, 162–68. See also Fouad Ajami, *The Vanished Imam: Musa Al Sadr and the Shia of Lebanon* (Ithaca, NY: Cornell University Press, 1986).

81. On the latter two, see el-Khazen, *The Breakdown*, 238.

82. Goria, *Sovereignty and Leadership in Lebanon*, 161.

83. Jumblatt supported Taqi al-Din al-Sulh until his resignation in October 1974, After a failed attempt by Sa'ib Salam to form a government, Rashid al-Sulh was able to form a government with Jumblatt's support. el-Khazen, *The Breakdown*, 231.

84. Ibid., 248.

85. Goria, *Sovereignty and Leadership in Lebanon*, 170.

86. el-Khazen, *The Breakdown*, 239.

87. AAD, Beirut 4286, Apr. 11, 1964.

88. Pakradouni, *Curse of a Nation*, 141.

89. AAD, Beirut 14537, Dec. 21, 1973.

90. See, e.g., AAD, Beirut 3056, Mar. 14, 1974; Beirut 3348, Mar. 21, 1974.

91. AAD, Beirut 5095, Apr. 30, 1974.

92. Al Jazeera, *Harb Lubnan*, Episode 2, 39:00; Sayigh, *Armed Struggle*, 358.

93. Niqúlá Násif, *The Deuxième Bureau: Ruling in the Shadow (Al-maktab al-tháni: hákim fi-l-zul)* (Beirut: Dár mukhtárát, 2007), 484.

94. FAOH Interview, Robert Oakley.

95. Lowell Bergman, "Arms Dealer Faces Charges in Laundering and Tax Case," *New York Times*, Dec. 29, 1999; T. Rees Shapiro, "Sarkis G. Soghanalian, Arms Dealer Dubbed 'Merchant of Death,' Dies at 82," *Washington Post*, Oct. 10, 2011.

96. Náṣíf, *The Deuxième Bureau*, 480–86.

97. Ibid., 486.

98. RG 59, CF 70–73, Box 1085, FT LEB, Memcon, Raffio, Ward, Sep. 20, 1973.

99. Philip Taubman, "Intrigue at the C.I.A," *New York Times*, Aug. 25, 1984.

100. Author Interview, Forrest Hunt, Jan. 18, 2010.

101. Goria, *Sovereignty and Leadership in Lebanon*, 172.

102. Júrj al-Baṭal, "Reading the Life Story of a Communist Leader (Qirá'a fi síra qá'id shiyú'í)," in *George Hawi: Positions of the Leader and Testimonies of Comrades (Jurj ḥáwí: muwáqif al-qá'id wa shahádát al-rifáq)* (Beirut: Dar al-Nahár, 2005), 62–63.

103. Ziad Hafez, "Independent Nasserite Movement: Interview with Ziad Hafez," *MERIP Reports* 61(1977).

104. NPM-NSC-CF, Box 621, Lebanon Vol. III[2 of 3], Beirut 5842, May 25, 1973.

105. AAD, Beirut 6768, Jun. 8, 1973.

106. Salibi, *Crossroads to Civil War*, 78; el-Khazen, *The Breakdown*, 224.

107. RG 59, CF 74, P740005-2234, Airgram, Beirut A-11, "The Situation in Lebanon," Jan. 25, 1974.

108. AAD, Beirut 11970, Oct. 2, 1974.

109. Quandt, *Peace Process*, 157–59.

110. GF, National Security Advisor, Presidential Country Files for Middle East and South Asia [henceforth GF-PCF-MESA], Box 25, Lebanon, From State— NODIS (2), State 230805, Oct. 19, 1974.

111. GF-PCF-MESA, Box 25, Lebanon, To State—NODIS (1), Beirut 12617, Oct. 22, 1974.

112. Karim Pakradouni, *The Curse of the Nation: From the Lebanon War to the Gulf War (La'na al-waṭan: min ḥarb lubnán ila ḥarb al-khalíj)* (Beirut: 'Abr ash-sharq l-al-munshawarat, 1991), 141.

113. AAD, Beirut 11657, Sep. 25, 1974.

114. Quandt, *Peace Process*, 159–63.

115. Goria, *Sovereignty and Leadership in Lebanon*; el-Khazen, *The Breakdown*, 223.

116. AAD, Beirut 8947, Jun. 30, 1974.

117. AAD, Beirut 9020, Jul. 31, 1974.

118. Goria, *Sovereignty and Leadership in Lebanon*, 159.

119. Ibid., 166. See also *Al-Nahar*, Sep. 23, 1974.

120. Goria, *Sovereignty and Leadership in Lebanon*, 167.

121. Salibi, *Crossroads to Civil War*, 85.

122. Jonathan Randal, *Washington Post*, "Lebanon: Rot, Impending Disaster," Sep. 15, 1974.

123. GF-PCF-MESA, Jordan, To Secstate—NODIS (2), Amman 6059, Oct. 9, 1974.

124. GF-PCF-MESA, Jordan, To Secstate—EXDIS (1), Amman 6155, Oct. 15, 1974; AAD, Beirut 12406, Oct. 15, 1974.

125. Jonathan Randal, *Going All the Way: Christian Warlords, Israeli Adventurers, and the War in Lebanon* (New York: Viking Press, 1983), 156–58.

126. SLF, Box 18, Memcons, Sisco and Kabbani, Nov. 22, 1974.

127. GF, NSA Presidential Correspondence File, Lebanon—President Frangie, Letter, Ford to Frangie, Nov. 15, 1974; AAD, Beirut 13851, Nov. 19, 1974.

128. AAD, Beirut 13897, Nov. 21, 1974.

129. See AAD, Beirut 14027, Nov. 21, 1974; Beirut 14033, Nov. 21, 1974.

130. AAD, Beirut 13607, Dec. 6, 1974.

131. AAD, Beirut 15234, Dec. 21, 1974.

132. AAD, State 281497, Dec. 25, 1974.

133. GF-PCF-MESA, Box 25, Lebanon, From State—NODIS (1), State 281788, Dec. 26, 1974; AAD, Beirut 15412, Dec. 30, 1974.

134. AAD, Beirut 14607, Dec. 6, 1974.

135. AAD, State 157526, Jul. 20, 1974.

136. AAD, Tehran 10611, Dec. 16, 1974; Beirut 15060, Dec. 17, 1974; State 277711, Dec. 19, 1974; State 278772, Dec. 20, 1974.

137. AAD, Beirut 15424, Dec. 30, 1974.

138. AAD, Beirut 644, Jan. 16, 1975.

139. Fred J. Khouri, "The Arab-Israeli Conflict," in *Lebanon in Crisis: Participants and Issues,* ed. P. Edward Haley and Lewis Snider (Syracuse, NY: Syracuse University Press, 1979), 166.

140. Interview, Karim Pakradouni, Beirut, Lebanon, May 19, 2009.

141. AAD, Beirut 14592, Dec. 6, 1974.

142. AAD, Beirut 180, Jan. 6, 1975.

143. Goria, *Sovereignty and Leadership in Lebanon,* 161.

144. Salibi, *Crossroads to Civil War,* 92–93.

145. GF, Presidential Country Files, MESA, Box 24, Lebanon (1), Tel Aviv 134, Jan. 8, 1975.

146. GF-PCF-MESA, Box 1, Middle East—General (4), Memo, Oakley through Scowcroft to Kissinger, "Lebanese/Fedayeen/Israeli Situation," Jan. 15, 1975; Box 24, Lebanon (1), Colby to Kissinger, "Intelligence Alert Memorandum: Possible Ramifications of Serious Hostilities in Southern Lebanon," Jan. 30, 1975.

147. SLF, Box 19, JJS Memo Chrons 1975, Memo, Sisco to Atherton, Jan. 15, 1975; Memo, Sisco to Atherton, Jan. 27, 1975.

148. GF-PCF-MESA, Box 1, Middle East—General (4), Beirut 630, Jan. 15, 1975.

149. GF-PCF-MESA, Box 24, Lebanon (1), Memo, Oakley to Kissinger, "Lebanese-Israeli Border Problems," Feb. 6, 1975.

150. Naomi Joy Weinberger, *Syrian Intervention in Lebanon: The 1975–76 Civil War* (Oxford: Oxford University Press, 1986), 144.

151. Salibi, *Crossroads to Civil War,* 92.

152. *New York Times,* Feb. 27, 1975, 15.

153. Facts on File, "Fishing Clashes Kill 19," Mar. 8, 1975.

154. Local groups continue to view Saad's death as an "assassination." See for instance the biography of Saad on the website of the Maarouf Saad Cultural Centre, www.maaroufsaad.org.

155. Salibi, *Crossroads to Civil War,* 92.

156. Marius Deeb, *Syria's Terrorist War on Lebanon and the Peace Process* (Palgrave Macmillan, 2003), 8; Azzim, *Liban: l'instruction d'un crime,* 129; el-Khazen, *The Breakdown,* 267–79.

157. AAD, Beirut 3256, Mar. 14, 1975.

158. AAD, Beirut 3501, Mar. 20, 1975.

159. Salibi, *Crossroads to Civil War*, 95; Weinberger, *Syrian Intervention in Lebanon*, 144–45.

160. Salibi, *Crossroads to Civil War*, 96.

161. AAD, Beirut 3203, Mar. 12, 1975.

6. Disturbing Potential

1. Henry Alfred Kissinger, *Years of Renewal* (New York: Simon and Schuster, 1999), 1024.

2. Jonathan Randal, *Going All the Way: Christian Warlords, Israeli Adventurers, and the War in Lebanon* (New York: Viking Press, 1983), 170–71.

3. See, e.g., "Lebanese Fascists Attack Palestinians," *MERIP Reports*, no. 37 (1975): 30; Kamal Salibi, *Crossroads to Civil War: Lebanon 1958–1976* (Delmar, NY: Caravan Books, 1976), 117–18; Edgar O'Ballance, *Civil War in Lebanon, 1975–92* (New York: St. Martin's Press, 1998), 1–2.

4. Farid el-Khazen, *The Breakdown of the State in Lebanon, 1967–1976* (London: I.B. Tauris, 2000), 289; Salibi, *Crossroads to Civil War*, 97–102.

5. el-Khazen, *The Breakdown*, 285–86.

6. O'Ballance, *Civil War in Lebanon, 1975–92*, 4.

7. Salibi, *Crossroads to Civil War*, 99–101.

8. Jüssi Hanhimäki, *The Flawed Architect: Henry Kissinger and American Foreign Policy* (Oxford: Oxford University Press, 2004), 379–80.

9. Ibid., 399.

10. GRFL, NSA Memcons, Box 10, Memcon, Ford, Kissinger, Scowcroft, Ambassadors to Middle East, Apr. 14, 1975.

11. AAD, Beirut 4749, Apr. 14, 1975.

12. AAD, Beirut 4916, Apr. 17, 1975.

13. John Robert Greene, *The Presidency of Gerald R. Ford* (Lawrence: University Press of Kansas, 1995), 112.

14. Hanhimäki, *The Flawed Architect*, 420.

15. AAD, Beirut 4947, "Beirut Sitrep—1500Z," Apr. 17, 1975.

16. *Al-Nahar*, Apr. 14, 1975.

17. See "Le Livre Blanc Libanais: Documents Diplomatique (1975–6)," (Beirut: Ministère des Affaires Etrangères et des Libanais d'outre-mer, 1976).

18. AAD, Beirut 4830, Apr. 15, 1975; Damascus 1467, Apr. 22, 1975; Beirut 5954, May 9, 1975.

19. AAD, Beirut 4794, Apr. 14, 1975; Beirut 4844, Apr. 15, 1975.

20. AAD, State 84399, Apr. 14, 1975.

21. AAD, Beirut 4830, Apr. 15, 1975.

22. AAD, Beirut 5438, Apr. 28, 1975. The meetings were with Victor Moussa, who Godley described as a "not too scrupulous but extremely wealthy Christian lawyer," and George Abou Adel, a "local ricissimo."

23. AAD, State 99338, Apr. 29, 1975.

24. Ya'ari, in "The War of Lebanon (Ḥarb lubnán)," Episode 5, 2:30–3:30. Schulze cites interviews with Ralph Eitan and David Kimche, who was the Mossad

contact with the Phalange during the early phases of the civil war. Schulze, *Israel's Covert Diplomacy*, 86.

25. FOIA Request #U-13-8,048/FAC2A1, response dated Aug. 22, 2013. DIA Information Report, Report # [Classified], Jun. 23, 1975.

26. AAD, Damascus 1563, Apr. 29, 1975.

27. Yezid Sayigh, *Armed Struggle and the Search for State: The Palestinian National Movement, 1949–1993* (Oxford: Clarendon Press, 1997), 361.

28. Helena Cobban, *The Palestinian Liberation Organisation: People, Power and Politics* (Cambridge: Cambridge University Press, 1984), 66.

29. Salibi, *Crossroads to Civil War*, 102–3. Karame, the former Chehabist, was a rival zaim of Frangie in the north of Lebanon, while Chamoun had not spoken to Karame since the 1958 crisis.

30. el-Khazen, *The Breakdown*, 294.

31. AAD, Beirut 6678, May 26, 1975.

32. NA, CREST #CIA-RDP79R01142A000600100001-1, Intelligence Alert Memo, "Prospects for Lebanon," May 25, 1975.

33. AAD, Beirut 6664, May 25, 1975.

34. AAD, Tel Aviv 3191, May 25, 1975; State 122341, May 25, 1975.

35. AAD, Beirut 1993, May 29, 1975.

36. AAD, Beirut 6966, Jun. 3, 1975.

37. Salibi, *Crossroads to Civil War*, 109–10.

38. *New York Times*, "U.S. Cautions Israelis against Raids into Lebanon," May 28, 1975.

39. AAD, Beirut 6825, May 29, 1975; State 125125 Tosec 20108, May 29, 1975.

40. AAD, Beirut 7685, Jun. 17, 1975.

41. AAD, Beirut 7730, Jun. 18, 1975.

42. AAD, Beirut 7748, Jun. 18, 1975.

43. AAD, Beirut 7503, Jun. 14, 1975.

44. AAD, Beirut 7539, Jun. 14, 1975; Beirut 7609, Jun. 16, 1975; Beirut 9187, Jul. 18, 1975.

45. AAD, Beirut 9187, Jul. 18, 1975.

46. AAD, Beirut 8485, Jul. 5, 1975. Godley and Chamoun may have had other conversations in July, but records of these remained classified. See AAD Electronic Withdrawal Cards, Beirut 9220, Jul. 21, 1975.

47. AAD, Beirut 8591, Jul. 8, 1975; Beirut 8674, Jul. 9, 1975; Beirut 10964, Aug. 30, 1975.

48. AAD, State 133746, Jun. 9, 1975.

49. AAD, Beirut 7382, Jun. 11, 1975.

50. AAD, Tehran 6881, Jul. 17, 1975; State 19461, Aug. 15, 1975.

51. AAD, Amman 3989, Jun. 11, 1974.

52. AAD, Beirut 7473, Jun. 12, 1975.

53. AAD, Beirut 7435, Jun. 12, 1975. The latest assessment was Beirut 7382.

54. AAD, Beirut 10950, Aug. 29, 1975.

55. See William B. Quandt, *Peace Process: American Diplomacy and the Arab-Israeli Conflict since 1967*, 3rd ed. (Washington, DC: Brookings Institution Press, 2005), 167–68.

56. Salibi, *Crossroads to Civil War*, 122.

57. Ibid., 119.

58. Ibid., 120.

59. For more on the article and program, see el-Khazen, *The Breakdown*, 306–13.

60. AAD, Beirut 11075, Sep. 3, 1975.

61. AAD, Beirut 11540, Sep. 15, 1975.

62. AAD, Cairo 9610, Sep. 26, 1975.

63. AAD, Cairo 9631, Sep. 27, 1975.

64. Salibi, *Crossroads to Civil War*, 129.

65. GRFL-PCF-MESA, Box 31, Syria, To Secstate—EXDIS (2), Damascus 2976, Aug. 4, 1975.

66. Kissinger, *Years of Renewal*, 1019.

67. AAD, Beirut 11726, Sep. 19, 1975.

68. AAD, Beirut 12068, Sep. 29, 1975.

69. KLF, Box 15, Folder 4, Checklist, Sep. 30, 1975.

70. Salibi, *Crossroads to Civil War*, 126–27; Michael Johnson, *Class and Client in Beirut: The Sunni Muslim Community and the Lebanese State, 1840–1985* (London: Ithaca Press, 1986), 181.

71. Sayigh, *Armed Struggle*, 370.

72. AAD, Beirut 11392, Sep. 11, 1975.

73. AAD, Beirut 11688, Sep. 18, 1975.

74. AAD, State 223619, Sep. 19, 1975; Beirut 11693, Sep. 19, 1975.

75. AAD, Beirut 11800, Sep. 22, 1975.

76. AAD, State 227366, Sep. 24, 1975.

77. AAD, Beirut 11845, Sep. 23, 1975. See also AAD, State 227390, Sep. 24, 1975.

78. AAD, Beirut 12078, Sep. 29, 1975.

79. AAD, Damascus 3820, Sep. 30, 1975.

80. GRFL-PCF-MESA, Jordan, To Secstate—NODIS (2), Amman 6488, "Talk with King," Sep. 26, 1975.

81. GF-PCF-MESA, Israel, From Secstate, NODIS (4), State 225115, Sep. 22, 1975.

82. AAD, State 228384 "Secretary's Meeting with Foreign Minister Allon—September 24," Sep. 24, 1975.

83. DNSA, Memcon, Kissinger and Sauvagnargues, Sep. 27, 1975.

84. AAD, State 238271, Oct. 7, 1975.

85. AAD, Beirut 12621, Oct. 10, 1975.

86. AAD, Paris 25409, Oct. 1, 1975; Beirut 12448, Oct. 7, 1975.

87. AAD, Beirut 12689, Oct. 13, 1976.

88. GRFL, NSC Institutional Files, Box 20, WSAG Meeting, 10/13/75—Lebanon, Portugal and Italy (1), Memo, Atherton to Deputy Secretary, "Washington Special Action Group Meeting on Lebanon (October 13 at 1015)."

89. FRUS, 1969–1976, Vol. XXVI, Doc. 264.

90. SLF, Box 42, Lebanon January 1975–January 1976, "What Should the US Do about Lebanon," Undated [around Oct. 10–16].

91. FRUS, 1969–1976, Vol. XXVI, Doc. 265.

92. KLF, Box 14, Folder 4, Memo, "Lebanese at the Crossroads," Oct. 10, 1975.

93. GRFL-PCF-MESA, Box 24, Lebanon (2), "What Should the U.S. Do about Lebanon: If Israeli and Syrian Intervention Occurs," No Date.

94. FRUS, 1969–1976, Vol. XXVI, Doc. 265.

95. SLF, Box 43, Memo, "Chronology of U.S. Actions in the Lebanese Civil Conflict, March 1975–March 1976," No date [April 1976]; AAD, State 239611, Oct. 8, 1975; AAD, State 239610, Oct. 8, 1975.

96. AAD, Jidda 6847, Oct. 11, 1975; Kuwait 4152, Oct. 12, 1975.

97. AAD, Paris 26148, Oct. 8, 1975.

98. GRFL-PCF-MESA, Box 17, Israel, From Secstate—EXDIS, State 243279, "Lebanese Situation," Oct. 11, 1975.

99. GRFL-PCF-MESA, Box 18, Israel, To Secstate—EXDIS (4), Tel Aviv 6562, "Lebanese Situation," Oct. 11, 1975.

100. AAD, Tel Aviv 6750, Oct. 24, 1975. The electronic version of the cable states that the meeting took place on October "27"; however, the cable's sending date, as well as the later chronology (see below), suggest that it took place on October 22.

101. SLF, Box 43, Memo, "Chronology of U.S. Actions in the Lebanese Civil Conflict, March 1975–March 1976," No date [April 1976].

102. AAD, State 243490, Oct. 14, 1975.

103. AAD, Damascus 4027, Oct. 16, 1975.

104. *Al-Nahar*, Oct. 14, 1975; Salibi, *Crossroads to Civil War*, 131.

105. GRFL-PCF-MESA, Egypt–State Department Telegrams, From Secstate–Secstate (2), State 243488, Oct. 14, 1975; AAD, State 243489, Oct. 14, 1975.

106. AAD, Jidda 6949, Oct. 15, 1975.

107. GRFL-PCF-MESA, Egypt, To Secstate—EXDIS (5), Cairo 10240, "Lebanese Situation," Oct. 14, 1976.

108. GRFL-PCF-MESA, Box 4, Egypt–State Department Telegrams, From Secstate—EXDIS (2), State 244360, Oct. 15, 1975.

109. GRFL, NSA Memcons, Box 16, Memcon, Ford, Kissinger, Scowcroft, Oct. 16, 1975.

110. KLF, Box 15, Folder 2, Memcon, No Title [marked only Top Secret], No date [Conversation on Oct. 17, 1975].

111. GRFL-PCF-MESA, ME, Box 24, Lebanon (2), NSC Mem, Oakley to Scowcroft, "Israeli Support for Lebanese Christian Militia," Oct. 31, 1975.

112. GRFL-PCF-MESA, Box 24, Lebanon (2), Briefing Paper, "Flow of US Arms to Lebanon," No date [Oct. 1975].

113. DNSA, Memcon, HAK, Dinitz et al., Oct. 31, 1975.

114. AAD, State 252628, Oct. 23, 1975.

115. Both of these buildings remain today as shells in downtown Beirut. Salibi, *Crossroads to Civil War*, 131; O'Ballance, *Civil War in Lebanon, 1975–92*, 27–30.

116. AAD, Beirut 13096, Oct. 21, 1975.

117. AAD, Beirut 13334, Oct. 27, 1975.

118. On this failed effort, see Salibi, *Crossroads to Civil War*, 133.

119. Ibid., 134–35.

120. SLF, Box 43, Memo, "Chronology of U.S. Actions in the Lebanese Civil Conflict, March 1975–March 1976," No date [Apr. 1976].

121. FRUS, 1969–1976, Vol. XXVI, Doc. 266.

122. Salibi, *Crossroads to Civil War*, 141–42.

123. Ibid., 146–47.

124. See el-Khazen, *The Breakdown*, 323–24.

125. Already on November 9, Bashir Gemayel spoke with Boulos Naaman at Kaslik about the need to occupy Tal al-Zaatar camp and others in the area. Búlus Naʿmán, *Man, Nation, Freedom: Memoirs of the Abbott Búlus Naʿmán (Al-insán al-waṭan al-ḥuriyya: mudhakirát al-ʾabátí búlus naʿmán)* (Beirut: Sáʾir al-mashriq, 2009), 89.

126. Salibi, *Crossroads to Civil War*, 149–50.

127. Ibid., 155.

128. GRFL, MR 08–39, #11, Memo, Oakley to Atherton (in Damascus), No Subject, Dec. 16, 1975; AAD, Beirut 15263, Dec. 17, 1975.

129. AAD, Cairo 12739, Dec. 17, 1975.

130. AAD, Beirut 15373, Dec. 19, 1975.

131. AAD, State 297926, Dec. 18, 1975.

132. AAD, Damascus 5187, Dec. 29, 1975.

133. el-Khazen, *The Breakdown*, 327–28.

134. AAD, Beirut 15637, Dec. 30, 1975; Beirut 15684, Dec. 31, 1975.

135. AAD, Beirut 156, Jan. 7, 1976.

136. AAD, Tel Aviv 231, Jan. 9, 1976.

137. *New York Times*, "U.S. Opposes Intervention," Jan. 9, 1976.

138. DNSA, Memorandum, Secretary's Staff Meeting, Jan. 12, 1975.

139. SLF, Box 42, Lebanon January 1975–January 1976, Memo, Atherton to HAK (via Sisco), "Possible Syrian Intervention in Lebanon," Jan. 13, 1976.

140. SLF, Box 42, Lebanon January 1975–January 1976, Memo, Atherton to HAK (via Sisco), "Dangers in the Present Lebanese Situation," Jan. 13, 1976.

141. DNSA, "The Secretary's 8:00 a.m. Staff Meeting," Jan. 14, 1976.

142. SLF, Box 42, Lebanon, January 1975–January 1976, Memo, Atherton to Sisco, "Assistance to the Christian Right Wing in Lebanon," Dec. 9, 1976.

143. SLF, Box 43, Memo, "Chronology of U.S. Actions in the Lebanese Civil Conflict, March 1975–March 1976," No date [April 1976]; AAD, State 6146, Jan. 10, 1976; State 9963, Jan. 17, 1976.

144. See AAD, Paris 935, Bonn 531, London 649 and Brussels 397, all from January 1976.

145. AAD, Beirut 15639, Dec. 30, 1975.

146. KLF, Box 16, Folder 1, Memcon, Kissinger, Rabin et al., "Aid Requests; Jordan; Lebanon; Strategy for the Next Phase," Jan. 28, 1976.

147. KLF, Box 16, Folder 1, Memcon, Ford, Kissinger, Rabin et al., Jan. 28, 1976, 10:30 a.m.–Noon.

148. Salibi, *Crossroads to Civil War*, 150–51.

149. Sayigh, *Armed Struggle*, 373–77.

150. SLF, Box 42, Lebanon January 1975–January 1976, Memo, Sisco to HAK, Jan. 17, 1976.

151. Israeli intelligence provided to the US identified these as the Hittin and Qadasiyah brigades. AAD, State 14281, Jan. 19, 1976.

152. DNSA, Memcon, Kissinger, Dinitz, Bar-on et al., Jan. 19, 1976.

153. GRFL-PCF-MESA, Box 14, Israel, From Secstate—NODIS (4), State 14190, Jan. 20, 1976.

154. GRFL, Kissinger-Scowcroft Files, Box 3, Central Intelligence Agency— Communications (20), Memo, [Title Classified].

155. GRFL, Dale Van Atta Papers, Intelligence Documents, January 17, 1976, Bureau of Intelligence and Research, Intelligence Summary, Jan. 17, 1976. See also GRFL-PCF-MESA, Box 24, Lebanon (3), NSC Memo, Oakley to Hyland, "Attached Report on Mobilization of Egyptian Military Units Preparatory to Intervention in Lebanon," Dec. 18, 1975.

156. SLF, Box 42, Lebanon, January 1975–January 1976, Memo, Sisco to HAK, Jan. 17, 1976.

157. GRFL-PCF-MESA, Box 24, Lebanon (3), State 13261, Jan. 19, 1976.

158. GRFL-PCF-Europe, Box 4, France—From Secstate—NODIS (4), State 13818, Jan. 20, 1976.

159. GRFL-PCF-Europe, Box 5, France—To Secstate—NODIS (8), Paris 1870, Jan. 20, 1976.

160. Ibid., Paris 1979, Jan. 21, 1976.

161. AAD, State 15280, Jan. 21, 1976.

162. GRFL-PCF-MESA, Box 31, Syria, From Secstate—NODIS (6), State 14281, Jan. 21, 1976.

163. GRFL-PCF-MESA, Box 32, Syria, To Secstate—NODIS (10), Damascus 318, Jan. 21, 1976.

164. AAD, State 16251, Jan. 22, 1976.

7. Reluctant Interveners

1. See, e.g., Kamal Jumblatt, *I Speak for Lebanon* (London: Zed, 1982), 52; Robert Rabil, *Embattled Neighbors: Syria, Israel and Lebanon* (Boulder, CO: Lynne Reiner, 2003), 52. Rabil cites Zeev Schiff, "Peace With Security: Israel's Minimal Security Requirements in Negotiations With Syria," *Policy Papers,* No. 34 (Washington, DC: Washington Institute for Near East Policy, 1993).

2. Jonathan Randal, *Going All the Way: Christian Warlords, Israeli Adventurers, and the War in Lebanon* (New York: Viking Press, 1983), 195.

3. See Yair Evron, *War and Intervention in Lebanon: The Israeli-Syrian Deterrence Dialogue* (London: Croom Helm, 1987); Henry Alfred Kissinger, *Years of Renewal* (New York: Simon and Schuster, 1999), 1045.

4. Author Interview, Abdulhalim Khaddam, Paris, France, Feb. 10, 2009.

5. See Rabil, *Embattled Neighbors,* 52.

6. Kissinger, *Years of Renewal,* 1040.

7. Michael Kerr, "'A Positive Aspect to the Tragedy of Lebanon': The Convergence of US, Syrian and Israeli Interests at the Outset of Lebanon's Civil War," *Israel Affairs* 15, no. 4 (2009): 357.

8. Stocker, "The Limits of Intervention," 366–67; David Wight, "Kissinger's Levantine Dilemma: The Ford Administration and the Syrian Occupation of Lebanon," *Diplomatic History* 37, no. 1 (2013): 145–46.

9. Wight, "Kissinger's Levantine Dilemma," 145–46.

10. Ibid., 153.

11. AAD, Beirut 1025, Jan. 31, 1976.

12. Wade Goria, *Sovereignty and Leadership in Lebanon, 1943–1976* (New York: Ithaca Press, 1985), 218.

13. Farid el-Khazen, *The Breakdown of the State in Lebanon, 1967–1976* (London: I.B. Tauris, 2000), 329.

14. Itamar Rabinovich, *The War for Lebanon, 1970–1985* (Ithaca, NY: Cornell University Press, 1985), 50, 70–83.

15. AAD, Beirut 1224, Feb. 6, 1976; State 30980, Feb. 7, 1976.

16. Goria, *Sovereignty and Leadership in Lebanon*, 219. For more on the Muslim viewpoints, see el-Khazen, *The Breakdown*, 327.

17. Goria, *Sovereignty and Leadership in Lebanon*, 220.

18. Yezid Sayigh, *Armed Struggle and the Search for State: The Palestinian National Movement, 1949–1993* (Oxford: Clarendon Press, 1997), 378.

19. See GRFL, MESA Staff Files, Box 15, Lebanon (26), "Chronology," Undated, attached to Letter, Oakley to Hauser, Jun. 14, 1976.

20. AAD, Amman 894, Feb. 21, 1976.

21. NA, CREST, Interagency Memorandum, "Asad's Domestic Position," Apr. 9, 1976.

22. Sayigh, *Armed Struggle*, 375.

23. Samir Kassir, *La guerre du Liban: de la dissension nationale au conflit régional (1975–1982)* (Paris: CERMOC, 1994), 166.

24. GRFL, NSC MESA Staff Files, Box 2, Egypt (1), Cairo 950, Jan. 25, 1976.

25. GRFL-PCF-MESA, Egypt, To Secstate—NODIS (37), Cairo 992, Jan. 26, 1976.

26. GRFL, NSC MESA Staff Files, Box 2, Egypt (1), Oakley to "Bud," Jan. 27, 1976; AAD, Beirut 1486, Feb. 17, 1976; Cairo 2198, Feb. 19, 1976.

27. Kissinger, *Years of Renewal*, 1026.

28. KLF, Box 16, Folder 1, Memcon, Kissinger, Rabin et al., "Aid Requests; Jordan; Lebanon; Strategy for the Next Phase," Jan. 28, 1976.

29. el-Khazen, *The Breakdown*, 332–33; Sayigh, *Armed Struggle*, 379. See also AAD, Damascus 1176, Mar. 2, 1976.

30. el-Khazen, *The Breakdown*, 333.

31. Sayigh, *Armed Struggle*, 380.

32. el-Khazen, *The Breakdown*, 333.

33. AAD, Beirut 2285, Mar. 13, 1976; Beirut 2307, Mar. 15, 1976.

34. See el-Khazen, *The Breakdown*, 339–40.

35. Kissinger, *Years of Renewal*, 1040. For the exact date, see Damascus 1445 below.

36. SLF, Box 42, Damascus 1445, Mar. 13, 1976; GRFL-PCF-MESA, Box 32, Syria, To Secstate—NODIS (10), Damascus 1446, Mar. 14, 1976.

37. Kissinger, *Years of Renewal*, 1043.

38. GRFL-PCF-MESA, Box 32, Syria, To Secstate—NODIS (11), Damascus 1483, Mar. 15, 1976.

39. GRFL, RAC Files, Box 9–12, "NSC MESA Staff Files, Box 75," Intelligence Memorandum, "Syrian Intervention in Lebanon," Mar. 17, 1976.

40. DNSA, Kissinger Telcons, Dinitz, Kissinger, Mar. 15, 1976, 3:10 p.m.

41. DNSA, State Department, Memcon, Mar. 15, 1976.

42. NA, CREST #RDP85T00353R000100260011-6, Intelligence Memo, "Syrian Intervention in Lebanon," Mar. 17, 1976.

43. Kissinger, *Years of Renewal*, 1044.

44. GRFL-PCF-MESA, Box 32, Syria, To Secstate—NODIS (11), Damascus 1722, Mar. 23, 1976.

45. GRFL-PCF-MESA, Box 31, Syria, From Secstate—NODIS (6), State 71012, Mar. 24, 1976. The original instructions were in State 70097. For the delaying motive, see GRFL, NSA Memcons, Box 18, Memcon, Ford, Kissinger, Rumsfeld, Scowcroft, Mar. 24, 1976.

46. GRFL-PCF-MESA, Box 32, Box Syria, To Secstate—NODIS (11), Damascus 1742, Mar. 24, 1976.

47. DNSA, Memcon, Kissinger, Dinitz, Bar-on, Mar. 24, 1976.

48. FRUS, 1969–1976, Vol. XXVI, Doc. 268.

49. GRFL-PCF-MESA, Box 32, Syria, To Secstate—NODIS (11), Damascus 1865, Mar. 27, 1976.

50. GRFL-PCF-MESA, Box 29, Saudi Arabia, From State—NODIS (4), State 71007, Mar. 24, 1976; GRFL-PCF-MESA, Box 21, Jordan, From Secstate—NODIS (7), State 71008, Mar. 25, 1976.

51. GRFL-PCF-MESA, Box 23, Jordan, To Secstate—NODIS (23), Amman 1581, Mar. 24, 1976; Ibid., Amman 1589; GRFL-PCF-MESA, Box 32, Syria, To Secstate—NODIS (11), Amman 1572, Mar. 24, 1976; RG 59, Amman 1588, Mar. 24, 1976.

52. GRFL-PCF-MESA, Box 23, Jordan, From Secstate—NODIS (7), State 72124, Mar. 25, 1976.

53. GRFL-PCF-MESA, Box 23, Jordan, To Secstate—NODIS (23), Amman 1595, Mar. 25, 1976; Amman 1596, Mar. 25, 1976.

54. GRFL-PCF-MESA, Box 32, Syria, To Secstate—NODIS (11), Damascus 1808, Mar. 25, 1976.

55. DNSA, Kissinger Dinitz, Mar. 25, 1976, 2:50 p.m.; GRFL-PCF-MESA, Box 17, Israel, From Secstate—NODIS (6), State 73315, Mar. 26, 1976; State 73316, Mar. 26, 1976.

56. GRFL-PCF-MESA, Box 31, Syria, From Secstate—NODIS (6), State 73314, Mar. 26, 1976.

57. KLF, Box 16, NODIS Memcons—March 1976, Memcon, Kissinger, Murphy et al., Mar. 26, 1976; GRFL-PCF-MESA, Box 31, Syria, From Secstate—NODIS (6), State 74076, Mar. 26, 1976. A minor change was made the next day. Ibid., State 74116, Mar. 27, 1976.

58. GRFL-PCF-MESA, Box 32, Syria, To Secstate—NODIS (11), Damascus 1860, Mar. 27, 1976.

59. GRFL-PCF-MESA, Box 23, Jordan, From Secstate—NODIS (7), State 74893, Mar. 27, 1976.

60. GRFL-PCF-MESA, Box 23, Jordan, To Secstate—NODIS (24), Amman 1633 and 1634, Mar. 27, 1976.

61. GRFL-PCF-MESA, Box 21, Jordan, From Secstate—NODIS (7), State 74921, Mar. 28, 1976.

62. GRFL-PCF-MESA, Box 23, Jordan, To Secstate—NODIS (24), Amman 1636 and 1637, Mar. 28, 1976.

63. SLF, Box 43, Madrid 2379, Mar. 29, 1976.

64. FRUS, 1969–1976, Vol. XXVI, Docs. 273, 275; DNSA, Kissinger Telcons, Kissinger, Sauvagnargues, Mar. 29, 1976, 12:32 p.m.; SLF, Box 43, State 74932, Mar. 28, 1976; Paris 9225, Mar. 30, 1976; Paris 9285, Mar. 30, 1976; GRFL, Presidential Country Files for Europe, Box 4, France, From SECSTATE—NODIS (5), State 75938, Mar. 30, 1976.

65. DNSA, Kissinger Telcons, Kissinger Dinitz, Mar. 27, 1976, 5:30 p.m.; Mar. 27, 1976, 5:40 p.m.

66. DNSA, Kissinger Telcons, Kissinger Dinitz, Mar. 27, 1976, 7:30 p.m.

67. DNSA, Kissinger Telcons, Kissinger Dinitz, Mar. 28, 1976, 12:50 [p.m.]

68. FRUS, 1969–1976, Vol. XXVI, Doc. 278.

69. SLF, Box 42, State 68647, Mar. 21, 1976.

70. GRFL-PCF-MESA, Box 5, Egypt, From Secstate—NODIS (16), Kissinger, State 71006, GRFL-PCF-MESA, Box 9, Egypt, To Secstate—NODIS (40), Cairo 3885, Mar. 24, 1975.

71. GRFL-PCF-MESA, Saudi Arabia, To Secstate—NODIS (7), Jidda 2189, Mar. 25, 1976.

72. On the US-Egyptian exchanges, see GRFL-PCF-MESA, Box 5, Egypt, From Secstate—NODIS (16), State 74949, Mar. 28, 1976; State 74962, Mar. 29, 1976; Box 9, Egypt, To Secstate—NODIS (40), Cairo 4027, Mar. 28, 1976; Cairo 4028, Mar. 29, 1975; Cairo 4029, Mar. 29, 1975.

73. SLF, Box 42, Beirut 2619, Mar. 25, 1976.

74. GRFL, MESA Staff Files, Box 14, Lebanon (8), Beirut 2565, Mar. 24, 1976.

75. Ibid., Beirut 2666, Mar. 27, 1976.

76. GRFL, MESA Staff Files, Box 14, Lebanon (9), State 76265, Mar. 30, 1976.

77. SLF, Box 43, State 74955, Mar. 28, 1976.

78. GRFL-PCF-MESA, Box 25, Lebanon, To State—NODIS (3), Beirut 2684, Mar. 29, 1976.

79. SLF, Box 43, Box 43, State 74965, Mar. 29, 1976.

80. GRFL-PCF-MESA, Box 25, Lebanon, To State—NODIS (3), Beirut 2703, Mar. 29, 1976; Beirut 2724, Mar. 29, 1976; Beirut 2739, Mar. 30, 1976. See also Camille Chamoun, *Crise au Liban* (Beirut: No publisher listed, 1977), 79.

81. GRFL, President Memcons, Kissinger, Ford, Scowcroft, Mar. 15, 1976.

82. SLF, Box 43, State 76575, Mar. 31, 1976; GRFL-PCF-MESA, Box 19, Israel, To Secstate—NODIS (12), Tel Aviv 2301, Mar. 31, 1976; GRFL-PCF-MESA, Box 17, Israel, From Secstate—NODIS (6), State 80366, Apr. 3, 1976.

83. Kissinger, *Years of Renewal*, 1041–42.

84. Ibid., 1042.

85. GRFL, Mandatory Review Request 08–37, Amman 1599, Mar. 25, 1976.

86. GRFL, NSA Memcons, Box 18, Ford, Kissinger, Rumsfeld, Scowcroft, Mar. 24, 1976; DNSA, Kissinger Telcons, Kissinger, Ramsbotham, Mar. 24, 1976, 6:45 p.m.

87. GRFL, Presidential Memcons, Minutes, NSC Meeting, Apr. 7, 1976.

88. SLF, Box 42, Lebanon, Jan. 1975–Jan. 1976, Beirut 13787, Nov. 5, 1975.

89. SLF, Box 42, Lebanon, Jan. 1975–Jan. 1976, Memo, JJS [Sisco], Undated [Early November].

90. See also David Ignatius, *The Washington Post*, "In the End, CIA-PLO Links Weren't Helpful," Nov. 12, 2004.

91. See Rashid Khalidi, *Brokers of Deceit: How the U.S. Has Undermined Peace in the Middle East* (Boston: Beacon Press, 2013), 16n14.

92. See, e.g., AAD, State 170887, Jul. 19, 1975; AAD, SECTO 6002, Feb. 28, 1976.

93. "The Assassination of American Diplomats in Beirut, Lebanon: Hearing before the Special Subcommittee on Investigations of the Committee on International Relations," House of Representatives, 94th Congress, Jul. 27, 1976, Volumes 8–16, USGPO, 1976, 39.

94. Former CIA agent Duane Clarridge writes that Fatah's Force 17, under the command of Ali Hassan Salame, took charge of ensuring the embassy's defense. Duane Clarridge, *A Spy for All Seasons: My Life in the CIA* (New York: Scribner, 1997), 162–63.

95. SLF, Box 42, Lebanon (3), State 77656, Mar. 31, 1976.

96. Ibid., Message, Brown from the Secretary (Drafted by Sisco), Mar. 31, 1976.

97. GRFL-PCF-MESA, Box 25, Lebanon, To State—NODIS (4), Beirut [2]813, Mar. 31, 1976.

98. AAD, State 60139, Mar. 12, 1976.

99. DNSA, Kissinger, Dinitz, Apr. 3, 1976.

100. On April 9, Israel provided the United States with a long list of the armaments already provided for the Christian militias, including forty-four 82mm mortars, nine 160mm mortars, 1,060 light machine guns, 345 medium machine guns, and sixteen heavy machine guns, over eight thousand various types of rifles (including 2,900 M-16s) and over ten million rounds of ammunition. KLF, Box 15, Folder 7, Memo, No Subject [labeled Top Secret], Apr. 9, 1976. By early May, Israel had provided more than 1,200 tons of arms and ammunition without remuneration to the Christian forces, who also paid for close to 200,000 liters of fuel. KLF, Box 15, Folder 7, Memo, No Subject [labeled Top Secret], May 10, 1976.

101. Randal, *Going All the Way*, 177–78.

102. GRFL-PCF-MESA, Box 26, Lebanon, To State—NODIS (10), Beirut 4058, May 6, 1976.

103. GRFL-PCF-MESA, Box 25, Lebanon, To State—NODIS (5), Beirut 2865, Apr. 12, 1976.

104. Ibid., Beirut 2867, Apr. 1, 1976.

105. Ibid., Beirut 2906, Apr. 2, 1976.

106. Ibid., Beirut 2905, Apr. 2, 1976.

107. Ibid., Beirut 2930, Apr. 4, 1976.

108. Ibid., Beirut 2940, Apr. 4, 1976.

109. SLF, Box 43, Beirut 2942, Apr. 4, 1976.

110. SLF, Box 43, State 81280, Apr. 5, 1975.

111. GRFL-PCF-MESA, Box 25, Lebanon, To State—NODIS (5), Beirut 2979, No title, Apr. 5, 1976.

112. GRFL-PCF-MESA, Box 25, Lebanon, To State—NODIS (6), Beirut 3029, Apr. 7, 1976.

113. Ibid., Beirut 3119, Apr. 8, 1976.

114. Brown added that "it might be worth a footnote, when the history of this problem is finally recorded, that at one moment I stood on the brink of becoming

'Brown of Palestine.'" GRFL-PCF-MESA, Box 25, Lebanon, To State—NODIS (6), Beirut 3024, Apr. 7, 1976; Beirut 3164, Apr. 9, 1976.

115. SLF, Box 43, Beirut 3290, Apr. 13, 1976; AAD, Damascus 2168, Apr. 9, 1976.

116. AAD, State 82088, Apr. 6, 1976.

117. GRFL-PCF-MESA, Box 32, Syria, To Secstate—NODIS (12), Damascus 2118, Apr. 8, 1976.

118. SLF, Box 43, Damascus 2118, Apr. 8, 1976.

119. SLF, Box 43, Beirut 3109, Apr. 8, 1976; GRFL-PCF-MESA, Box 25, Lebanon, To State—NODIS (6), Beirut 3165, Apr. 9, 1976; GRFL-PCF-MESA, Box 31, Syria, From Secstate—NODIS (7), State 87620, Apr. 11, 1976.

120. GRFL-PCF-MESA, Box 24, Lebanon (4), Memo, Oakley to Scowcroft, "Lebanon," Apr. 2, 1976; GRFL, Outside the System Chronological File 4/1/76–4/14/76, Box 4, Memo, Scowcroft, "Meeting of the National Security Council: Lebanon, Apr. 7, 1976; GRFL-PCF-MESA, Box 24, Lebanon (4), Memo, Saunders to Secretary via Sisco, "Will the Syrian Presence in Lebanon Inevitably Lead Lebanon to the Left?" Apr. 14, 1976.

121. GRFL, Presidential Memcons, NSA Meeting, Apr. 7, 1976.

122. GRFL-PCF-MESA, Box 32, Syria, To Secstate—NODIS (12), Damascus 2183, Apr. 10, 1976.

123. GRFL-PCF-MESA, Israel, Box 17, From Secstate—NODIS (7), State 86650, Apr. 9, 1976.

124. GRFL-PCF-MESA, Israel, Box 19, To Secstate—NODIS (12), Tel Aviv 2570, Apr. 11, 1976; Tel Aviv 2571, Apr. 11, 1976.

125. GRFL-PCF-MESA, Box 31, Syria, From Secstate—NODIS (7), State 88187, Apr. 13, 1976; AAD, Damascus 2275, Apr. 14, 1976.

126. AAD, State 94273, Apr. 19, 1976.

127. AAD, State 87615, Apr. 11, 1976.

128. GRFL-PCF-MESA, Box 25, Lebanon, To State—NODIS (6), Beirut 3191, Apr. 11, 1976.

129. GRFL-PCF-MESA, Box 25, Lebanon, To State—NODIS (7), Beirut 3288, Apr. 13, 1976.

130. Ibid., Beirut 3291, Apr. 13, 1976.

131. AAD, State 91022, Apr. 15, 1976.

132. GRFL-PCF-MESA, Box 25, Lebanon, To State—NODIS (7), Beirut 3349, Apr. 15, 1976.

133. Ibid., Beirut 3350, Apr. 15, 1976.

134. el-Khazen, *The Breakdown*, 343–44. See also *Al-Nahar*, Apr. 18, 1976.

135. Sayigh, *Armed Struggle*, 387.

136. GRFL-PCF-MESA, Box 26, Lebanon, To State—NODIS (8), Beirut 3545, Apr. 21, 1976.

137. AAD, Beirut 3532, Apr. 21, 1976.

138. SLF, Box 43, "April 16–June 1976," State 97586, Apr. 22, 1976.

139. GRFL-PCF-MESA, Box 26, Lebanon, To State—NODIS (8), Beirut 3535, Apr. 21, 1976.

140. GRFL-PCF-MESA, Box 26, Lebanon, To State—NODIS (9), Beirut 3655, Apr. 23, 1976; Beirut 3656, Apr. 23, 1976.

141. GRFL, Kissinger-Scowcroft Files, Box 32, "USSR—"D" File [Dobrynin]— Items #175–180, 4/2/76–4/27/76," Note, Soviet Embassy, Delivered Apr. 2, 1976; Note, HAK's initials, Apr. 3, 1976; Note, Dictated by Vorontsov by telephone, Apr. 17, 1976.

142. GRFL, NSC Institutional Files, Box 25, Meeting Minutes—WSAG, March–April 1976, WSAG Special Actions Group, "Part I of II," Apr. 22, 1976.

143. DNSA, Memcon, Kissinger, Brown, Saunders, Rodman, Apr. 23, 1976.

144. Ibid., Tab A.

145. Kail Claude Ellis, "United States Policy toward Lebanon in the Lebanese Civil Wars of 1958 and 1975–6: A Comparative Analysis" (PhD diss., University of Michigan, 1979), 321.

146. GRFL-PCF-MESA, Box 24, Lebanon (3), Memo, Dubs to Sisco, "Your Meeting with Lebanese Deputy Raymond Edde, Friday, Dec. 19—11:00 a.m." Dec. 18, 1975; Memo, Oakley to Scowcroft, "Your Meeting with Raymond Edde, Tuesday, January 20, at 3:00 p.m.," Jan. 19, 1976.

147. GRFL-PCF-MESA, Box 25, Lebanon, To State—NODIS (7), Beirut 3425, Apr. 16, 1975.

148. GRFL-PCF-MESA, Box 25, Lebanon, To State—NODIS (7), Beirut 3425, Apr. 16, 1975.

149. GRFL-PCF-MESA, Box 26, Lebanon, To State—NODIS (10), Beirut 3887, May 2, 1976.

150. Ibid., Beirut 3930, May 3, 1976; Beirut 3951, May 4, 1976.

151. Ibid., Beirut 3978, May 4, 1976.

152. Ibid., Beirut 4004, May 5, 1976.

153. Robert Stookey, "The United States," in *Lebanon in Crisis: Participants and Issues*, ed. P. Edward Haley and Lewis Snider (Syracuse, NY: Syracuse University Press, 1979), 237.

154. GRFL-PCF-MESA, Box 26, Lebanon, To State—NODIS (10), Beirut 4260, May 6, 1976.

155. Ibid., Beirut 4055, May 6, 1976.

156. AAD, Beirut 4061, May 6, 1976.

157. el-Khazen, *The Breakdown*, 344.

158. George Hawi and Ghassan Charbal, *George Hawi Remembers: The War and the Resistance and the Party: Conversations with Ghassan Charbal (Jurj ḥáwí yatadhakir: al-ḥarb w-al-muqáwama w-al-ḥizb: ḥiwárát maʿ ghasán sharbal)* (Beirut: Dar al-Nahar, 2005), 100–101.

159. el-Khazen, *The Breakdown*, 344–45.

160. AAD, Beirut 4175, May 11, 1976.

161. GRFL, MESA Staff Files, Box 24, Syria (3), Memo, Scowcroft, "Telephone Conversation with President Hafiz al-Asad," No Date [May 8, 1976].

162. AAD, Beirut 4346, May 17, 1976.

163. SLF, Box 43, "April 16–June 1976," State 120536, May 16, 1976; Beirut 4336, May 16, 1976.

164. Ibid., Beirut 4432, May 19, 1976.

165. Ibid., Secto 13013, May 20, 1976; Beirut 4493, May 21, 1976.

166. GRFL-PCF-MESA, Box 29, Saudi Arabia, From State—NODIS (5), State 107447, May 4, 1976; SLF, Box 43, Memo, Atherton to Sisco, May 3, 1976.

167. GRFL-PCF-MESA, Box 30, Saudi Arabia, To Secstate—NODIS (12), Jidda 3229, May 5, 1976.

168. Ibid., Jidda 3363, May 10, 1976.

169. The United States received this information from Egypt. GRFL, MESA Staff Files, Box 15, Lebanon (23), Cairo 7053, May 22, 1976.

170. AAD, Beirut 4422, May 19, 1976; Beirut 4538, May 24, 1976.

171. AAD, Paris 15354, May 25, 1976.

172. See GRFL, MESA Staff Files, Box 15, Lebanon (26), Letter, Oakley to Hauser, Jun. 14, 1976.

173. Karim Pakradouni, *La paix manquée: le mandat d'Elias Sarkis (1976–1982)* (Paris: Fiches du Monde Arabe, 1984), 10.

174. DNSA, Memcon, "Guidance for Ambassadors Eilts and Pickering," Aug. 7, 1976.

175. Evron, *War and Intervention in Lebanon*, 51. See also Schulze, *Israel's Covert Diplomacy*, 88.

176. Sayigh, *Armed Struggle*, 390.

177. Author Interview, Abdulhalim Khaddam.

178. KLF, Box 17, NODIS Memcons—June 1976, Kissinger, Crosland, Sauvagnargues, Genscher et al., Jun. 21, 1976.

8. Taking Its Course

1. Farid el-Khazen, *The Breakdown of the State in Lebanon, 1967–1976* (London: I.B. Tauris, 2000), 188–346.

2. On the US initiative toward Syria, see Henry Alfred Kissinger, *Years of Renewal* (New York: Simon and Schuster, 1999), 1051–53.

3. DNSA, Kissinger Memcons, Memo, "Secretary's Staff Meeting," Jun. 1, 1976.

4. Evron, *War and Intervention in Lebanon*, 54.

5. GRFL, RAC Files, "NSC MESA Staff Files Box 77," President's Daily Brief, Jun. 6, 1976.

6. NARA, RG 59, NW 33909 Entry 07D 99, Amman 2921, Jun. 1, 1976.

7. GRFL-PCF-MESA, Box 23, Jordan, To Secstate—NODIS (26), Amman 2855, Jun. 2, 1976.

8. GRFL-PCF-MESA, Box 9, Egypt, To Secstate—NODIS (44), Alexandria 343, Jun. 3, 1976. The article in question was probably *New York Times*, "U.S. Views Syria's Entry into Lebanon as Helpful," Jun. 2, 1976.

9. *New York Times*, Jun. 4, 1976.

10. SLF, Box 43, "April 16–June 1976," State 137520, Jun. 4, 1976.

11. Ibid., Beirut 4820, Jun. 4, 1976.

12. GRFL, Kissinger Trip Files [KTF], Box 37, Latin America—TOSEC (2), State 13914 [*sic*] repeating Beirut 4878, Jun. 7, 1976.

13. SLF, Box 43, "April 16–June 1976," Beirut 4843, Jun. 4, 1976; State 138645, Jun. 5, 1976; GRFL-KTF, Box 37, Latin America—TOSEC (2), Beirut 4876, Jun. 7, 1976.

14. el-Khazen, *The Breakdown*, 246.

15. GRFL-PCF-MESA, Box 9, Egypt, To SECSTATE—NODIS (44), Cairo 8015, Jun. 10, 1976.

16. Istvan Pogany, *The Arab League and Peacekeeping in the Lebanon* (Avebury: Aldershot, England, 1987), 74–75.

17. GRFL-KTF, Box 37, Latin America—SECTO (2), SECTO 16053, Jun. 9, 1976; Box 38, Latin America Trip, TOSEC (5), "Lebanon," Jun. 10, 1976.

18. GRFL-KTF, Box 38, Latin America Trip, TOSEC (5), State 142348, Jun. 10, 1976. See also SLF, Box 43, Cairo 8015, Jun. 10, 1976.

19. GRFL-PCF-MESA, Box 9, Egypt, To Secstate—NODIS (44), Cairo 8087, Jun. 11, 1976.

20. AAD, Damascus 4486, Jul. 11, 1976.

21. GRFL-KTF, Box 37, Latin America Trip, SECTO (1), SECTO 16023, Jul. 7, 1976.

22. Ibid., Box 37, SECTO (2), Secto 16099, Jun. 11, 1976. For the instructions to Murphy see ibid., Secto 16081, Jun. 10, 1976; Secto 16087, Jun. 11, 1976.

23. AAD, Amman 3707, Jul. 14, 1976.

24. GRFL-PCF-MESA, Box 23, Jordan, To Secstate—NODIS (26), Amman 3102, Jun. 11, 1976.

25. In the AAD online archives, a still-classified message (Tel Aviv 4015) with the subject of "Lebanon," as well as a reference code to Allon and Kissinger, was sent by the US embassy in Tel Aviv on June 13.

26. GRFL-PCF-MESA, Box 17, Israel, From Secstate—NODIS (7), State 150156, Jun. 17, 1976.

27. GRFL-PCF-MESA, Box 6, Egypt, From Secstate—NODIS (18), State 146857, Jun. 15, 1976; Box 9, Egypt, To SECSTATE—NODIS (45), Cairo 8170, Jun. 15, 1976; Box 29, Saudi Arabia, From Secstate—NODIS (5), State 147178, Jun. 15, 1976; Box 29, Saudi Arabia, To Secstate—EXDIS (5), Jidda 4391, Jun. 20, 1976.

28. DNSA, Memcon, HAK, Avineri, Dinitz et al., Jun. 15, 1976.

29. GRFL-PCF-MESA, Box 17, Israel, From Secstate—NODIS (7), State 152887, Jun. 20, 1976.

30. GRFL, Presidential Memcons, Cabinet Meeting Minutes, Jun. 18, 1976.

31. el-Khazen, *The Breakdown*, 346; Samir Kassir, *La guerre du Liban: de la dissension nationale au conflit régional (1975–1982)* (Paris: CERMOC, 1994), 218.

32. Yezid Sayigh, *Armed Struggle and the Search for State: The Palestinian National Movement, 1949–1993* (Oxford: Clarendon Press, 1997), 399.

33. el-Khazen, *The Breakdown*, 346.

34. Kissinger, *Years of Renewal*, 1047.

35. Author Interview, Forrest Hunt, Jan. 18, 2010.

36. Abou Iyad, *Palestinien sans patrie: entretiens avec Eric Rouleau* (Paris: Fayolle, 1978), 189; Sayigh, *Armed Struggle*, 395.

37. GRFL-PCF-MESA, Box 17, Israel, From Secstate—NODIS (7), State 152887, Jun. 20, 1976.

38. AAD, Beirut 5822, Jul. 3, 1976.

39. *New York Times*, "Beirut Holds 8 in U.S. Envoys' Killing," Jun. 28, 1983.

40. GRFL-PCF-MESA, Box 26, Lebanon To Secstate—NODIS (12), Beirut 5944, Jul. 7, 1976.

41. Ibid., Beirut 6190, Jul. 13, 1976.

42. AAD, State 172951, Jul. 13, 1976.

43. GRFL-PCF-MESA, Box 24, Undated, Untitled Document [prob. Jun. 19, 1976].

44. GRFL-PCF-MESA, Box 4, Egypt, State Department Telegrams, From SECSTATE—EXDIS (2), State 152892, Jun. 20, 1975; Box 6, Egypt, To Secstate—EXDIS (5), Cairo 8294, Jun. 20, 1976.

45. GRFL-PCF-MESA, Box 26, Lebanon, To State—NODIS (11), Beirut 5343, Jun. 21, 1976.

46. Ibid., Box 26, Lebanon, To State—NODIS (12), Beirut 5353, Jun. 21, 1976.

47. AAD, Beirut 6216, Jul. 14, 1976.

48. GRFL-PCF-MESA, Box 26, Lebanon, To State—NODIS (13), Beirut 6448, Jul. 20, 1976.

49. AAD, Beirut 5792, Jul. 2, 1976; Beirut 5829, Jul. 3, 1976.

50. FRUS, 1969–1976, Vol. XXVI, Doc. 290.

51. GRFL-PCF-MESA, Box 25, Lebanon, To Secstate—EXDIS (2), Beirut 5573, Jun. 27, 1976.

52. AAD, State 177762, Jul. 17, 1976; Beirut 6375, Jul. 18, 1976.

53. *New York Times*, "U.S. Staff in Beirut Lives in Isolation," Oct. 6, 1976.

54. FAOH Interview, Talcott Seelye.

55. On Syria's cooperation with the Christian factions, see *Wall Street Journal*, "Mideast Intrigue," Feb. 10, 1983; Chamoun, *Crise au Liban*, 147.

56. NARA, RG 59, NW 33909 Entry 07D 99, Beirut 5754, Jul. 1, 1976.

57. Kassir, *La guerre du Liban*, 218.

58. GRFL-PCF-MESA, Box 31, Syria, From Secstate—NODIS (8), State 163263, Jul. 1, 1976.

59. GRFL-PCF-MESA, Box 32, Syria, From Secstate—NODIS (14), Damascus 4223, Jul. 1, 1976.

60. State Department Virtual Reading Room, Kissinger Telcons, Mr. Day/Secretary Kissinger, Jul. 1, 1976.

61. Helena Cobban, *The Palestinian Liberation Organisation: People, Power and Politics* (Cambridge: Cambridge University Press, 1984), 73.

62. Yevgeny Primakov, *Russia and the Arabs: Behind the Scenes in the Middle East from the Cold War to the Present* (New York: Basic Books, 2009), 181. He cites Igor Grenevsky's book *Secrets of Soviet Diplomacy* on Kosygin's reaction.

63. *New York Times*, "Kosygin and Syrians Agree on Lebanon," Jun. 5, 1976.

64. *New York Times*, "Truce in Lebanon Urged by Soviet Union," Jun. 10, 1976.

65. See GRFL, President Country Files, Europe, Box 21, USSR, To SECSTATE—NODIS (12), Moscow 9400, Jun. 14, 1976; Moscow 9756, Jun. 16, 1976.

66. GRFL-PCF-MESA, Box 23, Jordan, To Secstate—NODIS (27), Amman 3751, Jul. 17, 1976; Amman 3752, Jul. 17, 1976; Amman 3753, Jul. 17, 1976.

67. AAD, State 177829, Jul. 18, 1976.

68. AAD, Amman 3761, Jul. 18, 1976.

69. GRFL, Presidential Memcons, Ford, Kissinger, Scowcroft, Jul. 19, 1976.

70. AAD, Moscow 4796, Jul. 20, 1976.

71. Kissinger, *Years of Renewal*, 1049.

72. AAD, Damascus 4639, Jul. 16, 1976; Amman 3753, Jul. 17, 1976; Damascus 5202, Aug. 7, 1976.

73. Kissinger, *Years of Renewal*, 1049.

74. GRFL-PCF-MESA, Box 31, Syria, From Secstate—NODIS (8), State 178824, Jul. 20, 1976. See also Box 32, Syria, To Secstate—NODIS (14–15), Damascus 4752, Jul. 20, 1976; Box 31, Syria, From Secstate—NODIS (8), State 180072, Jul. 21, 1976; Box 32, Syria, To Secstate—NODIS (14–15), Damascus 4771, Jul. 21, 1976; Box 31, Syria, From Secstate—NODIS (8), State 180101, "Soviet Pressures on Syria," Jul. 21, 1976.

75. GRFL-PCF-MESA, Box 32, Syria, To Secstate—NODIS (14–15), Damascus 4858, Jul. 22, 1976. The Tripoli incident was also discussed in Amman 3753, para 8.

76. GRFL-PCF-MESA, Box 23, Jordan, To Secstate—NODIS (27), Amman 3894, Jul. 26, 1976; Amman 3923, Jul. 26, 1976.

77. Kissinger, *Years of Renewal*, 1049.

78. GRFL-PCF-MESA, Box 32, Syria, To Secstate—NODIS (14–15), Damascus 5147, Aug. 4, 1976.

79. GRFL-PCF-MESA, Box 6, Egypt, From Secstate—NODIS (19), State 177831, Jul. 18, 1976.

80. GRFL-PCF-MESA, Box 29, Saudi Arabia, From State—NODIS (5), State 177860, Jul. 18, 1976; AAD, State 177832, Jul. 18, 1976.

81. KLF, Box 17, NODIS Memcons—July 1976, Kissinger, Bar-on et al., Jul. 20, 1976.

82. An interim response was given the next day. KLF, Box 16, NODIS Brief Notes, 1975–76, Memo, Atherton to HAK, Jul. 21, 1976. The main response is found in KLF, Box 15, Folder 7, Memo, No Subject [labeled Top Secret], Jul. 26, 1976. The record of another conversation with Bar-on on July 31 remains classified.

83. el-Khazen, *The Breakdown*, 346.

84. GRFL-PCF-MESA, Box 23, Jordan, To Secstate—NODIS (27), Amman 3965, Jul. 29, 1976.

85. GRFL, NSA Memcons, Box 20, Memcon, Ford, Kissinger, Scowcroft, Murphy, Jul. 31, 1976.

86. Kissinger, *Years of Renewal*, 1053.

87. FRUS, 1969–1976, Vol. XXVI, Doc. 290.

88. AAD, Beirut 6206, Jul. 14, 1976; Tel Aviv 4953, Jul. 16, 1976; Cairo 10048, Jul. 27, 1976.

89. Kissinger, *Years of Renewal*, 1054–55. DNSA, Memcon, "Guidance for Ambassadors Eilts and Pickering," Aug. 7, 1976.

90. DNSA, Memcon, "Guidance for Ambassadors Eilts and Pickering," Aug. 7, 1976.

91. See GRFL, MESA, Jordan, To Secstate—NODIS (28), Amman 4167, "Talk with King—Area Developments," Aug. 10, 1976; Amman 4168, "Talk with King—Lebanon, Syria, Egypt," Aug. 11, 1976.

92. Kissinger, *Years of Renewal*, 1049–50.

93. The cable that contains Kissinger's message is unavailable. GRFL-PCF-MESA, Box 32, Syria, To Secstate—NODIS (14–15), Damascus 5202, Aug. 7, 1976.

94. Ibid.

95. GRFL-PCF-MESA, Box 19, Israel, To Secstate—NODIS (13), Tel Aviv 5613, Aug. 16, 1976.

96. GRFL, Kissinger-Scowcroft Files, Box 32, "USSR—"D" File [Dobrynin]—Items #182–#189", Message dictated by Minister Vorontsov, 12:05 p.m., Aug. 18, 1976.

97. Ibid. Note, No Title, August 18, 1976.

98. DNSA, Memcon, Kissinger, Atherton, Houghton, Mack, Aug. 18, 1976.

99. *New York Times*, "Special U.S. Aides Arrive in Lebanon," Aug. 23, 1976.

100. AAD, Nicosia 2516, Aug. 25, 1976.

101. AAD, Nicosia 2518, Aug. 26, 1976; Nicosia 2546, Aug. 26, 1976.

102. AAD, State 215513, Aug. 31, 1976.

103. AAD, Nicosia 2677, Sep. 6, 1976.

104. Kassir, *La guerre du Liban*, 231.

105. *New York Times*, "Syria Charges Sadat Balks Beirut Peace," Sep. 21, 1976.

106. Kassir, *La guerre du Liban*, 231; Karim Pakradouni, *La paix manquée: le mandat d'Elias Sarkis (1976–1982)* (Paris: Fiches du Monde Arabe, 1984), 39–40. Khaddam confirmed to this author that the Palestinian attack was the impetus for the second offensive. Author Interview, Abdulhalim Khaddam.

107. Sayigh, *Armed Struggle*, 407; Kassir, *La guerre du Liban*, 232.

108. GRFL-PCF-MESA, Box 23, Jordan, To Secstate—NODIS (28), Amman 4387, Aug. 25, 1976.

109. *New York Times*, "Moscow Asks Syria to Leave Lebanon," Aug. 30, 1976.

110. *New York Times*, "Damascus Rebuffs Soviet on Lebanon," Oct. 2, 1976.

111. GRFL-PCF-MESA, Box 31, Syria, From Secstate—NODIS (8), State 225449, Sep. 12, 1976.

112. GRFL-PCF-MESA, Box 32, Syria, To Secstate—NODIS (14–15), Damascus 6154, Sep. 14, 1976.

113. Ibid., Damascus 6286, Sep. 17, 1976.

114. GRFL-PCF-MESA, Box 31, Syria, From Secstate—NODIS (8), State 233918, Sep. 21, 1976.

115. GRFL-PCF-MESA, Box 32, Syria, To Secstate—NODIS (14–15), Damascus 6392, Sep. 22, 1976.

116. GRFL-PCF-MESA, Box 23, Jordan, To Secstate—NODIS (29), Amman 5131, Oct. 5, 1976.

117. GRFL RAC Files, Box 9–12, "NSC MESA Staff Files, Box 55, Peace Negotiations," Amman 5267, Oct. 12, 1976.

118. GRFL-PCF-MESA, Box 23, Jordan, To Secstate—NODIS (29), Amman 5293, Oct. 14, 1976.

119. GRFL, RAC Files, Box 9–12, "NSC MESA Staff Files, Box 55, Peace Negotiations," Damascus 7042, Oct. 15, 1976.

120. AAD, State 257219, Oct. 17, 1976.

121. AAD, Amman 6366, Oct. 17, 1976.

122. GRFL-PCF-MESA, Box 23, Jordan, To Secstate—NODIS (29), Amman 6367, Oct. 18, 1976.

123. Ibid., Amman 6365, Oct. 18, 1976.

124. el-Khazen, *The Breakdown*, 353–54.

125. AAD, Beirut 8129, Oct. 22, 1976.

126. AAD, State 268211, Oct. 31, 1976.

127. AAD, State 268703, Nov. 1, 1976.

128. AAD, Beirut 8366, Nov. 9, 1976.

129. AAD, Beirut 8380, Nov. 10, 1976

130. AAD, Beirut 8379, Nov. 10, 1976.

131. AAD, Beirut 8402, Nov. 11, 1976.

132. AAD, Beirut 8605, Nov. 25, 1976.

133. Naomi Weinberger, "Peacekeeping Options in Lebanon," *Middle East Journal* 37, no. 3 (1983): 348.

134. KLF, Box 17, NODIS Memcons—July 1976, Kissinger, Bar-on et al., Jul. 20, 1976.

135. Ahmad Beydoun, "The South Lebanon Border Zone: A Local Perspective," *Journal of Palestine Studies* 21, no. 3 (1992): 39–43.

136. AAD, Damascus 7287, Oct. 26, 1976.

137. AAD, Damascus 7377, Oct. 28, 1976.

138. AAD, State 267579, Oct. 30, 1976.

139. AAD, Damascus 7452, Oct. 31, 1976.

140. DNSA, Memcon, Kissinger, Dinitz, Bar-on et al., Nov. 1, 1976.

141. GRFL-PCF-MESA, Box 17, Israel, From Secstate—NODIS (8), State 276331, Nov. 10, 1976.

142. GRFL-PCF-MESA, Israel, To Secstate—NODIS (14), Tel Aviv 7653, Nov. 10, 1976.

143. AAD, Tel Aviv 7709, Nov. 12, 1976.

144. See AAD, Damascus 7821, Nov. 15, 1976; Damascus 7839, Nov. 15, 1976.

145. Jüssi Hanhimäki, *The Flawed Architect: Henry Kissinger and American Foreign Policy* (Oxford: Oxford University Press, 2004), 443–44. For a portrayal of Kissinger as anti-Israel, see William Safire, "Henry's Private Scorn," *New York Times*, Oct. 18, 1976.

146. AAD, Tel Aviv 7705, Nov. 12, 1976.

147. *New York Times*, "Galilee Is Shelled from Lebanon after Long Lull," Nov. 22, 1976.

148. AAD, Damascus 8036, Nov. 22, 1976.

149. AAD, Damascus 8062, Nov. 23, 1976.

150. DNSA, Memcon, Kissinger, Dinitz, Nov. 23, 1976. See also KLF, Box 19, NODIS Memcons—November 1976, State 239698, Nov. 25, 1976.

151. DNSA, Memcon, Kissinger, Dinitz, Nov. 23, 1976.

152. GRFL-PCF-MESA, Box 17, Israel, From Secstate—NODIS (8), State 288030, Nov. 24, 1976.

153. AAD, Tel Aviv 8024, Nov. 29, 1976.

154. GRFL-PCF-MESA, Box 31, Syria, From Secstate—NODIS (8), State 289092, Nov. 25, 1976.

155. GRFL-PCF-MESA, Box 32, Syria, To Secstate—NODIS (16), Damascus 8133, Nov. 26, 1976.

156. AAD, State 286777, Nov. 23, 1976.

157. AAD, Beirut 8605, Nov. 25, 1976.

158. AAD, State 289090, Nov. 25, 1976; Beirut 8605, Nov. 25, 1976.

159. AAD, Beirut 8652, Nov. 29, 1976.

160. AAD, Beirut 8577, Nov. 25, 1976.

161. AAD, Beirut 8698, Dec. 3, 1976.

162. GRFL, Kissinger-Scowcroft Files, Box 19, Israel—Unnumbered Items (13), Memo, "Southern Lebanon: Talking Points," Dec. 1, 1976.

163. GRFL-PCF-MESA, Box 17, Israel, From Secstate—NODIS (8), State 296250, Dec. 5, 1976.

164. GRFL-PCF-MESA, Box 31, Syria, From Secstate—NODIS (8), State 296266, Dec. 5, 1976.

165. GRFL-PCF-MESA, Box 32, Syria, To Secstate—NODIS (16), Damascus 8306, Dec. 5, 1976.

166. AAD, Beirut 8718, Dec. 5, 1976.

167. KLF, Box 19, NODIS Memcons—December 1976, State 301768 Tosec 320225, "Briefing Memorandum—Your Meeting with Israeli Defense Minister Peres Monday, December 13, 3:00 p.m.," Dec. 11, 1976.

168. KLF, Box 19, NODIS Memcons—December 1976, Memcon, Atherton and Saunders to Kissinger, "Analysis of Arab-Israel Developments," Dec. 23, 1976.

Epilogue. The Cycle Continues

1. David Hirst, *Beware of Small States: Lebanon, Battleground of the Middle East* (New York: Nation Books, 2010), 116–21.

INDEX

Abbas, Mahmud, 202
abd al-Nasser, Gamal, 5, 7, 13, 22, 30, 32, 36, 47–48, 74, 90; and Arab nationalism, 24; Cairo Accord, 61, 65–66; impact on Lebanon of death, 85, 91, 162
Adwan, Kamal, 103–4
Ahdab, Abd al-Aziz, 173
American University of Beirut, 24, 28, 36, 42, 182
anti-Americanism, 28, 33, 71, 104, 121, 186, 221
Arab Deterrent Force, 213–16, 219
Arab League, 107, 143, 146, 160, 202, 213; 1964 Cairo Summit, 23, 27; 1967 Khartoum Conference, 35; 1969 Rabat Summit, 75; 1974 Rabat Conference, 135; reaction to 1976 Syrian intervention in Lebanon, 199–200
Arafat, Yassir, 82, 98, 100–104, 106, 109, 146–50, 178, 198–99; 1974 UNGA speech, 135–36; arrest and interrogation, 25; attitude toward Sinai II, 153; contacts with the United States, 112–13, 123, 183, 185–86, 189; Damascus Accord, 164; invitation to Riyadh conference, 213; meetings with Lebanese officials, 48, 53–54, 66, 88, 95, 103, 120–21, 130; as a moderating influence, 93, 102, 148, 182, 192; peace plan for Lebanon, 188; reaction to Syrian military intervention, 201–2; relationship with Nasser, 74; role in splitting the Lebanese army, 173
Armenians, 71, 73
Arqub (Fatahland), 38, 80–82, 94, 96, 144, 176, 215
al-Asad, Hafiz, 90, 164, 170, 191–93, 197–99, 201–2, 216, 219; attitude toward and relationship with the United States, 160, 183, 186–88, 200, 205–6, 209, 211–13, 220; consolidating power, 12;

meeting with Frangie, 139–40, 146; phone call to the White House, 192; relationship with Pierre Gemayel, 163; relationship with King Hussein, 152, 154, 156, 176, 178, 193, 197, 199–200, 205–7, 209, 212–13; tensions with Palestinians, 172. *See also* Red Line Agreement; Soviet Union: threat to cut off arms sales to Syria; Syria: commitment to control fedayeen in the Golan
Atassi, Nur al-Din, 29
Atherton, Alfred "Roy," 116, 140, 161, 164–65, 175, 215
Ayn al-Rammana incident, 143
Azimov, Sarvar, 71, 87, 109

Baath parties (Lebanon), 24, 38, 40, 49, 74, 87, 130
Baath Party (Syria), 35
Barak, Ehud, 103
Barbour, Walworth, 37, 40, 42, 95
Belgium, 101, 103, 166, 172
Biqa Valley, 12, 120, 152–53, 155, 177, 195
bishops (Greek Catholic and other), 76, 82, 108
Black September. *See* Jordan: 1970 Civil War
Black September Organization (BSO), 19, 94, 96, 101–3, 105–6
Brown, L. Dean, 17, 169, 171, 180–92, 197, 201, 204, 206; as ambassador to Jordan, 102, 111
Buffum, William, 93, 98, 100, 105, 115–16, 121–22, 210; on the comparison between Jordan and Lebanon, 102, 107; relationship with Suleiman Frangie, 94, 96; replacement of Porter, 90
Bulgaria, 132–33
Bustany, Emile, 31, 33–34, 48–49, 63, 65–66, 71, 74

CPSIA information can be obtained at www.ICGtesting.com
Printed in the USA
LVOW08*2304010316

477342LV00006B/11/P